Britain's Top Employers
2005

Britain's Top Employers

2005

Best Examples of HR Management

Editor: Guy Clapperton

Corporate Research Foundation

Guardian Books

First published in 2005 by Guardian Books
Copyright © Corporate Research Foundation 2005

The Guardian is a registered trademark of the
Guardian Media Group plc and Guardian Newspapers Ltd.

The right of Guy Clapperton to be identified as editor of this work
has been asserted in accordance with section 77 of the
Copyright, Designs and Patents Act, 1988.

A CIP record for this book is available from the British Library
upon request

ISBN: 1 84354 992 1

Distributed by Atlantic Books
An imprint of Grove Atlantic Ltd., Ormond House,
26-27 Boswell Street, London WC1N 3JZ

Cover Design: Two Associates
Text Design: www.carrstudio.co.uk

Printed in Great Britain by Cambridge University Press

1 2 3 4 5 6 7 8 9 10

Contents

Corporate Research Foundation

The Corporate Research Foundation (CRF) is an independent organisation that initiates and coordinates international research projects in business worldwide. CRF aims to contribute to a better awareness and understanding of corporate culture, effective human resource management, and the business strategies of successful enterprises by researching the key factors behind their success and publishing its findings.

The CRF represents a combined initiative of business journalists, analysts, trade associations and international publishers; and has been active since 1991 in the UK, South Africa, Germany, The Netherlands, Belgium and Switzerland.

Other titles in the CRF series include:

Top ICT Companies in the UK
Top UK Companies of the Future
Top Marketing and Media Companies in the UK

Martin Williams
UK Manager
Corporate Research Foundation
Kinetic Centre, Theobald Street
Elstree, WD6 4PJ
Tel: (0) 20 8387 1400
Fax: (0) 20 8387 1410
Email: martin@crf-uk.com
www.researchfoundation.com

Foreword

If one phrase has characterised the HR/employment arena over the last 12 months then it's 'work/life balance'. UK legislation has led to employers being obliged to consider requests for working from home or otherwise flexibly, and a lot of people are taking it up – although not as many as was at first anticipated.

Aiming to offer an employee a decent work/life balance is of course an excellent thing, but there's a possibility that the trend is moving too far in one direction. This theory can be tested in a very simple way – ask yourself 'what is work/life balance'?

If you're a student or a recent graduate then the caricatured image projected by the media says you'll regard work/life balance as the provision of a lively social life and could everyone go for a drink after work, please.

If you're not, then the fun starts. Say you're a man in his early 40s and want nothing more than to get home and see your family – UK working culture is among the most time-consuming in Europe, so you'll want any time you can claw back. Speaking personally, as a self-employed editor approaching his 40s, I find that any approach to work that increases my time with my family and yet allows me to fit in sports club membership without damaging deadlines is a fine thing indeed.

It is of course down to the employer to try to accommodate whatever his or her employees deem to be 'work/life balance' and it's difficult because it can mean so many things. In spite of the imprecision of this obligation, the companies that follow in this book have made admiral attempts to do so. Smaller companies are ironically among the most forward-looking in this respect; some will offer to spend money on evening classes in wholly irrelevant subjects if their employees will feel fulfilled as a result.

It appears likely that the issue has 'peaked' as a new phenomenon; everyone now acknowledges the importance of work/life balance so by the time we publish again it will go without saying. The question that badly needs answering, though, is that if everyone's 'done' work/life balance in the UK, how is it that we still have the longest working hours and some of the highest incidence of coronary heart disease in Europe?

Each of the companies in this book has been shortlisted then selected by an expert panel including HR practitioners, academics and journalists. It can never be an exhaustive list; some companies didn't have the time to take part, others will no doubt come to our attention after publication. Each inclusion, however, has been earned by a degree of excellence as an employer – they are all ahead of the market in their own particular sector.

NB: The companies involved have contributed to the cost of producing this book. This has in no way prejudiced their coverage, which remains strictly independent.

Guy Clapperton
Editor
December 2004

The Employer/Employee Deal

The stability of the UK economy and the steady rate of growth experienced over the past decade have produced a buoyant labour market. The total number of people employed has risen to record levels. Competition for talented people is severe, especially for skilled labour and for professional, technical and managerial staff.

The data from the Recruitment Confidence Index, a quarterly survey of these labour markets in the UK, shows employers have consistently reported difficulties in recruiting at senior levels. For example, over the last five years around a third of employers seeking to recruit graduates have experienced difficulty in doing so, and around 50% of employers recruiting at senior levels have also experienced difficulty.

One way modern organisations seek to gain and to sustain a competitive advantage is through the effectiveness of their talent management. This is well documented by the high-performing businesses described in this volume. The process of potential identification, career development panels, coaching, mentoring and similar processes are well known. What distinguishes organisations where talent management is taken seriously is firstly that these processes are coordinated and systematically applied, incorporating a focus on recruitment, leadership development and total rewards; and secondly that these processes are applied at all levels so that talent is not seen as the attribute only of a few high flyers – organisations need skills and leadership at all levels. The very fact that organisations do take talent management seriously is an attraction for potential employees.

In a world where potential recruits have more choices than ever before, what are the critical factors that affect their decisions on job offers? Improved employment prospects have come at a time when values about work are changing.

For potential employees, the key influences on their choice include not only the reward package but also the need to match the work style of the company with the lifestyle they desire. Values are important for organisations and for individuals alike. Finding a match may not be difficult. There are many public sector opportunities, and in the commercial sector a strong corporate social responsibility agenda is commonly found amongst the best employers. Corporate values also embrace ideals such as commitment to customers, to excellence, and to the long-term development of their employees. Such a commitment is only possible if companies satisfy their shareholders and are able to deliver added value. The "balanced scorecard" has become a mechanism to make such commitments clear and measurable.

In addition to a convergence in values, people choose organisational roles where the working style appeals; for example, where they can find opportunities, challenges, learning, autonomy, and an environment which helps them to become what they seek for their own identity – a constant search in a world which embraces work and non-work ambitions. Corporate reputations and the brand image are also significant factors in a choice of job. Adding a famous company to one's CV is likely to give the individual's career a boost. The psychological contract, "the deal" from the employee's viewpoint, includes very often a high degree of flexibility; providing opportunities to work on task time rather than clock time, if that is possible, so there is a high degree of autonomy. Careers are often built between companies, and for some people a portfolio career is desirable. Flexibility of all kinds is desirable – flexibility of time, flexibility of contract and flexible benefits – and in return employers often seek flexibility of task.

Employer demands are changing. Fast-paced work (with time as a competitive weapon) means staff are often required to hit the ground running – to make an immediate contribution. The expansion in jobs has been at the higher end of the range;

over 4 million new jobs were created in the decade to 2002 in the professional, technical and managerial fields. Additionally, clerical and administrative jobs have been drawn into this bracket (having been enriched to cover managerial tasks as part of efficiency drives) so that advanced computer skills, good interpersonal skills, and the capacity to deal with rapid change are requirements for most roles.

Employees are expected to have an interest in their employer's products and services and in their customers, and to acquire specialist company-specific expertise quickly. Employers must also respond to a rapidly shifting business environment. From 2006 age discrimination will become illegal. All the evidence so far indicates that young people feel most discriminated against, but the consequence of the new legislation may be that it helps towards a solution to the demographic problems currently emerging of an aging workforce – almost 50% of the population are over 50 years of age. The need for a diverse workforce to represent and to take advantage of all the potential in the population is driving competitive companies to make diversity policies and practices a priority. Competition is global, and an international mindset is required amongst the workforce.

The capability of the organisation and its capacity to develop and grow is a function of the people it employs. The awareness of this motivates boards of management to treat all the processes that sustain their human resources as a strategic priority.

Professor Shaun Tyson
Cranfield School of Management

Graduate Recruitment in 2005

Few businesses – large or small, private or public, local or global – do not recruit graduates these days. For the graduate job seeker, there is a need to know which are the "top businesses" to work for. This publication should be a great source of useful information.

The first question I pose is "Why should employers recruit graduates?"

Put plainly, they form the largest fresh talent pool. With 160,000 plus graduates entering the labour market each year, it's hard to ignore them. But, six years working as the chief executive of AGR (The Association of Graduate Recruiters) has taught me that there are other compelling reasons for recruiting and developing graduates.

- Graduates by definition have undertaken at least three years higher education when they will have gained detailed knowledge and understanding of a subject area. As importantly, they will have learnt how to manage their learning and that's vital in the fast changing world of work and lifelong learning.
- A degree is, in itself, rarely enough to satisfy employers who increasingly recruit against a set of competencies. However, it's wrong to assume that a fresh graduate will lack the competencies that employers look for. Studying and participating in extra curricular activities both help to develop skills in students. But perhaps the most important point here is that few students have not had extensive work experience. They learn and earn at the same time.
- Being at university, often away from home, helps emotional as well as intellectual development. That extra maturity should help them to be clear about what they want to achieve in life and how to go about it.
- Employers know that recruiting and retaining top talent is crucial to ensure that they maintain their competitive edge.
- Most graduates are at the starting line as far as their career is concerned. They are open to new ideas and approaches, eager to learn and prove themselves. In short, they fit the "grow your own" model to a tee.
- Many businesses want their workforce to be representative of the communities they serve. The current crop of UK graduates is the most diverse ever.

I will return later to the business benefits of operating a graduate programme but let's now consider what it takes to be a graduate employer of choice.

How can employers attract graduates?

The war for top talent continues unabated, irrespective of the state of the economy. However, the indications are that competition for graduates will intensify as the number of vacancies continues to expand.

Yet with more graduates year on year, the challenge is to identify and compete for those you really want to attract to your business.

Graduate attraction is the cornerstone of any campaign. Be clear about why you want to recruit graduates, what you want them to do, and how you are going to train them to do it. In other words, what do you expect from graduates and what can they expect in return? Utilising your market brand is important, although easier for some businesses to exploit than others – especially those that are new to graduate recruitment.

The search for the right graduate can be described as looking for a needle in a burgeoning haystack. All the more reason to adopt an integrated marketing approach incorporating written materials, media advertising, website content, and other activities such as on-campus presentations and careers fairs. It is a myth that spending lots of money is the only way to make a big splash in the graduate pool. It's not a big splash you are after, but a campaign that gets the right messages across to the right types of candidates. Recruiters strive to move from a high-volume/low-success formula to a low-volume/high-success model requiring a focused and integrated approach making the best use of resources, including online technology and face-to-face contacts.

Recruiters may still have large numbers of applicants to consider, and narrowing down the field to manageable proportions is quite a challenge. Screening criteria have to be lawful and fair. It's worth bearing in mind not just existing employment legislation but taking note of the impending age discrimination bill, which will outlaw selection criteria based upon dates of birth.

Increasing use is made of telephone screening, online testing, and self-deselection tools designed to help potential candidates decide whether the vacancy is suitable before making a formal application. There's huge scope here but tools need to be carefully vetted to ensure fair access and to avoid missing out on the unpolished diamond!

Outsourcing parts of the selection process is now commonplace in employer strategies. There is a growing awareness of recruitment costs and businesses are constantly looking at ways of reducing the costs per hire. Outsourcing is one approach, greater use of technology another, but a balance has to be struck between price and quality. Businesses must never forget the old maxim – today's candidate may be tomorrow's customer. All those who take the trouble to enquire after vacancies should be treated with respect, courtesy and efficiency.

Mention was made earlier of the use of competency sets, and once shortlisted candidates are chosen, many recruiters of graduates use assessment centres as a key stage in the selection process. Perhaps the best assessment tool is extended work experience, where both the business and the individual get the opportunity of an "employment trial". There is a range of such arrangements from summer internships to year-long sandwich placements. Not forgetting the part-time student employee. Too few employers target this pool when marketing vacancies. As with most good things, there is a potential downside to work experience. If the student experience is negative, then it will potentially damage rather than enhance your brand. Only offer placements when the quality is guaranteed.

So, is it worth recruiting graduates with all these factors to consider? As chief executive of AGR, consisting of over 600 businesses with a shared interest in recruiting and developing graduates, you would expect me to say yes – and I do!

But don't just take my word for it. In 2004, AGR commissioned Dr Anthony Hesketh – of the Management School at the University of Lancaster – to undertake research into the added value that graduates, and in particular formalised graduate programmes, bring to organisations.

Adding Value Beyond Measure demonstrated a raft of benefits to operating graduate programmes including:

• The capacity to articulate innovations and the ability to cope with the changes that this brings. They can see the wood for the trees!
• Developing faster than other employees and adding value more quickly. They hit the road running and demonstrate leadership qualities at an accelerated rate.
• The skills to articulate ideas into the cut and thrust of working life, despite their limited experience.
• Stimulating change in a fast moving world – not just accommodating it.
• Not looking at things and thinking "that's too difficult", but coming up with a solution and being innovative because they want to make their mark.

Hesketh's research suggests that graduates contribute a massive £1bn of added value to the UK economy each year.

Ultimately the choice lies between growing your own or buying in experience. As one employer in Adding Value Beyond Measure put it, "Do you do a Chelsea or do you have your own academy?"

Graduate recruitment is not a cheap option, but building your own talent pipeline is going to have a much healthier impact on your bottom line than being at the mercy of the experienced hire market.

Carl Gilleard
Chief Executive
AGR

Contact details:
The Innovation Centre, Warwick Technology Park, Warwick CV34 6UW
Tel: 01926 623236
Web: www.agr.org.uk

The Adding Value Beyond Measure research publication
can be purchased directly from AGR.

Contributors

Simon Barrow is chair of management communication consultants People in Business, a leading HR and management consultancy specialising in internal communications, leadership, culture and employee relations. In 1990, People in Business created the concept of the Employer Brand ™ to focus attention on the factors that make organisations "employers of choice".

Bryan Betts is a freelance journalist specialising in business and technology. As well as working for print and online publications, he is an occasional commentator on radio and TV. He also writes on topics as diverse as beer and history, and has recently completed a teaching qualification.

Frank Booty is a freelance editor and writer, contributing to many market-leading print titles, websites and books in the fields of business, IT and networking, facilities management, manufacturing, and chemicals and feedstocks. An award-winning journalist, he has also devised and chaired many conferences in the facilities management market.

Paul Bray read Modern History at Oxford and spent five years in the computer industry before entering journalism in 1988. He was deputy editor of Which Computer? for two years and went freelance in 1991. Since then he has written for the Daily Telegraph, the Sunday Times and the Guardian; many magazines including Computing, Computer Weekly, Director and NASDAQ International; as well as publications such as the Hutchinson Encyclopedia and Almanac. He lives in Kent, where his hobbies include opera singing, walking and providing a one-man taxi service for his two daughters.

Guy Clapperton (editor) is a journalist of some 16 years standing. He is editorial associate to the Guardian's Business Solutions supplement and contributes to several sections of that newspaper including Rise and the media pages. He also contributes to the Observer, the Times and the Radio Times. This is his fourth book as editor for the Corporate Research Foundation.

Paul Donkersley is a professional writer covering marketing, business, employment, sports and travel. Previously twice-editor of Britain's Top Employers, he has had freelance work published in the Guardian and various magazines and wrote the first UK book on fantasy football: Dream League – a Guide to Success. He is a communications copywriter and publications consultant through his own agency, IKON Associates. Also, a mad skier and mountain biker.

Jim Dow has been a newspaper journalist for more than 40 years. He spent 23 years at the Scotsman, latterly business editor for nine years, and now runs his own public relations/ freelance journalist business in Edinburgh.

Carl Gilleard is chief executive of the Association of Graduate Recruiters. Founded in 1968, AGR is an independent not-for-profit organisation dedicated to supporting employers in all areas of graduate recruitment. AGR represents over 600 organisations that, between them, offer a high proportion of graduate opportunities in the UK. Carl Gilleard was appointed chief executive of AGR in June 1998 following nine years as executive director for METRA Services Ltd. – a national human resource agency charged with, among other things, improving the recruitment and retention of graduates into local government. He was also part-time director of the West Midlands Employers Organisation.

Candice Goodwin has worked for 20 years as a journalist specialising in technology and how people use it at work. Based in London, she has contributed to a range of UK business and technical publications including the Telegraph, New Scientist, Computer Weekly and Computing.

Elspeth Farrar, a graduate of the University of Stirling and Manchester Polytechnic, has worked in the areas of student support and careers guidance in a variety of education environments including schools, colleges, and for the last 10 years, in the university sector at Middlesex University and in her current role with Imperial College London. With involvement in national professional training and careers information writing, Elspeth is an active member of the Association of Graduate Careers Advisory Services (AGCAS); she was, until recently, a member of the board of directors and the organisation's vice president.

Dennis Jarrett is a corporate communications specialist with a background in professional journalism. He has edited a number of IT publications and currently runs a newsletter for SMEs. He also produces e-books (mainly on IT and marketing), operates a small-business consultancy, and contributes regularly to national newspapers and specialist magazines.

Jon Lamb is a writer, editor and researcher, focusing mainly on HR and management issues. He has contributed to publications including the Guardian and the Times, and has undertaken projects for the Chartered Management Institute and the Chartered Institute for Personnel and Development. Jon is the founder of WordGhost, a communications and editorial services provider.

Helen McCay trained as a teacher and has worked in a variety of schools over the past 20 years. Subject specialisms include mathematics and careers education. She took up her current post as senior careers adviser in the University of Ulster in 2000 and has recently been appointed to the board of directors of AGCAS (The Association of Graduate Careers Advisory Services in HE) as the coordinator for quality.

Mark Reardon, Corporate Childcare Solutions Group. One of the UK's leading productivity groups measuring and reporting on initiatives that improve corporate productivity. They provide a full menu of HR outsourcing services, which enable any trade association or employer to be regarded as an employer of choice.

Rachelle Thackray has written for publications including the Independent and the Guardian, and published her first book in 2002 – 20/20 Hindsight, a Virgin Business Guide with a foreword by Richard Branson.

Roger Trapp is an experienced business journalist and corporate writer with in-depth knowledge of management issues, enterprise and related matters. He was on the staff of the Independent and the Independent on Sunday for more than a decade, and while there took responsibility for the Independent on Sunday's pioneering annual survey of fast-growing companies. He currently edits the paper's monthly section devoted to growing businesses as well as continuing to contribute to a range of magazines. He is married with three daughters.

Professor Shaun Tyson is professor of Human Resource Management, head of the People and Organisations Group, and director of the Human Resource Centre at Cranfield University. He has experience of human resources management in the public sector and in corporations such as the Thorn Group, and has held faculty positions at the Civil Service College in Sunningdale. He holds a PhD from the London School of Economics and is a fellow of the Chartered Institute of Personnel and Development, a fellow of the Royal Society of Arts, and a member of the British Psychological Society. He has published 18 books on HR management and broadcasts regularly on employment topics.

Andrew Walker knows what makes a good employer having worked for companies who are amongst the leaders in their respective fields (Rank Xerox, Sony, Manpower). His current role is as business director of remuneration specialists Croner Reward, a division of Wolters Kluwer (UK) Ltd., where he focuses on helping clients get the best out of their reward strategies, policies and practices.

David Vickery is an award-winning financial copywriter. His career has included freelance work, writing for blue-chip clients through leading advertising agencies, and holding senior writing positions with companies such as Abbey National Treasury Services and the London Stock Exchange. Currently, he acts as a consultant to the UK's largest national independent financial advisory company. He is married to Angie and they have a daughter, Zoe.

Ian Wylie, 36, is the editor of Rise, the Guardian's weekly careers advice section for students and graduates. Ian also writes on business and career issues for a wide range of magazine titles here and in the US including Management Today, Fast Company and Men's Health.

Company profiles

3M

3M United Kingdom PLC
3M Centre, Cain Road, Bracknell, RG12 8HT
Tel: (0) 870 536 0036
Web: www.3m.com/uk

Pay and Benefits	6.4	Innovation	7.8
Promotion and Development	7.0	Diversity	4.6
Training	6.8	Social Responsibility	6.0
Travel opportunities	5.4	Corporate Governance	6.8
Culture	6.6	Environment	7.4
Total			**64.8**

From early days making sandpaper, 3M is now a global business spanning electronics to transport markets. Over the hundred years since it started as the Minnesota Mining and Manufacturing Corporation, 3M has grown to be one of the world's most respected companies with operations in more than 60 countries outside the USA. The UK is its oldest subsidiary.

3M's record for innovation continues with products such as: display enhancement films which make electronic displays brighter (eg in notebook computers and colour mobile phones); a new class of drugs for the treatment of skin cancer in healthcare; and 3M™ Composite Conductors for use in overhead power transmissions, which represent a huge advance for the power industry.

Around 2,000 of the 3,500 UK staff work in manufacturing. White-collar recruitment is mainly for engineering and process graduates. This is evenly split between manufacturing, IT, sales and marketing, and other areas.

Executive summary

3M is an $18bn diversified technology company with operations in some 60 countries. In 2003, its growth continued with net sales rising 11.6% and net income rising 21.7%, to $2.4bn. Since 1998 its earnings have outperformed both the Dow Jones Industrial Average and Standard & Poor's 500 (it is a component of both indices).

Despite its profitability, the company's share price suffered somewhat during the dotcom boom, as some investors perceived the company was beginning to lose its way. However, CEO James McNerney (recently voted CEO of the Year by Industry Week) took over the helm in 2000 and proved them wrong – in the last two years the company's stock price has outperformed NASDAQ, for example.

Global competition poses a real threat to UK manufacturing and 3M has addressed this directly with its trade unions. Together, they have found realistic ways forward, moving from a complex, adversarial industrial relations structure to single union agreements – a partnership approach. This was piloted at 3M Gorseinon and is seen to be beneficial to both parties, leading to more opportunities and site efficiencies. In addition, unlike some manufacturers, 3M's strength is its diversity and technology platforms and so it continues to identify new growth sectors – for example the area of biometric security where it is working on pioneering biometric document issuance and authentication and biometric verification.

Pay and benefits

3M positions its compensation and benefit levels at the industry average, with new graduates starting from £22,494 a year. The company has social and sports facilities at its larger bases, runs employee/family open days and operates a childcare voucher scheme. There is a company car scheme and medical insurance, plus a range of voluntary benefits such as life assurance.

In 2003, its existing defined benefits pension scheme was replaced by a defined contributions (retirement stakeholder) scheme. The company says it wants the benefits to be the same as under the old plan, the difference being who carries the risk – under defined benefits it was the company, while under defined contributions it is fund-based.

It also operates very flexible bonus and special recognition schemes. This includes team and long-service awards, but perhaps the most interesting element is its Star (special thanks and recognition) scheme that empowers all employees to reward other employees with £25 with no authorisation required. Higher awards are available, but do require authorisation.

"The power of the Star scheme is massive," says Jeff Skinner, 3M UK's general manager of human resources. "Peer recognition is a huge motivator."

"However, recognition schemes cannot replace a simple 'thank you' from a line manager. Our staff surveys show that although the core recognition schemes are used most at HQ, employee satisfaction is rated equal across most locations – that tells us that day-to-day management recognition and behaviour is also important."

Promotion and development

Over 90% of 3M's management-level recruitment is internal, so there are good opportunities for promotion. There are also opportunities to change careers and move within the global 3M organisation, and for management and supervisory training. The company estimates that 90% of its management joined before they were 25, and says staff turnover is just 5%.

Where 3M UK does recruit strongly is at graduate and undergraduate level. It takes around 40 students a year for 12-month work placements and estimates that around 30% of these later apply to join full-time as part of its graduate intake, which also numbers 40 a year.

Graduate recruitment increasingly starts out on the web, with the initial sifting process using online tests, and continues with a two-day assessment. This involves group exercises, interviews and presentations; and involves line managers as well as HR staff.

Within the organisation, coaching and mentoring are encouraged. There are also considerable opportunities for development. Managers have their own training budgets – the aim being to provide job-specific training where appropriate, such as core supervisory skills for managers and leaders, with general learning used in other areas.

"Where there isn't a strong learning culture, for example in manufacturing, general learning can give people belief in themselves," says Jeff Skinner. "The more we empower people to take responsibility, the more productive and effective they are."

The company also runs a leadership development course in association with the London Business School. "It's like a one-year mini MBA, to broaden your business expertise and provide networking opportunities – that's the bit that costs least, yet is most highly valued," Skinner says. "You have to find good business reasons to talk, you can't just tell people to network. And people have to see the benefit and feel the time was well spent."

Company culture

3M is a supportive organisation with high standards of integrity, driving innovation through collaboration. Allied to its preference for promoting and recruiting internally, this has resulted in the average length of service in the UK being 15 years.

"3M attracts outgoing, friendly people and the company has a supportive feel," says Jeff Skinner. "We are also proud of our professionalism and our approach to people – there is a lot around the company culture that's supportive yet stimulating.

"The people who fit best at 3M are capable, naturally collaborative teamworkers," he adds.

The company has Investor In People accreditation at two sites, and takes a progressive and constructive attitude towards employee councils and the like, with industrial relations devolved to local plants. The company encourages a partnership approach, most strongly represented at its Gorseinon plant where it has a benchmark partnership agreement and from which it chairs an all-Wales initiative on partnership with ACAS. The company also conducts bi-annual employee satisfaction surveys with a good response rate (72% in 2004).

3M aims to keep its talent by helping people change roles if necessary, and by welcoming them back should they choose to leave and then rejoin. Skinner, for example: joined in finance, moved to manufacturing, left the company, and then rejoined in HR. "Working outside made me appreciate what I valued about 3M," he says.

More recently, a management team has been working to understand the work/life balance question. Their mission was to get ahead of the issue and develop plans and policies to deal with it before it becomes a problem.

The team has come up with several initiatives, says Skinner. "They include cultural and leadership messages; optional HR practices, such as flexible working and homeworking; core health support with help from a private health provider; and because a basic cause of stress comes from not feeling in control, we provide training in self management and clear objective setting, for example.

"It's a big challenge but also an opportunity – we now understand the issues and have a plan in place," he adds.

Innovation

3M, like many companies of its scale, is going through a corporate transition – increasing its globalisation without losing the local touch. It argues that faster communication means less need for autonomy and duplication in subsidiaries; and that a consistent, more process-driven approach can have advantages (a core set of definitions for performance measurement and appraisal is more cost effective than several local versions, for example).

It is a fine balancing act: continue to boost growth, improve productivity, cut costs and generate more cash – without denting 3M's hallmark creativity. Innovation continues to be vital. Not only does it provide a constant stream of new products, it is also a supreme motivator – a source of challenge and excitement for every employee.

"The success of the company is based on its ability to grow using its core technologies – whether that's abrasives or adhesives. Then, to make strategic acquisitions to complement these advances – such as in biometrics or optical," says Jeff Skinner. "3M is a huge multinational but the culture enables every employee to be entrepreneurial and innovative in their own area.

"On top of this, you're working in a company that does things the right way based on a strong ethical history matched by financial success."

Diversity and social responsibility

The company has formal policies in place to ensure that employees are judged on competence, knowledge and experience – rather than what it sees as other irrelevant concerns. Managers are trained in behavioural interviewing, and when recruiting, the aim is to supply them only with relevant information about candidates to avoid potential bias in who gets selected for interview.

A third of the company's staff is female, although this figure falls to 15% at management level. 3M does not hold information on the percentage that come from racial or religious minorities. It says it has no plans to actively change employee diversity, but adds that it recognises the importance of diversity in meeting stakeholder needs.

3M supports the communities around its UK locations with gifts of cash, products and usage of facilities. It encourages employees to work as volunteers, and via a two-year-old scheme called 3M 4Good, it will also pay each employee to spend a day working in the local community.

Via another scheme called care&share, the company agrees to match individual and team fundraising on a £ for £ basis up to a set limit. 3M UK says that its 2003 contributions to charitable, community and educational causes totalled £533,300 – of which £300,000 was in cash and the rest in employee time and gifts in kind.

Corporate Governance

3M has a single set of global Business Conduct Policies defining its corporate values and its ethical and lawful approach. This includes complying fully with applicable local rules and legislation such as competition laws, health and safety laws and regulatory requirements.

To address the governance issue, 3M UK and Ireland recently carried out a risk assessment and identified areas for attention, including specific regulation such as Sarbanes-Oxley.

The company provides managers and employees with training to help them understand the legal and policy requirements that apply to their jobs. Managers are also responsible for distributing and sharing the company's values and policies, while staff are provided with routes for feedback such as a facility on the company intranet where they can put confidential questions to senior management with the answers posted in the same place.

Environmental record

The company takes the position that using fewer resources and causing fewer environmental problems is a more efficient way to operate. It has an environmental health and safety (EHS) management system and uses EHS scorecards to evaluate the progress at various levels within the organisation.

It also requires its business units to conduct life cycle management (LCM) reviews on new and existing products; looking at their environmental, health, safety and energy effects from manufacturing right through to disposal. All UK and Ireland manufacturing sites are now ISO 14001-certified and it expects them all to be ISO 9000-certified by 2005.

3M says it can profit from producing products that are more environmentally friendly. It argues that society in general is moving that way, so if it develops those products before they are generally mandated it will gain an edge on its competition.

"We want to be ahead of the game, for example we were the first to invent CFC-free inhalers," says Jeff Skinner. "We feel if we can keep moving society's demands on, we can be successful.

"Environment and ethics are very good for the brand – it shows people you are genuine and can be trusted. 3M regularly scores highly on business surveys (for example it was ranked 17th in the Financial Times list of the world's most respected companies) and that says a lot."

AMV BBDO

Abbott Mead Vickers BBDO
151 Marylebone Road, London, NW1 5QE
Tel: (0) 20 7616 3500
Web: www.amvbbdo.com

A
M
V

B
B
D
O

Pay and Benefits	6.9	Innovation	4.8
Promotion and Development	6.4	Diversity	6.6
Training	6.1	Social Responsibility	6.6
Travel opportunities	6.4	Corporate Governance	6.3
Culture	7.5	Environment	5.7
Total			**63.3**

Abbott Mead Vickers (AMV) is the largest advertising agency in the UK, part of the worldwide BBDO group, and the winner of numerous industry awards. The AMV Group also covers a wide range of other activities such as PR, contract publishing and web design, thanks to a policy of diversification to build a broad communications offering for its clients.

AMV employs around 300 people in its core agency operations, whose recent successes have included campaigns for the Economist, Guinness and the RSPCA. The company's aim is to create the most effective campaigns, bringing business success to its clients and growth to AMV. It aims to continue growing in an advertising market that is static or declining, which means it must capture market share.

Executive summary

Founded in 1977 by the eponymous trio, Abbott Mead Vickers was acquired by BBDO (formerly a minority stakeholder) in 1998 in a £346m deal. BBDO is itself owned by Omnicom, the world's largest advertising conglomerate.

AMV has since served as a model for BBDO's other lead agencies, in particular for its diversification tactics. It is the UK's No 1 advertising agency with declared billings of £357m.

The market in which it operates is inevitably as cyclical as the economy, and is now coming out of a downturn during which money had flowed out of advertising-oriented activities. Fortunately, AMV's robust long-term client relationships, and its entry into areas other than advertising, have helped it emerge healthily from the downturn.

Advertising is a business which depends most heavily on its people – their talents and their passion – as all agencies have essentially the same other resources to work with whether they be offices, computers, and so forth.

AMV's plans to continue growing rely on it winning a bigger market share, and that in turn relies on how well it serves and treats its talent as well as its clients.

"We are on a trajectory; we are the biggest in London today, with the best client list and talent," says Farah Ramzan Golant, AMV's CEO. "We want to continue that growth in a static or declining market – we want a disproportionate share of the client's business."

Pay and benefits

Research by the Institute of Practitioners in Advertising puts AMV in the upper quartile of its industry for pay and benefits. On top of the starting salary of £19,000 for a graduate there are performance-based pay increases, spot bonuses and awards – such as one for account manager of the month, and another of £5,000 annually for an outstanding employee. Around 6% of staff own shares in the company by participating in the Omnicom share incentive plan (SIP).

The company also has a number of contractual benefits such as a pension plan (with opt-out), life assurance and a private health plan. Also on the well-being side, benefits include access to a nutritionist, a masseur and a complementary health practitioner.

Part-time working is an option; AMV has staff at all levels from senior management down working restricted hours for various reasons such as family commitments. Sabbaticals are used as a long-service reward – one month after 10 years, two months after 15 years, and three after 20 years.

"Then there are things to try and create an enjoyable working environment – a free breakfast and free fruit all day, a subsidised office, and when we do a party, we do it well," says Alison Chadwick, AMV's people director.

Chadwick argues that socialising promotes teamwork and rewards people for their commitment. The company therefore holds staff Christmas and summer parties, and arranges a subsidised ski-trip plus football and tennis tournaments, departmental social events and so on. "It's a virtuous cycle – if you hire the right people and treat them right, they reward you with better ideas," she says.

"We do celebrate our successes and the team involved," adds Farah Ramzan Golant. "It helps that your operation is very visible, and we try to make everyone and every department feel part of that creative drive; it's part of our pride in our work."

Promotion and development

One of AMV's achievements, in an industry notable for high staff turnover, is to make it possible for people to advance without changing companies. As well as training, it uses a number of other ways to retain staff, such as making it relatively easy for them to change roles within the company.

The result is that people tend to stay longer than the industry average, and although its top four managers were recruited externally, all have been there more than 12 years now.

"People pay a lot of lip-service to transferable skills but don't put the training or soft benefits in place. Getting one person to change offices is not enough," says CEO Farah Ramzan Golant. "We try to understand that good people are few and far between.

"We recruit six or seven graduates a year from universities and creative courses at colleges, typically via placements in account management or planning. At senior level it is more often from other agencies or companies, depending on the skillset."

The company has a section of its website devoted to graduate recruitment, aiming to give a sense of the organisation and the sort of work and daily experience an employee can expect.

New account managers begin with 10 weeks of basic training on the industry. After this comes a role as part of an account team and a residential course in communications planning. Training then continues via the company's annual development programme.

"We put a lot of effort into making sure our managers know how to manage. We use coaching, and part of a manager's performance review is focused on how well they manage," adds Alison Chadwick.

"Everyone has performance reviews. It's important for us to know how people feel, and formal reviews are so we can agree on the development needed to help people fulfil their potential. We know though that while having a formal process is very important, it's important to combine it with regular dialogue."

Company culture

"Some agencies do great work, others are great places to work; we manage to combine both," says Farah Ramzan Golant. "Trust is an important part of that. We expect a lot from people so we need to treat them like grown-ups. We don't want to homogenise people's ideas.

"The people who flourish here have all the required skills – creativity, good work – but over and above that they want to be part of creating solutions in a thoughtful and intelligent way. It's not a place where ego is the driver, but it's full of people who know their worth. Individualistic tramplers don't survive."

This is a company which expects emotional commitment, yet sees no reason why people can't debate and create in a relaxed environment. In addition, simply wanting its staff to balance work and life is not enough – it absolutely needs them to have a life outside work, says account director Mark Mulhern, as it's a necessary part of the job.

"You need to live in the real world to see what people are buying, what ads they see, and so on," he says. "We all love ads and how they work. Brands can be used against you if they're managed wrongly.

"People tend to stay a long time. There are a lot of women, and very good maternity policies," he adds. "We also have a very mature attitude to people coming and going. We will try to keep them, and if they come back it's almost like we've won them back."

He says that people who leave tend to go into something different, not join other agencies in the same field, because of the difference in attitude between AMV and its competitors. "Some other agencies can be aggressive, so our people wouldn't fit there," he explains.

Innovation

AMV looks for new and better ways to deal with the problems that plague its sector, such as high staff turnover and the issue of outsourcing skills that may have been peripheral in the past, but are now becoming core instead.

"We are formally instituting a best-before date," says Farah Ramzan Golant. "People tend to get worn out on an account, so we proactively move them before they burn out – to a new portfolio, say. It's more important to catch them then rather than wait for their sell-by date, which is when they may leave."

She adds that the agency is also adapting to an increasingly digital culture, and to the digitisation of media such as video and the web. For example, some creative production work that would previously have been passed out to specialist companies is now done in AMV's own studios, while staff have been supported in learning related skills.

"We are experimenting with doing our own post-production work, using freelance operators where needed, so we can keep the craft skills and control more of the process," she says.

"You need to hold onto the things that built your success, but be open to the unexpected – it's in the mindset of your people. I'm not building the business, I'm building the people who make up the business."

Diversity and social responsibility

The company's gender ratio is 60:40 (women to men) across management and staff, although people director Alison Chadwick notes, "There tends to be a higher proportion of women in some areas, eg management and client service, than in others, eg creative, which is typical of the industry."

It does not monitor the ethnic origins of its staff, but supports the Institute of Practitioners in Advertising's initiative to help attract, recruit and retain a more diverse range of graduates to the advertising and media industries.

On the social side, it is known as "an agency with a conscience" – in particular for its work on social issue and charity campaigns. Its pro bono work tends to be ad hoc, but recent examples include creating a free series of poster ads for its local church to encourage church attendance from the community, and elements of its work on the Big House project.

The latter is a halfway house for the homeless, which AMV conceived in association with a local day-care centre run by West London Mission. Staff at the company organised events to raise funds and worked with other organisations in the field to make Big House a reality. AMV says that, so far, it has a 100% success rate for residents moving on into their own accommodation.

Corporate Governance

As part of a US conglomerate, despite its UK location and focus, AMV's regulatory environment includes the likes of Sarbanes-Oxley alongside local factors such as UK corporate law. It also tests quarterly for compliance with US SEC (Securities and Exchange Commission) regulations.

It is very much a human organisation, operating as it does in a business where the ability to influence individuals at a personal level is key. Aspects such as its recruitment philosophy, its non-contractual schemes for rewarding teamwork and quality, and its management and appraisal techniques are therefore designed to reflect its company values.

AMV lists its values as: humanity, quality, teamwork and energy. It says that those values ultimately derive from its three founders; all of whom stayed with the agency for over 20 years, and who during that time hired people that shared their ideas.

Environmental record

Operating as it does in central London, AMV provides interest-free loans for season tickets, and as well as having car parking on site, it has cycle storage too. It also took part in a pilot scheme with Transport for London to offer discounted travel for part-time workers.

As a knowledge-based and office-centred operation, the company does not have the pollution concerns that a manufacturer might have; it still has a policy, overseen by its head of facilities, of recycling as much waste as possible. For example, IT equipment is donated to charity for re-use where practical, or otherwise recycled, while paper is recycled, after shredding if needed.

Adecco

A

Adecco House
Elstree Way, Borehamwood, WD6 1HY
Tel: (0) 20 8307 6000
Web: www.adecco.co.uk   www.adecco.com

Pay and Benefits	5.5	Innovation	6.2
Promotion and Development	6.3	Diversity	6.7
Training	5.8	Social Responsibility	5.8
Travel opportunities	5.0	Corporate Governance	6.1
Culture	6.5	Environment	6.0
Total			**59.9**

Adecco is the UK subsidiary of Adecco SA, a publicly listed company, which is headquartered in Switzerland and is the world's top employment services company. Within the UK it employs 1,350 of its own staff, known as colleagues, and every day it supplies over 30,000 contract staff and temporary workers, which it refers to as associates.

It works in all areas of human resources, and especially in recruitment and contract staff. It is the biggest recruitment firm in the UK, having its roots in Alfred Marks and now including such well-known names as Office Angels and Computerpeople.

Executive summary

In 2003, Adecco SA had revenues of €16.3bn and net income of €305m, up 26% on the previous year. The company says that Adecco UK's 2003 sales were up 5% and its "profitability increased substantially" helping to offset business declines in other European regions. Adecco SA has two principal shareholders and has been profitable for the last eight years.

Adecco staffing's core work in the UK is recruitment for permanent or temporary staff. It has high street branches, off-high street offices, a corporate managed service division, and offices located on site with large clients. Its onsite work varies from basic recruitment to complete outsourcing of full departmental operations.

Not surprisingly, Adecco locations vary hugely in size from branches with just one or two staff, to large corporate operations which employ up to 100 people.

It is becoming harder to be profitable as a recruiter, because these days you are dealing with procurement rather than HR departments and "large procurement projects can equal ever tightening profit margins for the recruitment provider," says Mark Bloxham, Adecco UK's marketing and communications manager.

He adds that, "With the advent of the web, it's easier than ever to apply for a job – you can place an advert and get 25,000 replies," but points out that this can make specialist expertise even more valuable, because rarely do pressured managers or HR departments have the resources or knowledge to sort through that many applications.

"Recruitment can often be seen as a simple business, but we offer a complete range of services – everything from single local job placement to outsourcing managed services such as whole internal departments," he adds.

Pay and benefits

Adecco positions the basic pay of its colleagues at or above the industry average, aiming to compete instead on bonuses and benefits – this is a sales business, and bonuses can potentially double the salary of a good and hard-working consultant, it argues.

The company's high proportion of female staff means that it has had to offer good maternity benefits, such as childcare vouchers and flexible working. It says that 58% of those returning from maternity leave go on to flexible working – typically this means reduced hours. Some also work from home, although obviously this depends on the role.

Flexible benefits are purchased via a salary sacrifice. There are company cars (or the equivalent cash allowance) for specific roles, and some 13% have shares in the company. The pension plan is under review, however the existing plan allows colleagues to contribute from day one with company contributions depending on job grade.

The biggest learning curve for the recruitment industry is at eight to nine months; new starters can find our industry tough, says Mark Bloxham. "Once you get past that point, you stay. The average is probably three to four years now, five to six years at head office. We have 164 people with over five years service."

Compared to its competitors, Adecco also takes an enlightened attitude to its associates; putting them on contract rather than treating them as freelance contractors.

"What we offer is different from what others do, for example a travel scheme and support schemes for temporaries with flexible working," says Mark Bloxham. "The welfare of associates is as important to us as the welfare of colleagues, because they are our major asset."

Promotion and development

Adecco makes extensive use of internal promotion, to the extent that all of its board directors and the bulk of its regional and departmental managers were internally promoted. It estimates that some 40% of all vacancies are filled internally, and although some of these vacancies are the result of staff turnover, many are new roles that are created as the business grows.

In 2004, Mark Bloxham said: "We opened 100 branches last year, we will open over 70 more this year, and every one needs a manager. We rarely recruit managers – it's an internal push. Turnover is at entry level because of peaks and troughs in the economy." The company has worked to reduce staff turnover too: Bloxham says it is now coming down to around 25%, at a time when the average for its industry is above 40%.

Once inside the organisation, Adecco colleagues can expect an average of eight training days a year. The company uses a range of techniques, including e-learning, and defines four core skillsets plus another 120 courses – not all of which are vocational. For example, the core includes the rules and regulations affecting recruitment, their implementation, plus the effects of minimum wage legislation.

The company admits that it can be harder in some departments – for example, in teams where people have individual roles – than in others, but says that continual development and access to training is now a directive from the board.

"There is a lot more onus on flexibility, as a huge number of people don't want to work five days a week, although it is difficult to balance," says Bloxham. He points out though that the company already does that "load balancing" for its associates.

Company culture

Adecco has been through drastic structural and cultural evolution in the last few years, driven by the appointment of a new global MD in 2001. In particular, all the management reporting lines have been flattened and significant extra emphasis has been placed on internal communications. The result is an organisation which its own staff describe as consultative, empowering and reactive.

Tools and systems for internal communications are especially important in a business where 1,000 of its 1,350 UK employees are branch-based and therefore remote from head office. In Adecco's case, they include its own monthly TV programme called Echo and an intranet called Doo Lally – both of them named by staff polls.

"People have said they didn't choose recruitment as a first industry choice; they fell into it. A lot of our people have huge amounts of knowledge from other industries," says Mark Bloxham. "We touch every area of the business in all environments, dealing with a variety of people, so we need that variety of people too. We need that diversity to meet client business needs."

He says that there is no single profile of the ideal Adecco colleague, but that the pressure means they tend to be "go-getters, forward-looking people with big personalities, and relationship builders. People who are scared of keeping up can get lost along the way. We don't have easy days, no one's never busy."

The company is also working more globally now, both to support the recruitment needs of its multinational clients and to ensure that expertise is shared where feasible. For example, its Commitments programme, which promises better service for clients and candidates alike, has now been rolled out in 28 countries.

In addition, the global organisation means that there are opportunities for overseas assignments or permanent moves to Adecco offices abroad – the company has on occasion used the latter to retain staff who would otherwise have left the organisation when emigrating.

"We are working more globally now, so people get an opportunity to see other accounts. We also have a number of second-language speakers," Bloxham says. "We want a single corporate identity but we are also very aware of cultural differences; we look for the shared message within that's going to work."

Innovation

The company claims that its Commitments programme is the recruitment industry's first service guarantee scheme. The programme lists six commitments made by Adecco to its clients, six more to candidates, and another six to colleagues. It says that it is also the first company in its sector to use TV for internal communications and sharing best practice. It has also brought in new systems to monitor diversity, and improve working conditions and pay for its candidates.

Adecco's position within the recruitment industry gives it access to just about the broadest possible range of HR expertise and knowledge from many different industry sectors. This in turn allows it to bring innovative ideas and best practice to candidates, its clients, and its own staff. For example, it is able to monitor the progress of bespoke HR solutions implemented for clients, and plan further innovations based on that.

Diversity and social responsibility

The recruitment business relies heavily on people skills, so it is little surprise to find that a relatively high proportion of Adecco staff are female – the company estimates it is over 80%. Around three-quarters of branch and regional managers are women too, although the proportion falls above that; men make up 57% of the company's UK board of directors.

Diversity monitoring is voluntary, making it difficult; however, Adecco believes that it is in line with its localities as regards employment of racial and religious minorities. It has also been working to combat age-related discrimination – it says that some of its most successful branches are run by people over 40, as they understand the clients and candidates well and can make very good tutors.

The company supports local charities through Business in the Community (BITC) and via funds that it allocates for sponsorship, often to causes identified by its branches. It prefers to provide support in areas that it can influence, such as the ageing population, diversity and equal access.

Through its parent company's Adecco Foundation (a non-profit association based in Italy) and its local Adecco Plus programme, Adecco UK also focuses on unemployment and integrating (or reintegrating) disadvantaged groups into the workforce. It involves its clients in this where possible, for example it has recruited homeless people to jobs in liaison with IBM UK's main CSR programme.

Corporate Governance

As well as UK employment, health and safety, data protection and anti-discrimination legislation, Adecco highlights its responsibilities under US compliance and corporate governance rules such as the Sarbanes-Oxley Act. "We have had a team working on Sarbanes-Oxley for 18 months; we want certification a year early," says Mark Bloxham. "The big thing is knowing how it will affect you."

The person ultimately responsible for this within Adecco SA is a British lawyer Tunde Johnson, who was appointed in September 2003 to the role of compliance and business ethics officer.

Fortunately, after ½100m-worth of extensive investigation and audit work (and the departure of a number of its US managers) the company came through with a completely clean bill of health – and perhaps the most accurate set of accounts in the business.

As well as its involvement with BITC, Adecco UK has Investor In People accreditation, is a City & Guilds approved centre, and holds a number of other accreditations including ISO 9001:2000.

Environmental record

The paperless office is one of Adecco's stated aims – in the meantime it encourages staff to make communications brief, to recycle paper, re-use envelopes and use recycled paper. Printer and copier cartridges and other waste materials are also recycled where possible, and mailing lists monitored to reduce wastage.

Company cars are allocated only where required for business responsibilities, and branch managers are required to share the use of their company cars with branch staff. The company also promotes the use of public transport where practical.

Adecco's head office and all its branches are non-smoking areas, and staff are encouraged to switch off lights and electrical equipment when not in use.

Adidas UK

Adidas UK Ltd
Pepper Road, Hazel Grove, Stockport, Cheshire SK7 5SA
Tel: 0161 419 2500
Web: www.adidas.co.uk

Pay and Benefits	6.2	Innovation	7.0
Promotion and Development	6.0	Diversity	6.2
Training	6.6	Social Responsibility	6.2
Travel opportunities	6.7	Corporate Governance	6.2
Culture	7.3	Environment	5.6
Total			**64.0**

One of the best-known brands in sport, Adidas was founded by the eponymous Adi (Adolf) Dassler in 1949. Floated in 1995, the company acquired winter sports specialist Salomon two years later, renaming itself Adidas-Salomon AG. It now employs 15,700 people and claims approximately 15% of the world sporting goods market. As well as Adidas (footwear, clothing, bags and balls), the company's brands include Salomon and Bonfire (winter sports), Mavic (cycling), TaylorMade and Maxfli (golf), Arc'Teryx (outdoor) and Cliché (skateboarding). Adidas Area North (UK, Ireland, Belgium and the Netherlands) is a marketing, retail and distribution operation employing about 740 staff, with its HQ at Stockport, near Manchester.

Executive summary

Adidas is the world number two in sports goods; the company is trailing Nike by a short head in Europe, by several lengths in Nike's US heartland. Sports goods form a mature, fairly flat market in which Adidas has returned a solid performance: consolidated net sales climbed from ½5.8bn to ½6.3bn from 2000–03, with earnings per share showing steady growth.

Behind the scenes, however, Adidas must work hard to maintain its position. The market is highly competitive; while Adidas pursues its worthy, if optimistic, strategic aim of toppling Nike from its perch, it must keep innovating and streamlining even to stand still.

The Area North business unit (UK, Ireland, Belgium and the Netherlands) was created in 2003 and is now the company's best performing unit in Europe. In 2005, Adidas plans to significantly increase its retail operation in the UK – almost doubling its tally of 13 shops and moving into more prestigious, high street locations. This will entail a cultural shift from a predominantly marketing and distribution operation to a fully-fledged retailer and could, if successful, add 20% to UK turnover. The company is also expanding into fashion goods (see below).

Pay and benefits

Adidas aims to pay middling salaries, benchmarked against sports and consumer goods companies, but backed up by a healthy benefits package. The company's success in achieving its targets means every employee has received a bonus in each of the last 12 years; the level depends on personal performance, ranging from 8–25% for management grades. Whenever the company breaks a record or hits a significant target all staff receive token rewards such as gift vouchers, while individuals may be rewarded with a weekend break or a trip to a major sporting event (four shopfloor workers went to Portugal for the 2004 World Cup). Staff with 100% attendance records will also receive incentives.

The company's position as a major sponsor (think Olympics, World Cup, British Lions) means it often has access to sporting events in the UK and abroad; many workers get tickets to Manchester United, Manchester City, Newcastle United and Liverpool games which they might not otherwise be able to afford. There is also a free Wellness Centre at the company's Stockport HQ, with a huge gymnasium and a medical centre. More conventional benefits include free BUPA for managers (and at discounted rates for other ranks), life assurance, discounts on company products, a subsidised restaurant, Christmas parties and long-service awards.

All staff may join the pension scheme, with contributions of 4% from the employee and 5.5–8.5% from the company. Cars are provided for essential users and for senior managers, who can take a cash option instead. Holiday allowance is 25 days, rising to 28 with service. A few very senior managers receive stock options, but there is no company share purchase scheme. The company is considering moving to a fully flexible benefits system. It is also considering giving childcare vouchers, as there is no childcare on site.

Promotion and development

"Adidas Area North has developed a reputation as a breeding ground for talent," says the company's director of human resources, Tony Cooke. "When there are roles available within the wider group, the recruiters tend to come looking here first."

Adidas has devised eight personal archetypes (with – you've guessed it – a sporting theme) under which to classify people: spectator, solid player, emerging player, champion etc. Energy is then focused on developing the emerging players and champions rather than the linesmen. Personal development will almost certainly involve changes of function, as the person "zigzags" (their own phrase) along their career path. "We deliberately try to recruit people who don't want to develop their careers vertically," says Cooke. For example, the current directors of business process development and range management both joined the company as sales people.

Adidas recruits at graduate level, but not enough to have a formal programme. The organisational structure is flat, and annual staff turnover is 8%. The company's retail expansion will precipitate a very significant recruitment campaign for experienced retail staff at all levels from manager to sales assistant.

There is no formal training quota, but most staff get about 2–4 days a year; Adidas spends the equivalent of 1.5% of payroll on training. The employee development manager creates a training and development plan for each business function, and helps identify key talent and ensure these people receive the right training – with a lot of emphasis on people management and personal skills. The company partners with Loughborough University and Dale Carnegie to provide recognised managerial qualifications. Finance and HR professionals study for professional qualifications, and one person has been sponsored to take an MBA. Potential high flyers may be whisked off to Adidas-Salomon's Campus Europe in Germany, from where they enjoy postings around Europe supported by a structured development programme.

Company culture

If you don't like sport, don't apply to Adidas. There's a gym, badminton league and running club, and staff are as likely to meet customers on the company's private soccer pitch as in a meeting room. "The vast majority of people we recruit are users of our products, and everyone here is passionate about sport," says Cooke. They are encouraged to wear company products to work too, since dress codes are very informal, "like dress-down Friday every day," says Cooke. Almost anything goes (unless, of course, it sports a Nike logo).

This informality reflects the company's rather laid-back style. "We're not big on meetings for meetings' sake, and not very long-winded with our decision making," says Cooke. Passionate pragmatists thrive; bureaucrats and procrastinators don't. The layout is very open-plan; the managing director, Gil Steyaert, queues up in the canteen and sits with the staff; and the firm prides itself on a culture of fair play and freedom of speech.

All staff receive a quarterly briefing from Steyaert on business performance, new products etc., at which they can ask questions. They can also send him direct emails and make suggestions via a "clearing house" with a guaranteed response. In the latest staff survey (the second the company has conducted), 90% of respondents said they were proud to work there.

Official working hours are 8.45am–4.45pm, but the offices are open on Saturday and Sunday and Cooke admits that there is a long-hours culture: "people are passionate and they do spend a lot of time here." There is no formal policy on work/life balance – managers are left to their own initiative – but the company does seem at last to be waking up to the issue. On the positive side, the company supports flexitime, job-sharing and part-time working; staff must take their full holiday entitlement; and the Wellness Centre offers counselling on stress and personal issues.

The company's offices are in a pleasant location, in well-to-do Cheshire within easy reach of Manchester and Liverpool, but there are excellent opportunities to go further afield. More than a quarter of staff travel abroad, especially to other Area North countries. Positions often come up at Adidas-Salomon HQ in Germany, and there are opportunities in the USA, eastern Europe and the far east.

Innovation

Adidas believes success in the sporting goods sector is intrinsically linked to innovation in both technology and design. The company has a long history of product innovation and plans to launch at least one major new technology every year. Recent examples have included Climacool breathable shoes and fabrics, the Roteiro thermal-bonded football, Ground Control System shock-absorbing footwear and T-MAC 4 laceless basketball boots.

Recently the company has diversified into fashion goods – some sportswear, some not directly related to sport such as retro fashions. To assist in this, Adidas has gone into partnership with top designers, including Stella McCartney and Yohji Yamamoto – an innovative step for a sports goods manufacturer.

Diversity and social responsibility

Adidas is a young company, with an average age of 31; even board members average only 39. The company has the usual policies on equal opportunities. Women make up 47% of all staff and 14% of the management team. Ethnic and religious minorities account for 3% of staff, which the company is working to increase by forming relationships with local schools and colleges.

The company supports two charities: Action Heart, and Genesis Trust Cancer Care. It sponsors local children's sports events with gifts of kit, and offers work experience and student placements.

Corporate Governance

Although Area North is allowed some autonomy, many of the strategic decisions are taken at Adidas-Salomon HQ in Germany including product design, PR strategy and guidelines on headcounts, remuneration etc. Being a wholly owned subsidiary, Area North does not publish separate financial statements. There is no union representation only a motivated works council.

Area North has received its fair share of external recognition, including The Sunday Times 100 Best Companies to Work For 2004, The Dale Carnegie Leadership Award, and the 2004 Sports Industry Award for the best TV sports commercial for ads featuring David Beckham and Johnny Wilkinson.

Environmental record

Adidas cannot judge its environmental performance since it does not benchmark it. There are corporate environmental guidelines, and the facilities manager is a member of the Institute of Environmental Management and Assessment. The company recycles cardboard, paper and toner cartridges; and disposes of unusable IT equipment and fluorescent tubes as special waste. There are bike sheds on site, but access by public transport is limited.

AEGON UK

AEGON House, Edinburgh Park, Edinburgh EH12 9XX
Tel: (0) 870 600 0337 **Fax:** (0) 870 600 0338
Web: www.aegon.co.uk **Email:** groupcom@aegon.co.uk

Pay and Benefits	5.8	Innovation	5.8
Promotion and Development	5.6	Diversity	5.0
Training	6.7	Social Responsibility	5.7
Travel opportunities	4.8	Corporate Governance	7.1
Culture	6.3	Environment	6.4
Total			**59.2**

AEGON UK has assets under management of over £34bn and is a member of the AEGON Group, one of the world's largest listed insurers, employing 28,000 people worldwide and about 5,000 in the UK. It is currently on track towards its vision of being recognised as a leading provider of long-term savings and protection products. The businesses (grouped according to the core activities of manufacturing and servicing, asset management and advice) are Scottish Equitable, Scottish Equitable Protect, Scottish Equitable International, Guardian Financial Services, AEGON Asset Management UK, Origen, Positive Solutions, HS Administrative Services and Benefit Solutions.

Executive summary

AEGON UK is a key player in the UK long-term savings industry, and its goal is an average autonomous annual earnings growth of at least 10%. Over the last couple of trading years pre-tax profit has been what it describes as "extremely stable" – £130m in 2003, £146m in 2002, £231m in 2001.

Revenues have increased steadily over the past five years from £3.45bn to £4.28bn, and total assets have gone up from £32.6bn to £34.45bn.

The company says that the figures demonstrate that it has the reserves in place to weather future storms, and it places much emphasis on the fact that AEGON UK has brands that are household names, such as Scottish Equitable.

Nevertheless, incoming chief executive Otto Thoresen, who takes over in the early part of 2005, has authorised a strategic brand review – a clear indication that AEGON UK does not hesitate to challenge the accepted, and is prepared to change in its desire for continued success.

Pay and benefits

Ian Tomlinson-Roe, director of human resources and communications, states: "We have to ensure that we pay the appropriate level to attract and retain quality staff; we benchmark annually what we pay within the financial services sector and across other sectors as the employment market becomes more competitive."

It is accepted that people have different priorities, and that means a flexible pay and benefits scheme that compares favourably with what is provided by other financial services companies. All the right ingredients are there – a defined contribution pension scheme (the final salary scheme is closed to new recruits), long-service awards, a top achievers' conference for sales staff, stock options, a car scheme, life assurance, childcare vouchers, and line managers are allowed to sign "supercheques" for individual or team achievements.

The gross starting salary of a graduate is around £18,500 and he or she can take advantage of flexible working – 13.2% of staff work part time and employees can also opt to work in ways that suit their circumstances.

The addition of Tomlinson-Roe to the team is interesting. In 2003, the company had to make around 800 people redundant. It was painful and AEGON UK did all it could to help and counsel affected staff.

It called in an expert to help them get it right – the managing director of People Solutions with KPMG in London. That was Tomlinson-Roe, and they liked his style so much that he is now in a role elevated from group personnel manager to director of human resources and communications.

The cynics might say that is because they might have to go through a similar process again, a more enlightened view is that it is giving even more priority to dealing with and communicating with people.

Promotion and development

AEGON UK's view is that if it fails to offer development opportunities to its staff it will lose them, and if it does not maximise the potential of people in the organisation it is failing them. Line managers are in constant discussion with staff over their needs and promotion opportunities – to get to where they want to be it is likely that they will need training and that is given priority at AEGON UK.

It calls on leading business schools and educational establishments for help and has its own virtual AEGON University which is run out of Holland and operates for three weeks a year in different global venues. About 60 people a year take part and it is all about sharing knowledge that is within the AEGON Group.

Through the company's Professional Development Scheme, staff have a chance to develop by undertaking a course of study leading to professional qualifications. The company pays the costs and time off is allowed for studying.

Under this scheme, a number of staff are sponsored through some high-level qualifications, including an MBA. The need for coaching and mentoring is generally identified through a performance management system or by discussion with an organisational development consultant.

The same performance management system is used to identify those with talent. Development will be tailored to their needs and can include a wide range of methods such as training and development and secondments, and there is a succession planning process which will also identify key successors and those with high potential.

Company culture

AEGON UK's motto is centred on three phrases – respect people, make money and have fun. These are described as guiding principles, but constant hard work and dedication are required to stick to them. Like many organisations, AEGON UK has gone through a challenging couple of years; people have been made compulsorily redundant for the first time and that had to be tackled in a sensitive, caring way.

This would put a strain on any company culture but AEGON UK stuck to its core values of respect, quality, transparency and trust. It did not lose the trust of the staff in difficult times, and did not incur the ire of the trade unions with the way it dealt with the situation.

The company culture could be changing with the arrival of the new chief executive, Otto Thoresen. He has made it clear that nothing is forever and that AEGON UK needs to undertake a review of its various brands.

It is stressed that at this stage it is simply a close examination of the brand structure, which any well-run company should do, and it might not result in any major change; but should AEGON UK decide to drop the 170-year-old Scottish Equitable brand, it will herald a change in the company culture – and certainly be a cultural shock.

Innovation

The cornerstone of the company's success to date has been innovation. It is innovative in its use of technology to bring products to the market and improve communication with its customers, and it sees itself as being a market leader in developing a number of products ahead of its competitors.

Can it be innovative simply to acquire companies? It is the AEGON UK way. There are considerable changes in the independent financial adviser (IFA) market. Costly regulatory compliance has put a question mark over the future of many IFAs and the distribution channel that is so important for providers of financial products.

While others have hesitated, AEGON UK has boldly taken minority stakes in national IFAs and acquired five IFAs outright; amalgamating five of them into one entity, calling it Origen and bringing to the market a bold new brand.

It has set Origen ambitious business development targets over the next three years and it has also taken a majority investment in Positive Solutions, a dynamic national IFA business.

Acquisitions and taking stakes in companies are old hat, but in the IFA sector it is innovative.

Diversity and social responsibility

The view is that the customers are diverse in their nature and that should be reflected in the people the company employs. The company policy quite clearly states that no members of staff or applicant for employment will be discriminated against on the grounds of race, sex, religion, marital status, nationality or disability. It says this policy will be followed at all times and in particular will apply to recruitment, selection, promotion and training opportunities.

The Executive Board has signed up for a project to review and broaden the company approach to diversity, which accepts the principle that it will be a mainstream business issue. The project involves reviewing all areas of HR policy such as recruitment, training and development, and reward. "We don't do it because we have to do it – we do it because we are a responsible corporate employer" is the company answer to the diversity question.

The company has developed a Code of Conduct to support corporate responsibility; this includes creating a positive workplace, influencing others, complying with laws and regulations, making responsible investments and respecting the environment. Three charities are selected each year, and through a mixture of staff activity and company support, each charity receives around £20,000 a year.

Corporate Governance

According to the outgoing chief executive, David Henderson, in the company's 2004 corporate brochure, Synthesis, AEGON UK is committed to maintaining a robust corporate governance structure for the protection of its stakeholders' interests.

It operates in a heavily regulated sector and complies with the requirements of the Financial Services Authority (FSA).

That covers a multitude of possible sins to the extent of sometimes seeming to be overbearing – but AEGON UK accepts that the laws that govern its relationship with its customers and the requirements of the FSA are key, and every aspect of its operation complies with these laws.

Although the AEGON Group promotes a decentralised management approach, there is a code of conduct – developed by employees across the group – which outlines a series of business principles, rules of conduct and core values which cover all businesses and all employees.

Environmental record

AEGON UK is doing all the right things. It sees its environmental responsibilities as being global as well as national and local, as befits its business. It has a UK-wide environmental management scheme, which aims to balance the need for resources and the impact of their output on the environment and is focused at the local market levels.

The company has various contracts with a specialist company, which segregates and recycles waste where appropriate. This can mean recycling something in the region of 70% of all waste. IT waste is disposed of and recycled through an accredited company.

At the Edinburgh Head Office there is cooperation with relevant bodies to improve train and bus links to the office, and there is a complementary bus service from the train station to the office that replaces a 15–20 minute walk. But it has to be said that the public transport provision is poor.

Argos

Argos Ltd
489-499 Avebury Boulevard, Saxon Gate West, Milton Keynes MK9 2NW
Tel: (0) 870 600 3030
Web: www.gusplc.com   www.argos.co.uk

Pay and Benefits	5.5	Innovation	6.0
Promotion and Development	5.8	Diversity	6.5
Training	4.8	Social Responsibility	6.3
Travel opportunities	3.0	Corporate Governance	6.3
Culture	5.0	Environment	6.5
Total			**55.7**

Argos is a major retailer of general merchandise. It employs more than 20,000 people (plus around 20,000 seasonal temps between October and January) and operates over 560 stores throughout Britain and Ireland, which it says puts it within 10 miles of more than 95% of the UK population. It estimates that two-thirds of UK households now have an Argos catalogue.

Its sales are based on catalogues which are published twice a year; customers can consult these in-store, or take one home, and order goods for collection on the spot. In recent years it has added a home delivery service, telephone ordering for collection at a nearby store or delivery, and an award-winning website.

Executive summary

Argos is owned by the retail and business services group GUS plc, which acquired it in 1998 for £1.9bn. GUS has spent the ensuing years repositioning Argos from a value brand to become the leading UK retailer in many sectors (eg toys, small electrical appliances and Christmas gifts). Christmas is its busiest time of year, accounting for 40% of annual sales, with smaller peaks in January/February and August when it publishes its new catalogues; during these busy periods HQ staff help out in the stores.

Argos has been one of the fastest growing large retailers in the UK. In 2004, it had sales of £3.4bn and profits of £297m – a growth rate of 45% and 76% over the last three years. It is currently opening 35 new stores each year.

Argos is a multi-channel catalogue retailer, and while it has high street stores nationwide, its fastest growing channel is its website. As well as allowing customers to order online for home delivery, the website also lets them check stock levels and reserve items for collection at a local store.

The company's aim is to be the UK's No 1 non-food, non-clothes retailer, doubling its business over the next five years. It recognises the threat posed here by the supermarkets in particular, as they grow their non-food business. However, it believes that it can compete – for example by offering a convenient delivery service, and by careful investments in pricing as well as in the necessary systems and infrastructure (including its distribution centres).

Pay and benefits

The company aims to be in the top quartile for retailers, according to its Retail HR manager Sonia Astill. She adds that the basic pay differential between it and its competitors could decrease; Argos awarded an inflation-based general increase of 3% while the National Minimum Wage rose 7.5%, choosing instead to make substantial investment in performance-related pay rises and bonuses.

Those bonuses are based on overall company performance and on local areas that staff can affect, for example customer service in their store, using techniques such as mystery shoppers to check performance. There is also a discount scheme for staff and their immediate family.

Argos has uniforms for its store staff, while the head office dress code is smart-casual. Benefits such as a pension plan and health insurance are provided to certain grades within the company – these grades apply broadly across the organisation, not just at head office.

Of its staff, around 1,100 are at Avebury (head office) in Milton Keynes, an average of 400 work at each of its seven regional distribution centres, and most of the rest are in its high street stores – each of which has a management team of three or four. Many staff work as part-timers, particularly in the stores.

Staff can also participate in the Sharesave Scheme of its parent company GUS, which was introduced in 2001. This allows them to buy shares at a 20% discount using a tax-free savings account; they can save between £5 and £250 per month, then after three or five years the account matures and can be used to buy the discounted shares, or the accrued savings can be taken in cash.

The first issue of the GUS Sharesave Scheme matured in 2004, with an average profit per member of £2,590 and the top investors receiving over £10,000 each. 31% of Argos staff currently participate in the scheme.

Promotion and development

"We expect people to some extent to take the initiative and manage their own development," says Lucy Calver, Avebury HR manager. She adds that each area of the business has two elements to development; one being the standard functional and behavioural elements for an individual's current job, the other being training to help them move through the business.

Training programmes exist at several different levels. Internet-based learning is also used within the stores and the company has invested in human resources and learning support. Argos spends 5.4% of payroll on training.

"We are advanced in internal and external executive coaching," says Calver. "We have staff appraisals at least annually. It is an ongoing process with formal mechanisms and a formal link to pay; it also links to development and our corporate values.

"We use 360-degree appraisal only in specific areas, but there is feedback from employees on managers – it is a tool to help people develop, not a way to force them to do things."

The company also aims to promote internally where possible, as well as enabling staff to change roles or even to leave for another job and return later. Retail HR manager Sonia Astill, says that many store management teams include at least one person who originally joined as a Christmas temp.

"In stores, we encourage people to gain different experiences," she says. "Management turnover is under 10% – it's a loyalty thing. There is also crossover between stores and head office."

Company culture

Argos has undergone significant developments in its corporate culture in recent years. At its Milton Keynes head office, the change programme has included a move to open-plan working to encourage teamwork, internal communication and general openness; and the stores have been refurbished as part of its brand reinvigoration, says the company's HR director Carol Kavanagh.

The company has also worked hard to establish its new values and become more customer-focused. For example, it uses its internal publications to focus on its values – which are expressed in succinct and practical language – and how its people fulfil them.

"It's a positive culture which gives you the ability to be master of your own destiny. It's an excellent working environment, with a sense of fun and people who are supportive and approachable," Kavanagh says. "There is very little bureaucracy – people come in expecting big company bureaucracy but say it's not what they expected.

"It is a fast pace though, so it can be stressful – that's true for non-management staff too. People have to handle change well and take ownership of issues. One blocker is an inability to work with ambiguity; we expect people to take a lead fairly early on. We look for a can-do attitude – here's a challenge, get on with it."

In the past, graduate recruitment has been relatively ad hoc, Kavanagh says. Now though, Argos is planning to bring around 50 graduates a year into function-based roles as part of its fast track development programme and as it plans for future growth that could see its business volumes double over the next five years.

Innovation
One of the company's big innovations has been its development of multiple retail channels, alongside strengthening and repositioning its brand. The latter process has been accelerated recently by a successful TV advertising campaign starring Richard E Grant and Julia Sawalha.

The Argos Direct channel makes 10,000 customer home deliveries every weekday and its website is one of the most visited sites in the UK – it became the most visited high street retailer on the web during the Christmas 2003 trading period.

It has now added mobile e-commerce channels too, allowing customers to order via Vodafone Live! and text messaging; and made innovative use of technology in its stores, for example installing kiosks where customers can check stock levels and pay online.

Diversity and social responsibility
Over half of the company's employees are female, including the managing director and many of its part-time workers. Women occupy nearly half of all its store management positions, and the company adds that the percentage of racial and religious minorities on staff maps to the local catchment areas too.

Argos supports a different national charity each year – in 2004 this was Whizz-Kidz, which improves the mobility of disabled children, and in 2003 it was disability charity Scope. Staff are encouraged to get involved in fundraising activities, such as carrying out stunts under the Argos Olympics banner and collecting redundant mobile phones and inkjet printer cartridges for recycling, says corporate responsibility manager Laurence Singer.

The company prefers people-related charities and community projects, especially those relating to children. As part of this, the company's stores are supplied with video and educational materials to donate to local schools.

Argos, and the charitable trust of its parent GUS, support a range of other initiatives too – for example the National Association of Toy and Leisure Libraries' Good Toy Guide and its associated awards. At Avebury, Argos runs a scheme to provide around 200 children in local authority care with Christmas presents.

The company is also involved in supporting the government's fire safety campaigns, as a Partner in Fire Prevention. These campaigns aim to reduce the consequences of household fires.

Corporate Governance
Argos believes in good practice and good corporate citizenship, and five years ago it defined a set of company values during a culture change programme. These include customer-focus, teamwork, taking ownership, and respect and support for colleagues. Among other ways, it builds these into its organisation via induction courses, its benefits and appraisal schemes, and its publications.

As a retailer and provider of financial services, Argos is directly affected by a range of regulations and legal requirements. These include the British Retail Consortium Best Practice Code on Extended Warranties on Electrical Goods, and the Association of British Insurers Code of Practice for General Insurance. Its Argos Card Services arm is a member of the Finance and Leasing Association, which has its own Consumer Code of Practice.

Argos has partnership agreements with the USDAW and T&G trade unions.

Environmental record

Corporate responsibility manager, Laurence Singer, says that Argos takes its responsibilities seriously in areas such as recycling and sustainability. The latter is especially important for a retailer carrying many thousands of different product lines, any of which could raise questions over their environmental impact.

"We are in the upper quartile for corporate responsibility," Singer says. "We have audited over 60% of the supplier base for direct imports, looking at environmental and supply chain issues. We are setting targets for waste minimisation, energy reduction, timber from sustainable sources, and so on."

Argos encourages customers to recycle its catalogues and flyers, saying they are sought after by newspaper print manufacturers because they help to improve the quality of the recycled paper in newsprint. It also aims to become more efficient in catalogue distribution – in 2004 it used 73,700 tonnes of paper to produce its catalogues, a 38% decrease on the previous year.

It also recycles mobile phones and inkjet printer cartridges for charity, and offers a free collection service for old white goods such as cookers and washing machines (though not fridges and freezers at present) when a customer orders a new appliance for express delivery. Within its warehouses, the company is installing balers so it can recycle more material such as cardboard.

ARM

ARM
110 Fulbourn Road, Cambridge CB1 9NJ
Tel: (0) 1223 400400 **Fax:** : (0) 1223 400410
Web: www.arm.com

ARM

Pay and Benefits	7.1	Innovation	7.5
Promotion and Development	6.9	Diversity	6.7
Training	6.6	Social Responsibility	7.2
Travel opportunities	7.2	Corporate Governance	6.9
Culture	7.2	Environment	7.3
Total			**70.6**

ARM designs low-cost, power-efficient chips to power mobile electronic devices such as phones, digital cameras, games consoles and automotive systems. Rather than manufacturing chips itself, it pioneered the concept of licensing its technology to a network of partners that includes 19 out of the top 20 semiconductor vendors worldwide. ARM was established in November 1990 as Advanced RISC Machines Ltd – a UK-based joint venture between Apple Computer, Acorn Computer Group and VLSI Technology – and went public in April 1998. It now employs approximately 1180 people in 10 countries, and is the leader in reduced instruction-set computing (RISC) chip technology.

Executive summary

If you own a mobile phone, a digital camera, a games console or MP3 player, chances are that there's an ARM chip inside it. Efficient, cost-effective chip technology is what makes today's portable electronic devices possible and ARM has established itself as the pioneer in low-cost reduced instruction-set (RISC) computing, a technology that makes it possible to produce fast, low-power chips ideal for use in handheld computers. According to analyst estimates, nearly 75% of the 538m RISC chips shipped in 2001 were based on ARM technology.

Apple and VLSI both provided funding, while Acorn supplied the technology and ARM's 12 founding engineers. Rather than manufacturing chips itself, ARM took the route of licensing its intellectual property to partners, and signed up its first licensee in 1991.

The arrival of Nippon Investment and Finance (NIF) as a major shareholder in 1993 brought ARM the investment it needed to start establishing a global presence. It opened offices in Asia, the US and Europe, and in April 1998 listed on the London Stock Exchange and NASDAQ. ARM is now a global corporation, employing more than 790 people in facilities in 10 countries and on three continents. This number is growing fast, since ARM is actively recruiting in line with demand for its products in the marketplace.

ARM has been hit over the past three years by the downturn affecting the whole technology sector and by the weakness of the dollar, and its share price has suffered accordingly. However, thanks partly to tight cost control, it continued to make a profit throughout the downturn and its cash position has improved steadily year on year. As the industry emerges from recession, the company is looking forward to improved profits and revenues once more.

Pay and benefits

Though ARM keeps a watchful eye on industry pay rates to ensure its salaries are in line with the market, it believes in offering employees a total reward package that includes benefits and quality of working life as well as money. As an innovator, it naturally attracts staff who want to work with other talented people in a company respected for its ground-breaking chip design. And as a "big small company" it aims to offer all the benefits you would expect from working for a major organisation – plus some others besides.

There are twice-yearly pay reviews, with an element of pay differentiated on individual "contribution" – not just in terms of contribution to profits, but also based on qualities such as teamwork, responsiveness and proactivity. It's possible for employees who perform well to double their pay increase. ARM believes that all employees have the right to share in the organisation's success, so everyone is on an annual bonus linked to overall company performance.

As well as this, ARM employees are offered a range of benefits including private healthcare, permanent health insurance, travel insurance, a pension scheme, life assurance; and a confidential employee assistance programme, which offers a phone advice line including legal advice and counselling.

ARM's equity package is particularly impressive, with all employees – from the most junior right up to the top – being awarded share options. In addition, there is a Save As You Earn (SAYE) scheme, which allows employees to buy shares at a discount without risk.

Many ARM employees have said that the thing they value most is time, and the company has adapted its reward package with that in mind. Employees can work flexible hours, and are entitled to buy or sell extra days holiday. After four years of service they can take a four-week sabbatical on full pay. ARM also offers enhanced maternity leave, with six weeks on full pay then 50% pay for the remaining 20 weeks. Fathers can have two weeks paternity leave, with the first week on full pay.

Promotion and development

For a company like ARM, whose intellectual property is its prime asset, attracting and retaining skilled employees is vitally important. Figures suggest the company is good at it: staff turnover has been consistently low at around 5% per annum since 2000. A committed and enthusiastic workforce has enabled the company to grow from 12 people in 1990 to more than 700 in 2003.

ARM has also received a number of independent accolades for its employment policies, for example it was named as the Employer of the Year in the UK National Business Awards for 2003.

The company believes that continual self-improvement through reflection and feedback, coaching and mentoring, training and education, is the lifeblood of personal and organisational change. Through on-the-job and formal training, it aims to promote employee development on both an individual and team level.

The company runs generic core training courses, but also training tailored to individual needs. As well as being used to assess pay increases, the ARM performance monitoring system is also used to identify training support needs.

Those on ARM's two-year graduate scheme are assessed every six months for promotion. It is a relatively young company and has some senior people still in their 30s. However, the company needs excellent engineers as well as general managers, and recognises that not everyone has to be promoted in order to progress in the company. You can be a valued employee and see your pay increase while staying at the same grade.

Employees can expect to receive a week to 10 days of training each year, but this does not include the regular conferences ARM holds to get different communities in the organisation together. In any given year, a quarter to a third of the organisation will have attended a conference of some kind. Each year, for example, the company holds an innovation conference; this is a cross-functional event not limited to a certain type of person.

Company culture

If you're passionate about electronic engineering, then ARM is the place for you. What the company describes as "the ARM adventure" attracts the brightest and best engineers from top universities, keen to join ARM in pushing back frontiers in chip technology. Even non-engineers joining the company (in finance, HR, sales or marketing) will need to be enthused by the company's products and their potential – and can enjoy the satisfaction of seeing the company's work translated into ground-breaking electronic devices three or four years along the line. Some might find this nerdy; others will find it exciting and challenging.

ARM describes itself as "a small company playing in the big league". It maintains a small company feel, and qualities like selflessness and teamwork are valued highly. The company recognises that as it grows it will be harder to maintain this culture, but it is working to preserve it by, for example, rewarding altruism and a helpful attitude as part of pay and performance reviews.

Management works to foster a culture of participation and involvement, and employees can contribute to decision-making processes through a number of internal conferences and briefing sessions. The ARM Consultation Forum has been established to represent the 500 or so employees in its UK offices, and a worldwide employee satisfaction survey is carried out every two years to measure ARM's performance as an employer and ensure it is meeting employees' expectations.

ARM aims for an informal environment where creative people can flourish. There is no dress code – if engineers want to come to work in shorts and a bobble hat that's not a problem, though sales staff tend to wear more conventional clothing. Working hours are relaxed too; in the Cambridge site it's not uncommon to find people playing chess in the atrium at 2pm, and the onsite gym is used throughout the day.

Though the main site is in Cambridge, the company designs its products across design centres worldwide and employees are encouraged to go on assignment to different offices.

Innovation

ARM's business is all about innovation: finding new ways to make smaller, faster, cheaper chips to meet demand for ever more compact and powerful handheld electronics. Chips using its designs can be found in leading-edge products in markets including automotive, consumer entertainment, imaging, microcontrollers, networking, storage, security and wireless.

The company was the first to produce a low-cost, low-power RISC chip design suitable for use in portable and embedded devices, and has won several awards for its innovative technology. It continues to innovate with elegant, power-efficient chip designs that in turn make it possible to build ever more compact mobile products, which cost less and have a longer battery life.

Technology is not the only area in which ARM has innovated: in the early 1990s, it pioneered the concept of openly licensable chip designs. By licensing, as opposed to manufacturing its chip technology, the company established a new business model that redefined the way microprocessors are designed, produced and sold.

ARM aims to be proactive rather than reactive in its product design. It talks constantly with its customers to find out what mobile devices will be like in five years' time in order to be able to innovate around future needs. This forward-looking approach is enabling it to stay ahead of its field and play an important part in shaping where the digital world is going.

Diversity and social responsibility

ARM is committed to the statements in the Good Corporation Charter, and is verified against them annually. It gives donations and sponsorship to a range of educational institutions working in the areas of science, mathematics and IT; for example, it has sponsored a degree course in semiconductor design at Loughborough University. It sponsors the Royal Institution Mathematics Lectures, which aim to stimulate school students' interest in mathematics, and contributed to the training costs of the UK's International Maths Olympics team. ARM also supports a number of organisations that promote engineering as a potential career to young people.

Based in Cambridge, ARM has provided financial backing to specialist schools in the Cambridge area, and given money towards a new ICT suite for a local junior school. It is also one of the sponsors of Cambridge Arts Theatre.

But as well as giving its money, the company encourages its employees to give their time and skills to help with local causes. Several of its UK employees are local school governors, and others help coach young people through their first business projects. ARM employees in Austin, Texas have worked at the Austin Food Bank and got involved in the Texas Special Olympics, while California employees distributed and unloaded food at a local distribution centre.

ARM strives for equal opportunities for all present and potential employees. It recruits on the web and employs a wide range of different nationalities. The company is, frankly, male-dominated – but that just reflects the fact that the vast majority of engineering graduates emerging from universities are still men.

It also works hard to make company information accessible to all employees. Many of its documents are published in PDF format, which enables the text size to be manipulated to suit individual needs; and since November 2003, new technical document PDFs have been designed to be able to use screen-reading software for visually impaired users.

Corporate Governance

ARM is taking steps to ensure it complies with the Financial Services Authority's Combined Code on Corporate Governance.

Its board is currently made up of five executive directors – the chief executive officer, chief operating officer, chief financial officer, chief technology officer and executive vice president for marketing – plus four independent non-executive directors and the chairman. A resolution to change the company's Articles of Association to increase the maximum number of directors from 10 to 12 was approved at the 2004 AGM. This would enable further non-executive directors to be appointed, with the intention that they will make up at least half the board.

The board is aware of the principle in the Combined Code that it should undertake an annual performance evaluation, and the first review of board effectiveness took place during 2004. In 2003, the executive committee (which includes the executive directors other than the chairman) also worked with third-party facilitators on a board effectiveness programme that included collective and individual performance evaluation.

During 2003, the chief technology officer and executive vice president for marketing attended a three-day training course for plc directors run jointly by Henley Management College and Ashridge and Manchester business schools. Further training for directors is planned.

Environmental record

ARM's production processes are largely intellectual rather than physical, and as a result the company is graded as a low impact business in environmental terms by EIRIS, The Ethical Investment Research Service. Nevertheless, the company acknowledges that all business activity has some impact on the environment and is aiming to measure and improve its performance by using Department of the Environment, Transport and the Regions (DETR) guidelines. It monitors its energy usage and business travel, and aims to reduce consumption of resources such as paper, water and packaging through recycling and improved efficiency.

As well as measuring its business travel, the company collects data on the transport methods its employees use to and from work. It encourages greener commuting by providing cycle sheds, showers and changing rooms at its UK offices. There are fewer than 20 company cars in the entire organisation.

ARM has a rolling programme of measures to reduce paper usage. In 2002, it sent electronic greetings cards rather than traditional printed ones, and its Corporate Social Responsibility reports have only ever been published electronically for environmental reasons. It has aluminium can recycling bins in most of its offices, and aims to use less environmentally damaging refrigerants in its air conditioning systems.

Ascent Media

Ascent Media Group Ltd.
1 Stephen Street, London W1T 1AL
Tel: (0) 20 7208 2200
Web: www.ascentmedia.co.uk **Email:** topemployers@ascentmedia.co.uk

Pay and Benefits	6.4	Innovation	7.3
Promotion and Development	6.6	Diversity	6.6
Training	6.6	Social Responsibility	6.5
Travel opportunities	5.7	Corporate Governance	6.6
Culture	6.6	Environment	6.5
Total			**65.4**

Ascent Media is a world leader in end-to-end media services for the entertainment industry, providing post-production resources and next-generation digital media techniques. Highly creative, Ascent Media talent brings feature films, hit TV series and commercials to life – including recent blockbusters such as King Arthur, Troy and Alfie. Ascent Media's global divisions include creative services, media management services and network services. With over 3,000 clients worldwide – including the leading names in media, entertainment and advertising – Ascent Media Group has over 50 locations in the US, UK and Singapore. Over 1,200 people are employed at a dozen facilities and studios situated in London's trendy, vibrant Soho and colourful Camden Town.

Executive summary

Imagine it's 9.15am, you've just finished your first cappuccino, and you get down to work. And work is creative input to the images in a Hollywood blockbuster movie yet to be released or a major TV drama series. That's what working at Ascent Media is about. People really touch the product – a highly visual product.

There aren't many industries in which Britain is an inspirational world leader, but the sexy world of film and TV post-production is one of them. "Our people are at the front end of the back end of production. It's highly creative – our people think of themselves as artists," says Brenda Smith, Ascent Media's personable UK group managing director. A glittering collection of Oscars and other awards is proof. This is a fun, energetic business – and its people love it.

Owned by the Liberty Media Corporation, whose UK investment stands at £80m, Ascent Media is financially secure. UK turnover is £80m, and Ascent Media has tripled earnings (before interest, tax, depreciation and amortisation) in three years. In a recent customer survey, 68% said that Ascent Media was "better" or "much better" than its rivals. "We do serve big global clients, but no job is too big or too small," says Smith. "We can be an 800-pound gorilla or a cuddly pussycat."

Ascent Media is a very young company – a baby really. It's just five years since Liberty bought and merged a number of smaller legacy companies and leading studios in London, which it recently re-branded as Ascent Media. It has fast become one of the largest and most recognised forces in the UK for technological innovation, creative talent and complete media solutions.

The talented people at Ascent Media help deliver content in its most creative form; processing film, adding special effects, sound mixing, editing, formatting and sub-titling. It also provides technical services in media management – including digital asset management, restoration and duplication – and delivers content (transmission) through network services.

Pay and Benefits

"You can earn a lot working in the media, but first you must earn your stripes," says Jo Dolman, UK HR director. "We're very fair, even though we don't have to chase people." This is a highly attractive company to work for. But Ascent Media wants to retain the people it has invested in and participates in an annual independent survey of 20 media companies to check that it pays competitively within the sector.

Everyone is salaried, and increases reflect inflation and individual performance. A percentage of senior managers' pay is variable, depending on business unit and company performance. Bonuses are awarded for sales generation. Everyone is eligible for a Summit Award worth £250, where anyone can nominate a colleague for doing something beyond normal duty.

Benefits are fairly standard and include life assurance, pension (5% matched contributions), private health cover and private medical insurance at a certain management level. Maternity and paternity pay are above statutory levels.

Unsurprisingly, a highly creative workforce spills over into a buzzy social life – a double benefit of working in the media and in Soho. Work and social lives invariably intertwine. Employees run the social committee. Apart from the high-octane parties, "gallery nights" (where employees exhibit their own work over a glass of wine) are highly popular, as are "band nights" where Ascent Media people are the live entertainment.

Promotion and development

Ascent Media is bursting with creative and technical wizards: editors, graphic designers, transmission controllers, schedulers, sound mixers, DVD authors, producers, telecine operators and videotape operators to list but a few. Professional, managerial and administrative functions are found in the corporate unit, but are also very much integrated with the individual business units. Each has an MD and retains its own brand identity, but operates within an overall Ascent Media matrix. The joins are seamless and people work across all operations.

A media industry tradition, many people join Ascent Media as "runners". "They literally run errands and get to know Soho like the back of their hand," says Dolman. "There's lots to do for clients, so they have to make themselves useful – preparing rooms, making tea and coffee, and cleaning up." The upside is that in their free time, runners can sit in on all the studio production processes, watch the experts, learn and decide which path they wish to follow after about six months. "Runners need a great can-do attitude," says Dolman. "That's what gets you noticed and weeds out those who really want to get ahead." Around 50–60 runners start the race each year. Two of Ascent Media's managing directors began as runners.

Seniority reflects competence. Assistants acquire technical skills and progress onto small projects; but, effectively, promotion means working on the bigger, more prestigious jobs. Juniors sit in with experts who, having benefited from this process themselves, are extremely willing to share their skills and knowledge. In addition, Ascent Media has an in-house technical trainer, whose courses are so popular that clients ask to join them.

Everyone has an annual performance and development review where personal targets are set. Management courses are based on leadership and soft skills development, and managers receive mentoring and coaching. Ascent Media also runs specialist workshops on topics including employment law, recruitment skills and policy implementation. Professional membership and examination qualifications are paid for, and Ascent Media contributes to MBA study if appropriate.

Some 50% of vacancies are filled internally. "Although you need good technical skills, because we work so closely with clients, attitude, interpersonal and teamworking skills are more important," says Dolman. Ascent Media people move across different business units and there are opportunities to work in the US, full time or on project secondments.

"The great thing about this business is that you don't have to have super academic qualifications to be very successful," concludes Dolman.

Company culture

Buzzy, fun, happy and creative are all good descriptors. But Ascent Media focuses relentlessly on its clients – the biggest household names in the media industry – and this requires teamwork. Smith joined Ascent Media because: "I liked the way in which the US and UK teams interface and work together collaboratively. With so many owner-manager businesses to meld together the company has done fantastic things on limited resources."

"Jeans and T-shirts are the norm, but you shouldn't be fooled by this," says Dolman. "The underwear is a real professionalism, work ethic and talent."

In the annual survey, employees said overwhelmingly that they love the people they work with. Ascent Media urges employees to mix. "If they know one another and their talents, they work effectively as a team, even though they might be in different locations," says Dolman. Communication is key. Smith sets the tone, keeping people informed on everything. She holds regular "meet the masses" briefings at each facility but is just as likely to drop in for a chat over coffee. US senior management flies across the pond twice-yearly for "town hall" meetings with managers (to then cascade to staff). There are newsletters, intranet and an employee communications group. An offbeat channel is "Ken Talk Radio" where the US CEO records a downloadable interview on what's happening in the business.

HR – the department and policies – has grown tremendously recently, revealing how seriously the company takes people issues. HR is very people focused; is staffed with professional CIPDs; and has worked hard to establish a uniform approach, standardise procedures and achieve parity across a collection of individual businesses. Ascent Media operates flexible or part-time working for employees with childcare commitments (men and women) and has 15 homeworkers, including one in Norway!

Innovation

"The fantastic thing about Ascent Media is that it supports this can-do approach," says Smith. "People have the freedom to move into anyone else's territory, without inhibition, and all ideas are considered." This licence to interfere has spawned many innovations. For example, Blade – an exciting digital interface tool for storing and managing high-value assets that clients can easily download and view. "We're constantly identifying how to help clients adapt to where media services will be in five years," says Smith.

Indeed, four facilities in the UK – with additional support from the US – collaborated to define the workflow process for a new digital intermediary process that takes film to data, enables data manipulation for colour and special effects, and then "churns back out" to film. It was first used on King Arthur.

A spirited initiative called the Rushes Soho Shorts Festival allows young, aspiring film producers to submit short films, which are viewed and judged over a week-long event around Soho. The winner of the short film award, which is sponsored by Ascent Media, gets access to studio services, including Blade, to enhance their project.

Diversity and social responsibility

Ascent Media is very much an equal opportunity employer, giving everyone the same chance of progression. Diversity is not an issue here. The managing director is female and her predecessor was of Asian origin. Half the UK managing directors are women. The media business has never worried about cultural differences, personal beliefs, gender or gay issues, and so on. In fact, Ascent Media positively encourages a richly diverse workforce.

Disabilities are accommodated in the workplace – Ascent Media works closely with the National Library for the Blind, makes adaptations for wheelchairs, and shifts are changed for people receiving hospital treatment. "Media is a young people's business," says Dolman, "but some of our people in the film labs are 70. Others retire and then come back – they can't keep away!"

Ascent Media excels in community work, harnessing its media credentials as a potent means for engaging young people. The company visits schools in disadvantaged areas, explains the media business and offers work placements. In conjunction with Kodak student commercial awards, Ascent Media processes and transfers film at no cost to the students. Ascent Media works closely with Business in the Community, and with Skill Set has helped to devise a training programme for the industry. At the request of employees, Ascent Media operates a Give-As-You-Earn scheme.

Corporate Governance

Ascent Media takes all aspects of corporate governance very seriously. In-house legal affairs and company secretariat teams ensure that Ascent Media is fully compliant on all matters including employment law, finance and data protection; and Ascent Media puts everyone on PAYE unless they prove they are genuinely self-employed.

It provides training in its Code of Ethics for every single employee, including a 40-minute programme giving guidance on issues like business behaviour, confidentiality and receiving gifts. There is even a Code of Ethics helpline for employees to ring if they are concerned about anything. Issues raised are almost always investigated.

Environmental record

Ascent Media is hardly a polluter, but it does its bit to be as environmentally friendly as possible. There are recycling bins for toner, cartridges and paper in all offices and studios. Everyone has access to a computer and email to avoid wasting paper unnecessarily: HR policies, communications – everything is available online. The maintenance team's mantra is "repair it – don't chuck it out". Also, the company pension scheme has an option to invest in ethical and environmentally friendly funds.

Bacardi-Martini

B

Bacardi-Martini Ltd
West Bay Road, Southampton, Hants SO15 1DT
Tel: (0) 23 8031 8000
Web: www.bacardi.com

 BACARDI-MARTINI LIMITED

Pay and Benefits	6.6	Innovation	5.8
Promotion and Development	6.8	Diversity	6.2
Training	6.3	Social Responsibility	5.7
Travel opportunities	5.8	Corporate Governance	6.0
Culture	6.7	Environment	5.2
Total			**61.1**

Bacardi-Martini is the UK subsidiary of the family-owned, global manufacturer and distributor of premium-brand alcoholic drinks including Bacardi rums, Martini vermouth, Bombay Sapphire gin, Bacardi Breezer ready-mixes and Grey Goose vodka. The company's site at Southampton docks, acquired during the merger with Martini in 1993, is its largest in Europe – mixing, bottling and distributing Bacardi-Martini products to the UK and 50 other countries. The company also distributes Glenmorangie malt whisky and Drambuie liqueur; as well as Jack Daniels, Southern Comfort and Finlandia vodka in a cost share arrangement with Brown-Forman. Most of its 540 staff are based at Southampton, with around 100 field sales staff working remotely.

Executive summary

Bacardi-Martini is a successful company in a declining market. Sales peaked in 2001 at £409m, partly thanks to the success of ready-mixed drinks such as Bacardi Breezer. Since then, the general fall in ready-to-drink sales have seen turnover stabilise at £327m in 2003–04.

But Stella David, the company's dynamic and charismatic managing director, is not downhearted. "We're a very sustainable business," she insists. "If you invest in them, successful spirits brands last a very long time – Bacardi is more than a century old. We don't get involved in things which are here today and gone tomorrow."

Sales of Bacardi rum, still the company's core product, have grown 25% over five years; Bombay Sapphire gin sales have quintupled since 1998 and still have big potential, says the company. Partnerships are also important, especially the cost sharing agreement with Brown-Forman, owner of the Jack Daniels, Southern Comfort and Finlandia vodka brands.

Bacardi-Martini was confident enough to pay a 10-figure sum in 2004 for the Grey Goose premium vodka brand (little known in the UK but a major player in the super premium vodka category in the USA, says the company), and would consider further acquisitions to gain complementary brands. The company is still owned by the Bacardi family, but the feeling is that flotation is a possibility in the longer term.

Pay and benefits

Service beyond the call of duty at Bacardi-Martini is more likely to be rewarded with a pen and a pat on the back than with hard cash. This is not meanness, but culture: nobody expects to be paid extra for working hard or having good ideas, since these are part of their job. "We pay in the top quartile and offer great benefits and a great working environment, and in return we expect people to go the extra mile," says Kathryn Jackson-Day, director of human resources. Thus the company eschews performance-related pay and commissions for sales staff, preferring managers to "surprise and delight" deserving staff in simple, human ways, for example taking them out for an ice cream on a hot day.

Not that the firm is stingy. Salaries are benchmarked to keep them in the top quartile, and everyone is eligible for a performance-related bonus of up to 10% of salary. In addition there is an annual company bonus of up to 15% (actually 4% in 2003–04, probably around 6 or 7% in 2004–05). The company is still owned by the Bacardi family, so there can be no staff share ownership.

Benefits are generous and are identical for staff at all levels; they include free health care for staff and their families, free eye tests, free restaurant offering three-course meals, free hot and cold drinks, long-service awards of up to £600, occupational health checks and counselling for staff and families, residential retirement seminars, and some liquid cheer for Christmas and birthdays.

The non-contributory pension scheme is also open to all, with company contributions of 7–13.5% depending on age. Holiday allowance starts at 24 days, rising to 29 days after five years' service. Car allowances are provided for mobile sales staff and management grades.

Promotion and development

Jackson-Day is refreshingly honest about Bacardi-Martini's attitude to promotion. "In a lot of companies promotion happens too fast," she says. "On average, we like someone to be in a job for at least two years so they can become really proficient before they move on."

Moving on is important, however. Developing people's careers occupies a lot of management time, even at board level for senior staff, and it is company policy to challenge people (eg making a young brand manager the marketing manager for Grey Goose) and encourage them to move between disciplines as they progress. The company is divided into commercial (mostly sales and marketing, plus product innovation, accounting, IT, HR etc.) and production (bottling, warehousing, distribution etc.), and it is common for people to move between the two.

Recruitment takes place at all levels, principally for junior sales reps, but the preference is to promote from within –more than 70% of posts are filled this way. Staff turnover is 11% pa, mostly among junior sales people; there is a core of long-serving staff and nearly half of the managers started their careers with the company. Two of the five board members are aged under 50 (including David) and most of their direct reports are under 40.

Each staff member averages at least five days' training a year, and the training budget is 3% of the total salary bill. The aim is to develop management and people skills as well as technical capabilities. One person has taken an MBA with the firm and many have qualified or are qualifying in accountancy, procurement, HR etc.

The Bacardi Learning Centre, a newish computer-based training suite with remote access capability, provides a range of computer software training and is being extended to offer non-vocational courses. Talented staff may also be sponsored to take external training; one technician learned photography and film making, and now produces the company's videos and brochures.

Company culture

When we met Stella David she had just finished a tête-à-tête with one of the warehouse staff, her standard practice with all recruits on completion of six months' service. On her desk was a pile of birthday cards awaiting her personal signature – everyone gets one every year, plus something with which to drink their health. This approach is typical of the company's management style ("high-energy but very informal," says David, which just about sums her up) and it's reflected in the cheery demeanour of its staff – the security guard even called me "young man" as I signed in.

David's approach is simple. "I come to work to enjoy myself and I expect other people to do the same," she says. "But I don't want anyone to enjoy themselves unless they're doing a good job." She also believes in "catching people doing something right, not doing something wrong," and says "we evaluate people by how they behave as well as what they achieve."

Being privately owned makes the company entrepreneurial. "Because there are no City shareholders to please, if you have a good idea and you can justify doing it, you can," says Jackson-Day. The annual staff attitude survey is taken very seriously ("listening is a waste of time unless you're prepared to change things," says David) and there is an Involvement Group for staff consultation. There seems to be no "us and them" divide between the commercial and production operations, and the company says union relations are excellent.

The docks area of Southampton is rather grotty with little lunchtime interest (hence, in part, the free restaurant and onsite shops) so the lunch break is only 30 minutes, with an earlier finish. People work hard, but it's not a long hours culture and there's a subsidised gym on site for relaxation. Flexible working is supported including homeworking, part-time working, flexible hours and a couple of job-shares.

Because Bacardi-Martini is a global company there is plenty of opportunity to travel. About 40% of staff travel abroad each year, especially on the sales and marketing side; and people have been posted to India, South Africa, Australia, Mexico and the Asia-Pacific region.

Innovation

Creativity is one of Bacardi-Martini's management maxims, and although its best-selling product was drunk by the Victorians, the firm knows it must keep innovating to remain successful. It's a team effort, says David: "Innovation isn't just about new products, but how you promote them and how you involve your people in the development of the brand."

One of the firm's most startling successes was Bacardi Breezer, still selling well after more than a decade. The next big thing, the company hopes, will be Kalyr – a long, creamy, fruity drink trialled in Northern Ireland in 2004 for UK-wide launch in 2005.

The firm believes in continuous incremental improvement in business processes too, and cites its single-tier benefits package and computer-based learning centre as examples of its innovative approach to HR.

Diversity and social responsibility

"I think Bacardi-Martini is all about individuals," says David. "I'd be horrified if I thought there was a 'company type'. I think you need diversity of opinion and experience."

The company has an equal opportunities policy linked to recruitment procedures, and employee liaison and union representatives are trained in these procedures. About 5% of staff come from ethnic minorities (slightly above average for the Southampton area), while 31% of staff and 34% of managers are women; David is the only woman on the five-person main board. Focus groups are run on ethnic minority and women's issues.

Bacardi-Martini is aware of the social and health problems of drinking, but claims its attitude is responsible. Its products are premium brands, aimed only at adults, and it frowns on happy hours, 2-for-1 deals etc. It helps educate local groups, such as students, about safe drinking; and although its own products are much in evidence on site, all the bottles remain full.

The company gives modest support to charities. Staff have raised £20,000 in two years for local animal and hospice charities, and the firm will match staff members' fundraising efforts for other causes.

Corporate Governance

Being privately owned, Bacardi-Martini is not subject to the full rigour of accounting scrutiny, but it believes it fully complies with all relevant employment, health and safety, environmental and commercial regulations.

The company is one of only two to be placed in the top 10 in all four years of the Sunday Times 100 Best Companies to Work For (fifth in 2004); it was Batley's Supplier of the Year in 2002; and in 2003, Bacardi-Martini was acknowledged by Tesco as its best wines and spirits distributor.

Environmental record

Bacardi-Martini rates its environmental record as "fair". It is working towards ISO 14001 certification for the elimination or recycling of waste, and has recently audited all its waste contractors. The company uses movement sensors and low-energy lightbulbs to save electricity, and recycles plastic cups and waste paper. Most staff have to drive to work because access by public transport is not appropriate in the docks area.

Barclays

Barclays Plc
54 Lombard Street, London EC3P 3AH
Tel: (0) 20 7699 5000
Web: www.barclays.com

Pay and Benefits	6.5	Innovation	6.3
Promotion and Development	6.3	Diversity	6.8
Training	6.0	Social Responsibility	8.0
Travel opportunities	5.0	Corporate Governance	7.3
Culture	6.3	Environment	6.8
Total			**65.3**

Barclays is one of the world's largest financial services groups, employing 82,000 people around the globe – 80% in the UK, where Barclays is the third-largest banking group, behind HSBC and RBS. Its principal operating groups are Personal Financial Services (UK banking and the Woolwich, between them servicing 14 million personal customers); Barclaycard (11.4 million customers – one in five credit cards in the UK is a Barclaycard); and Business Banking (over 730,000 customers). Barclays is a full-service operation and also includes investment banking, asset management, and Barclays Private Clients (high net worth customers) as well as Barclays Africa.

Executive summary

In terms of market capitalisation, Barclays is one of the top ten largest banks in the world. A leading high street name with the best-known UK credit card operation, it also provides investment banking, investment management and coordinated services to multinational corporations and financial institutions worldwide.

Like most of the big-name banks, Barclays has been doing rather well of late. For 2003 Barclays reported profits up 20% at £3.8bn, and the first half of 2004 continued the good news with a 23% rise in profits (£2.4bn, well above City forecasts).

Pay and benefits

People are critical to Barclays – the group argues that its business is driven by how energised and committed the staff are, and says this is reflected in the rewards structure. Base pay is targeted at the market average, but there is potential for earning large bonuses at all levels – the more you are able to impact the business, the bigger your potential bonus, but it's typically 10–15% even for clerical staff.

The good news is that bonuses (and performance appraisals generally) are based not just on what the individual achieves, but how they achieve it. So, for example, growth and development are as important as any sales outcomes. And this is a systematic approach: Barclays has developed a sophisticated scorecard scheme based on customer service metrics to assess staff progression.

Like most employers, Barclays has moved away from a final benefit pension scheme, replacing it with the award-winning "afterwork scheme" that combines a guaranteed retirement fund with the opportunity to invest in the stock market. It requires employees to contribute a minimum of 3% of their salary.

Barclays has an extensive benefits catalogue that includes deals on Barclays products and discounts on other products.

All employees have the right to ask for flexible working arrangements and where possible the company is keen to take a supportive view. That's seen too in unpaid parental leave and adoption breaks that exceed the government's minimum rules; and maternity "buddying" is an interesting idea, giving new mothers the chance to talk to a friendly maternal mentor.

As you would expect from a bank, the financial options are extensive, with an SAYE monthly savings plan that enables staff to purchase Barclays shares at a 20% discount; and the Sharepurchase share incentive plan which lets you contribute between £10 and £125 per month towards tax-free share purchases. Barclays estimate that 65% of their employees have a stake in the company through their employee share plans. Together, they represent the biggest private shareholder group. There are also recognition schemes (awards and rewards for exceptional contributions), tax-free saving for childcare and car purchase deals for managers.

Private medical cover is available immediately for most management levels, and to all staff after one year's service. Cover can be extended to include partners and dependent children.

Barclays offers up to 30 days' paid leave, with additional time off available for family or compassionate needs as well as for participation in voluntary organisations. You could also apply for an unpaid career break where your job will be held open for between one and five years.

Promotion and development

All banks tend to be formally structured with established hierarchies and the clear lines of responsibility that are required for financial transparency and probity. Barclays is no different, but there's a flipside: the structure means clear career development opportunities, with an easy-to-read CV resulting from it. The company's size also allows for sideways moves as well as simply upward progression – there is a huge variety of roles and career paths available throughout the organisation that bring all kinds of opportunities to develop new skills.

Barclays has always been highly regarded for the quality of its training – available via the intranet as well as in conventional face-to-face courses. The award-winning Barclays University lists courses for work-related and personal development, and there's a grant of £150 pa towards any extra training anyone might want. Essentially any and all training is available, though obviously Barclays will target its resources on what it feels will be of most benefit to the business. Barclays also considers requests to support professional qualifications and MBAs.

The HR department at Barclays has a sophisticated, market competitive and highly developed approach to the professional development of its talented individuals, and runs many specifically designed development programmes to identify and grow talent.

The Business Leadership Programme (graduate recruitment) is highly rated – graduates are recruited for specific professional streams, but all spend three months in customer-facing training followed by up to 12 months in placement with the relevant department. It's a fast-track programme with a good success rate of quick entry to management-level jobs.

Company culture

Barclays has a set of "behaviours" which it believes set the tone for the company. They include the common goal of "delighting customers" and the equally important "protect and enhance our reputation". They also emphasis performance (encouraging achievement, avoiding complacency) and dynamic execution (taking ownership of collective decisions and pushing through change where it is needed).

This sounds at odds with the traditional representation of banking as old-fashioned and stuffy – this is because Barclays has put a great deal of effort into changing that image. From the new employee's viewpoint, Barclays comes across as a consensus-oriented organisation that makes much of internal networking and team operations, but also wants the individual to contribute positively.

It seems to be working: Barclays is an employer that can retain its staff – the average length of service is 11 years and individuals now have the right to request to work up to the age of 70.

Barclays is an international group, operating in 60 countries. Some 30% of the workforce is outside Britain, and while there is a policy of staffing with local nationals, there are some international opportunities for expatriates.

Employees are continuously encouraged to have their say via a range of mediums such as the annual Employment Opinion Survey, interim surveys, roadshows, company magazines, events and conferences.

Innovation

While retaining a strong sense of heritage and a culture of responsibility, Barclays thinks of itself as especially innovative within its sector. Certainly it has racked up a number of UK firsts – the first bank to install computers, the first with ATMs, the first with a website, the first credit card in Britain and the first to offer customers a personal banker.

More recently, there has been a highly praised and successful deal with the union on offshore outsourcing, an ongoing experiment with non-PVC materials to produce a more environmentally friendly credit card, the new award-winning pension scheme, and a switch from an extended graduate training curriculum to a shorter, more intense programme that gives trainees real responsibility within their first year on the job.

Diversity and social responsibility

Barclays is a highly responsible organisation, and not just because of the stringent regulations that apply to this sector. The group has a strong brand and a good reputation for being leading edge, and it wants to maintain both.

As part of that, Barclays has a strong culture of community and social responsibility within the group. Indeed, Barclays aims to become a leader in its attitude to CSR; and to that end it has set up an impressive structure of oversight and compliance.

The whole CSR agenda is driven by the group's vice-chairman, who heads a Brand and Reputation Committee that includes five board directors. Barclays sees a seamless link between its brand and CSR, and the main role of this committee is to ensure conformity, identify areas of non-compliance and act as a CSR think-tank. It has three subcommittees on CSR itself, the environment, and equality and diversity.

In 2003 Barclays was named in the top ten of the Employers Forum on Disability Global Inclusion Benchmark, and in the top five of private sector companies by Race for Opportunity for promoting global diversity.

The group certainly has positive policies in the equality and diversity field, including the establishment of Spectrum – a group for employees interested in gay, lesbian, bisexual and transgender issues that acts as a consultation forum and a support network. There is a similar group for employees interested in disability issues, and a further network for those interested in cultural diversity. More broadly, some 30,000 staff have completed special awareness courses on diversity issues.

People from an ethnic minority background made up 2.7% of senior executives in September 2004, up from 1.1% two years before. Two of the 20 members of the board are women and Barclays is committed to ensuring that the representation of women in senior positions will hit 22% by the end of 2005 (from 11% in 2001).

In 2003, £32.8m was given to the community, including a continued commitment of 1% of UK pre-tax profits. The national Make a Difference Day is now in its ninth year – 10% of the whole group took part last time, contributing their time as well as money to local projects and charities. Barclays sees this as good for teambuilding and good for giving something back to local communities. Also, their £ for £ scheme matches the money employees raise for charity (up to a maximum of £750 for each initiative).

In Africa, Barclays is doing more to support families with HIV/AIDS than some governments; in the UK, Spaces for Sports will transform 300 sites over 3 years to convert under-used and derelict land into community sports facilities.

At the National Business Awards 2004, Barclays won the award for being the organisation that can best demonstrate company-wide commitment to corporate social responsibility. Judges looked for evidence of a clearly articulated and widely communicated CSR strategy embedded in the company's business strategy, and policies and projects that positively impact on the local community in terms of the environment, local employment, local education and charitable work.

Corporate Governance

Barclays takes corporate governance very seriously, as befits an organisation that places so much emphasis on its reputation. The responsibility of the company secretary, it is overseen by an Audit Committee of the board.

The corporate governance report (included in the group's annual report) has a great deal of detail on the board structure and its remuneration (including itemised share holdings and options). It complies with the Combined Code on corporate governance except for the formal appointment of a senior independent director to oversee it – that is "a priority for the board during 2004".

Environmental record

Barclays has a defined policy on environmental management, administered by an environmental director and overseen by an Environmental Steering Group (senior management from major business areas and functions). The policy is based on compliance with local environmental legislation and international accords on sustainable development.

The company's environmental management policy and reporting has been rated "exceptional" by the EIRIS Guide to Responsible Banking 2003. A list of key environmental targets is monitored and a detailed annual report is published (the group is currently on track for all targets except paper consumption and overall energy consumption). However, by purchasing 50% recycled paper, recycling all confidential waste and ensuring no redundant electronic equipment is sent to landfill; Barclays are making good progress in achieving these targets.

Barclays recently ranked 4th out of 13 banks in the Economic Index of Corporate Environmental Engagement and are, to their knowledge, the only bank to have achieved ISO 14001 accreditation.

The new HQ that Barclays has built in London's Canary Wharf has been rated "excellent" under the Building Research Establishment's Environmental Assessment Method. It has also won a Green Apple award for its high environmental standards.

Barnardo's

Barnardo's
Tanners Lane, Barkingside, Ilford, Essex IG6 1QG
Tel: (0) 20 8550 8822
Web: www.barnardos.org.uk

Barnardo's
GIVING CHILDREN BACK THEIR FUTURE

Pay and Benefits	7.5	Innovation	7.1
Promotion and Development	6.5	Diversity	8.0
Training	7.3	Social Responsibility	6.6
Travel opportunities	3.4	Corporate Governance	7.3
Culture	6.7	Environment	6.7
Total			**67.1**

Barnardo's is the UK's leading children's charity, supporting 100,000 children and their families through 361 services in England, Northern Ireland, Scotland and Wales. Its aims are to help children, young people and their families to deal with issues such as abuse, homelessness and poverty, and to tackle the challenges of disability. With an annual turnover of £20m, partly derived from central and local government and partly from voluntary donations, it employs 6,000 staff across its nine regional offices, 360 children's projects and 330 shops throughout the UK. Its headquarters are in Barkingside with a staff of 500.

Executive summary

The charity dates back to 1867, when Thomas John Barnardo set up a school for poor children in the East End of London, and went on to set up a number of children's homes and to establish the first fostering scheme in the UK.

Barnardo's no longer operates the children's homes for which it is best known. Its work now focuses on a wide range of projects aimed at helping children and young people. For example, it works to support foster carers and adopted families; operates drop-in centres for children whose parents are affected by drug and alcohol abuse; runs schools for children excluded from mainstream education; teaches life skills to disadvantaged children; and provides services to support young carers.

Barnardo's is not an international organisation, but it has sister organisations in Canada, Australia and New Zealand.

Pay and benefits

Barnardo's aims to stay within the upper quartile of pay for the charity sector and takes part in salary surveys to make sure its salaries remain competitive. New graduates joining the organisation can expect to be paid from £17,409 to £19,092, and IT graduates are paid from £19,713 to £23,313. Thereafter, pay will depend on the job role in question, with the aim of matching market rates. For example, social workers will earn around £30,000 while managers will earn in the region of £35,000.

The organisation offers a final salary pension scheme to which employees contribute 6%. The scheme offers four times final salary, plus a two-thirds salary spouse or dependant pension which includes partners of either sex, and a one-third salary children's pension. There is also an ill-health pension and a death-in-service scheme amounting to four times salary.

At its London head office, Barnardo's has an onsite pre-school nursery which is available to staff and the general public. The nursery is not subsidised, but staff have priority for places. It also offers childcare vouchers to staff across all of its sites.

Barnardo's operates a flexitime working scheme whereby employees are contracted to work an agreed number of hours over a set period, but can choose their own start and finish times each day around fixed "core" hours of attendance, with maximum and minimum periods for breaks. Excess hours can be carried over from one accounting period to the next, or used as time off in lieu. Similarly, a limited number of deficit hours can be made up.

The organisation also has other flexible working schemes – many staff do job-sharing, and term-time working is also available as long as it fits around the employee's responsibilities.

Promotion and development

In the past, Barnardo's recruitment policies did not particularly favour internal applicants, but the organisation is now actively working to encourage them, for example by advertising vacancies internally first and developing its existing staff to take on new responsibilities.

Job appraisals are carried out annually, with a review every six months. Opportunities for training and development are available for all staff, and personal development paths are identified through performance reviews.

Overall, the organisation spends just over 3% of its budget on training. Employees' learning and development needs are aligned to the objectives set out in Barnardo's five-year corporate plan, and learning and development activities are explicitly linked to business need.

For example, admin staff have opportunities to attain NVQ level 2 and 3 in administration, and the organisation has an internal management course – Foundations of Management – that has been accredited by the Institute of Leadership and Management. Project management staff can work towards qualifications including Management level 4 and 5, TDLB level 4, A1 and V1 Assessor/Verifier, Care Awards, Playwork levels 2 and 3, and Customer Services. On average, employees will spend between five and 12 days a year on learning and development activities including e-learning, courses, mentoring, coaching, videos and reading.

Barnardo's has a succession planning and career management programme, which identifies talented individuals through their regular performance appraisals and then provides opportunities to enable them to fulfil their potential – such as secondments, special projects, shadowing and sideways moves.

The organisation runs a small graduate development programme. In 2002–03, it took on six graduates for its marketing and communications department, and as part of their development these trainees are completing the Open University Certificate in Management. The organisation has sponsored a number of employees to study for MBA and MSc qualifications at Roffey Park, Ashridge Consulting, and other professional institutions. It also has links with the Institute of Marketing and Fundraising on their Certificate programmes.

At present, Barnardo's does not have a formal mentoring system in place, though it plans to introduce an in-house coaching programme in 2005–06. Informal coaching and mentoring is, however, an integral part of the way the organisation works. A number of staff have had external coaching relationships and this has been used as a basis for the in-house transfer of knowledge and experience. The organisation also actively seeks to build mentoring and coaching relationships that draw on the expertise of its corporate partners, and is in the process of developing such a scheme with Barclays.

Company culture

Barnardo's is an organisation with a strong mission to improve the lives of children and young people. Its employees need to be dedicated individuals who are committed to the organisation's goals – and who aren't primarily motivated by money.

To give some idea of the organisational ethos, most staff join from caring professions; many are qualified social workers, nursery nurses, and youth and community workers. Whatever their background, employees are expected to be innovative, open to challenge, and able to deliver in what are often difficult circumstances. Those working with children need to be good listeners who can empathise with young people, but also be strong emotionally and resilient enough to deal with harrowing situations and damaged individuals.

Since most of Barnardo's work is focused on strong project teams, employees also need to be good teamworkers with strong people skills – this isn't a place for loners.

Innovation

Barnardo's has always been an innovator in the field of childcare, coming up with cutting-edge approaches in a number of fields and raising public awareness of hitherto concealed issues.

By lobbying government, it has changed the public view of child prostitution from one where the child was perceived to be at fault. It was instrumental in changing the law so that child prostitutes are now accepted as the victims of abuse and the adults who use them have become criminalized.

It has also made the public aware of the number of children who act as carers, and provided them with support networks and drop-in centres where they can go to seek advice and support.

Another of Barnardo's groundbreaking approaches has been its work with children who have life-limiting illnesses, helping them to come to terms with their situation by talking about what will happen to them and their relatives. Following its work in Northern Ireland with children who lost their parents in the fighting there, it provides support to children with terminally ill parents.

Diversity and social responsibility

Barnardo's welcomes difference in its staff and volunteers, and encourages applications from disabled people. This positive attitude is reflected in that fact that it won the British Diversity Awards Fellowship during 2004.

Currently, 82% of Barnardo's staff are women and 38% are men. Just over 11% are from racial and religious minorities. Barnardo's is happy with the overall figures, but believes that more work is needed to raise the percentages within some local regions. Departments and regions are being challenged to develop local action plans to address this issue.

As this suggests, Barnardo's is committed to taking active steps to eliminate unfair or unlawful discrimination or prejudice within its organisation. It is in the process of examining all its structures and practices to identify and remove those which might perpetuate discrimination. For example, it is adapting all its premises to make them more readily accessible to disabled people.

It plans to continue to check its progress in tackling disadvantage and discrimination by implementing a thorough monitoring and evaluation system, consulting with under-represented groups, and developing an integrated equalities/diversity strategy.

The chief executive has overall responsibility for the implementation of the organisation's equal opportunities policy, assisted by the director of human resources.

By its very nature, Barnardo's works closely with local communities to pursue its goal of supporting disadvantaged children and their families. Members of Barnardo's staff are also invited to help charities by allowing donations to be deducted from their pay. The suggested minimum amount to be donated to each of the charities chosen by members of staff is 50p per week. Since this is deducted from pay before tax is calculated, the true cost of the donation is lower to the member of staff.

Corporate Governance

Barnardo's works in a multicultural society but derives its values from the Christian faith. Its values include respecting each person's unique abilities; encouraging people to fulfil their potential; and exercising responsible stewardship to help children, young people and their families to overcome severe disadvantage. All meetings and new pieces of work are underpinned by these values.

The organisation's chief executive and the Barnardo's council are responsible for ensuring these values are upheld. The council meets every six months and consists of about 20 people who work for the organisation unpaid. Council members are brought in for the skills they can offer and their ability to cover different geographical locations. Some members have been involved in Barnardo's work; some are from the commercial sector; some are childcare and legal specialists; one current member is the mother of an adopted Barnardo's child. Barnardo's is always looking for new council members and recruits actively through press adverts.

The organisation has a formal recognition agreement with Unison, the local government union. Management decisions are broadcast via email and the organisation's Weekly Bulletin. It is a Licentiate Member of the Institute of Assessors and Internal Verifiers.

Environmental record

Though its responsibilities to children and their carers take top priority as part of the responsibilities implicit in its basis and values statement, Barnardo's aims to be an environmentally conscious organisation contributing towards a safe and healthy environment. Its director of properties and facilities management is responsible for ensuring that its environmental policy is carried out.

At present, the company recycles its lightweight paper and other waste; and also recycles garments, shoes, bottles and glass through its network of shops.

Use of public transport among staff is encouraged by offering season ticket loans. Company cars are given to fundraisers and others who need to travel as part of their job, but the organisation strives to ensure that cars are as environmentally friendly and economical as possible. A fixed mileage allowance is given to those using their own cars.

To improve its environmental performance, however, Barnardo's is working on an action plan and a management system to monitor progress. The first stage of the action plan will be to generate staff support for tackling environmental issues. Next, it plans to identify and implement environmentally friendly actions that could be introduced at no cost to the organisation. Thirdly, it will tackle environmental issues that need some funding, particularly those with a lower payback period.

Big Yellow Group

Big Yellow Group Plc
2 The Deans, Bridge Road, Bagshot, Surrey GU19 5AT
Tel: (0) 1276 450708
Web: www.bigyellow.co.uk **Email:** jobs@bigyellow.co.uk

Pay and Benefits	6.7	Innovation	6.7
Promotion and Development	6.2	Diversity	5.2
Training	6.0	Social Responsibility	4.5
Travel opportunities	3.0	Corporate Governance	4.5
Culture	6.0	Environment	4.7
Total			**53.5**

Big Yellow Self Storage was one of the earliest entrants into the now-burgeoning self-storage market. As an industry, the business straddles sales and service, and working in the company is likely to appeal to workers currently engaged in both of these areas. Since its entry in the last Top Employers book, the organisation has continued to develop its original focus in the south-east, with 31 stores now open and a further 10 stores committed. Its growth record and history of internal promotions augur well for anyone wanting a long-term career with prospects.

Executive summary

Big Yellow, alongside a couple of early competitors, essentially invented the concept of self-storage and has been pleased to deliver its maiden profits during 2004 (of £1.2m), after start-up years in which investment in growing the number of stores was deemed more of a focus. Prior to profits, the losses had been shrinking and the size of the business growing ahead of most expectations; it can be gathered easily that Big Yellow is a well-run company with its focus firmly on sales and controlled growth for the future.

Entrants into the company can expect to see extensive literature about their new place of work including an entire booklet on benefits you wouldn't necessarily see in other companies, and if the business case can be made, they can look forward to rapid promotion internally – the company continually looks to improve benefits for its staff, balanced with recruiting externally as appropriate.

In spite of its relative youth, Big Yellow Self Storage is a publicly quoted company. It takes its branding, service and cash flow very seriously without losing sight of the employees' need to enjoy their jobs. It shows every sign of being able to sustain its growth into the future.

Pay and benefits

Big Yellow aims to keep its pay and benefits above its sector's average, and it ensures the package it offers is up to the mark by conducting a bi-annual survey. In addition to hard cash, which varies according to the level at which an individual is recruited, all staff are eligible to receive a performance-related bonus and 65% of the staff have shares, with a Sharesave scheme having recently been introduced. Big Yellow also offers a pension scheme where the company matches the employee's 3% salary contribution and tops this up to 6% after two years.

The business also has a Pleasure Points scheme under which employees gain points that can be exchanged for Red Letter Day experiences. Staff can accrue points in a monthly prize draw in which ten awards comprising of £1,000 in points are allocated; the Department of the Quarter gets £100 in points for each member of the winning team; similar allocations are on offer for customer service, a suggestion scheme, sales and marketing awards, and the "introduce a friend" scheme.

Away from the points scheme, the business encourages its staff to have fun and be more productive by:

- Allocating a social budget of £75 per head, which stores may use as they see fit
- An extra day off for your birthday
- Engagements, weddings, births, passing exams and other life events recognised through gifts and vouchers
- A high-profile Christmas party
- An annual staff and partners meeting
- Giving everybody an Easter egg!

The company has a flexible working policy, and stores are encouraged to work out their rotas so that individual needs are catered for as far as is possible whilst fulfilling the corporate objectives.

Promotion and development

Big Yellow has reasonably low turnover compared to the retail sector in general. It is worth mentioning that the head office's turnover rate during the period preceding the 1Corporate Research Foundation's assessment of the business was precisely zero.

The company takes the development of its employees very seriously, and will finance driving lessons and other training when it serves the business as well as the personal need – in other areas it may contribute anything from all to part payment if something is work or partly work-related. All new staff are recruited to a probationary period during which time they receive continuous coaching and training. A full review of personal performance concludes the probationary period, and objectives are set and revisited on a quarterly basis. Every member of staff receives an annual performance review between November and February thereafter.

The organisation works on personal development in other ways. It has a succession plan that it revises every year after the personal performance reviews. This plan outlines strengths, areas for development, career development and other issues; together with a training needs analysis, these become the templates for development over the coming year. The business is aware that there won't always be a natural way forward in a small concern like Big Yellow, which still employs fewer than 200 people, but when this appears to be an issue the organisation looks to build opportunities such as further education, professional qualifications and further responsibilities. The company spends 2.5% of the payroll budget on training; all store staff get two weeks' training in a training store before they start work and there are a further 11 training courses specific to sales, operations and management development.

Managers are trained and encouraged to spot talent from very early on in the company.

Company culture

Big Yellow aims for a lively, fun environment without losing sight of a committed service ethic and total customer focus. There is a lot of emphasis on the social side of the business; for example, in June 2004 the company had a meeting/social gathering at The Clink Hall of Arms in London, where the directors reviewed the group's recent performance and recognised individual contributions in sales and customer service through the presentation of awards, as well as discussing future strategy.

As the business has grown, it has had to formalise some of the means by which ideas are disseminated around the company, although it has never lost sight of the fact that its employees are individuals. The hierarchy remains relatively flat; the idea is that everybody knows who their line manager is, but anyone can contribute an idea or approach another individual. Formal structures and events include executive meetings with directors every other week in stores, monthly operations meetings involving senior managers and senior store managers, and other meetings for management at various levels. The key to understanding the company is to note its focus on communication all the time; it is as proud of its informal communications as it is of its formalised structures.

As a young company, it has employee satisfaction surveys as one of its targets for the future; it has started, meanwhile, working on its accreditation as an Investor In People.

Innovation

Big Yellow's first appearance in a Corporate Research Foundation book happened two years ago. At that stage it was necessary to explain the concept of self-storage as it was much less commonplace than it is now. One of the company's main innovations was that it was founded in the first place; more recently it has stayed at the forefront of the industry with high-level security for its customers, remote out-of-hours monitoring, and a combined TV and radio advertising campaign, which is the first from a company in this sector.

Cheryl Hathaway, HR controller, also considers the non-contractual benefits package (see above, including extra holiday for a birthday, Easter eggs and other ideas) an innovation in itself – as is the establishment of 8 designated training stores, and courses and development materials branded into a single package called "The Big Yellow Career". The company is also proud of its internet and intranet, which are packed with information for its customers and staff.

Diversity and social responsibility

The business regards itself as an equal opportunities employer although the board, comprised of the founders, is entirely male. This is the only level at which this is true – once senior managers are taken into account the sex balance becomes more even. Incoming employees are trained on the company's equality policy as a matter of course and there is a formal policy in place should there ever be a complaint. 35% of the staff are from racial and religious minorities, and Big Yellow plans to retain its current policies on equality and objectivity whilst recruiting and developing people.

The company is active in supporting numerous charities, whether through cash donations or through sponsoring employees involved in charitable activities.

Corporate Governance

At its current size, Big Yellow does not have a dedicated compliance officer as such, but it acknowledges the importance of the highest standards of corporate governance and complies with the Combined Code. Its values have led it to invest in quality locations (the location is of prime importance to the company) and staff, and it believes it has invested more heavily in these than its competitors.

Environmental record

Big Yellow is not in manufacturing and is therefore not a great consumer of materials; it does, however, ensure that it exceeds all laws and regulations on the environment where they apply to its activities. It encourages staff to work for branches which are local to their home; a number of the properties it has acquired for development are brownfield properties; and there is a paper recycling system operating at head office and in some stores.

The company believes its record in these matters to be better than those of its competitors.

BLP

Berwin Leighton Paisner
Adelaide House, London Bridge, London EC4R 9HA
Tel: (0) 20 7760 1000   **Fax:** (0) 20 7760 1111
Web: www.blplaw.com

*berwin leighton paisner

Pay and Benefits	7.5	Innovation	6.0
Promotion and Development	6.3	Diversity	5.8
Training	6.0	Social Responsibility	5.8
Travel opportunities	4.2	Corporate Governance	6.3
Culture	5.8	Environment	5.8
Total			**59.5**

Formed in 2001 by the merger of Berwin Leighton and Paisner & Co, Berwin Leighton Paisner (BLP) has grown to become one of the City's top 15 law firms. Operating in four main areas – corporate, real estate, finance, and litigation and dispute resolution – its clients range from major corporations and financial institutions through to public sector organisations and individuals. Based at London Bridge, the firm also has a Brussels office and alliance offices in New York, Paris, Milan and Rome. In addition, BLP has relationships with professional firms in all major centres around the world.

Executive summary

Berwin Leighton Paisner is a full-service law firm, which also operates through an international alliance.

Since 2001, the firm has focused on developing its corporate, finance and real estate businesses and international alliances. The success of this strategy is evidenced by a 40% growth in profitability in 2003–04, and the firm being named Law Firm of the Year in June 2004 by The Lawyer magazine.

BLP focuses on creative and innovative ways to achieve commercial solutions and provides teams who "go the extra mile" to achieve service excellence. The firm encourages its lawyers to think laterally and values original thought.

Pay and benefits

BLP's salaries are in the upper quartile for the profession as a whole, and on a par with other leading City firms. Trainee lawyers can expect to start on £28,000 and newly qualified solicitors earn £50,000.

In addition, the firm offers an impressive package of core, flexible and voluntary benefits available to all employees. For employees 25 and over, BLP pays 5% of salary into a group personal pension plan delivered by a choice of three providers. If the employee chooses to pay 2.5% themselves, BLP will pay an additional 2.5%. Employees under 25 have access to a stakeholder pension plan.

BLP offers private medical insurance and permanent health insurance, plus regular health screens and flu jabs. Staff can benefit from season ticket loans, an employee assistance programme, and a flexible benefit package including travel insurance and gym subscription.

Women on maternity leave get enhanced maternity pay, and childcare vouchers are a recent benefit to emerge from employee consultation. All staff can buy the vouchers and take advantage of NI savings on their childcare.

With the aim of improving work/life balance, the firm has also laid on an in-house concierge service which will take care of tasks such as booking theatre tickets, delivering and picking up dry cleaning, finding plumbers and electricians, and so on – enabling staff to make better use of their leisure time.

Voluntary benefits include online discount shopping, a DVD delivery service, in-house sales, and arrangements with local retailers.

Long-serving employees are recognised via holiday entitlement, which increases with years of service; and through gift vouchers, which are awarded at completion of 10, 15, 20 and 25 years. There are bonus schemes in place to recognise the introduction of new staff and new clients.

BLP is keen to promote flexible working where possible and will grant requests to work a non-standard pattern if employees present a convincing business case. 17% of support staff, 19% of secretarial staff and 7% of solicitors work flexible hours.

Promotion and development

The career path BLP offers its staff is reflected in low staff turnover rates of 17% for fee-earners and 10–11% for support staff. Most partners are promoted internally, though some senior staff have been recruited from outside to provide the firm with expertise it lacks in a certain sector. Vacancies are advertised internally.

Rather than being sent on a specific number of courses each year, BLP staff can choose which courses they want to attend from the firm's training programme – though solicitors have to attend a minimum number of hours per year to maintain their practising certificates. There are tailored development programmes for lawyers, secretaries and support staff which include specific technical training and general business skills training (covering communication, coaching, leadership and participating in change).

Staff are also given funding to take relevant professional qualifications. Details of completed training, as well as plans for the next six months, are recorded on a personal development plan and discussed at bi-annual reviews.

As part of the induction programme, new joiners are assigned a "buddy" who helps with their transition into the firm. Trainee solicitors are mentored by designated training partners and share a room with a partner or senior fee-earner who will help with their technical development. HR carries out new-joiner meetings with staff around two months after joining, and partners or managers will also have meetings with staff three and six months after they join to check they have settled in well and are receiving appropriate training and support.

All staff have two performance reviews each year based around a personal development plan. Partner candidates are coached by mentors.

Company culture

BLP is increasingly attracting recruits from larger firms, drawn by its open, unstuffy, entrepreneurial culture.

New staff joining the firm can expect to be given responsibility and high levels of autonomy early on. Staff are also encouraged to share their views and ideas with the firm, both informally – through an open-door policy – and through official feedback forums such as new joiner meetings, departmental meetings and the staff liaison committee.

The firm's Project Leo initiative (see below) is one example of how it actively works to foster an open, entrepreneurial climate. It has also run a series of Client Service workshops with individual practice teams, including both fee-earners and support staff. Underlying these initiatives was the key principle that all members of the firm have a role to play in client service and in the success of the firm.

BLP staff are high achievers, but the firm also aims to promote a good work/life balance through flexible working where feasible, through benefits such as its concierge service, and by providing information on health, time management and stress management.

Most of BLP's work is for clients headquartered in London. However, solicitors will occasionally be sent on secondment to the firm's Brussels office or its alliance offices in New York, Paris and Milan. At partner level, foreign travel to international clients or alliance offices is more common.

Innovation

Though the law is a traditional profession, BLP nevertheless aims to be an innovator through its business processes. One of its most successful innovations has been Project Leo, an initiative launched by managing partner Neville Eisenberg to keep the firm on track to achieve its vision and goals for the next three to five years. As part of the initiative, all practice groups and support departments within the firm set up task forces to review all aspects of its work, report on its findings and make suggestions for change. The initiative proved to be very successful, generating a host of new ideas – such as childcare vouchers for employees – and a detailed agenda for future change.

In 2004, BLP took the unusual step of signing up England rugby captain Lawrence Dallaglio for a three-year contract to provide motivational and teambuilding tips for employees and clients.

BLP also aims to make innovative use of technology to provide better support to clients and staff. For example, its "beprofessional" service, a joint venture with Deloitte, was established to provide web-based information for smaller and medium-sized enterprises.

Flexible working for staff is supported by the firm's well-developed IT infrastructure and systems, and by its recently introduced digital dictation service.

Diversity and social responsibility

Over 60% of BLP's workforce and more than half of its recent trainee intake are female, and the proportion of women in management roles (currently 30%) looks set to grow. The firm supports its female employees through initiatives such as childcare vouchers and flexible working. In 1997, it founded The Adelaide Group, a networking forum for women business leaders.

The firm is keen to play a part in attracting more black and Asian candidates into law. Via a link with business campaign group London First, it has started to provide short-term work placements to non-white students.

BLP is committed to the wider community through a variety of activities ranging from pro bono work to contributing to national and EU policy initiatives. It has a Give As You Earn scheme, which enables employees to give a regular donation via their monthly salary.

The firm also has a Charities group, which each year selects a local charity to receive all money raised from charitable activities within the firm for that year. In August 2004, for example, some 50 members of the firm took part in a London to Paris cycle race to raise money for the Greater London Fund for the Blind.

Corporate governance

As a law firm, BLP is bound by the Solicitors' Accounting Rules and is audited annually to ensure it complies with them. It has also developed its own internal quality assurance systems, tailored to the needs of its clients. Client Relationship Partners have overall responsibility for clients' affairs and are responsible for service quality.

Each practice area in BLP is up to speed with the laws relating to its work and clients' sectors. As well as the technical training programme delivered to all staff, the firm also has a number of professionals whose role is to disseminate information on changes in legislation and to feed information into the various online tools the firm has developed.

A member of the HR team is responsible for ensuring that all qualified staff members' practising certificates are kept up to date. Checks are carried out when recruiting new fee-earners to ensure practising certificates are current.

All fee-earners are required to attend training on the subject of money laundering and a senior partner is responsible for this area.

Environmental record

Environmental issues are one of the regular items on BLP's staff liaison group agenda, and staff members are encouraged to come up with ideas for reducing the firm's environmental impact.

The legal profession generates a lot of paperwork, but BLP is taking steps to cut the paper mountain down to size. It is working to make staff aware of the amount of paper they use; the BLP intranet features a Tree-o-meter, which shows how much paper the firm uses year on year and the environmental impact this has. It also promotes paper-saving measures such as copying double-sided wherever possible. Environmentally friendly paper is used in all photocopiers. Growing use of electronic systems, such as electronic disclosure, is also helping to reduce the amount of paper consumed. Paper, toner cartridges, ring binders and plastic cups are all recycled.

Low energy lighting has been installed in BLP's new building, and movement detectors automatically switch off lights within unoccupied areas.

BLP is based near London Bridge station, and apart from a small number of evening staff, nearly all staff travel to work by public transport. The 20 or so parking spaces next to the firm's buildings are intended for use by clients. Any staff wanting to use them – from the most junior to the most senior – have to pay a parking fee.

BPP Law School

BPP Law School
68-70 Red Lion Street, London WC1R 4NY
Tel: (0) 20 7430 2304
Web: www.bpp.com **Email:** lawrecruit@bpp.com

Pay and Benefits	6.1	Innovation	5.6
Promotion and Development	5.8	Diversity	7.2
Training	6.5	Social Responsibility	7.2
Travel opportunities	3.4	Corporate Governance	6.4
Culture	5.7	Environment	6.6
Total			**60.5**

BPP Law School is one of the UK's largest providers of postgraduate legal training for budding solicitors and barristers. It employs about 240 staff and trains 3,500 students a year at its schools in central London, Leeds, and soon Manchester. BPP Law School is part of BPP Professional Education plc, a £112m turnover firm specialising in professional business training, which claims to train for more qualifications than any other company in the world (subjects include: accountancy, tax, law, insolvency, financial services, marketing, HR and languages). The Law School is BPP's fastest-growing division.

Executive summary

Since its foundation in 1992, BPP Law School has grown rapidly to become one of the UK's largest training grounds for professional lawyers. It claims to train nearly a third of students on conversion courses (for non-law graduates), a fifth of students on legal practice courses (for solicitors), and a sixth of those studying for the bar. It is a preferred provider for City law firms, and from 2006 will be the sole training provider for five of the largest.

Peter Crisp, BPP Law School's chief executive, ascribes this success to the company's professional and focused approach. Unlike the universities, which provide most of the UK's legal training, BPP is teaching-led. "We treat our students as business clients; providing top quality facilities, committed teachers and a dynamic experience," says Crisp. Despite the company's growth, Crisp says its courses are consistently full.

While most of the BPP group (accountancy, tax, financial services etc.) has seen demand for its courses pegged by the overhang from the recession, the Law School has grown by more than 25% a year since 2001 and says it has comfortably outperformed its direct competitors. Now it is expanding further, with new law schools in Leeds (opened to students in September 2004) and Manchester (opening September 2005), each designed to take up to 600 students.

Pay and benefits

Since most of its direct competitors are in the public sector, BPP can reasonably claim to pay well above the average for its market, and it does some informal benchmarking to ensure this remains the case. Jobs are graded to reflect the nature of the work, but salaries of both academic and support staff are individually negotiated and reflect the employee's abilities and performance. Most of the academic staff also earn very good extra money by teaching additional evening or weekend courses; with a regular teaching load of only about 16 hours a week they can do this without the risk of overwork.

Actions well beyond the call of duty may be rewarded with a small bonus, and there is a set fee of several hundred pounds for anyone who introduces a new staff member. Otherwise there is no bonus scheme – although the BPP group is introducing one in 2005 – and recognition is usually of the pat-on-the-back variety. There are rolling sharesave schemes, and 40% of staff have executive share options.

Benefits include healthcare and private medical insurance for all, onsite gym and monthly massages, season ticket loans, and an independent counselling service for staff and their families. There is a stakeholder pension scheme, to which the company makes no contribution except a National Insurance rebate. Annual holiday allowance is 30 days for academic staff, and 25 days for support staff rising by increments to 30 days after six years, plus a total of seven extra days at Christmas and Easter. Support staff can also take up to two duvet days (no-questions-asked sick leave). From 2005, a new flexible benefits scheme covers holiday, pension, life assurance and childcare vouchers.

Promotion and development

Almost two-thirds of BPP's 240 employees are teaching staff who provide and manage students' tuition; the other third provide a wide variety of support functions including accounts, IT, marketing, HR, library, careers advice and administration. Most of the teaching staff have worked in legal practice, and the company does not necessarily require previous teaching experience. The principal recruitment vehicle is the company's website. Annual staff turnover is about 10%, and in 2005 there will be a big push to recruit support staff for the new Manchester law school, while the Leeds school will continue to expand.

Where possible, BPP fills vacancies internally; and promotion every year or two is common. Crisp joined the company in 1997 as a tutor and rose to be chief executive within 6 years, and the whole board of directors have been promoted from the ranks. "This is a company that rewards performance," says Crisp.

As you would expect from a professional education company, training is taken seriously. Everyone gets an annual personal training budget (£750 for academics, £400 for support staff) to spend as they like. Necessary business skills take precedence, but support staff can spend their budgets on anything from music lessons to massage courses. More expensive training can be considered, if necessary. Staff can also attend any of the BPP group's courses free of charge. There is no limit, as long as it does not affect their work, and many have qualified in accountancy, law, HR and marketing, and taken MBAs etc.

There is a formal Teaching and Learning Certificate scheme (TLC) for all tutors at the Law School. Certification takes place annually based on teaching and training portfolios. However, entrepreneurial flair is encouraged, whether it is setting up summer schools during the long vacation, or a stationery shop in the school library. "If anyone comes up with a good idea they'll get to be involved with it, and may share in the profits," says Annie Begley, the Law School's financial controller.

Company culture

Anyone joining the staff of BPP Law School in the hope of prolonging their student days will be in for a shock, since the company is run on purely corporate lines; with corporate facilities and a corporate attitude.

"We have staff who are very passionate and love what they do," says Crisp. However, he also characterises the company as flexible and anxious for its employees to be happy. Almost all the academic staff work from home one day a week, and support staff can do likewise if commitments allow. The BPP group is planning to set up a stress management policy, but the law school is not highly pressurised or a long-hours culture. "It's a much less stressful environment than legal practice," says Crisp (who has experience of both).

The leadership style is collegiate. "We have a culture where we listen to staff, keep them informed and involve them in decision making," says Crisp. Even the cleaners have email addresses, so literally everyone is kept in the loop. Academic and support staff are treated equally, and there is a lot of contact between the two; many support staff work alongside the academics.

"The management style is very approachable," says HR manager Suzanne Emmings. "It's very open-door. You can speak directly to the chief executive or the chairman if you want." There is a "red envelope" scheme allowing staff to make suggestions or raise concerns (anonymously if they wish), and the company is beginning a full-scale staff survey in 2005.

Although the company has no policy on work/life balance, it is quite flexible. It supports part-time working, compressed hours and other flexible arrangements; and staff can decide when to start and finish work, commitments permitting. Everyone has remote access to the office computer system to facilitate homeworking; and staff occasionally take sabbaticals of up to a year. Monthly drinks parties, a film club, sporting fixtures, and regular awaydays to exotic locations all help to oil the wheels.

Innovation

In a market where most tuition is provided by university law schools, BPP's corporate approach and focus on pure training are somewhat unusual. Although up to half its students have their fees paid by their employers, the remainder are self-financing, and the company tries to treat all its students like customers. For example, IT facilities for both staff and students are sophisticated, with remote access, a lively intranet, well-resourced library, and a self-service HR records system for staff.

In 2001, the school designed a new legal practice course for City firms in conjunction with Nottingham Law School and the Oxford School of Legal Practice, and it claims to have the widest range of elective courses of any legal training institution in the country. The company's flexible approach to timetabling, with a wide range of part-time, evening and weekend courses, is also instrumental in attracting students.

Diversity and social responsibility

Many of the faces at BPP are young, and not just among the students. The average age of staff is around 30, with middle managers averaging early 30s and the board mid-to-late 30s. Women make up 58% of staff and 44% of management, while 27% of staff are from racial or religious minorities. The company is happy with these ratios and has the usual policies on equal opportunities, etc. It has recently begun blocking out applicants' names on application forms before vetting them, to help eliminate any unconscious bias during the selection process.

The company has no policy on charitable giving, but it invests £100,000 pa in its pro bono legal advice clinic, which gives free legal advice to over 100 people each year. It supports ad hoc charity initiatives such as dress-down Fridays, and redundant computer equipment is donated for refurbishment and re-use in developing countries.

Corporate governance

Operating as it does in the legal sphere, BPP Law School is regulated by the Law Society and the Bar Council, as well as complying fully with corporate best practice as part of BPP Professional Education plc. The Law School has its own data protection officer and risk assessment team, and regularly uses mystery shoppers to check the quality of its courses. It is considering applying for Investor in People accreditation.

The school has won several accolades and awards, including a rating of "excellent" for its London Legal Practice Course from the Law Society, and being chosen as sole training provider by five leading City law firms.

Environmental record

The Law School has no formal environmental policy, but believes in doing its bit. There are recycling bins for paper on every floor, staff are trained to switch off lights etc. when leaving rooms, and equipment such as air conditioning are turned off overnight. There are no company cars and no parking on site. The city centre locations of all four schools mean almost all staff travel by public transport, for which the company offers interest-free season ticket loans.

Broadway

Broadway
Chaucer House, White Hart Yard, London SE1 1NX
Tel: (0) 20 7089 9500 **Fax:** (0) 20 7089 9501
Web: www.broadwaylondon.org **Email:** broadway@broadwaylondon.org

Pay and Benefits	7.5	Innovation	6.8
Promotion and Development	6.7	Diversity	7.4
Training	7.0	Social Responsibility	7.1
Travel opportunities	3.7	Corporate Governance	6.8
Culture	7.8	Environment	6.9
Total			**67.6**

Broadway is a leading London-based homeless service provider. It employs 200 full-time staff and a varying number of volunteers in the capital, and had a turnover of £8.4m in 2003–04, up from £7.5m the previous year.

Executive summary

Broadway is a young organisation, formed in 2002 from the merger of two long-standing organisations. It provides a full range of services designed to enable homeless people to make the journey from street to home. Clearly the provision of accommodation is the core service, but other activities aid the transition for homeless or vulnerably housed people to independent living. The client base varies significantly, ranging from individuals with severe support needs who may have serious mental health and substance misuse problems, to those who have only recently found themselves homeless.

The organisation has a diverse presence in the capital. As well as an outreach service, it owns a large day centre where people receive a number of support activities, and has four direct-access hostels – one of which is for women only; another aimed exclusively at people with substance misuse problems. A large matrix division hosts a client learning centre, which caters for a wide spectrum of learning needs from basic literacy skills to help finding employment. Broadway provides support to people in around 500 accommodation units and has a dedicated property services team to deal with maintenance issues. It also provides floating support to clients who are living in permanent independent accommodation.

Broadway manages the Combined Homelessness and Information Network (CHAIN), an internet-based information system collating data on rough sleepers in London. The Clearing House is another pan-London Broadway service that coordinates lettings to a pool of 4,000 rooms and flats developed for former rough sleepers under successive phases of central government's Rough Sleepers Initiative.

The main challenge for Broadway (and indeed similar organisations) is the shortage of available housing in London. Through a consultative arm it maintains a dialogue with the government and other agencies on this and related issues of concern.

Funding arrangements have changed in recent years. Once largely resourced from central government, Broadway now receives most funding from local authorities. Charitable donations make up around 7% of their income.

Pay and benefits

"In an organisation like this, what people want is a pay deal that's fair, and terms and conditions that are fair," says Helen Giles, director of human resources. "Performance-related pay is anathema to our people. Recognition for them is the feedback they get from their clients – they are not in competition with one another."

Broadway benchmarks itself against both the social housing sector, and the broader charitable sector. In doing so it aims to reward in the upper quartile for salaries and benefits alike. The organisation is generous in its leave provision: everyone is entitled to 30 days annual leave, no matter how long their tenure of employment. The opportunity for flexible working is also unlikely to be matched by many other organisations. While the core working hours are 10.30am to 3.30pm, people who opt to work longer days can accrue up to 21 hours' leave in reserve per month. Annually this represents a potential maximum of 10 weeks' leave. Broadway believes the demands of the work make this a positive measure in proactively tackling potential stress amongst the workforce.

Other benefits include a stakeholder pension scheme, into which the company will match contributions up to 5% of salary, and a raft of life-friendly policies, such as a provision for up to 10 days' compassionate leave on full pay.

Promotion and development

Broadway does not have a prescriptive approach to training and development; rather, it promotes the idea of a learning culture in which there is a high level of freedom for employees to develop their own skills. However, because the organisation recruits people from a variety of work backgrounds, there is a strong focus on induction. This takes the form of six to eight weeks' on-the-job training and some offsite modules. The core service delivery programme for employees involves acquiring skills to help them interact with their clients and positively influence their behaviour, through applied motivational interviewing and conflict management techniques.

Many employees eventually decide to move into specialist areas, such as welfare rights. As well as supporting training up to NVQ level 3, Broadway favours the use of mentors to deliver this type of training package. This is an obvious way of keeping costs down. Notwithstanding this, 2–3% of payroll is allocated to training – about £850 per person each year and well above the sector average. The practice also helps mould future managers, though there are, in addition, dedicated "getting that promotion" courses on offer.

"Some companies boast of a flat structure but we are against de-layering because it reduces career opportunities," says Giles. "With this in mind, we have a lot of supervisory positions. People who have regularly provided cover for others will also advance their claim for promotion. We are very careful, however, not to promote people beyond their level of competence."

Company culture

Broadway people are professional people, who use their skills to support and enhance the lives of London's most marginalised population. In exit interviews, the supportive environment is most frequently cited as the aspect of the organisation staff will miss more than any other. As an example, line managers are expected to spend at least 50% of their time actually line managing – that is, paying attention to employees' needs. This focus on people no doubt accounts for 84% of staff claiming job satisfaction in the most recent staff survey, compared to a sector average of 68%.

There is no doubt that the opportunity to make a real difference and change people's lives for the better makes for tremendously rewarding work. However, as it can also be emotionally demanding Broadway's employee assistance programme is more important than in many businesses. In a sector characterised by high levels of absence through sickness, Broadway fares very well – averaging five days per person compared to a median of 10. Turnover levels are also below average for the charitable sector and much of the turnover that does occur is healthy.

There is a lot of social activity at Broadway. Formal events are laid on at its end-of-year party and following the annual staff conference held in summer. Most social interaction between staff outside work, however, happens spontaneously. Much of it will also involve clients, with whom staff forge strong relationships. Barbecues and five-a-side football matches – to cite but two examples – are typical events.

Innovation

Like other organisations in the social housing sector, Broadway faces a real challenge in recruiting people. Unlike others, however, it takes the view that prior experience in the sector is not mandatory. Instead, it puts faith in potential and transferable skills.

According to Giles: "A lot of organisations shoot themselves in the foot by saying they only want people with experience. So what they do is set the entry level to let in people who are often no good. We'd rather have someone with good communication skills and the right values, than someone in the same field who is moving sideways."

From a service delivery perspective, Broadway has had to place innovation at the centre of its identity. This is because of the changing nature of the client base. Once it was primarily single homeless people, now it increasingly supports individuals with additional multiple health and learning needs. In order to engage effectively with this population, Broadway has moved away from a prescriptive approach to support, to one that is much more participative. In 2004, it organised a "speak out" event at which the voices of homeless people were heard by key decision-makers, and conducted a survey which found out that seven out of ten clients were satisfied with its services. The Greater London Authority has recently asked Broadway to lead its consultation with homeless people on the future London Housing Strategy.

Diversity and Social Responsibility

The majority of employees in the organisation are female, which is characteristic of the charitable sector; more significantly, a majority of managers are too. The workforce is generally relatively young (the majority falling within the 25–40 band), though Broadway is keen to change the perception that working with the homeless is a "young person's game" (the oldest employee is 57).

As a London-based organisation, Broadway is keen to adequately reflect the ethnic diversity of the capital in its people. Currently, 25% of all staff and 16% of managers are from a minority background. Under an active diversity strategy, a fast-track scheme exists which provides additional leadership development for minority junior managers. In addition, a diversity working group meets quarterly to discuss other ways of reducing the "snowcap effect" in the organisation. There is also a disability strategy.

Though its core activities are intrinsically socially responsible, Broadway maintains a broader commitment to CSR. This takes a variety of forms – recent examples include work placements for people from disadvantaged groups, and a bring and buy sale at the day centre to raise money for Great Ormond Street Hospital. Because of the way it is funded, however, the organisation has less freedom in the way it spends money than corporate equivalents.

Corporate Governance

Overseeing all activities is a 12-strong board of trustees, recruited on the open market and appointed on the basis that they can each bring a different strength and skillset. As with employees, the induction process for board members is taken very seriously. They will attend and actively participate in a number of meetings before they are formally co-opted onto the board.

The board meets every six weeks and receives detailed reports from the senior management team on all aspects of the business, from cash flow to rent collection to sickness absences. There are 8 operational strategies – all have been approved and are mutually complementary and in line with corporate objectives. The board will also receive regular quantitative and qualitative feedback on organisational health and client satisfaction to ensure the business is being conducted with integrity.

"Our statement of values was developed from the bottom-up so it has a great deal of buy-in," notes Giles. "Because of their adherence to these values, most people would not normally need to look at our code of conduct, but it is communicated to them as part of the induction."

Environment

Broadway has an explicit environmental policy and recycles everything from mobile phones to items of clothing. Around the office, efforts are made to use energy efficiently, for example by switching off photocopiers after use; while tea and coffee are invariably free-trade label brands. Many of these types of initiatives originate from the staff themselves rather than as directives from management.

Bromford Housing Group

Bromford Housing Group, Central Office, 9 Shaw Park Business Village,
Shaw Road, Bushbury, Wolverhampton WV10 9LE
Tel: (0) 1902 773618 **Fax:** (0) 1902 311373
Web: www.bromford.co.uk **Email:** hr@bromford.co.uk

Pay and Benefits	6.5	Innovation	6.6
Promotion and Development	6.8	Diversity	8.5
Training	6.5	Social Responsibility	6.8
Travel opportunities	3.6	Corporate Governance	6.8
Culture	6.9	Environment	6.6
Total			**65.6**

Formed in 1963 by a group of voluntary board members, with just a handful of properties, Bromford Housing Group has grown to become one of the UK's leading providers of affordable housing; with a national reputation for excellence in housing management, development, and associated care and support services. Bromford has more than 15,000 homes under management and 550 employees. Based in the West Midlands, through organic growth and occasional acquisition its homes now stretch from Staffordshire to Wiltshire. Friendly, approachable and flexible, Bromford was recently named No 1 employer in the Midlands. Bromford regularly outperforms its competitors in most areas of service, and came top in the public sector category of the Unisys Customer Service awards in 2004.

Executive Summary

In the "third sector" of not-for-profit organisations, Bromford Housing Group's mission is "creating homes and supporting communities where people really want to stay". It prides itself on having real social purpose where its people ("colleagues") can make a real difference to peoples' lives.

Bromford's activities encompass building affordable homes for rent and shared ownership; letting and running these homes; and providing support services, particularly for special needs. It does this with distinction, regularly featuring at the top of the Housing Corporation's key performance indicators.

Funded partly through government grants and the balance through financial instruments, Bromford must be sound financially – it has to satisfy both lenders and regulators – and its approach to risk management is sophisticated. It performs quite a balancing act, raising the necessary funds while keeping housing rents affordable. It does generate profits, but these are used to grow the business and provide more housing for people who need it. In the year to March 31 2004 it made an operating surplus of £18.1m on turnover of £51.6m (in 2003 and 2002 these figures were £16.6m/£43.1m and £14.9m/£36.8m respectively).

Bromford is adding additional homes at the rate of over 800 a year, which includes development and management. Much depends on getting preferred partner status with local authorities and private developers. It is extremely proud of its "voids performance" – remarkably reporting no empty homes at year-end for the past two years.

Pay and Benefits

Bromford is currently migrating away from traditional incremental pay scales to a competency-based reward structure. This gives Bromford the opportunity to reward performance with non-consolidated (bonus) payments and move people quickly along pay bands. "Colleagues don't come into our business to earn big money," says Marianne

Skelcher, director of human resources. "But a lump sum, equivalent to a whole increment, does make a real difference." Bromford measures group performance and individual competencies based on assessments made by managers. This allows Bromford to pay above average in a competitive marketplace, and provide the best total package.

"It's the total reward package – including flexible working, personal development, and our ability to offer fresh career challenges – that really retains people," adds Skelcher. True enough, but Bromford also offers colleagues a wide array of tangible benefits.

The final salary pension scheme requires members to contribute 3–5% of pensionable earnings. BUPA health cover is free to all colleagues, and family cover is available at reduced cost. The Personal Support Line offers a confidential, 24-hour support service for everyday issues and more serious problems. Maternity and paternity leave and benefits vary with length of service; as does occupational sick pay and holidays, which range from 23–26 days. Senior managers receive a Total Benefits Statement, which includes a reminder of non-financial benefits – an initiative that is being rolled-out across the business.

Promotion and development

Bromford offers a wide range of careers and roles. Customer service advisers work in areas such as repair and maintenance, and regional housing centres. Support workers interact more closely with customers with special support needs. On the property side, there are asset managers, building surveyors and estate managers – and of course tradespeople and maintenance staff. These are supported by finance and accounting, communications, HR and ICT.

Graduates might join at entry level in any of these roles. Many catch the "Bromford Bug" and resist pursuing more lucrative careers. "Growing our own is important," says Skelcher. "We target 75% of management appointments from within. This sometimes means promoting someone we realise isn't quite there yet, but with a structured personal development plan and stretch targets they can grow into the role."

The objective is to give colleagues the opportunities to realise their potential and become highly skilled, motivated team players able to contribute fully to Bromford's success.

This is the challenge that Bromford colleagues cherish so highly; and it helps significantly in both recruitment and retention. "99% of people raise their game if given the opportunity," adds Skelcher.

Bromford encourages movement across roles. Sarah Flaherty started in customer service in supported housing, but became a property development manager; Keith Nelson joined as a temp for two weeks and is now a professional analyst, being supported in acquiring educational qualifications. Bromford actively uses project secondments to give people exposure to different parts of the business – "Experiencing It", as it's known.

"We want people who share our values and actually behave that way," says Skelcher. "We recruit for attitude; train for skill." The driver is the personal development plan supported by a substantial in-house training and development programme. Business knowledge training might be in heath and safety, landlord-tenant law, anti-social behaviour, complaints procedures or home ownership. Personal development includes "softer" areas such as assertiveness and presentation skills. Management development focuses on leadership, coaching, and recruitment and selection. Bromford supports colleagues financially in achieving professional qualifications, while ensuring that they must support the business – it must show it is investing money wisely.

Company culture

Chief executive Mick Kent, who has given Bromford leadership and continuity for 20 years, says: "Our culture is strongly focused on results and high performance, but at the same time it is one that supports our people to achieve their full potential through career development plans, training programmes, and assisting them to balance their careers and home life. Through this, we aim to create a fun place to work, great teamwork, and excellent customer service."

Bromford claims it is "more than bricks and mortar". And cementing its culture are its core values of customer focus, teamwork, and continuous improvement. In its seventh year of Investors in People accreditation, Bromford has created a workplace where people really want to stay. "We want to bend over backwards for our people and have created a framework that enables us to do this," says Skelcher. "If you have itchy feet and want a different role, we say: 'come and talk to us about it – don't leave for another place.'" Bromford culture is natural, organic and can-do – unusual for its sector. For example, the remarkable achievement of having no unlet properties at year-end was a target set on the front line – not by managers.

Recognition plays an important role. The Colleague Award scheme runs in each of Bromford's four regions, and provides a shortlist for the annual award at the high-profile "Bromford Bash". People are nominated for (and win) industry and national awards, which reflects on the whole team. Managers have personal recognition budgets to use at their discretion. And then there are the little things. A balloon in the coffee station indicates a new starter is in the office. Find the matching balloon at the newcomer's desk, say "hello", and you win chocolates!

Flexible working is integral. With a culture that encourages open discussion, Bromford recognises that everyone is different – so there's no "one size fits all" approach. Instead there is a range of flexible working options at managers' discretion including homeworking, equipping people with laptops and mobile phones, nine-day fortnights, and even annualised hours. The only non-negotiables are that customer service and performance must not suffer and the whole team must sign up to the arrangements.

One colleague was approached by a building contractor partner and offered a bigger job and more money. He didn't know what to do. Bromford offered him a one-month secondment to see if he enjoyed working for his potential new employer. He came straight back! Others have left and begged to return within a couple of weeks – and Bromford usually has its doors and arms wide open.

Innovation

Driven at local team level, all colleagues are encouraged to think about their part of the business, contribute fresh thinking, tweak processes, and go out and find new ideas and come back and implement them.

Bromford has done much innovative work in the area of anti-social behaviour, making people feel safer in their homes. For example, they have provided designated, specialist community safety managers, whose role is focused on people experiencing difficulties with their neighbours. They are trained to mediate and work with groups of residents, in partnership with local police forces, to help them feel comfortable in taking a stand. This resulted in one group of residents winning a Home Office award.

Bromford is at the leading edge of income recovery, recognising that it is their job to help people manage their money properly and get them back on track in order to pay their rent. "It's better to be supportive than punitive," says Anna Pickering, communications manager. "It's also better to keep existing customers rather than have to find new ones."

Diversity and social responsibility

Using a specialist company, Equality Foundation, Bromford takes an expansive approach to equality and diversity – going well beyond the workplace to scrutinise everything including customers, accessibility to services and contract awards.

Bromford sets workforce diversity targets relative to Census figures. It is currently on target for 8.5% black/ethnic minorities. In fact, it attracted 11% for new recruits, and on internal promotions is hitting 16%. It's a similar situation with their age profile, being evenly spread 30/30/30 between the main "box bands". Two of the five-strong executive team are women, and overall, 65% of the workforce is female.

"Social responsibility? That defines what we do!" says Skelcher. Bromford is dedicated to building sustainable communities, and designs mixed-tenure developments that really contribute to the community infrastructure. And with community regeneration projects (Bromford has heavy involvement in post-war council estates in Birmingham and Cheltenham), it goes out of its way to involve local residents and let them have their say.

Corporate Governance

Bromford is regulated by the Housing Corporation and a raft of legislation. The regulator attends at least one board meeting and a one-to-one meeting with the chairman annually. Bromford is also inspected by the Audit Commission. It has an explicit code of governance; and detailed, transparent terms of reference for employees. There is a non-executive board (three female members), a full-time company secretary, and quality assurance roles in each of its main business areas. For example, on revenue funding for supportive housing, there are minimum grades to meet in the quality assurance framework. Bromford always exceeds these.

Environmental record

Bromford has clear policies on affordable warmth. Using modern methods of construction, it builds "standards of lifetime" homes that must be energy efficient. The Eco Homes project in Wolverhampton is a good example. Customers are also provided with information on energy efficiency in the home.

The issue of sustainability is a core one, both in terms of construction and surrounding infrastructure. Bromford is looking to create a safe and clean community, and to this end operates a Medal Scheme in which its customers rate the environmental quality of public areas and landscaping. It also costs-in the provision of an estate caretaker so that negative issues of litter, abandoned cars or fridges can be dealt with on the spot.

In its offices, Bromford has invested considerably in IT infrastructure, aspiring towards paperless offices. Most company documents are already found on its intranet.

Bucknall Austin

Bucknall Austin
Millennium Point, Curzon Street, Birmingham B4 7XG
Tel: (0) 121 503 1500
Web: www.bucknall.com **E-mail:** info@bucknall.com

Pay and Benefits	7.2	Innovation	6.4
Promotion and Development	7.0	Diversity	6.4
Training	6.9	Social Responsibility	6.2
Travel opportunities	4.6	Corporate Governance	7.0
Culture	6.5	Environment	6.2
Total			**64.4**

Bucknall Austin specialises in project management, quantity surveying and building surveying. It is based in six locations around England; at Birmingham, Bristol, London, Manchester, Sheffield and Thames Valley. Following a management buyout in early 2003 from Citex, its former acquirer in 1998, the company has stamped its mark once more in UK construction's premier league. The firm recently posted profits after tax of £443,000 on turnover of £27m in its first reported trading period since its reformation. Such success is firmly rooted in the fact that over 60% of the company's turnover is generated from long-term framework agreements.

Executive summary

Bucknalls has invested heavily in recruitment, training and IT; and in developing a dynamic cost-modelling tool linking capital and whole-life costs, and a state-of-the-art intranet-based process map called Intelligence.

Bucknalls has also published its Best Value Review, measuring its performance against industry standards and assessing its ability to meet Best Value objectives. Scores were "well above industry standards in several areas" including value for money, quality of service, environmental impact and whole-life performance. Against the industry benchmark standard, Bucknall Austin consistently performs in the upper quartile in all areas. This marks the third year running that the consultancy has achieved a top quartile rating.

Pay and benefits

"Our pay and benefits package is well in line with the market sector," says Ann Bentley, operations director. Graduates, for example, have starting salaries in the range of £18,000–£25,000. The basic benefits include private medical insurance for all employees, permanent health insurance, stakeholder pension scheme with employee contributions of 4% and employer contributions of 5% (1% of which is for life assurance cover of four times salary death-in-service benefit), and 25 days holiday for all employees. Depending on professional qualifications and status in the company, there is a five-tier car allowance. On promotion to associate (band three), employees are entitled to reimbursement of all private fuel costs.

"But we also offer alternative benefits to enable employees to achieve a better work/life balance," says Bentley. "For example, there's a flexible holiday policy and a system for getting more value from their basic salary through the use of Inland Revenue-approved tax and NI-effective salary sacrifice schemes – such as home PC, bicycle and childcare voucher purchase schemes."

Bucknall Austin is a wholly employee-owned company and all employees are offered the opportunity to purchase shares in the company. To date, the take-up rate is 32%.

Employees may opt to purchase shares annually, with the company offering a six-month timeframe in which to pay.

There is also a two-tier bonus scheme. Tier one, the Business Performance Bonus, is for all employees; 10% of profits are put into a pot and shared among staff for doing a good job and returning profits to the company. Tier two, limited to 20% of the company, is the Business Improvement Bonus for people who have made the biggest improvement in business performance; it is limited only by the size of the improvements made.

Promotion and development

"Everyone is offered the opportunity for training. We don't pick people out; it's provided as you need it," says Bentley. In the 2003–04 financial year there were 900 days of training, which equates to 3.5 days for each person on average. "We currently have eight staff pursuing MSc and one MBA qualifications, and 23 graduate employees awaiting professional qualifications," says Bentley. "Over 60% of employees are professionally qualified, with Royal Institution of Chartered Surveyors (RICS) or Chartered Institute of Building (CIOB) accreditation." Over 50% of the staff are graduates, with 15% having second degrees.

There are opportunities for promotion, with employees encouraged to discuss their particular aspirations both at a formal review and also at any time with their line manager. The company has initiated the Bucknall Austin Academy "to encourage employee development along lines of pre-set principles, objectives and philosophy". Essentially this embodies a single group culture where everyone is afforded the necessary training, education and development opportunities they need, rounded off with a two-way commitment from the company and each employee. The company provides the training, and employees are motivated to make the most of opportunities offered to enhance skills and knowledge.

A vigorous coaching and mentoring system is in operation. Line managers act in supervisory or coaching roles. Coaching is now being developed consistently as a management style company-wide. "We are focusing on staff being stretched and accepting accountability, and emphasising effective recognition, feedback and coaching skills for everyone's benefit," says Bentley.

Company culture

There is an open culture at Bucknall Austin where the age range of employees reflects society, with a span of 18 to 66. Each of the six office environments at the company occupies one floor plate, which is "good for communications and openness". There are no offices for managers, just meeting rooms which are available on a "first come, first served" basis. The culture is also described as honest, respectful, professional, challenging, fair, customer-focused – and fun. It's very much: work hard, but enjoy yourself too. There's a low rate of sickness absence; people like to come to work here.

The work/life balance is good. Take flexible working, where the company has extended existing legislation to cover such areas as job sharing, reduction to part-time hours and working from home on specific days to cater for childcare. Each case is assessed to fit with the individual's and the business's needs. And where any employee – irrespective of whether they meet criteria covered by the legislation – may need flexibility of working hours, there's a sympathetic ear.

There is also a flexible holiday policy aimed at suiting personal needs, and enhanced maternity and paternity policies to enable employees to have more financial support to enjoy time with their families.

The company invested over £500,000 in a state-of-the-art IT system, enabling staff to work from home as though they were in the office. As a new company, Investors in People accreditation is expected in early 2005, while Bucknall Austin recently achieved ISO 9001:2000.

Innovation

"We run a senior management group called the Innovation Forum where people can introduce new ideas for review, debate and decision," says Bentley. "Support will be granted for those ideas which show clear benefits for the business. We have a R&D budget of 0.5% of turnover, to support initiatives such as these right through to implementation." An example is the four-dimensional cost model (4DCM), which has found a way to include time, the fourth dimension, into standard three-dimensional construction cost models. This dynamic cost model could slash whole-life costs on building projects by millions of pounds, and equally builds sustainability into cost plans for the future. That is innovation.

There is also an HR forum underpinning the key belief that involvement of as many employee disciplines as possible enables a continual review and update of the company's HR offerings. The HR forum is composed of volunteers from all parts of the company. Ultimately these people become ambassadors for any new initiative agreed in the forum. All staff are encouraged to provide ideas for the forums and also to volunteer for membership.

"We tend to be more developmental rather than innovative," says Bentley. "We find specific solutions."

Diversity and social responsibility

While women constitute 26% of the total headcount at Bucknall Austin and 9.5% of total management, and 5% of staff are from racial and religious minorities, the company is not happy with the balance. "Remember first that we are about construction," says Bentley. "We are not complacent, but are seeking to improve on these figures. A key way of tackling this issue is to target schools and colleges to encourage students at an earlier age to consider construction as a career."

The company is offering sponsorships for college and holiday work experience for some students nationwide in an effort to encourage people from a cross-section of backgrounds into construction.

"We're committed to playing an active role in supporting charitable and other community activities through our Serious Partners in Community and Education, SPICE, programme," says Bentley. "We'll consider any proposals from staff under our charitable policy, eg one graduate asked for support for a two-week project in Rwanda – he took one week's holiday and we paid the second week. The Birmingham office decorated a scout hut; while Manchester is involved in local school projects through the Salford Business Education Partnership, where staff give their time."

Corporate governance

"Our core corporate functions are managed by professionally qualified competent people," says Bentley. "The finance director also acts as company secretary and is a clear point of accountability. Where we employ freelance support we ensure specific rules are followed on section IR35 issues, and that limited companies we work with are up to date with their VAT and tax returns."

"We are registered under the Data Protection Act and use external legal advisers, because everybody is fallible," says Bentley. There are compliance officers – for example a health and safety manager with clear responsibilities, and a quality manager to ensure the company adheres to its business promises. Under active development are initiatives in corporate social responsibility embracing health, safety and environmental issues. There is a professionally qualified nine-person HR team, plus fully accredited accountancy and IT teams.

A major investment is the one Bucknall Austin makes in its staff. There is no union. "We feel we have established good employee communications forums," says Bentley. "We are, however, aware of the new Information and Communication with Employees (ICE) legislation, effective 6 April 2005, and thus we have a fresh and formal policy to ensure our communications procedures are totally compliant."

Environmental record

"We regard the maintenance of the environment as a vital part of sustainable business development," says Bentley. "We support responsible environmental and resource management in balance with sustainable business development." There's a board – the Future Initiatives Team – comprising volunteers with the remit to generate ideas and follow them through to implementation. So far, the group has ensured all offices recycle paper and toner cartridges. Old computers and mobile phones are donated to charity. The board (actually a young board) also passes out tips and hints such as "remember to turn off all taps and lights at home and work" in an effort to make sure the issues remain in people's consciousness.

Interest-free loans on season tickets are available to encourage the use of public transport. Inter-office travel and visits to clients are conducted using trains.

Bucknall Austin considers itself at the forefront regarding sustainability issues. There's the new 4D Cost Plan Model for example, with sustainability for the future as a key external focus. "When we look internally, we regard ourselves as ahead of the game too, compared with the rest of our sector," says Bentley. That can be borne out through customer references and many referrals.

Cadbury Schweppes

Cadbury Schweppes Plc
25 Berkeley Square, London W1J 6HB
Tel: (0) 20 7830 5095 **Fax:** (0) 20 7830 5157
Web: www.cadburyschweppes.com

Cadbury Schweppes

Pay and Benefits	7.3	Innovation	6.2
Promotion and Development	6.8	Diversity	6.8
Training	6.0	Social Responsibility	7.2
Travel opportunities	6.6	Corporate Governance	7.0
Culture	7.5	Environment	6.0
Total			**67.4**

Cadbury Schweppes needs little introduction: the range of beverages and confectionery products it manufactures, markets and distributes around the world are household names. As well as Cadbury chocolate and Schweppes drinks, its product range includes other well-loved brands such as Halls, Trident, Dr Pepper, Snapple, Trebor, Dentyne, Bubblicious and Bassett's. With origins stretching back over 200 years, the group's products are today enjoyed in almost every country worldwide. Its purchase of Adams Confectionery in 2003 made it the world market leader in sugar and functional confectionery and a strong number two in chewing gum. It is also the world's third-largest soft drinks company. The group employs around 55,000 people in 60 countries.

Executive summary

Cadbury Schweppes is one of the world's largest international beverage and confectionery companies, with a 2003 turnover of nearly £6.5bn.

The company's history began in 1783 when Jacob Schweppe perfected his process for manufacturing carbonated mineral water; forty years later in Birmingham, John Cadbury set up in business selling a range of products including tea and coffee, with cocoa and chocolate becoming Cadbury's main business within a few years. In 1969, these two household names merged to form Cadbury Schweppes.

Since then the company has expanded worldwide through both acquisition and organic growth, strengthening its beverage and confectionery portfolio to include the household names listed above as well as Canada Dry, 7 Up and Orangina.

Cadbury Schweppes has a record of being solidly profitable for many years and operates in a mature market. As the corporate website puts it: "Our brands become old friends with whom our consumers have special relationships". The company's challenge for the future is to find ways of spicing up that relationship to generate new top-line growth.

On one hand it is looking at new ways of marketing and presenting old and well-loved brands. On the other, it is responding to consumers' changing preferences and innovating to suit new tastes. During 2003, the company organised around five regional operating units supported by 6 global functions in order to give its focus on growth and efficiency the strongest possible structural foundation. The new organisation requires new behaviours – a key one being collaboration. Employees across Cadbury Schweppes have been introduced to the new behaviours through the Working Better Together programme introduced by the CEO, Todd Stitzer.

Pay and benefits

As an international company, rewards and recognition policies inevitably vary between regions and divisions, depending on factors such as local conditions and local legislation. The company aims to offer competitive levels of pay, benefits and employment terms. Most countries offer an annual performance-based incentive plan for managers; and benefits often include a retirement plan, a company car and private medical care for senior employees. In some countries, performance incentives will extend down below management level.

The company actively encourages share ownership among its employees, and in many countries this is supported through access to all-employee share plan arrangements. For example, in the UK there is a share purchase scheme and also a sharesave scheme, which has proved extremely popular with the workforce. This scheme enables employees to buy shares at a discount, then at the end of a certain period opt to either take the money and interest from their investment, or to reinvest the money in further shares. Similar schemes are being extended to all regions, depending on local legislation.

In the UK, a specialist shared-service team based in Birmingham coordinates a range of employee benefits. These range from vouchers for childcare support through to pet care insurance, and offers such as health club membership and discounted car insurance.

There is also a company pension scheme in the UK, which provides defined benefits linked to pay during your career with the company.

Promotion and development

Cadbury Schweppes prides itself on offering strong internal career progression and excellent opportunities for employees to maximise their talents: that's why people tend to stay with the company for a long time. Most hiring at management level happens internally; around 90% of company executives have been recruited from within the organisation. All businesses are required to advertise jobs locally, and the company increasingly uses electronic systems to make sure staff are aware of vacancies.

New graduates joining the company can expect an individually tailored career and development plan, and promotions based on merit and performance. As well as local graduate recruitment programmes – in the UK, 10–20 graduates are taken on each year – Cadbury Schweppes aims to broaden its pool of talent by recruiting finance and business graduates through the international student organisation AIESEC.

The company invests in staff training at a local, functional and global level. New graduates joining the company can expect to receive general training in business skills such as time and team management, but also training tailored to the specific business function they work in. Employees who want to study for professional qualifications related to their job are given study time off as well as financial support; all finance graduates are expected to study for the CIMA qualification. Where staff need to work abroad, the company also offers one-to-one tuition in a range of languages.

Globally, the company has a number of training programmes centred on strategic objectives such as product development, sales and operational planning, and building commercial capability.

Cadbury Schweppes is made up of over 30 businesses, which share the same values but have distinct operating styles. That's part of what gives the company its unique atmosphere. As a global business, it recognises the value of cross-cultural awareness and international experience; many roles have multi-country or regional responsibilities, and at any one time around 150 employees will be on international assignment. This is likely to increase with growth in the size of individual operating regions. The company is also actively looking at ways of increasing movement between functions in the organisation.

Company culture

Cadbury Schweppes offers its employees the close-knit team spirit involved in working in a collaborative business, together with the challenges and opportunities that come from being part of a large global organisation. Many of the brands that now form part of the Cadbury Schweppes group were originally small family-run companies – many with Quaker origins or strong community ethics – and their history has helped to form the Cadbury Schweppes culture.

The company aims to strike a balance between meeting commercial goals and contributing to the local community. The culture tends to suit people who want to make a positive impact and a difference to the business and the communities in which Cadbury Schweppes operates.

Cadbury Schweppes may be well established, but it isn't staid. Company style is relaxed, with smart-casual wear the norm in most operations. Employees are expected to make a difference within the company; renewing their skills, and being prepared to change and grow with the organisation are part of that. A number of global training programmes are aimed at supporting organisational change.

The company also prides itself on fostering individuality and allowing staff to use their talents in their own way. For example, it aims to make it possible for employees to work flexibly around the needs of their personal life. In the UK, several senior women and a few men work part time. People can work from home where their job responsibilities allow it; sales people are based mainly at home, coming into the company only for sales meetings. Employees who want time off to travel can take sabbaticals – not all of them at the same time though!

The acquisition of companies around the world has created a multicultural board which includes executives from around the world.

Innovation

With a history that goes back over 200 years, Cadbury Schweppes has brands that are well known and loved by consumers and have become part of people's lives. But the company also recognises the need to stimulate top-line growth and is continually seeking ways to innovate. One of its themes for the future is to find new ways for people to enjoy its products, and this is creating opportunities for employees across a number of different business areas to make their mark.

Cadbury Schweppes has always looked to innovation because it is the lifeblood of any consumer company. Examples are the company's relaunch of its flagship Dairy Milk brand with new packaging and varieties such as "wafer" and "bubbly"; and the launch of two new varieties of Flake made of white chocolate, and praline.

On the production side, innovation can mean innovative packaging techniques, or a different type of chocolate such as Snaps (individual waves/curves of chocolate).

Cadbury Schweppes is also looking to innovate by bringing out new products. In response to consumers' increasing health awareness, it has launched new sugar-free products such as sugar-free mints and gum. As well as this, it is acquiring companies that specialise in products that are free from artificial colours and additives, such as The Natural Confectionary Company.

Diversity and social responsibility

When John Cadbury set up his grocery business in Birmingham in 1824, he wanted the company to reflect his own Quaker principles. Cadbury became well known for its pioneering welfare work: providing housing, education, welfare and recreation facilities for the local community. Though Cadbury Schweppes is now a global company, it's still passionate about being a responsible corporate citizen.

The company has a formal strategy for growing community value around the world. This provides guidelines to locally operating companies as well as ideas and suggestions for action. Specifically, it asks businesses to:

- Build community investment into mainstream business practice
- Aim for a contribution of around 1% of pre-tax profits
- Encourage the inclusion of community objectives in the development of brands, people and reputation
- Report details of community investment annually as part of year-end returns

Cadbury Schweppes is a member of the BiTC PerCent Club, which requires members to donate a minimum of 1% of UK pre-tax profits. In the UK, most corporate giving is channelled through the Cadbury Schweppes Foundation, which makes grants to projects and partner organisations; or via the main UK operating company, Cadbury Trebor Bassett. In addition, operating companies around the world support community activity through their own programmes.

Corporate Governance

By having ordinary shares listed in London, and American Depository Receipts listed in New York; Cadbury Schweppes has to comply with the Combined Code, the New York Stock Exchange Corporate Governance rules, and with securities laws in both the UK and USA.

However, the company goes beyond these basic requirements, with a list of business principles that every employee is required to subscribe to. This covers issues such as ethical business practices, respecting the environment, equal opportunities, diversity in the workplace, health and safety at work, and ethical trading. As well as this, the board has adopted a code of ethics that applies to the chief executive officer and senior financial officers in the group. Both sets of guidelines are available for public viewing on the company's website.

Environmental record

Cadbury Schweppes is committed to responsible environmental, health and safety (EHS) management. A steering group regularly reviews its EHS management systems and recommends any changes in policy to the board, and EHS accountability cascades down from the main board through each business unit to every individual. Health and safety is seen as the responsibility of every employee in a factory, and they are asked to be vigilant and respond to any incident that might damage the environment.

Each year, the company carries out training programmes to raise awareness of how to conserve energy and water, undertake risk assessments, improve machine guarding, reduce waste, promote recycling, and respond to spills and emergencies. The group's factory processes are regularly reviewed by corporate or group auditors who are independent of the site's management. Auditors' recommendations are reviewed during subsequent follow-up visits.

In 2004, the company started to roll out a new set of integrated EHS standards, including management system requirements based on ISO 14001 and OSHAS 18001. Data on the group's EHS performance is made available on its website and in its annual reports.

The Capita Group

The Capita Group Plc
71 Victoria Street, Westminster, London SW1H 0XA
Tel: (0) 20 7799 1525 **Fax:** (0) 20 7799 1526
Web: www.capita.co.uk

CAPITA

Pay and Benefits	6.1	Innovation	6.9
Promotion and Development	6.0	Diversity	6.5
Training	5.9	Social Responsibility	6.4
Travel opportunities	4.1	Corporate Governance	6.2
Culture	6.0	Environment	6.2
Total			**60.3**

The Capita Group is one of Britain's leading business process outsourcing (BPO) groups, delivering professional support services to businesses and organisations across the UK and Ireland. Through its portfolio of companies, it offers functions including back office business processes, IT and software services, customer services, human resources, financial services, and management and property consultancy. Within recent years, it has set up London's congestion charging scheme and taken on the BBC's television licensing contract. Founded by its current executive chairman within the Chartered Institute of Public Finance and Accountancy (CIPFA) twenty years ago, Capita floated on the London Stock Exchange in 1989; it now employs 22,000 people in more than 250 workplaces.

Executive summary

Over the past fifteen years, Capita has seen rapid and steady growth. Rod Aldridge, who started the company within CIPFA in 1984 and led the management buyout three years later, remains Capita's hands-on executive chairman. Paul Pindar joined Capita from 3i during that period and is now chief executive, and other members of senior management boast similar lengths of tenure. Turnover rose from £898m in 2002 to £1,081m in 2003; and in 2004 the group delivered another period of strong financial results, with revenues increasing to £620m for the half-year.

Capita takes over and transforms all manner of services for public and private organisations, and has led the way in broadening the concept of outsourcing from solely IT to other essential functions such as human resources. In the process, it has won accolades including Management Today's Most Admired Support Services Company for three consecutive years. Capita was also named Company of the Year 2003 in The Royal Bank of Scotland Sunday Times Business Awards.

The group concentrates on eight key markets: central and local government, education, health, transport, insurance, life and pensions, and private sector companies. While some growth has come through acquisition, which has taken the group into new market sectors and deepened penetration in others, Capita sees much present and future growth as being organic: through the winning of major contracts and cross-pollination, for example identifying opportunities to introduce existing and new customers to new services.

Capita attributes its success to a "very simple business model" and a high degree of selectivity about which contracts to bid for in a market worth a potential £65bn.

Pay and benefits

Around 60–70% of Capita's employees come into the group through contract wins and acquisitions, so the group operates a variety of terms and conditions. In cases where

Capita inherits a legacy of union partnership, the group operates a collective bargaining pay element and embeds its own performance management system. For the rest of the workforce, there is individual performance-related pay.

In principle, Capita steers away from status to keep core benefits the same throughout the group. Salaries tend to be in the middle quartile, depending on sector; although some of the most highly paid people in the group are in sales. There are bonus arrangements for senior executives linked to the performance of particular businesses.

Capita operates three share schemes: the most popular, a protected sharesave scheme, has 40% take-up by employees; a share ownership plan has about 5% take-up; and a share option scheme, available only to the group's top 300 employees, is allocated annually.

Core benefits, including free daily refreshment, are supplemented by other benefits such as car allowance and corporate healthcare; more flexibility in terms of choice is gradually being introduced. Where the group prides itself, however, is in the range of discounts it offers employees through its intranet on everything from mortgages to spectacles, insurance to will-writing, home computers to high street goods. "These discounts are a big plus for us," explains Joanne Bacon, group HR director. "We have a great amount of buying power and we pass that on to our clients, but also to our employees."

Non-financial recognition includes a scheme in which employees can be nominated by their peers for innovation, excellence, teamwork and community contribution. Winners' achievements are celebrated within their teams. They receive a certificate and a bottle of champagne, and are invited to an annual Service Excellence Dinner.

Promotion and development

As an organisation devoted to improving the way things work, it's hardly surprising that Capita makes a priority of training its own staff. This falls into two broad categories: technical training, giving employees necessary expertise to deliver the service required; and personal development, delivered in partnership with their Learning & Development business (recently acquired from The Industrial Society).

With a relatively flat structure, Capita prefers to train its line managers to become coaches, encouraging them to highlight the training needs of individuals in their teams and point them towards the appropriate course of action – whether that is accessing a specific programme through the group intranet or enrolling on an outside development course, such as an MBA.

Every employee goes through an annual performance appraisal to set objectives and deadlines, which are reviewed quarterly. Everywhere within the group, a fast and effective report-back is key to ongoing success. Though progress is closely monitored, the culture is entrepreneurial: one young man who began as a temp, for example, was coached so effectively by his line manager that he is now, in his mid-twenties, still with Capita and running one of its business development teams.

While few opportunities exist for international travel, employees may be mobile within the UK; and because teams vary widely, "cross-cultural" working is common. Most senior managers have been with Capita for some years, and all vacancies are advertised internally, but the group maintains a 75:25 split – intentionally bringing in new blood to keep ideas fresh.

Managers are encouraged to be mobile and generalist within the group, and to find opportunities for growth in roles that, within larger organisations, may have been under-rated. "Sometimes people have been running back-office administrative functions which were not previously given a lot of attention. We take people from the back office into the front line," says Shona Nichols, group marketing director.

Company culture

Capita is a meritocracy: it matters less that you went to university than that you can contribute within a fast-moving, vigorous team environment which prizes integrity and reliability. "We give autonomy to people so that they can take responsibility within a clearly defined set of rules. Within these boundaries, they have a lot of freedom. The aim is to keep politics to a minimum," says Nichols.

The group operates a number of "monthly operating boards" at which small numbers of managers examine profit and loss, and re-forecast. They look "not just at the numbers, but at what the numbers tell us. If you are reviewing very regularly, it is okay to raise problems and mistakes and seek solutions with your colleagues. This strengthens collective responsibility in solving the problem. It's the opposite of a blame culture," says Nichols.

Capita works with several unions, but has three main relationships: with UNISON, PCS (civil service), and CWU (communications workers). The group has partnership agreements in place, which have been refined over the years; these mechanisms have enabled minor falling-outs to be rectified at an early stage, and the relationship built upon. The approach is preventative, rather than reactive.

As an organisation that tends to privilege human interaction over formal policies, the group depends on the discretion of line managers to implement work/life balance policies. Employees in different locations may do flexitime, shift work, term-time hours, zero hours (the employer does not guarantee work, paying only for work actually done) or, if they are particularly mobile, work from home. As Nichols puts it, "one size doesn't fit all".

Inheriting different working cultures, winning people's trust and integrating new employees into the "Capita way" is a challenge the group relishes. It dealt with one organisation's high absenteeism rate, for example, by changing a formal policy to a softer, more attentive approach. After another contract win, staff helped to design a new office that was then purpose-built for them.

Innovation

As it constantly takes on new business, and its modus operandi is to find ways to better existing services, innovation comes as second nature to Capita. When it was setting up the congestion charge in London, for example, it soon saw that getting motorists to text their information to the centre would save time and money. The success of the implementation was such that Capita was asked to submit a paper to the government on its achievements.

"Innovation is what our business is about," says Nichols, citing the way Capita bid for and re-won a contract to administer teachers' pensions for the government's DfES. "We are operating against different competition in all of the areas we are in. We had to show, in this contract re-bid, what would be innovative over a further seven years."

Diversity and social responsibility

With such a broad base of businesses, and so many employees coming from outside organisations, the workforce is "a real mix of people". In general, the group prefers to monitor diversity and equality by supporting and providing adequate training for its managers, rather than going around with a checklist; although in some cases, with an inherited set of conditions, it does aim to meet existing targets.

Half of Capita's workforce are women, and the number of female managers has increased to 34%. "Our standard is equality for all, and the best person for the job," says Bacon. "From a human resources point of view, we look at data on a monthly basis to analyse where we need to go. It's about what is relevant and works for the organisation, rather than having targets which are unrealistic."

Capita's executive chairman and chief executive have built individual, long-standing relationships with The Prince's Trust and the NSPCC, and a third charity is chosen annually by staff to benefit from their support. The group recently launched a dedicated annual charity week, issuing an A-Z of Fundraising pack to all workers.

Employees are also encouraged to give their time on a 50/50 basis (half from the group's time, half from their own) to community work: for example, to become leaders on a Prince's Trust xl programme for young people, or offer accountancy on a pro bono basis. The group is keen to promote regeneration in areas such as Blackburn; and works with other agencies to encourage mothers to return to work, and to engage those with learning disabilities.

Corporate governance

Capita has a dedicated team of people who deal with risk management across the group. One advantage of being a company to which key services are entrusted by other businesses, is the fact that Capita is constantly being subjected to intensive due diligence; hence its own internal processes have to be watertight.

"Parts of our business are regulated by the FSA, but we take risk mitigation very seriously ourselves," explains Nichols. "We need to understand where all the risks are and mitigate them – and, if necessary, price that into the deal."

Capita prides itself on "top-end" accountancy practices and on tightly managing finances – making sure that those who are responsible have the right level of training.

Environmental record

While not considered a business of high impact to the environment, Capita uses the principle of continuous improvement to ensure that all of its practices are environmentally friendly.

In particular, Capita's property businesses are actively monitored against legislative requirements, and Capita Infrastructure Consultancy are certified as compliant with the ISO 14001 environmental standard.

At present, it sources 100% of its electricity from renewable sources; and recycles printer cartridges, paper and computers where it can. Individual employees are also rewarded for taking the initiative: one engineering assistant received an innovation award for piloting the use of recycled glass within pavement layers of the carriageway as part of Capita's strategic partnership with Cumbria county council.

The recent appointment of a safety, health and environment officer – who reports at board level on progress – demonstrates Capita's commitment to going green.

Claridge's

Brook Street, Mayfair, London W1A 2JQ
Tel: (0) 20 7629 8860
Web: www.claridges.co.uk **Email:** recruitment@claridges.co.uk

Claridge's

Pay and Benefits	6.6	Innovation	6.6
Promotion and Development	6.5	Diversity	7.1
Training	6.0	Social Responsibility	6.2
Travel opportunities	4.2	Corporate Governance	6.4
Culture	6.7	Environment	6.8
Total			**63.1**

Claridge's is one of London's most exclusive and successful hotels. Founded in 1854 and rebuilt in 1898, the Mayfair hotel's 203 rooms have housed royalty and statesmen from all over the world, as well as countless business people and mere mortals who have saved up to treat themselves. In 1894, Claridge's joined a group which also included classic London hotels the Savoy, the Berkeley and the Connaught; but the group changed hands in 2004 and the Savoy has been sold off. Claridge's employs around 350 people, 90% of them in operational roles. Profit in 2004 was £17m on turnover of £38m.

Executive summary

Claridge's is the living embodiment of success on the Monopoly board – a hotel in Mayfair – and its own success story is just as impressive. Less than a decade ago it was stumbling, with fewer than half its rooms occupied and annual staff turnover at nearly 75%. By 2004, it had more than doubled its revenues and was making a remarkable 45% pre-tax profit. It is more profitable than its sister hotels, the Connaught and the Berkeley, and benchmarking itself against similar London hotels, it claims to have the highest occupancy and second-highest room rates.

Although revenues suffered in 2001 (the year of foot-and-mouth and 9/11) and 2003 (because of the Iraq war), Claridge's says it is less vulnerable to world events than most hotels. Occupancy rates bounced back just six weeks after 9/11, compared with 18 months for some competitors.

With average room rates of £356 a night, Claridge's does not pretend to be egalitarian. With its rooms and food-and-beverage facilities almost full to capacity, it is actually in a position to raise prices, and therefore profitability, still further.

Quinlan Private, the Irish investment company which bought the four-hotel group in 2004, has sold off the Savoy – leaving it free to invest in Claridge's and its sisters. Future plans include refurbishment of the existing portfolio and expansion of the new brand overseas.

Pay and benefits

Claridge's aims to pay salaries in the top quartile for the hotel industry, and benchmarks itself to see that it does. There are grades, but these are fairly fluid and there are no set pay scales. Although there is no performance-related pay, the company gives a twice-yearly flat-rate bonus based on the hotel's financial performance to all staff up to manager level (totalling about £1,000 per person in 2004). In addition, managers get a performance-related bonus, while individual bonuses for senior managers are determined by both personal and company performance.

There has been a big shake-up in personnel practices at the hotel since the 1990s trough, including several recognition programmes for staff at all levels. "We work hard to recognise people who aren't necessarily high flyers, but without whom the hotel couldn't function – like the gentlemen who operate the ironing machine in the Linen Room," says Claire Thompson, the hotel's director of HR. Awards include employee of the month, nominated by colleagues and worth £150; and employee of the year, who wins a big prize like a cruise.

The final salary pension scheme is still open to new recruits, in return for a 3.5% contribution. Other benefits include a daily free meal in the staff restaurant; occupational health support and eye care vouchers; uniform and free laundry (the latter also available to office staff); long-service awards; discounts on osteopathy, chiropody and beauty therapy; and private health insurance for senior managers. The hotel has a hostel providing cheap accommodation for new recruits if required. All staff, however junior, also get to spend a night as a guest of the hotel when they pass their three months' probation, to introduce them to the Claridge's philosophy.

There are no company cars, and no share scheme as the group is privately owned. Holiday is 20 days a year, rising to 22.5 days after five years and 25 days after seven years.

Promotion and development

"We always try to recruit from inside before we look outside, and our absolute ideal would be to recruit everyone at the bottom and promote from within," says Thompson (who began her own career at Claridge's before returning as HR director in 2004). About 70% of management and supervisor vacancies are filled internally, and more than half of the current management team have been promoted from the ranks.

The hotel usually recruits two or three graduates a year, generally with hotel-related degrees, and welcomes sandwich-year undergraduates and school pupils on work experience. As well as operational roles in housekeeping, food and beverage, maintenance etc., the hotel has most of the back-office functions of any medium-sized business including accounts, IT, procurement, public relations and HR (but not sales and marketing which are handled at group level). There is plenty of scope to take further qualifications, but these will mostly be on the practical or hotel management side since the company is more interested in practical experience than paper qualifications.

Promotion can be swift – after as little as nine months – and good people can make assistant manager in three to five years. Occasionally, Claridge's staff transfer to the Connaught or the Berkeley, but this is unusual since the three hotels are very different. As far as possible, people are encouraged to shape their own careers; and succession planning takes place down to assistant manager level.

Everyone has a personally tailored training and development plan, and there are training coordinators in every department. Staff typically get four or five days' formal training a year, often in-house in the new training suite (set up at the request of staff thanks to a generous bequest from a long-time resident of the hotel).

To develop and stretch people, the hotel sets up cross-functional teams of seven or eight managers or assistant managers to cooperate on projects outside their usual area of work – ranging from redesigning the staff newsletter to increasing in-room dining sales or developing facilities and services for children.

Company culture

At the end of the 1990s, Claridge's was not a happy ship; staff turnover was high, morale was low, and communication, teamwork and pay were poor – so a new management team was brought in to shake things up.

Today the hotel's heart of house areas teem with noticeboards celebrating staff successes, highlighting satisfied customers, listing bi-monthly social events, and picturing everyone in the hotel so new recruits can always put a name to a face. People are friendly and industrious, staff turnover has fallen from 73% to 27% (low for the hotel industry), and 97% of staff say they are proud to work at Claridge's.

"People feel that it's their hotel, and they take responsibility for it instead of just expecting the general manager to do so," says Debbie Hole, the hotel's learning and development manager. This is helped by "back to the floor" days and managers serving food and drink at staff parties, but it goes much deeper. The management strive for a no-blame culture, where staff are empowered and given the opportunity to make decisions and learn from their mistakes.

Personality and attitude are more important than five-star hotel experience. "You can train people to lay a table or cook a steak, but you can't train them to smile," says Hole. Although it welcomes high flyers, the hotel also makes room for quieter types who just want to do a good job.

"There's a great sense of pride now," says Thompson. "People get a real buzz from knowing that they work for one of the best hotels in London, and they work extremely hard; not just because we're busy, but because they care."

Staff certainly do work hard, and Claridge's admits there is still a long-hours culture – not just operationally but throughout the hotel. Management does what it can by giving time off in lieu, encouraging people to take their full holiday allowance, and providing congenial restaurant facilities and subsidised gym membership. Part-time working is possible, and although the hotel must be staffed round the clock, this does mean that many staff can choose their own hours.

The hotel is tough on sickness absence, paying only the first two weeks for people with up to two years' service, with an extra week per year's service thereafter (up to three months). No unions are recognised but industrial relations are generally good.

Innovation

Much of the appeal of Claridge's lies in its classic, almost timeless nature – it still has lift attendants, and the last major restoration (in 1999) was done in 1930s art deco style. However, in contrast, the hotel is subtly innovative and extremely forward thinking, particularly with regards to technology. Claridge's is cutting edge and thrives on keeping up to date with guests' high expectations, with developments such as high-speed internet and Wi-Fi connections.

Heart of house, the hotel was one of the first to introduce an online system for staff appraisals, enabling both appraiser and appraised to gather and share their thoughts before the annual appraisal interviews. It has also introduced a pioneering drug and alcohol awareness programme for staff – not because Claridge's has a particular problem, but simply recognising that these issues are endemic in the hotel industry. The HR professionals keep their knowledge up to date through membership of the Hospitality and Catering Personnel and Training Association.

Diversity and social responsibility

With 52 nationalities among its 350 permanent staff, Claridge's must be one of the most diverse employers in the UK; it is unusual for a foreign guest to arrive at reception for whom a translator cannot be found somewhere in the hotel. The age range is equally wide, although the management team is quite young: the average age is 35 among the executive team, 28 for managers and under 25 for assistant managers. Women account for two of the eight executives and more than a third of managers.

The hotel has several links with the local community. It has built a relationship with a shelter for homeless people, taking residents on work placements to help them get back into employment, and regularly talks to local schools and provides places for work experience. It also supports Hospitality Action, a benevolent association for former hospitality workers, and donates prizes to local charities.

Corporate Governance

The safety and wellbeing of its customers and staff are of the highest importance to Claridge's, which undertakes regular health and safety audits and gives full training in subjects such as food hygiene. The director of security, health and safety and fire prevention reports directly to the general manager. Responsibility for data protection is split between the director of HR (for staff) and the general manager (for the business as a whole).

The hotel gained Investors in People accreditation in 1999 and 2002, and has won many awards – including Employer of the Year in the National Business Awards 2002, and many hotel and leisure awards.

Environmental record

Claridge's claims to be London's second-greenest hotel, recycling virtually anything that can be recycled including paper, glass, batteries, printer cartridges and even cooking oil. Staff are trained to recycle during their induction. Resource-saving measures include lights operated by movement sensors and water-saving taps. There is no parking at the hotel, and all staff are offered season ticket loans. The hotel also pays a contribution to taxi fares for staff who start or finish work late at night.

Clifford Chance

Clifford Chance
10 Upper Bank Street, London E14 5JJ
Tel: (0) 20 7006 1000 **Fax:** (0) 20 7006 5555
Web: www.cliffordchance.com

C L I F F O R D
C H A N C E

Pay and Benefits	8.1	Innovation	6.2
Promotion and Development	6.6	Diversity	7.3
Training	7.1	Social Responsibility	7.0
Travel opportunities	7.1	Corporate Governance	6.2
Culture	6.6	Environment	6.6
Total			**68.8**

Clifford Chance is one of the "Magic Circle" top 5 UK law firms, and the largest in terms of revenue. Formed in the mid-1980s through the merger of law firms Clifford Turner and Coward Chance, it went on to form a tripartite merger with two other major law firms – Pünder Volhard Weber Axster in Germany, and Rogers & Wells in the US – and is now a global organisation with offices in 19 countries. The London office is the largest in the network, generating 40% of the firm's business. Clifford Chance employs 7,000 staff worldwide and around 2,500 in the London office, approximately half of whom are lawyers. Its 2003–04 global revenues were £950m.

Executive summary

Most of the firm's clients are major organisations: large multinationals such as Altria and Siemens; financial institutions including Citigroup, JP Morgan Chase, Aviva and UBS; and government bodies such as the European Commission.

The London office is organised into six client-facing practice areas: finance; capital markets; litigation and dispute resolution; corporate; real estate; and tax, pensions and employment. Each of these is led by a practice area leader who sits on the London Management Group.

Pay and benefits

As befits one of London's biggest law firms, Clifford Chance pays good money. Its salaries are benchmarked against those of other leading law firms and city institutions; trainee lawyers start on £29,000, rising to £33,000 after one year and £50,000 once they qualify. Once qualified, lawyers are eligible for bonus awards of up to 40% of salary; while support staff can receive bonuses of up to 15% of salary depending on their year of qualification or grade.

On the benefits side, there is a money purchase pension scheme, and employees receive private health insurance, life assurance amounting to four times their salary, and long-term sick pay of 75% of salary if they have to be off work for more than six months. There is also the option of unlimited season ticket loans, and interest-free personal loans of up to £1,500. The firm is currently piloting a childcare voucher scheme.

All employees can apply for flexible working arrangements. Requests are considered on their merits – flexible working is not always possible in some areas of the firm's business – and granted where possible. Many employees work part time and some work term time only.

Clifford Chance moved to new premises in Canary Wharf in 2004. As well as stunning views, the 30-floor building has a staff restaurant, onsite gym, swimming pool and exercise studios, and a shop offering services such as dry cleaning and DVD rental.

Promotion and development

Around 5% of Clifford Chance's payroll budget – £1.35m – is currently invested in training its staff. Everyone joining the firm goes through a week-long, office-wide induction programme intended to familiarise them with the organisation, its processes and information systems.

The firm takes on around 120 trainee lawyers each year, all of whom undergo a two-year training period with four six-month "seats" in different practice areas within the firm. Once qualified, all employees have the option of booking themselves on to training courses, with their supervisor's approval. Uptake varies, but lawyers attend four days training a year on average, and support staff attend around 1.5 days.

Most training is internal. It includes skills training courses tailored for specific target audiences – such as junior support staff, trainee solicitors and mid-level lawyers – plus some e-learning courses relevant to all employees. Occasionally, employees also attend external training courses; and the firm will sponsor staff to take external qualifications if these are considered relevant to their job role.

All staff can expect a formal appraisal each year, but frequent informal performance feedback is encouraged. There are a number of informal mentoring schemes in place and the firm has also introduced a career management guide known as Profile, intended to provide career development guidelines for all lawyers. It aims to encourage lawyers to take responsibility for their own development by giving them benchmarks, against which they can review their work and skills at each stage of their career. It also includes regular meetings between lawyers and a designated mentor or supervisor.

To develop the skills of its mid-level lawyers, Clifford Chance holds a programme known as the Lawyers' Development Centre, during which participants carry out exercises enabling them to be benchmarked against the firm's global performance standards for lawyers two years' senior to them. After the event, they receive a report summarising their development and highlighting areas to focus on. For senior staff, there is another event called the Senior Development Programme, which works in a similar way.

Clifford Chance recruits very broadly, visiting around 60 locations (including individual Oxbridge colleges) for its trainee intake. Business services (support) staff are drawn from across the whole commercial sector.

All lawyers can potentially progress to partner level. Around 90% of management started at the company, and 40% of vacancies are filled internally. Staff turnover is approximately 15%.

Company culture

As you would expect of one of the UK's top law firms, Clifford Chance aims to attract and develop the highest-quality people in order to deliver a top-quality service. To thrive there, people need to be not only well qualified, but also highly ambitious, committed and hardworking.

That's not to say, however, that employees are expected to do nothing but work. The firm recognises that hardworking people also need to unwind. Its new building in Canary Wharf has a large in-house gym, squash courts and a fifth-floor swimming pool with views over London. A full programme of classes from aerobics to yoga takes place in its exercise studios.

There is also a film club, wine club and arts club, as well as sporting events, and the firm is about to open a bar for employees.

The firm looks outwards as well as inwards; it has a strong commitment to serving the community, and encourages employees to take part in programmes such as reading to local schoolchildren and mentoring secondary school students.

As an international firm, Clifford Chance has a more cosmopolitan culture than many law firms. Many of its clients are multinational, and during 2003 around 600 members of staff travelled abroad on the firm's business.

There is also a flow of staff between the international offices; at any given time, around 150 members of its London office will be on international secondment or on secondment to a client, for anything from one month to three years. All trainees are offered the chance to spend one of their four six-month training periods abroad.

Innovation

Though the legal sector is generally fairly conservative, Clifford Chance has established a reputation for innovation on several fronts. One of these is its significant European, and especially US, expansion; it is still the only UK law firm with a significant New York operation. It was the first law firm to move to London's Canary Wharf – a daring move in terms of law firms, which tend to define themselves as City firms with offices in the Square Mile.

Within the firm, it is seeking to innovate by reorganising the HR function so it is more closely aligned with the business. Practice area HR managers will provide a more strategic HR service and deal with most day-to-day HR enquiries through a central enquiry line. A new Centre of Expertise, consisting of specialists in major HR areas, is being set up with the aim of providing an overall HR service that surpasses anything in the external marketplace.

Clifford Chance is in the process of launching the London Employee Forum, a consultative body with employee representation. One of its goals will be to more actively involve employees in the business and in developing innovative business solutions.

Diversity and social responsibility:

Clifford Chance is in the process of rolling out a global diversity strategy. As part of this it is reviewing all its induction and training processes, and ensuring all recruiters and trainers are trained in diversity awareness. One of its senior partners has been appointed diversity champion.

At present around 50% of its employees overall are women, and it estimates that around 20% of its graduate recruits are from ethnic minorities – though employees are not obliged to give information on their race or religious beliefs. It is involved in Global Graduates, a programme run for ethnic minority students at the top 30 universities worldwide who are interested in a legal career. It takes part in Legal Chances, an open day organised with seven other City firms for ethnic minority law students; and supports African Caribbean Diversity, an educational charity which aims to raise the aspirations and achievements of African-Caribbean school students. The firm provides a multi-faith prayer room for employees.

Over 100 volunteers from within the firm read for 30 minutes with a child at a local primary school each week, and help the children develop their numeracy skills. Staff are also involved in mentoring local secondary school students, and over 40 of them work as school governors.

Each week, the firm provides meeting room facilities for one of its pro bono partners; or for charities such as the National Autistic Society, Thamesmead Law Centre and Reprieve. Its match-funding policy effectively doubles all funds staff raise for UK-registered charities.

Employees are given credit for time spent volunteering and taking on pro bono work. A full-time team of three manages the firm's community work and pro bono programmes, which include free evening legal advice sessions held three times a week in London, and pro bono legal work for Death Row prisoners in the US.

Corporate Governance

As a law firm, Clifford Chance is obviously aware of all the relevant laws governing its operations, such as the Law Society Rules which govern the profession in England and Wales; the rules and regulations governing conflicts of interest, which dictate what work it is able to take on; the Proceeds of Crime Act, which stipulates the checks law firms have to carry out before accepting a new client; the laws governing legal professional privilege; and the laws governing limited liability partnerships.

In addition to this external legal framework, however, the firm is seeking to self-regulate internally by instilling key corporate values throughout its organisation. Focus groups involving staff and partners have identified four core values: commitment, ambition, quality and community. Its goal is to ensure that these values are instilled in its global organisation and "hardwired" into its corporate processes. It is planning to incorporate them into performance appraisals for all staff, including partners, and into its staff development programmes.

Environmental record

Clifford Chance aims to meet, and where possible exceed, legislation on environmental issues, and has a number of policies aimed at minimising its environmental impact. It aims to reduce its use of energy, paper, water and other raw materials; minimise waste through reduction, re-use and recycling; and minimise noise.

It has a paper-recycling programme, which it estimates has saved the equivalent of 44,693 trees. The firm is also involved in a tree-planting programme in conjunction with conservation organisations Paper Planet, Highfield Park Trust and the Woodland Trust, which has planted 2,629 trees.

The gleaming new Clifford Chance building in London's Canary Wharf has a Building Research Environmental Assessment Method (BREEAM) rating of "excellent" for its energy conservation features. Canary Wharf has good public transport links by tube, bus and Docklands Light Railway. Employees are charged £1,000 per year car park charges and parking spaces are strictly limited. Free cycle racks plus shower and changing facilities are provided for cyclists.

ClinPhone Group

ClinPhone Group Ltd
Lady Bay House, Meadow Grove, Nottingham NG2 3HF
Tel: (0) 115 955 7333 **Fax:** (0) 115 955 7555
Web: www.clinphone.com **Email:** hr@clinphone.com

Making the clinical trial connection

Pay and Benefits	6.4	Innovation	6.8
Promotion and Development	5.0	Diversity	4.4
Training	6.6	Social Responsibility	6.4
Travel opportunities	5.8	Corporate Governance	6.5
Culture	6.6	Environment	6.0
Total			**60.5**

ClinPhone Group provides specialist technology services to manage clinical trials for the pharmaceutical industry worldwide. This is a specialised area that ClinPhone has made its own; using its novel Interactive Web Response (IWR) and telephone-based Interactive Voice Response (IVR) systems, ClinPhone has been involved in more than 1,200 clinical trials across 75,000 sites in 80 countries (and using 70 languages). The company has grown substantially since its foundation in 1993, and was on course for sales of £28m in 2004. It employs over 400 people, most at its Nottingham HQ; there are sales and project management offices in the USA and Europe.

Executive summary

In the global pharmaceutical industry, getting a new drug to market quickly is critical to a company's success. But the need to conduct clinical trials of all drugs before they can be made available to the public can be a real brake on the process. ClinPhone was established to accelerate the management and reporting of clinical trials by automating the data collection functions, enabling the drugs manufacturers to speed up the testing and get on the market sooner.

This has proved a potent message: ClinPhone is a highly successful company and the market leader. It has built specialised technology, but it has also developed specialised 24/7 support and project management teams who understand this world. The company has an impressive collection of awards, including two Queen's Awards.

Ten years ago ClinPhone had ten people; now it employs 412. It is based in Nottingham and three-quarters of the staff are there, but ClinPhone also has sales and project management offices in five US locations as well as facilities in Brussels and Heidelberg.

The average age of ClinPhone's employees is just 31.

ClinPhone's financial results are pretty spectacular. Sales up to year-end 2004 were £28m, a 44% increase on the year before, and profits were £4.5m, up 45%. 2005 was forecast to calm down a bit, with sales growth of just 21% and a mere 16% increase in profits. This is a company that's going places.

Pay and benefits

ClinPhone aims to pay well and offers 25 days paid annual holiday. There's also a contributory pension scheme (employees contribute a minimum of 5% of salary), a generous private health insurance scheme, a death-in-service policy that pays twice the salary to your named beneficiary, and enhanced maternity/paternity/adoption benefits which exceed the government's minimum requirements.

Other benefits include subsidised membership at a commercial gym and fully funded membership of a well-equipped local leisure centre. There is an active staff suggestion scheme; length-of-service awards; and a discretionary annual bonus for all staff based on a proportion of profits, which so far has produced 3–5% extra on annual salaries. There are also individual performance-related bonuses of 10–20% of salary for key sales-generating and support staff. The company holds two "huge" staff parties each year.

ClinPhone is just introducing salary conversion schemes for childcare vouchers and the Computers at Home scheme. Considering the size of the company, it does well on benefits. There's also the chance to share in the organisation's success: ClinPhone is a private company, but it intends to go public in 2006. The founders, and the venture capitalists who funded their idea, will then be able to see the value of their investment – and so will the staff, all of whom qualify for share options at no cost after a year's service.

Promotion and development

In order to get the most out of its investment in people, ClinPhone aims to keep staff turnover to below 5% (it is currently less than 2%). In fact, ClinPhone takes the view that its people are central to the success of the organisation and it is vital that they are skilled, flexible and motivated.

This implies a lack of preconceptions about the people ClinPhone recruits; there's a high geek quotient, for instance, and some of those people might not have found it so easy to get a job elsewhere.

ClinPhone achieved the Investors in People standard as long ago as 2001. Now it is one of only 16 organisations to be named an Investors in People Champion, a best-practice programme that recognises employers which have boosted the performance of their businesses through the way they manage and develop their staff.

As the company grows it still prefers to develop its managers in-house because of the special needs of ClinPhone's niche and the company's own special qualities. To that end it has invested substantially in a management development programme developed with the Chartered Institute of Management.

More broadly, ClinPhone aims to foster a "life-long learning environment". ClinPhone runs its own training department and has a generous annual allocation of £800 per person for training.

Sophisticated training and professional development programmes have also been developed, featuring management by objectives and the internally developed Competency Framework. This provides a visible role-graded career pathway that demonstrates the opportunities for individual members of staff; it also includes a company-wide benchmark for desired and expected behaviours and skills.

ClinPhone has funded PhDs, MBAs, MCSEs and other qualifications, usually via subsidised loans. ClinPhone encourages its people to obtain further qualifications and will cover subscriptions to professional organisations.

Company culture

ClinPhone's two founders (who are still the joint MDs, an unusual division of responsibility that works well) had a vision of a bureaucracy-free company – one that imposed no rules unless they were required. This was to be supported by a very flat management structure and a deliberate lack of hierarchy.

These principles appear to have continued as the company has grown; ClinPhone is now getting large enough to need more structure and some more explicit rules, including for instance a degree of sickness monitoring. Previously, the company was able to rely on peer pressure and the individual's sense of responsibility – both of which still apply – but there's a need for everyone to see that the playing field is indeed level. There's still an informal culture of "management by peer group", however.

There's also awareness that the transition from university to employment is a major lifestyle change for new graduates.

The recent annual staff satisfaction survey had 90% of respondents saying they were "proud" to work for ClinPhone, and 87% agreeing that they were "pleased to come to work". The free-fruit-at-work policy might help: its sends all the right messages. ClinPhone also operates totally flexible working hours, and there's little clock-watching.

Innovation

ClinPhone was founded on an innovative business idea. Specifically, ClinPhone was the first company to develop an automated touch-tone telephone response system linked to a database that collects and collates details from doctors, patients, carers and pharmacists. The company now counts 18 of the top 20 pharmaceutical companies amongst its clients, and through continual innovation and development it has managed to maintain its lead in this specialised market despite the arrival of several eager competitors.

ClinPhone has developed significantly from its early days, adding more (and more sophisticated) methods of collecting and processing testing data from clinical trials using automated telephone and online systems.

The company runs its own blue-sky R&D subsidiary employing 10% of the staff roster.

ClinPhone is also quite imaginative in terms of the way the organisation operates – a very flat management structure, emphasis on finding and keeping the right people, a benefits package that is unusually rich for such a small company, and the promise of a flotation that will allow everyone to share in the company's progress.

ClinPhone won the Best Growth Through Technology category for companies with more than 100 members of staff in the 2004 Sage/Daily Telegraph Business Awards. The award recognises the best correlation between the implementation of an IT solution and growth in profits, customer base and employees over the previous 12 months.

Diversity and social responsibility

ClinPhone operates and enforces equal opportunities policies, and the idea that people are valued for their contribution and their potential is ingrained into the culture.

So is a strong sense of commitment to the local community. Nottingham has some areas of serious social deprivation, and ClinPhone has a considerable commitment via its work with Nottingham County's Football in the Community scheme.

Staff are encouraged to participate in local charity events, with the company typically paying entrance fees and providing organisational assistance. There's also support for charitable giving, with matched funding for staff fundraising projects and a "charity day" when staff can take a paid day to do charitable work.

Corporate Governance

ClinPhone is a private company, and as such does not need to conform to the codes of corporate governance required of public companies. However, ClinPhone does have a good track record of community awareness and employee care that will stand the company in good stead when it does go for a Stock Exchange quotation.

Environmental record

ClinPhone's business does not have much direct environmental impact, but the company is an enthusiastic recycler and actively seeks suppliers with a similarly responsible attitude. It also promotes lift sharing; it encourages cycling to work; and to minimise the impact of parking by those staff who do drive, ClinPhone has acquired two warehouses near its offices to get staff cars off the streets.

Cobra Beer

Cobra Beer Ltd.
Alexander House, 14-16 Peterborough House, London SW6 3BN
Tel: (0) 20 7731 6200 **Fax:** (0) 20 7731 6201
Web: www.cobrabeer.com **Email:** cobrabeer@cobrabeer.com

COBRA
PREMIUM
BEER

Pay and Benefits	5.5	Innovation	7.2
Promotion and Development	5.5	Diversity	5.5
Training	6.0	Social Responsibility	7.5
Travel opportunities	6.5	Corporate Governance	6.0
Culture	7.5	Environment	6.0
Total			**63.2**

Cobra Beer is one of the fastest growing beer brands in the UK with a current turnover of £56.9m at retail value, 90% of which is in its home market. Having been exported to over 30 countries worldwide, Cobra is stocked in over 6,000 restaurants, in most major supermarkets and off licence chains, and to more than 5,000 pubs, style bars and clubs in the UK. Cobra Beer is brewed in the UK, India and Poland; and has subsidiary operations in India, South Africa and the US.

Executive Summary

A classic entrepreneurial tale, Cobra Beer is the creation of Karan Bilimoria who saw a gap in the market for an extra-smooth, less gassy lager that would complement spicy food and appeal to ale drinkers and lager drinkers alike. Launched in 1989, the business targeted the Indian restaurant sector and imported its product from Bangalore, India. However, rising demand meant production switched to the UK in 1997, since when Cobra Beer has been brewed by Bedford-based Charles Wells.

For the last ten years sales growth has been constant – an average of 42% compound – and distribution has been extended to most major supermarkets and a large number of pubs, bars and clubs. However, Bilimoria's mission is to turn Cobra Beer into a global brand and so brewing commenced in Poland in 2004 – in order to expand in the export market and to offer new formats, such as cans; and Rajasthan, India – to brew for the domestic Indian market.

Cobra Beer is a limited company and its founder holds 72% of share capital, with the remainder in the hands of private investors. With growth and brand awareness the cornerstone of business strategy, net profit is a comparatively modest £1m. Helping along its increasingly high profile, Cobra Beer has garnered a number of accolades: most notably two Grand Gold Medals and four Gold Medals in the 2004 Monde Selection, Brussels World Selection of Quality; and Gold for three successive years at the 2003, 2002 and 2001 Monde Selection awards. Monde Selection also presented Cobra with the International High Quality Trophy in 2003 for its achievements.

Pay and Benefits

The company does not benchmark its pay and benefits package against its generally much larger beverage competitors, however, Cobra Beer employees are thought to enjoy pay in line with that of the sectoral average. Nonetheless, the graduate starting salary is a healthy £22,000 and high-performing salespeople will earn bonus payments worth around 30% of their base salary. There is also an annual company bonus to be shared out among employees.

Other benefits include a stakeholder pension scheme, medical insurance and provision of company cars for senior and sales staff. The company has also recently introduced a share option scheme. Then there is the free beer...

As with many SMEs, there is an informal approach to flexible working. In the past, equipment has been provided for homeworking by a pregnant employee, while senior staff can work irregular hours. Maternity leave is by arrangement; previously the company has paid out three months' full pay and footed the bill for a nanny.

Promotion and development

Karan Bilimoria has a number of personal business principles, two of which are: "staff are recruited for attitude not qualifications" and "providing an environment for employees to flourish". In practice, this reinforces the informal, flexible approach to people management that exists at Cobra Beer. That is not to say there are no formal mechanisms in place. There is an annual appraisal at which individuals assess themselves as well being assessed by their manager. But appraisal also takes place on a continuous informal basis.

The same informality extends to promotion opportunities. Take Bilimoria's own senior assistant: four years ago she was delivering sandwiches to the company. The team suggested she try a stint at telesales; she impressed in the job, switched to a full-time position and was soon promoted to telesales manager.

Certainly staff at Cobra Beer appear loyal to the business – turnover is just 8%. Yet the company is no less loath to lose its employees; in fact, it pays out one month's salary to individuals who leave for every year they have worked there. According to the chief executive, at least one senior manger has been headhunted for a position elsewhere, realised what they have left behind and decided to come back.

Training accounts for 4% of company expenditure and is growing rapidly. Depending on the role or project, it is delivered in-house or via external trainers – sometimes from the US or South Africa. Cobra embraces an ethos of "lifelong learning" which exists in everything that it does. Bilimoria himself is a believer in this cause and champions it within the organisation.

Company Culture

While Bilimoria is from a distinguished Parsi family (his father was a general in the Indian army), the business he has created is extremely down-to-earth. There is no formal dress code for staff – unless they are meeting clients, naturally – and the atmosphere is one of easy interaction between employees of all rank and seniority. Underpinning the business ethos throughout is trust; trust in customers that they will recognise the strength and quality of the product (this being reflected in the fact that Cobra Beer never asks for exclusivity), and trust in employees that they will give of their best in order to repay that recognition.

It is the sort of place where people will work long into the evening to meet personal targets – not because they have to, but because they want to. Appropriately, Cobra Beer was ranked in an annual list of top SMEs to work for in the UK in 2004, and within that survey, placed first for people feeling they had control over their work. At the same time, talented individuals are encouraged to become involved in tasks that would benefit from their valuable input. This in turn often leads to promotion or movement elsewhere in the business, and makes for a hothouse environment where versatility and a hunger to learn are actively encouraged.

Cobra Beer is also the place for budding entrepreneurs. Aside from the example of its founder, the company benefits from the number of interns it hosts from high-class institutions such as the London Business School, Cranfield, and Cambridge University (where Bilimoria was recently appointed as honorary visiting entrepreneur). Staff may also learn about foreign markets and the logistics of growing a global business through secondments to international offices.

Innovation

This is a business that truly pays more than lip service to the idea of innovation. Why would it be otherwise? Cobra Beer has had to innovate to thrive in one of the most competitive of UK industry sectors. It was the first beer maker to supply its product in larger-size (660ml) bottles, and pioneered a "story of the product" approach to bottle design that helped drive a significant increase in sales over the following six months.

When it is not winning design, packaging and entrepreneurial awards, the company is encouraging team members to share their ideas. Managers actively seek their input into the processes and policies of the company. An Idea of the Month scheme has firmly established itself, with cash prizes awarded to the first three winning suggestions. Sometimes the ideas are simply about morale boosting. A recent example was the suggestion that clocks showing the times at all of the company's locations be hung on the wall – reminding people there that they were now working for a global business.

Will, rather than skill, is prized at the recruitment stage, and there is a real belief that individuals can learn and contribute to the business in a non-conventional way. Accordingly, all types of training that embrace wider skills are encouraged. For example, the marketing communications executive took writing courses to refresh her writing skills, while a member of the administration team took a two-month sewing course for one morning a week.

Diversity and social responsibility

In keeping with its global focus, Cobra Beer has an appropriately diverse and international workforce. Nationalities represented include, among others, Indian, Spanish, Portuguese, Sri Lankan, Italian, Canadian, Bangladeshi and South African. Ironically, as Cobra Beer moves further into the mainstream beverage market, the proportion of ethnic minority staff is actually likely to fall; however, with a male to female ratio of 70:30 the company is keen to recruit and develop more women, who currently represent only 2% of managers.

A large number of good causes have benefited from the company's patronage in recent years – often in the form of free wine and beer at fundraising events. Cobra firmly believes in fulfilling its responsibility at all levels, which includes community support. Beneficiaries of its largesse include literacy projects in India, MacMillan Cancer Relief in the UK, The Loomba Trust for the education of children of poor widows in India, and Rethink severe mental illness – to name a few. Keen to formalise these charitable donation activities, the company is setting up a foundation that is scheduled for launch in spring 2005.

Corporate Governance

The informality that characterises its organisational culture does not mean that Cobra Beer has a laissez-faire attitude to corporate governance. Its chief executive is chairman of the government's National Employment Panel SME Board, and sat on a government-appointed task force in 2003 to look into the recruitment and development of non-executive directors. According to Bilimoria, this helped cement his belief that diversity and accountability at board level are a pre-requisite for sustainable growth. Consequently, Cobra's board and management team are heterogeneous in character: a stockbroker, a lawyer and a technical expert among its multinational membership.

The culture of openness, informality and entrepreneurialism is apparent to all who work at Cobra Beer – and indeed to its various external stakeholders and partners, many of whom get invites to its AGM. Bilimoria talks of a commonsense approach to operational matters, which will inevitably have to become more formalised when a planned IPO materialises. However, the company has spent two years preparing itself for Investors in People, and the processes and procedures for effective people management would appear to be largely in place.

Environment

Cobra Beer proclaims a commitment to integrate sound environmental management practice into the business. How seriously does it take this? Well, in the UK, employees do what happens in a lot of businesses today – they use recycled paper and separate waste for efficient recycling.

At a corporate level, however, an ongoing dialogue with shareholders, suppliers and customers has led to genuinely innovative developments. In India, at the brewery in Rajasthan, local farmers have benefited as the company buys the waste created from their crop production and uses it to generate power. Also, waste water is treated and used to irrigate fields. Bottle production plays a part too. For quality reasons Cobra Beer only uses new bottles; once used they are donated to be recycled and can be used up to 15 times elsewhere. This greatly increases the pool of recyclable bottles in a country where bottles are often in short supply.

Deloitte

Deloitte
Stonecutter Court, 1 Stonecutter Street, London EC4A 4TR
Tel: (0) 20 7936 3000 **Fax:** (0) 20 7583 1198
Web: www.deloitte.com

Deloitte.

Pay and Benefits	7.5	Innovation	6.0
Promotion and Development	6.5	Diversity	5.3
Training	7.0	Social Responsibility	5.5
Travel opportunities	5.2	Corporate Governance	6.8
Culture	5.7	Environment	6.5
Total			**62.0**

Deloitte, one of the "big four" UK accountancy firms, prides itself on being the UK's fastest-growing major professional services firm. Its offering can be summed up by saying that the expertise of its people and the broad range of its services enables it to deliver a complete business solution to a wide range of clients. The UK operation is part of Deloitte Touche Tohmatsu, an organisation with a global reach that serves more than half of the world's largest companies. Deloitte's services include audit, consulting, emerging markets, enterprise risk services, corporate finance, legal, and tax. It employs 10,000 people in the UK; and is the only "big four" firm to retain a consultancy service.

Executive summary

In 1833, William Welch Deloitte became an assistant to the Official Assignee at the Bankruptcy Court in the City of London. This led him towards the foundation of a firm that would rise to become one of the leading UK and global accountancy practices throughout the next 170 years.

Since then, mergers have taken the firm through a bewildering series of name changes; most recently Deloitte Haskins & Sells (1978), Deloitte & Touche (1990), and the naming of the international firm Deloitte Touche Tohmatsu (1993).

Following the collapse of Arthur Andersen in 2002, 3,500 partners and staff joined Deloitte, considerably boosting its numbers.

Deloitte's revenue figures have risen impressively in recent years. In 2001, revenue was £822m; in 2002, £924m; and in 2003, £1,228m – a rise of 33%. DTT's figures have also risen consistently: $12.5bn in 2002, $15.1bn in 2003.

Until 2003, Deloitte as a professional services partnership – rather than a plc – needed only to show revenue figures, not profitability. However, its partners believe that it was the most profitable firm over the last three years at least – and the latest figures confirm that this is now the case.

Pay and benefits

HR partner Steve James: "We look to bring hundreds of graduates into the business each year: in 2004, for instance, we aimed to recruit 800 new graduate entrants. We therefore need to be highly competitive in terms of pay. At graduate level, we benchmark ourselves not only against the other big three accountancy practices, but also other key players – consultancies, investment banks, and the like."

To give one example, a graduate joining the Audit Department in London would receive a starting salary of around £24,000 in 2004. And just three years later, he or she could expect to earn a figure in the mid £40,000s.

At the very top of Deloitte's structure are 600 partners. These are equity partners and share in the profits of the firm. Most recently, their average earning was £600,000 before various deductions and any investments they may make in Deloitte. Suffice it to say that they have a significant stake in the firm! Nor is this the preserve of the venerable; a number of those who became partners in 2004 were in their early thirties.

Everyone at Deloitte enjoys the usual benefits associated with large firms: life assurance, a pension scheme, and so on. However, since 2002 a flexible options scheme has been in place. Deloitte employees receive a payment (from a minimum of £500 to considerably more for senior staff) which they can spend on one or more benefits such as additional holiday, cars, private health care, travel insurance, laptops, childcare vouchers, etc.

There is an Outstanding Contribution Award scheme, allocating quarterly one-off payments of between £500 and £2,500. In 2003, 600 awards were made. There is also a performance-rated staff bonus scheme, which rises from zero to 40% of salary. Finally, managers and above participate in the firm-wide bonus scheme. In 2004, it paid out £15m.

Promotion and development

Deloitte offers early responsibility, challenge and opportunity backed by extensive personal and career development. For instance, the 800 graduates of 2004 will first experience a major induction programme over several days. Thereafter, most move on to training programmes – which in some cases last for months.

Graduate or not, Deloitte staff enjoy four levels of development. The first is technical training, focusing on a person's specific business area. For instance, people working in audit will receive audit methodology training, culminating in their qualification as chartered accountants.

The second is the career and personal development programme. This is built around people's personal goals, allowing them to take stock every two years of their career direction and skill set.

The third centres on specific skills or knowledge training aligned to a specific industry. For instance, an individual might gain training in financial services or technology, adding to his or her personal offering for clients in those sectors.

Finally, the most senior grades can take advantage of developmental assessment centres. These are much more about personal and individual coaching on a one-to-one basis.

In addition to the technical training, Deloitte invests heavily in helping people gain professional qualifications – £6m in 2004. These tend to be accountancy-based; it is rare for an accountant to take an MBA, but support is there if desired.

The concept of coaching and mentoring runs right through the business. Through the performance management system, everyone has a mentor who will oversee his or her career. Such mentors can be external to the firm for senior people.

Company culture

At Deloitte, lots of people are travelling for a significant amount of time, both throughout the UK and globally. This is mostly work-related. There are also structured secondment programmes through the Global Deployment Programme: Deloitte exports over 100 people a year to the DTT network, and DTT companies similarly send people to the UK.

It's true to say that most partners will have been on secondment. It is seen as an important professional challenge (as well as being attractive to most). There is also an element of negotiation about where you go!

Regarding the work/life balance, James comments: "It's the nature of this business that we expect people to work hard. The vast majority of Deloitte people are driven and motivated, and find this no problem. As a result, people won't be leaving at 5.30pm very often. Having said that, we recognise the need to be flexible in terms of managing workload. We have a booklet on work/life balance that outlines opportunities for career breaks, returning from maternity, and secondments. In our latest survey, 60% of people were very happy with the work/life balance."

There are clear guidelines for dealing with stress, bullying and harassment; including ultimately the right to email the chief executive directly.

Those who flourish at Deloitte relish intellectually challenging environments and enjoy working with high-quality people, both within the firm and with clients.

Innovation

Given the recent furore over creative accountancy, innovation might not be seen as a good thing in this profession! But Deloitte, arguably, is innovative in terms of its commitment to quality and integrity. Where accountancy, banking and similar firms have been at the centre of scandals, these have tended to be caused by maverick individuals. This couldn't happen at Deloitte; all work is reviewed independently, as well as within the department, before it leaves the building.

Again, Deloitte stands out in terms of its flexibility. It is the opposite of bureaucratic and old-fashioned; on the contrary, it changes very quickly and responds to impetus, either internal or from the market. A good example is the Andersen transaction, where the firm's numbers rose from 6,000 to over 9,000 overnight. Even Deloitte's rivals admit that this was handled with amazing smoothness.

Deloitte is also innovative in its thought processes. When the other big firms decided to drop consultancy as a service, Deloitte stayed with it – because it saw the regulatory picture as less restrictive than its rivals did. As a result, Deloitte became one of the top two accountancy firms in the UK – and its rivals are reputedly rebuilding their consultancy arms.

Diversity and social responsibility

The firm has equal opportunities policies in place although Deloitte currently has only 60 female partners – out of a total of 600. It is conscious that this is less than admirable. However, the situation is improving year on year; it has two females on the board, for instance, one of whom was recently elected.

The problem is certainly not caused at recruitment level: the current graduate intake mix is roughly 50:50. Furthermore, the mix of those who leave the firm is approximately the same. The problem seems to lie in the fact that those who leave tend to go, not to another accountancy firm, but to industry – to become finance officers and ultimately chief executives. A number of these will then rejoin Deloitte at a later date, usually as partners.

Deloitte gives thousands of hours of management and partner time to various community bodies including the Prince's Trust and Business in the Community. Through Skills for Industry, it develops the IT skills of school-leavers, helping them to enter the job market with far greater skills. This won Deloitte several awards in 2003.

Corporate governance

Deloitte is a partnership, not a plc, and therefore its board structure is different. Having said that, the board is responsible for the corporate governance of the firm. Processes and systems are in place to safeguard aspects such as practice protection. The managing partner on the board has personal responsibility for these areas, indicating the importance Deloitte places on them.

Environmental record

Being a service industry, there is less Deloitte can do than some companies in this book to safeguard the environment. The impression of the writer, however, is that it certainly does what it can. Its offices have "green bins" on site and it uses environmentally friendly lighting and air conditioning, and recycled paper where possible.

Deloitte also tries to ensure that it has in place responsible purchasing policies, so that whatever it buys is produced in an environmentally friendly way.

As a result of all this, Deloitte was ranked in 2003 for the first time in Business in the Community, the corporate ranking of responsible employers.

Diageo

Diageo plc
8 Henrietta Place, London W1G 0NB
Tel: (0) 20 7927 5200 **Fax:** (0) 20 7927 4600
Web: www.diageo.com

DIAGEO

Pay and Benefits	6.5	Innovation	6.5
Promotion and Development	5.8	Diversity	4.2
Training	6.8	Social Responsibility	4.5
Travel opportunities	6.5	Corporate Governance	5.5
Culture	5.2	Environment	5.8
Total			**57.3**

Diageo is the world's leading premium drinks business, with an outstanding collection of brands across spirits, wine and beer categories. Its well-known brands include Smirnoff, Johnnie Walker, Guinness, Baileys, J&B, Captain Morgan, Cuervo and Tanqueray, as well as Beaulieu Vineyard and Sterling Vineyards wines. Operating in some 180 countries across the world, the company is becoming truly global. Listed on both the London and the New York Stock Exchanges, the company employs around 24,000 people worldwide, approximately 6,000 of whom work in the UK.

Executive summary

Although its roots go back to 1749, Diageo as a business was formed in December 1997 through the merger of GrandMet and Guinness. At the time of the merger, Diageo was a broad-based consumer goods company with food and drinks at its core.

Since 1997, Diageo has realigned its business to focus exclusively on premium drinks. This strategy has been developed by adding some more key drinks brands: for instance, in December 2001 it took on board some important Seagram spirits and wine businesses. It also moved to divest itself of its food brands, selling Pillsbury in October 2001 and divesting Burger King from its operations in 2003. As a result, 2004 was Diageo's first year as a business comprising exclusively premium drinks.

Charlotte Knight, director of employee engagement, commented: "The change of strategy was a significant move for us, and the results are now starting to come through."

Knight was speaking soon after the company's 2004 preliminary results were announced in September 2004, and those results bear out her view. Net sales after deducting excise duties were up 6%; operating profit was up 7%; earnings per share up 1%; and its free cash flow, at £1.5bn, was up by £241m.

Pay and benefits

Diageo says that its rewards reflect the market and compare favourably with those of competitors. In practice, this means very competitive salaries and a wide range of additional benefits.

Individuals have a two-tier reward system. Some rewards connect to the overall performance of the business, such as the Shares4all scheme (a share-savings vehicle) and a business-related bonus. Others link directly to individual performance, as monitored and developed by the employees' annual review.

The company takes on around 70 graduates each year. For these, the company closely monitors starting salaries in the external market to ensure it remains in the upper quartile. Other graduate benefits include good annual leave allocation, a chance to earn the equivalent of up to 10% of salary in free shares, an opportunity to buy shares at preferential rates, a generous product allowance to spend in the company shop, healthcare, relocation support if required, and a contributory final pension scheme.

Some graduates, depending on their role and location, also enjoy the use of an onsite gym, mobile phones or laptops if required, and cars if they need mobility in their job.

All staff, whether graduates or not, enjoy life assurance and personal accident insurance cover; private healthcare; a product allowance to spend in the company shop; and an element of flexible reward, which can be spent on various benefits such as increased holidays, private medical care or childcare. Company cars are allocated to those who need them for their job or by seniority (translatable into a cash payment if preferred); and there are special rewards for long service. Furthermore, the main office sites have bars, and many of them have social clubs.

Promotion and development

Knight says, "Our aim is to continue building a company that releases the potential of all our employees, and to provide a work environment where they can learn, grow and celebrate success." At Diageo, everyone participates in people performance management (PPM) where they receive regular reviews, which include constructive feedback on their job performance and insights as to how that potential could best be released. At all times, the employee takes ownership of his or her PPM plan and will track progress against agreed milestones, seek feedback on performance, and implement development priorities agreed under a "be the best" (BTB) development plan.

The BTB development plan focuses on priority development areas, strengths that can be built upon, and specific development activities the company will undertake to help the employee achieve set goals. Employee options could include on-the-job training; project work; new assignments; feedback and coaching (whether internal or external); formal development events such as courses, workshops and seminars; books and e-learning tools; or a community project.

As well as the reviews, and beyond the ordinary training opportunities, employees can take part in the Diageo Way of Brand Building (DWBB): a five-day course designed around its own best-practice brand building processes and skills, designed to drive top-line growth. Around 8,000 people have completed the full interactive learning experience to date.

High Performance Coaching (HPC) is an approach for Diageo managers, designed to stretch performance in others. Once mastered, coaching for high performance is ongoing, driven by both the coach and the employee being coached.

Company culture

The company conducts a Value Survey each year, covering a range of questions. Under the key question of "What is it like to work at Diageo?" over 90% of people declare themselves proud to work for the company. Since the returns are anonymous, that speaks volumes.

Diageo has a very performance-driven culture, but one which offers recognition and reward. It is also a very sociable company; its claim on its website to work hard but play harder seems to be borne out in reality.

There are many travel opportunities; travel is actively encouraged, and it is largely true that those wishing to become real high flyers may not, unless they move around the business.

Those who flourish at Diageo embrace the behaviours that will build a strong business culture and deliver excellent performance; in particular, having insatiable curiosity, taking ideas which work from one area and applying them elsewhere, and being "a team together even when we are apart". As Knight puts it, "We offer terrific support, but the onus is still on you; you're in charge of your own destiny. The company culture is incredibly passionate, and if you're the same you'll do well. If you're the kind of person who doesn't want to get noticed, Diageo may not be for you!"

Work/life balance is relatively new for the company, but it is pursuing those tenets enthusiastically. Although not a nine-to-five job, Diageo compensates with career breaks, sabbaticals, maternity/paternity leave and flexible hours.

Innovation

Diageo is energetic about driving original thinking, new ways of working and better business practices. To this end, hierarchies and conventions have no place in its business, and its approach is as relaxed and informal as it is driven and hardworking.

Managers are measured in part on their ability to generate new ideas and on what they bring to the fold. Recognition programmes are centred locally, and lots of recognition revolves around innovation.

At a company level, over 70 new brand or packaging innovations were introduced in the year to September 2004 alone. Recent examples include: introducing Cîroc across high-end urban bars; launching Smirnoff Cranberry Twist and Smirnoff Twisted V in the US, and Smirnoff Penka in the UK; launching Guinness Extra Smooth in Ghana; introducing Johnnie Walker Green Label; launching Bell's Special Reserve in the UK; introducing "Guinness Surger" (a new dispenser) to Japan...the list goes on. Innovation is key if the company is to meet what CEO Paul Walsh calls its ambition of becoming the number one in premium drinks in every market.

Diversity and social responsibility

In its first Corporate Report in 2003, Diageo reported specifically on diversity, and it has set out policies to support it in its workplace. In late 2004, it signed up to the UN Standard on Human Rights. It values diversity in the workplace and is committed to providing equal opportunities. The company acknowledges it could do better in this area, and is in the process of setting itself objectives to achieve this.

As a business focused on alcoholic drinks, Diageo takes its social responsibility very seriously. It reaches out to consumers through "sensible drinking" advertising campaigns, sponsors alcohol education initiatives, and participates in over 20 "social aspects" organisations around the world. The company is committed to self-regulation, and insists that those promoting its brands adhere to the highest standards of social responsibility.

The company also encourages and supports employees who give their time and effort to charitable and fundraising work. The Diageo Foundation provides funding and expertise to projects worldwide working in areas such as alcohol education and "water of life".

Corporate governance

According to Knight, corporate governance is "hugely important" to the company. It has a separate compliance department; all employees have to sign up to its principles.

Diageo is governed by a board of directors and is accountable to shareholders. The board agrees strategy and operational targets. The CEO, backed by an executive committee, runs the company on a day-to-day basis. Each member of the executive represents the key components of its business. Beyond the executive, core elements of its strategy are driven by market, functional and cross-business executive groups. These groups are either permanent executive committees or project-based executive working groups (EWGs). Each of the EWGs works to an agreed remit, and each is ultimately accountable to the CEO.

Environmental record

Diageo has a specific environment policy: this sets out its commitment to conduct its business in such a way as to support environmental sustainability and biodiversity, and to continually improve its performance in this regard.

The company has set standards for all its businesses in terms of greenhouse gases, energy, solid waste, water use, effluence, air emissions, packaging, hazardous substances and transport.

Diageo actively encourages its employees to contribute to its environmental programme. It also has equally high expectations of, and demands on, its suppliers.

Dixons

D

Dixons Group plc
Maylands Avenue, Hemel Hempstead HP2 7TG
Tel: (0) 870 850 3333
Web: www.dixons-group-plc.co.uk

Dixons Group plc

Pay and Benefits	5.9	Innovation	6.7
Promotion and Development	6.2	Diversity	6.7
Training	6.6	Social Responsibility	6.2
Travel opportunities	4.8	Corporate Governance	7.5
Culture	6.1	Environment	7.7
Total			**64.4**

Dixons Group is a major player in the European retail scene, with sales of £6.5bn and more than 1,400 stores across the UK, Ireland, the Nordic countries, France, Spain, Italy, Greece, Hungary and the Czech Republic. Its companies now serve more than 100 million customers across Europe every year. It includes some of Britain's best-known retail brands – Currys is the country's largest electrical chain, PC World is the UK's biggest computer superstore, The Link is a major player in mobile phones, and the Dixons name itself is part of the high street landscape. The group is also a major supplier of IT equipment and mobile telephony services to business and the public sector via PC World Business, now augmented by the recently acquired B2B IT provider Micro Warehouse; and through Genesis Communications, a leading mobile communications solutions provider to businesses.

Executive summary

Dixons Group began life in 1937 as a one-store photographic studio in Southend, and it has since grown into one of the most important retail groups in Britain. The Dixons stores no longer represent the major part of group sales – a third of the high-street outlets were closed in 2003, and now Currys and PC World are both much larger contributors – and in the last five years, Dixons Group has become a truly European operation with a significant presence in a dozen countries.

International operations include Elkjop, the market leader in the Nordic countries; Uni Euro, a major electrical retail chain in Italy; and Kotsovolos, the market leader in Greece. The international business contributed 27% of the group's sales in 2003–04 and £100m in profits (total group sales were up 13% at £6.5bn, pre-tax profits were 16% higher at £329m). A quarter of Dixons Group's 38,000 people are outside the UK.

The company has been returning a consistent year-on-year growth in sales, averaging over 15% each year for the past five years, and producing just under £6.5bn in 2004. Pre-tax profits have varied during the period as the group made investment and disposal decisions, but it's a long while since Dixons made anything like a loss – on average profits have been around 8% of sales in the past five years, a pretty decent margin for a fast-moving retailer with expansion plans.

Micro Warehouse, a £143m business that is one of the UK's largest and longest established direct resellers of branded IT products and services to business, was acquired in 2004 for an undisclosed sum; it now forms part of PC World Business, the business-to-business operation subsidiary of Dixons Group.

This is a fast-moving business: products have a very short marketing life, it's a fiercely competitive business, and increasing choice makes customers more discerning. Dixons feels that it's in a good position to capitalise on its traditional strengths – a wide range of products and a value-for-money reputation – and it also has the financial clout to see off most competitors.

Pay and benefits

As you would expect from a large and well-established company, there is plenty on offer for Dixons Group employees in terms of benefits – though eligibility for some benefits does depend on length of service and/or job level. The basics include a minimum of 21 days' holiday a year for new starters, which rises according to length of employment (at five years it's 25 days a year).

There are a number of performance-related bonus schemes, increasingly now tied to team performance (rather than the individual's) and to customer service (rather than sales) so that more employees can and do benefit from success.

Many of them have a tangible stake in that success. Impressively, more than 12,000 people throughout the group – nearly a third of all employees – are participating in discretionary share option schemes. There are several of these, including a sharesave scheme with around 5,000 participants that provides a fund for buying shares in Dixons Group at a discounted price. In addition, the company grants share options to employees depending on grade and length of service.

There's free life assurance for all (with cover at four times basic salary) when someone joins the company pension scheme. That's a contributory scheme (employees pay between 3% and 5% of earnings depending on age), which is available after a year's employment.

Discounts include 10% off all group products and services (available after three months' employment) plus deals on top brands from around 100 suppliers – from nursery places to wines, and including discounted gym membership at Fitness First.

Flexible working hours have been available for a long time now, and within the constraints of the retail environment, people are encouraged to come to their own judgements. Another example of the company's attitude is the offer of career breaks; employees with at least two years' service can take between three and 12 months with the opportunity to return to the company at the end of the break.

The group also operates an Employee Assistance Programme: a confidential advice, information and counselling service available to any staff on a 24/7 basis. This scheme – which is free and unrestricted – is provided via telephone helplines staffed by specially trained advisers.

Promotion and development

There is widespread acknowledgement that Dixons is particularly good at developing managers – not least by the people at the top of many of Britain's leading retailers, many of whom spent some of their most formative years at Dixons Group.

Dixons Group puts a lot of emphasis on performance management to identify and develop high flyers, but also to help employees more generally to be more effective in their roles. So personnel reviews emphasise goals and performance; and there is a wide range of bespoke training on offer from a dedicated internal training resource and specialist external consultants.

In fact, the group offers more than 500 training and development options to employees, including language training. These options use carefully structured modules, training workshops and a dedicated e-learning intranet service. In 2003, more than 12,000 hours of leadership training were delivered, and the group operates four levels of management development training run in conjunction with Henley Management College.

In addition, there's increasing emphasis on coaching and mentoring alongside the more conventional methods of developing people. Dixons Group says it aims to add value to the people it employs, and it is prepared to take a creative attitude to this.

Similarly, the group is determined to use the best ideas from any part of the organisation. Dixons is no longer a UK-focused operation; it is becoming a truly European group with operations in 13 countries. The growing internationalisation is being matched by more inter-country postings.

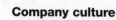

Company culture

Dixons Group's management talk about "the Dixons DNA", by which they mean a set of characteristics and values that are shared by Dixons Group's best people: optimism, high task orientation, a sense of humour, competitiveness, pride, commitment ... all those you might expect any large and successful organisation to claim. At Dixons Group they also include pragmatism, an awareness of where profit can be made, and an awareness both of the appeal of consumer technology and of the pace of technological change.

One manager summed it up: "Our retailing is about theatre, and we have to be enthusiastic about what we do". The essential Dixons message comes down to a broad range of the best products at a competitive price, plus good customer service. Understanding the value of audience reaction is what makes the difference at Dixons Group.

There's also a culture of commonsense – Dixons Group's management is aware it doesn't have all the answers all the time, and there's strong encouragement for individuals to contribute. Reviews are regular, systematic and performance-oriented; there's a strong sense that treading water is not an option (unless you can argue a case for it).

Innovation

Dixons Group has a good track record in commercial innovation. For instance, the development of the PC superstore in the shape of PC World effectively created a new market for PCs and associated products among a non-technical audience who can touch and feel a good range of products – and get informed comment from the salespeople as well as good post-sales support. The PC World model is now being rolled out in Europe as PC City.

Dixons launched the internet service provider Freeserve in 1998, offering internet access with free email and web space. This was a simple-to-understand ISP offering, probably the real mass-market rival to AOL in Europe. (Freeserve has since been sold on, generating a return for Dixons Group shareholders of £1bn, and AOL now has a deal with Dixons to preload its dial-up software on to the PCs and laptops Dixons sells.)

More recently, Dixons continues to look for imaginative retail offerings. It has, for example, announced an exclusive partnership with Napster, the first agreement of its kind between a British consumer electronics retailer and an online music provider. New store formats are emerging in Europe, and the pace of change is relentless.

Diversity and social responsibility

Dixons Group believes strongly in corporate social responsibility; the group operates a CSR committee that covers social, environmental, ethical and reputation issues. It reports to the group board.

Dixons Group actively seeks to provide equal opportunities to all its employees, and has developed explicit policies to support that goal. Any complaints of discrimination are treated seriously. There are formal and informal procedures in place for handling grievances, including a confidential helpline.

The group is a member of the Employers' Forum on Disability and has benchmarked its current activities in this area using their guidelines. The group has also been awarded the Positive About Disability "two ticks" mark.

The biggest source of community funding is the Dixons Foundation. This invests almost £1m a year in good causes – ranging from support for people with disabilities, to education, to health. More than 350 local organisations benefited in 2003. The foundation encourages applications for support from community groups and small charities, particularly in areas where Dixons employs a lot of people. The foundation also supports larger scale initiatives, particularly in education.

Dixons Group also provides financial and management support, resources and marketing expertise to CREATE (Community Recycling Enterprise And Training for Employment), a network of social businesses to which it provides end-of-life household appliances. The refurbished appliances are resold in the community to low-income families.

Employees in the UK choose charities to support in an organised campaign under the banner "Charity of the Year". The 2004 campaign supported a consortium of four disability charities; the group raised £450,000 from the campaign during the European Year of Disabled People.

Switched on to Volunteering is a new programme that rewards employees who volunteer by donating funds to the charity or group that they volunteer to help.

To improve local links and promote good community relationships, the group has also developed a novel Community Kit that provides ideas for local action. Employees are encouraged to get involved in local projects; and the group has introduced community-related training options including volunteering, mentoring and skills-transfer opportunities. The group will normally match any individual's fundraising.

Corporate Governance

Dixons Group says it maintains high standards of corporate governance for which the directors are collectively accountable to shareholders. Its corporate governance structure measures up to all the key principles in the Financial Services Authority's Combined Code on Corporate Governance as revised in 2003. The company's external auditors review compliance with this.

In 2003, the group held its first evaluation of the board's performance (on a self-assessment basis with external guidance). That is being followed up with formal appraisals of the performance of each director.

More generally, Dixons Group operates a policy of enabling employees to raise concerns (anonymously if they wish) about the group's conduct. This is facilitated by a helpline run by an independent third-party organisation, and the system has been benchmarked as one of the best available.

Environmental record

Dixons Group says that environmental responsibilities should be integral to the way it does business, rather than being treated as discrete activities. The group's overall score in the Business in the Environment Index of Corporate Environmental Engagement increased from 66% to 74% in 2004; and environmental performance is reported in some detail in the annual report, where for instance we learn that in 2003 the group cut 2% from its packaging waste and 4.5% from average CO_2 emissions from fleet cars.

But there are also many individual examples of the group's concerns: it has, for example, won awards for its 100%-recycled carrier bag; its Stevenage national distribution centre recycled 9.5% more waste in 2003; and other initiatives include Ink for IT (encourages schools, community groups and charities to collect recyclable inkjet printer cartridges in return for PC World vouchers), and Community Fonebak (offers the opportunity to turn old mobile phones into cash or Dixons Group vouchers). The spirit of many of these ventures is entirely consistent with the group's culture and style – a pragmatic approach; avoiding complexity where possible; and taking simple, practical steps that deliver sustainable results.

DLA Piper Rudnick Gray Cary

DLA Piper Rudnick Gray Cary LLP
3 Noble Street, London EC2V 7EE
Tel: (0) 870 011 1111
Web: www.dla.com

Pay and Benefits	7.0	Innovation	6.8
Promotion and Development	6.2	Diversity	6.2
Training	6.4	Social Responsibility	7.2
Travel opportunities	4.6	Corporate Governance	6.4
Culture	7.6	Environment	6.6
Total			**65.0**

DLA Piper Rudnick Gray Cary is now the seventh-largest UK law firm, with a significant presence in Asia and continental Europe that gives DLA offices in 21 countries with over 2,200 lawyers and 3,600 people in total. It provides a full portfolio of services; and aims to anticipate and then meet client needs, and build long-term relationships. This is an ambitious, imaginative firm with a genuine commercial awareness and an eagerness to show that it is not hidebound by the traditions of the legal business.

Executive summary

DLA Piper Rudnick Gray Cary really has been a success story in the legal world. In five years it has nearly doubled its revenues, while increasing the headcount of partners by less than 50%.

In the year to 2004, DLA's fee income was up again to £275m. DLA is one of the only full-service law firms able to offer a truly integrated service throughout the UK. It has achieved its growth primarily by focusing on commercial services – IT, employment, property, PFI, competition and regulatory issues, intellectual property – with a long-term emphasis on client relationships that represents a very different model from the high-yield one-off projects of many of its competitors. International expansion is clearly on the cards.

Pay and benefits

DLA offers a total benefits package that is above the sector average, and participates in benchmark surveys to make sure this is the case. In practice, remuneration aims for the top quartile in the regions; and in London, DLA aims to pay top rates outside the "Magic Circle".

The benefits have some genuinely novel features, especially those under the award-winning Lifeworks label. They include a concierge service – a freephone number to help manage time-consuming tasks from arranging a holiday to looking for a plumber. And the Lifeworks staff assistance service provides factsheets and 24/7 counselling on a range of issues from budgeting to managing stress.

Among other creative offerings, there's a Service Holiday – after three years' service, employees qualify for an extra 10 days' paid holiday which can be taken over two years. These benefits apply to all staff, as do the free private medical and health insurance, life cover, and enhanced maternity/paternity/adoption benefits. The pension scheme, with a choice of five different pension funds, is available to all after only three months' service. This is a defined contribution scheme with a standard monthly contribution rate of 5%, offering a choice of a 3% contribution for younger employees and trainees.

DLA sees clear links between the benefits package and the firm's values: there's an obvious concern for giving time back to individuals, serving the individual's day-to-day needs and making life easier rather than merely wealthier. DLA was awarded the HR Excellence Award for the Most Effective Benefits Programme in 2004.

Promotion and development

DLA places a good deal of emphasis on retention – on training and retaining people who grow up with the firm, who understand what it represents and who share its values.

This kind of attention to the individual combines with the firm's size and breadth of work to provide opportunities for staff to progress through new responsibilities, new roles or movement between offices. Personal development is emphasised for everyone.

For instance, DLA's solicitors average 60 hours' professional development training – well above the Law Society's requirement. DLA believes that lawyers need to focus on business and organisational issues – the practicalities of financial management and people management will be among the training objectives that will be discussed during performance reviews. There is an established set of development programmes, including an executive development programme for those with executive management responsibilities.

Company culture

DLA prides itself on not being a traditional law firm – it regards itself as down-to-earth and pragmatic, and encourages its people to share those values.

DLA believes that large law firms are also large service-sector businesses, with implications for what they do and how they are run. One result: issues of status don't permeate DLA as they do some other law firms – there are no distinctions between lawyers and business professionals. So, for example, the benefits are open to all.

Given its ambitions, and its willingness to break the mould of conventional legal firms (recently awarded Mould Breaking Firm at the 2004 MPF European Practice Awards), it's understandable that DLA is looking for a diverse mix of skills – sheer will to succeed is as important as academic qualifications. This is a high-performance culture, one that specifically eschews the clubbiness of the traditional Oxbridge/London background of the old-style law firm.

Nor is the job quote what the average law graduate might expect. Legal training is obviously important, but commitment to the client and understanding the commercial reality are more fundamental in determining the DLA personality.

Not that DLA represents an overly pressured environment for the newcomer; there is an eagerness and a gratifying buzz about the place, but it's not a case of putting the job above all else.

Flexibility is part of that make-up, and this works both ways. For instance, DLA will consider any requests for flexible working, including flexitime around a core set of hours.

Innovation

By its own admission, DLA likes to be different. It was one of the first UK firms to set up a lobbying arm in Brussels. It was one of the first in the wave of law firms to take on Limited Liability Partnership status.

Business opportunities have been spotted and seized early – with niche-filling specialisms now in regulatory legal advice, information technology, intellectual property and telecommunications.

DLA also has specialist groups, such as DLA Consulting which provides consultancy advice on a range of employment issues; DLA Upstream, an advance-warning service that helps clients to track political and regulatory developments both nationally and within Europe; and DLA Advance, which runs around 140 public training seminars and conferences annually.

A range of online services to speed up processes and increase transparency has been developed. They include a generic ClientZone as a secure portal for client access; an online medical database, MEDS, for the insurance industry to identify evidence in personal claims cases; SPACE, a system for providing legal approval of clients' advertising across Europe; and the Contract Matrix, an online guide to the legal niceties of commercial transactions for the non-specialist.

DLA is keen to foster these new developments, and set up an Innovation Centre in 2003 to test and prioritise new product ideas.

But perhaps the most innovative element of the DLA mix is simply the way a full-service law firm is being run like a business, and is talking to its clients on the same level. Most notably, DLA has an emphasis on customer relationship management that is unusual among its peers and is central to its business model – DLA aims to provide a full portfolio of services that will foster long-term relationships with its clients.

Diversity and social responsibility

DLA takes a positive view of diversity – welcoming difference and emphasising the firm's values of mutual respect, responsibility and teamwork.

Nearly two-thirds of the staff is female. More pertinently, 28% of partners and associates are women.

All DLA offices have local corporate social responsibility programmes for pro bono work and specific projects that have a notional value in excess of £1m. DLA's own charitable trust provided £75,000 to UK charities in 2003. Local offices also support local charities and community projects. The office managing partner has overall responsibility for distributing resources, with input from the local staff.

In addition there are large-scale exercises – in June 2003, DLA people walked from John O'Groats to Land's End (in 15-mile segments) to raise £500,000 for the WellChild Trust.

DLA also sponsors a high-quality art competition, with the results displayed in the firm's offices.

Corporate Governance

Within the constraints of client confidentiality, DLA is open about its operations. Each year DLA produces an annual report, which is widely available.

The firm also has a bespoke client service, which can advise on governance and regulatory audits, independent advice to directors, stakeholder engagement, and internal and external communications programmes. The aim is to help the client design governance programmes that are useful, valuable and right for their business.

Environmental record

DLA has an explicit environmental policy that centres on energy consumption and recycling. It uses suppliers with similar policies, runs twice-yearly risk assessments that include environmental issues, and has invested in technologies such as video-conferencing to minimise travel between offices.

Doncaster Metropolitan Borough Council

D

Doncaster Metropolitan Borough Council
The Council House, College Road, Doncaster DN1 3AJ
Tel: (0) 1302 737007
Web: www.doncaster.gov.uk **E-mail:** askus@doncaster.gov.uk

Pay and Benefits	7.3	Innovation	7.0
Promotion and Development	6.7	Diversity	7.0
Training	6.5	Social Responsibility	6.4
Travel opportunities	3.6	Corporate Governance	6.8
Culture	6.5	Environment	6.8
Total			**64.6**

Doncaster Council is the only local authority in the Yorkshire and Humber region, and one of only 11 nationally, to be led by an elected mayor. Doncaster is an area of great potential, with excellent road and rail communications links and now a new international airport. A £32m community sports stadium project is to be built, while Mayor Martin Winter is overseeing one of the biggest regeneration agendas in the country with an impressive leadership vision. There is key recognition that customers are at the heart of what the council does.

Executive summary

Doncaster Metropolitan Borough Council is led by an elected mayor, Martin Winter. By 2010, Doncaster expects to be a major contributor to regional and national prosperity, enjoying a high-growth economy with support from increasing educational attainments and commercial vibrancy. Much of this can be attributed to the keen leadership vision of Mayor Winter.

The Audit Commission conducts local authority performance assessments using five category ratings (poor, weak, fair, good, excellent). In 2002, when Mayor Winter assumed office, Doncaster was rated "fair". Now the rating is "good" – one year before it was expected to be so. The council is now ambitious to be "excellent" and to become a winning council in all they do.

One of the biggest regeneration projects in the UK is underway in the borough. The Robin Hood Doncaster Sheffield International airport opens in April 2005 on the former RAF Finningley site – creating thousands of jobs, directly and in ancillary services. Meanwhile, the council was shortlisted for the prestigious Personnel Today Employer Branding award for its modern approach to recruitment, work/life balance and diversity. This is a progressive local authority with clout.

Pay and benefits

"We cannot always compete on pay with the private sector," says Mandy Coalter, head of human resources. However, job satisfaction and the benefits on offer match and often exceed what's available in the private sector. "Our pay and benefits package is set out in the terms of the National Joint Council for local government employees, so we're in line with our market sector." Graduates can expect to start on a salary of £20,370, rising to £21,867 after two years.

The work/life balance package at Doncaster is excellent. "Mayor Winter has long championed the maintenance of a healthy balance between work and our lives outside work," says Coalter. The package includes job share, flexitime (with no core hours), term-time working, homeworking and career breaks; and leave for religious observance, bereavement, study for approved qualifications, volunteering in the community and "special purposes" – which can cover fertility treatment, medical issues or unexpected problems.

A good example of the council's positive approach to work/life balance is the career break scheme. This enables employees to request a break to undertake caring responsibilities, voluntary work or study. For example, an employee recently took a year's break in Australia to accompany her husband who was posted there.

There's a contributory final salary pension scheme, with employees paying 6% and the council paying the balance of 6% to provide the benefits package.

There's a recognition scheme for individuals and teams, with monthly awards for individuals of £50 and for teams of £100 within each of the council's directorates. Each year, the directorates award an Employee of the Year and Team of the Year, which attracts a further monetary award and recognition at a special ceremony led by the mayor.

There are monetary awards for any staff member producing an idea that is subsequently taken up in the "make a good idea count" (MAGIC) scheme. There are also long-service awards for staff notching up 20, 30 and 40 years' service.

Staff also enjoy 25% discounts at council-owned leisure centres, swimming pools and fitness suites. Anyone cycling to work and between sites for business purposes receives an allowance.

Promotion and development

"Training is offered depending on identified need rather than being defined in numbers of days per year," says Coalter. "There are opportunities for employees to attend courses for potential career development. We provide support for anyone acquiring relevant professional qualifications in a trade, care work, accountancy, law, social work, HR, etc.; and we pay relevant professional fees."

The council's top 250 managers are progressing through a Transforming Leadership programme that includes a two-day residential programme and 360-degree feedback. A Flying Start annual fast-track programme to identify and nurture future top managers has taken in its first 23 staff who will now receive training, mentoring and a secondment. There is also a range of learning and development opportunities available to all staff such as short courses and work shadowing. There have been 300 secondments in 2004, not all internal – "some have come to us". One employee, for example, recently spent a month working at the Office of the Deputy Prime Minister in London. Doncaster has taken on two graduates through the National Graduate Programme for Local Government on two-year assignments. The council is also sponsoring 12 employees on the Public Sector Foundation Degree and MA in Public Sector Management at Huddersfield University.

Appraisals are carried out annually with six-month review points, supported by regular staff supervision and one-to-one meetings at monthly/six-weekly intervals.

"Mentoring is offered to a wide range of employees", says Coalter. Coaching is available on request and promoted throughout the council as good management practice. Emphasis is placed on the manager's role as coach in leadership and management training programmes.

Company culture

The council is very much customer focused. "Again, this has been driven by Mayor Winter," says Coalter. "It's a key turnaround from being an inwardly-focused organisation. Indeed, the culture here is very much can-do, daring and innovative. We want our staff to live the values of the organisation, as demonstrated by our annual awards for Employee and Team of the Year. For example, our recent Employee of the Year had saved a member of the public's life through her actions."

The council is now rated as a "good" council. Half the organisation has achieved Investors in People accreditation – the Social Services directorate received a two-star rating for its service provision. The council is also subject to Ofsted education reports and Audit Committee assessments. An external peer team (favourably) reviewed the HR department, which has resulted in a new, more consistent approach to HR management.

The government has selected the council as one of 21 local authorities to pilot local area agreements in which Whitehall is granting local authorities greater freedom to decide how best to organise themselves. Doncaster is currently undertaking a major restructuring of the council and has a proposed structure of one managing director, four general managers, community directors, service managers and area managers.

"We've undertaken a work/life balance awareness-raising programme with over 500 managers," says Coalter. "This is a key initiative championed by Mayor Winter. Sick leave had proved a problem due to the physically demanding nature of some manual jobs. However, with positive support mechanisms – such as manual handling training, onsite counselling and flu jabs for some staff – sick-leave absences are beginning to decrease."

Innovation

"We are unique with our elected mayoral model," said Coalter. "There is a significant and ambitious programme of development underway for the Doncaster area, not the least of which is the opening of the international airport. Our recently appointed managing director is female, with international experience gained in local government roles in Cape Town, South Africa; and before that in Adelaide, Australia. She is in the process of transforming us into a winning council."

The Doncaster HR team has played a key role in securing funding from the Office of the Deputy Prime Minister for a unique career development talent management and recruitment web portal to be hosted in Doncaster. All the major employers in the region are to collaborate on this project including the hospital, the new airport and college.

The MAGIC suggestion scheme referred to earlier has encouraged staff to come up with new ideas, while the new HR structure emerging from the external peer review is expected to introduce competency-based job roles and fresh career ladders for the HR staff.

Every employee in the council received an extra half-day's holiday as a result of the "good" rating achieved in the Audit Commission's Comprehensive Performance Assessment.

Diversity and social responsibility

"Mayor Winter has published his own white paper on diversity issues in which he outlines the focus and actions on how the borough will work towards a better relationship and understanding with ethnic minority groups," says Coalter. The corporate equalities policy and strategy are underpinned by a corporate race equality scheme and corporate equality plan. That said, 1.34% of the council's 14,500 workforce are of black and ethnic minority origin, against 2.23% in the local community. The council is now also working with ethnic minority staff and local residents to look at how more can be done to promote opportunities for black and ethnic minority people.

Women, including a female managing director, hold 37% of the top offices. "Compared to other public and private sector organisations, we have achieved a high number of women in senior positions, but we want more women at the top to reflect the fact that 74% of our workforce is female," says Coalter. "In 2004, the council participated in a South Yorkshire Women's Development programme, where attendees had access to work-shadowing and mentoring exercises with senior women drawn from across the county."

The local community is what the council is all about. There's a "partnering in volunteering" scheme where staff do voluntary work one day a year. Recently a number of staff participated, lead by the mayor, in a voluntary programme at the local hospital to wrap Christmas presents for patients.

There are annual Spirit of Doncaster awards, hosted by the mayor, "to recognise the hard work and effort of citizens, done to help others without thought of recognition for their efforts."

Corporate Governance

"The key laws and regulations applying to the council are the Local Government Act, and all equalities and employment legislation," says Coalter. "Then, each service area has specific legislation relevant to that area; for example social care, education and welfare acts."

"We want to make it as easy as possible for residents to access our services, help and support," says Coalter. Plans to put the customer first include a one-stop shop "local access to services" philosophy; the enhanced provision of particular services where the local need is greater; fully coordinated and individually tailored service delivery; a new management framework to enhance joint working between services; and greater freedom, trust and accountability of staff for results.

Changes in the way senior management is organised started to be implemented in January 2005, with a subsequent review of changes affecting the rest of the council rolling through to spring.

A Working Together partnership with unions has been established and used as a model of best practice by ACAS. Meetings are held monthly between the head of HR and all unions. The council is aware of the new Information and Communication with Employees legislation, effective 6 April 2005, and has a formal policy to ensure its communications procedures are totally compliant.

Environmental record

"We are very passionate about environmental issues," says Coalter. In 2004, the mayor launched a Zero Waste strategy programme setting out how the authority would face the challenge of dealing with its waste. In 2003, the FLAG ("fight litter and graffiti") campaign was launched, intending to keep Doncaster clear of unsightly litter, abandoned vehicles and graffiti. A dedicated hotline phone number was set up for ease of reporting by the public.

Processes have been put in place to recycle paper, and office and computer equipment, under the guidance of the Waste Electronic and Electrical Equipment (WEEE) EU directive.

"We're negotiating with the South Yorkshire Passenger Transport Executive to offer travel discounts for those giving up their cars for commuting," says Coalter. There's a business TravelMaster ticket scheme, which allows staff to travel by bus/train/tram on business so they don't need to bring a car to work. Following a trial, it's expected that a pool car scheme for business travel is to be introduced. A cycle mileage allowance has already been introduced for those cycling to work and between sites on business.

All due to a mayor with vision, and a local authority with the clout to carry it out.

Eaton

Eaton Limited
Tayhouse, 300 Bath Street, Glasgow G2 4NA
Tel: (0) 141 331 7012
Web: www.eaton.com

Pay and Benefits	6.1	Innovation	7.3
Promotion and Development	5.9	Diversity	5.1
Training	6.8	Social Responsibility	5.7
Travel opportunities	6.9	Corporate Governance	5.8
Culture	6.5	Environment	5.8
Total			**61.9**

If there is a light under the British bushel, it belongs to Eaton Limited. It is a US-quoted company employing 55,000 people worldwide, over 3,000 in the UK, and it has been in the UK for around 50 years – yet it is hardly a household name.

Eaton is a diversified industrial manufacturer with sales of over $8.1bn. It is a global leader in fluid power systems and services for industrial, mobile and aircraft equipment; electrical systems and components for power quality, distribution and control; automotive engine air management systems, powertrain solutions and specialty controls for performance, fuel economy and safety; and intelligent truck drivetrain systems for safety and fuel economy. It sells products to customers in more than 100 countries, and has plants throughout Britain.

Executive Summary

Eaton traces its beginnings to the fledgling trucking industry of 1911 when it produced its first eight front and rear axles, and it was through its truck and auto markets that founder Joseph Oriel Eaton built the foundation for today's diversified industrial multinational. The company has continued to grow through its continued commitment to its auto and truck customers, and to this day Eaton holds product leadership positions in both markets.

Once characterised as a vehicle component supplier, Eaton's business base has undergone a significant transformation. Today, the company classifies its business into four distinct segments: fluid power, electrical, automotive and truck.

Eaton grows in part through acquisition – its purchase for $2.2bn of Aeroquip-Vickers, Inc. in 1999 made it a leader in the development and sales of fluid power products to industrial, mobile equipment and aerospace customers worldwide. It bought the Westinghouse Distribution and Control Business Unit to propel it to a leadership position in electrical power distribution and control equipment for industrial, commercial and residential markets.

The automotive business is driven by new product development, and global expansion and acquisition. Through its history, a primary tenet of the Eaton business has been that the company carries a responsibility to deliver breakthrough solutions to its customers. Innovative entrepreneurship continues to drive Eaton.

For example, where there is a significant advantage, Eaton takes the opportunity to standardize an aspect of the business by adopting and deploying common tools or business processes. The sum of all these tools and processes, aligned and integrated, is called the Eaton Business System (EBS). This pervades all Eaton processes, representing a philosophy of strengthening the overall enterprise and individual businesses through an integrated operating system.

Pay and Benefits

The Eaton Compensation Philosophy says it all: "Compensation at Eaton is fair and competitive for performance that contributes to the success of the business. Fair means that compensation should reflect the extent of our contributions – the greater the contribution, the higher the reward. Competitive means that we will have the opportunity to earn at least as much as we would in similar positions at other companies with which we compete."

Salaries are reflective of several factors, including the relative worth of the position as represented by salary grade and salary range midpoint, individual performance results, and individual skill and competence levels. There is an annual merit increase review by which salaries are adjusted to reflect the competitive pay position and level of contribution of each individual.

There are also a series of tiered corporate and local recognition and reward programmes to provide immediate acknowledgement for performance that goes above and beyond the call of duty.

Many facilities offer an Employee Guidebook for orientation purposes, and an additional Benefit book – this supplements the core benefits (such as sick pay, a final salary pension scheme, personal protective equipment and health screening) with offerings that include savings on home insurance, childcare vouchers, electrical discounts, holiday discounts, car rental and a personal hospital plan.

Promotion and Development

In the war for talent, Eaton recognises that employees demand greater control and choice in fashioning their careers. Tools and processes – the online performance management system, coaching tools, Eaton University and Eatonjobs.com – are provided to help employees take control of their own careers and maximise their potential.

There is an annual formal assessment of organisational capability to identify high-performers, and to ensure that they are being equipped with the necessary skills and experience to be business leaders of the future. Those with talent and ambition will be spotted and nurtured – and the world is their oyster. Eaton is always looking for high-calibre people to fill skills gaps, and the opportunities are worldwide.

Company Culture

The company's core values are: "making our customers the focus of everything we do; recognize our people as our greatest asset; treat each other with respect; be fair, honest and open; be considerate of the environment and our communities; keep our commitments; and strive for excellence".

Eaton is an advocate of "the power of one" and all that it brings in terms of best-practice sharing, knowledge transfer and economies of scale. The company has employees in 29 countries and six continents, but it is all within a framework aimed at creating one integrated operating company in order to exceed the rising performance expectations of its stakeholders. Eaton holds to the view that by providing a common philosophy, set of values, management tools and measures; it has the foundation for achieving operational excellence.

The company's vision is to be the most admired company in its markets, to achieve top priority goals of profitability and growth, make customers the focus of everything it does, and abide by the fundamental principles of global ethical behaviour. The company states: "We share a belief in measuring ourselves aggressively and consistently."

The chairman, Sandy Cutler, tells employees in the company newsletter: "High-performing organisations have an exceptional internal culture. There is always an opportunity to improve and we must continue to do so. Some locations or functions have further to go than others but we must all be committed to continuous improvement, which means driving to achieve the principles and working environment embodied in

The Eaton Philosophy." This commitment is cemented in the annual employee survey, and reciprocated by employees through a participation rate exceeding 96%. Similarly, the Eaton Philosophy work practices model reinforces "the power of one" and their dedication to excellence through people.

It's quite a culture. The newsletter with that message to employees from the chairman was printed in 17 languages.

Innovation

To Eaton, innovation means making meaningful change to improve an organisation's products, services and processes, and to create new value for the organisation's stakeholders.

Innovation should lead to new dimensions of performance. Innovation, the company states, is no longer strictly the purview of research and development departments: innovation is important for all aspects of the business and all processes. Organisations, it states, should be led and managed so that innovation becomes part of the learning culture and is integrated into daily work. "Innovation builds on the accumulated knowledge of our organisation and its employees. Therefore, the ability to capitalise on this knowledge is critical to managing our innovation."

The company has been founded on innovation. When founder Joseph Oriel Eaton said in 1911 that the company aimed to produce the highest quality products at costs which made them economically practical in the most competitively priced markets, that meant innovation – and it has been pursued avidly ever since.

The company has been driven by new product development since the early days when it invented and hand-manufactured the first truck axles in the industry. It delivers what it likes to call "breakthrough solutions" to customers, and that means innovation and entrepreneurship.

Diversity and Social Responsibility

Employees in 29 countries with 17 languages, 23% of them with multi-language skills, is diversity itself; and that is what Eaton is all about.

On social responsibility, the company believes that an organisation's leaders should stress responsibilities to the public, as well as ethical behaviour and the need to practise good citizenship. Leaders should be role models, focusing on business ethics and the protection of public health, safety and the environment. They should also be mindful of the lifecycle of the company's products and services.

The company states: "Organisations should emphasise resource conservation and waste reduction at the source. Planning should anticipate adverse impacts from production, distribution, transportation, use and disposal of products. Effective planning should prevent problems; provide for a forthright response if problems occur; and make available information and support needed to maintain public awareness, safety and confidence."

Eaton believes in practising good citizenship and supporting what it calls "publicly important purposes". These might include improving education and health in the community, environmental excellence, resource conservation, community service, improving industry and business practice, and sharing non-proprietary information.

Effective design strategies should anticipate growing environmental concerns and responsibilities.

Corporate Governance

The Eaton Business Excellence report, an evaluation of the entire organisation, says that with visionary leadership, the directions, values and expectations of the organisation should balance the needs of all the stakeholders. Leaders should ensure that there is the creation of strategies, systems and methods for achieving excellence, stimulating innovation, and building knowledge and capabilities: "Senior leaders should inspire and motivate the entire workforce and should encourage all employees to contribute, to develop and learn, to be innovative and to be creative. Senior leaders should also be responsible to the governance body for their actions and performance.

"The governance body should be responsible ultimately to all stakeholders for the ethics, vision, actions and performance of the organisation and its senior leaders.

"Senior leaders should serve as role models through their ethical behaviour and their personal involvement in planning communications, coaching, development of future leaders, reviewing organisational performance and employee recognition. As role models they can reinforce ethics, values and expectations while building leadership, commitment and initiative."

The governance policies of the board of directors say that one of its most important responsibilities is to ensure that the company's senior management is well qualified to conduct the company's business affairs.

Environmental Record

The company goes well beyond what is required. It supplements existing laws and regulations in different locations with an additional 26 regulations of its own, the first being the need to have one or more qualified individuals designated as primarily responsible for EHS matters for each facility or group of facilities. Each individual must be provided with adequate training, time and resources to fulfil these responsibilities; and each newly designated individual must participate in an orientation programme for EHS managers.

On materials and industrial waste management, the 26 additional regulations cover greenhouse gas reduction, underground tanks, chemical and waste storage, hazardous communication, chemical inventory, waste minimisation, sanitary waste water, and waste disposal. They are called the Environment, Health and Safety (EHS) Worldwide Directives. These additional regulations include remits for plant surveys and assessments (asbestos surveys are at the top of the list), corporate non-routine government contacts, financial issues and records management. Nothing is missed or taken for granted.

Edexcel

Edexcel
One90 High Holborn, London WC1V 7BH
Tel: (0) 870 240 9800
Web: www.edexcel.org.uk **E-mail:** hr@edexcel.org.uk

Pay and Benefits	6.2	Innovation	5.8
Promotion and Development	5.6	Diversity	7.6
Training	6.0	Social Responsibility	5.6
Travel opportunities	4.4	Corporate Governance	6.5
Culture	6.2	Environment	5.8
Total			**59.7**

Edexcel provides qualifications that help to shape and change people's lives. Formed in 1996 through the merger of two well-respected examining bodies, each a leader in its field of providing academic and vocational qualifications; Edexcel today provides a range of qualifications to cater for all needs and learning styles. It has a key belief in the parity of esteem of vocational and general qualifications. Some 90% of its business is in the UK, and 10% in servicing customers in over 100 countries. Edexcel is an operating company within the education and media organisation, Pearson plc.

Executive summary

Edexcel was formed as a result of a government initiative in 1996 to create unitary examining bodies. As the first of these bodies, Edexcel was formed from the merger of BTEC (Business & Technology Education Council) and ULEAC (University of London Examinations and Assessment Council). The other main awarding bodies are AQA, OCR and City & Guilds. At first, Edexcel was a not-for-profit organisation run by a committee of trustees. It became apparent, given the complexity of the UK's educational system, that there was a need to invest in new technology. It was not viable to remain a charity. A partner was sought, and London Qualifications Ltd (trading as Edexcel) was set up in 2003, 75% owned by Pearson plc and 25% by Edexcel Foundation (the original charity). Edexcel is now an operating company within Pearson plc. The transition from a charity making £7m losses on £91m turnover to a company making £7.5m profits on £121m turnover in 2003 has been a success.

Edexcel is organised to allow it to focus on its key customer markets of schools, further education colleges, higher education institutions, employer organisations and training providers. Customers are serviced through a network of six regional offices and out-based field staff. There are 1,000 employees, most of them in London, utilising the services of 15,000 examiners (contractors).

Pay and benefits

"Being part of Pearson gives us a lot more security as a business," says Tim Williams, HR and customer service director. "Our pay/benefits package is in advance of the market sector average, and we tend to offer a more comprehensive package of incentive payments and benefits than is offered by the education sector generally."

A regional business development manager at Edexcel, historically recruited from the education sector, has a base salary in the range £33,000–£50,000 with a median of £36,000; all higher than the public or semi-public education sector. In addition at Edexcel there is a potential 10% performance-related bonus; an annual car allowance of £4,800; pension scheme (the Pearson Money Purchase scheme with a wide range of risk preference and contribution choices); private health insurance; access to the company's save-for-shares scheme; and employee assistance programme. While there are no specific graduate jobs, a typical starting graduate salary is £16,500.

Some 20% of the staff are in Pearson's worldwide save-for-shares plan, while 84% of staff have shares in Pearson plc. The car allowance is given to those employees whose jobs require 10,000 business miles a year. Special rates have been negotiated with Lex Vehicle Leasing to enable leasing of high-quality fully maintained vehicles.

There are two schemes to recognise individuals' input. STARS offers recognition and financial rewards for good performance and outstanding work, while Eureka is a suggestion scheme which offers payment for implementable ideas. Special leave of up to five days a year is offered for a range of social responsibilities. Staff are also supported in involvement in charitable or community activities. A range of flexible working alternatives is also offered.

Edexcel recognises long service. A small financial token plus an extra day's leave for the year ahead is given every five years. Staff with more than 10 years' service are invited to an annual lunch with the chief executive and directors.

Promotion and development

"We try to talent spot our staff," says Williams. "In effect it's an annual review, partly aimed at senior level succession planning. Individuals we identify in this way receive additional development and are grouped for future potential promotion opportunities." About half of the staff in senior management positions have worked their way up through the organisation. Also, half the vacancies are filled from within the organisation.

Edexcel has undergone profound and positive change over the past few years, which has resulted in many opportunities for movement and progression. The onus is on the individual to pursue specific opportunities, a task which currently takes place informally during performance reviews and one-to-one meetings. A career review process is being introduced where employees can discuss career aspirations with their line managers.

There are full-year and mid-year reviews. The former measures past performance against objectives, competencies and review development; while the latter is designed to check progress made and carry out any refocusing if necessary. There is currently no formal policy on coaching and mentoring, but the approach is actively encouraged with some managers offering coaching to some of their staff.

Employees on average spend up to six days in formal training and about three days in on-the-job training. A variety of online training activities are available at no cost. If there is a specific need, involving external sourcing, the training must be relevant to the employee's role. The organisation invests £60,000 annually in supporting employees with their further education requirements, ranging from NVQs to post-graduate and professional programmes including MBAs. Edexcel has recently achieved Investors in People accreditation.

Company culture

The key words that are best used to sum up Edexcel's corporate culture are integrity, customer focus, teamwork, people development and innovation. "Historically, people who tended to flourish here came from the educational sector, for example moving on from teaching to become part of the assessment system," says Williams. "There's less of a dependency on that approach today, and more on professionals in a particular discipline that's required."

That the organisation is innovative can be shown in the move to marking exams online – it was 15% of scripts in 2004, moving to 50% for the next few years. "The relationship with Pearson gave us access to funding and access to technology they developed for our use," says Williams. "The process is more efficient, there's consistency, and overall it's faster. Ultimately there'll be moves to exams and assessment online."

Communication within Edexcel is handled in a variety of ways – a bulletin from the chief executive to employees each week, intranet, monthly newsletter, team meetings, and a works council which meets quarterly and where any issue can be discussed.

Instead of one work/life balance policy, a raft of seven policies addresses the area: adoption, maternity, paternity and parental leave; flexible working; career breaks; and homeworking. In the third (most recent) staff survey, the response rate was 74% – above the average rate of 58% for all such surveys conducted by the independent assessor, and above the online survey average of 69%. Overall, satisfaction with working at Edexcel is good.

Innovation

Edexcel is innovative in its use of technology, for example it offers web-based access to enable its customers to submit information and access records. On a wider scale, there's a rich website which provides information on all aspects of the organisation's work. In seeking to find ways to improve its processes and operations, Edexcel continually encourages staff to introduce new ideas through the staff suggestion scheme, dubbed Eureka.

There are teambuilding events involving process-based exercises, which are designed to develop people through working efficiently in small groups. For example, a marketing teambuilding event involved 50 staff producing a five-track CD in one day, which was sold to support a children's charity.

"We decided we needed to improve the quality and calibre of middle management," says Williams. "We constructed an eight module programme including topics such as leadership, project management, marketing, etc. – all leading to a formal BTEC qualification. Each module covers 30 hours. Staff members complete the eight modules, undergo an assessment and ultimately receive BTEC level 4 in management. An external examiner checks we are assessing to the right standard."

Edexcel has reached stream five of the programme, with 12 people in each stream. Six staff have already been successfully signed off the first stream.

Diversity and social responsibility

There is a rigorous equal opportunities policy in operation. Within Edexcel, 55% of the staff and 51% of the management are female, while 20% of the staff are from racial and religious minorities.

"We are happy with this state," says Williams. "However, as a company we are more concerned that at the highest levels Edexcel is not sufficiently representative of the communities which we service. We are working with Pearson plc's diversity team to explore all avenues, to help ensure our senior management pool becomes more diverse and more representative."

A corporate social responsibility strategy has been developed which will be used in the organisation's development tools.

An HR team was involved in a pilot project, linked to CSR activities, where a block of flats for homeless people was decorated. Each year, Edexcel utilises its Christmas card budget to help an education charity. Further to these activities, Pearson offers to match funding which has been specifically raised for charities. While there is no formal policy on charitable donations, the issue forms part of the new social responsibility policy. As a services business, there's a limit as to how much further these policies can be improved.

Corporate governance

There is a compliance team with the primary responsibility to monitor compliance for Edexcel from an educational regulatory point of view. The organisation is subject to close regulation through the Qualifications and Curriculum Authority (QCA), an arm of the government's DfES, Department for Education and Skills. "We have to adhere to their strict guidelines and ensure all our qualifications are fully accredited," says Williams. "We have to have the right standards of assessment regimes." Across the three bodies – Edexcel, AQA and OCR – an A grade in A level history has to be of the same standard.

There is a board of directors to ensure Edexcel complies with all legal requirements – the Data Protection Act, the European directive on communications, etc. The company's values are publicised generally and reinforced through its STARS programme, for example, where specific recognition awards are provided for staff exhibiting these values. There is no recognised union or partnership agreement, but there is a staff consultation forum called Dialogue.

Edexcel uses over 15,000 examiners who are contracted annually for their services. Some freelance staff will be used for exam marking, writing exams or syllabus writing. All freelances sign contracts. There is an arrangement with the Inland Revenue, which specifically covers provision of examiner services.

Environmental record

There is a natural limit as to how far Edexcel can pursue an environmental agenda, as it is a services business. That said, Edexcel ensures paper-recycling facilities are in place through the deployment of colour-coded receptacles, and toner cartridges are recycled. Use of public transport is encouraged wherever possible. There are season ticket loan facilities available. Automatic movement sensor switches control the office lighting system, which conserves energy.

Edexcel subscribes to Pearson's environment policy which pursues such key commitments as: complying with the relevant environment laws and regulations applicable to each country it operates in; taking account of environmental issues when placing contracts with suppliers of goods and services; and continuing to introduce energy efficient systems into its buildings and to manage energy requirements sensibly wherever it operates. Where no regulations exist, the company sets its own guidelines. The facilities and purchasing departments ensure all the environmental policies and procedures are known and adhered to by all staff through publicity (the newsletters, intranet, etc.) and monitoring.

Education is the future and Edexcel may be seen to be playing its part in seeing that students and young people are inculcated with the latest views on the environment, energy conservation and sustainability.

Egg

Egg plc
Waterhouse Square, 138-142 Holborn, London EC1N 2NA
Tel: (0) 20 7526 2500
Web: www.egg.com **E-mail:** askhr@egg.com

egg™

Pay and Benefits	6.6	Innovation	6.8
Promotion and Development	6.8	Diversity	5.8
Training	6.8	Social Responsibility	6.6
Travel opportunities	2.2	Corporate Governance	5.8
Culture	6.0	Environment	6.0
Total			**59.4**

The online financial services provider, Egg, was launched in 1998 with the aim of helping its customers understand and manage their money more effectively. It is now the world's largest purely online bank with a customer base of over 3.6 million. It operates in three main areas: banking, investments and insurance. In June 2000, Egg plc was listed on the London Stock Exchange. Egg is part of the Prudential Group, which owns 79% of its shares. Egg is itself the parent of a number of companies making up the Egg group, all of which trade under the Egg name. It has offices in London, Dudley and Derby.

Executive summary

In 2004, Egg announced a pre-tax loss of £103m, due to its withdrawal from the French market. The UK business made a pre-tax profit of £53m for the nine months to September 30 2004, compared to the £57m profit for the same period in the previous year. The company says the majority of business comes through unsecured lending – which principally means the credit card, and increasingly, personal loans. Egg remains committed to making use of its unique brand proposition to create substantial long-term value.

Pay and benefits

Egg's salaries are benchmarked against salaries in other financial services companies. The company estimates that when annual bonuses are taken into account, it pays in the upper quartile for the sector. Employees on its IT graduate training scheme get £22,000.

All employees automatically become members of the Egg group personal pension plan. Contributions range from 3–10% of salary, and when they retire, employees have the option of a pension for life or a reduced pension and tax-free lump sum. Those transferring to Egg from parent company Prudential have the option of continuing their membership of Prudential's staff pension scheme.

Employees are also covered by the group's life assurance plan, which provides death-in-service benefits of 3–4 times basic salary. Eligible employees get free private medical insurance, and other employees can opt for subsidised membership of the same scheme. The company also operates two share option plans: the approved share option plan, which about a third of the staff participate in, and a savings-related share option plan. Certain employees can opt for a company car or cash alternative.

A childcare voucher scheme enables employees to make savings of up to 11% on their childcare costs; and participating employees also have access to the BUPA Childcare at Work helpline, which offers advice on a range of childcare issues. All staff can also get discounts on a range of high street products. Annual leave starts at 22 days and builds up to 25 days, and the company has just introduced a scheme to allow employees to buy up to five days' extra holiday.

From April 2003, Egg has operated a flexible working policy available to all employees with children under six-years old or disabled children under 18. Requests for flexible working by other employees are considered on their merits.

Promotion and development

Prospects for promotion within Egg are good. The company only recruits externally as a last resort, and about 54% of professional grade staff and about 70% of managers come from within the company. Employees can expect formal performance appraisals twice a year. However, managers are also encouraged to give ongoing feedback and adapt their approach to suit what motivates each individual.

The pay system at Egg is graded on three levels: developing (the level at which most new staff are recruited), competent and expert. Pay reviews are normally carried out once a year for professional staff; as part of the review, staff are asked about their aspirations for career progression.

Employees are encouraged to give feedback about the organisation through a monthly opinion survey, which measures their views on issues such as feeling valued, knowing how they contribute to Egg's objectives, quality of line management skills, and scope of personal development. The survey results are used to help the company identify future areas of development.

During 2003, Egg spent £3m on training – 4% of total payroll costs. New employees can expect to receive four weeks of training followed by a further two weeks of coaching, usually carried out by the line manager.

For more senior employees, annual training can vary from one to 10 days a year depending on changes to products or systems or the requirements of their role. Managers' capabilities are assessed during development workshops, resulting in a personal development plan.

Company culture

Egg's mission statement is "to revolutionise the customer's experience of financial service, driven through unleashing the power of people". The company believes in challenging financial industry conventions by providing better products and services. It aspires to be vibrant, imaginative and fair in everything it does, and to encourage employees to develop their careers in a stimulating environment.

The company's Make A Difference scheme, launched in 2003, aims to empower employees and encourage them to be proactively involved in the company's development. The scheme enables employees to put forward ideas and suggestions for improvements, and be involved in seeing the idea through to conclusion by working closely with people in the relevant business area. People's voices are very much heard, and a strong policy on people's wellbeing is almost tangible.

Another important aspect of Egg's culture is to recognise that its customer-facing staff are the people best placed to know about customers' needs. It sends staff on road shows and workshops to collect customer feedback, and encourages them to put their findings about customer requirements and behaviour into its intranet-based feedback system.

The culture within Egg is very much about adult relationships. Leading policies are based on adult-to-adult relationships, and are concerned with giving enough information to enable decisions to be made. For knowledge workers in particular, there are a lot of homeworking possibilities and flexible hours opportunities. Associates, the people who operate the phones, have opportunities for flexible working, shift working, job sharing. There is respect for flexibility here.

Innovation

Since its inception, Egg has always been an innovator within the financial services industry. Its strategy has been to take advantage of the opportunities presented by the online services marketplace, and pass the cost savings and convenience of the online model on to its customers. It now has over 3.6 million customers, and is the largest purely online bank in the world.

Egg can point to a long list of financial industry firsts. In 1998, it took the financial services market by storm by launching a market-leading savings account offering 8% APR. Its Egg Card was the first online credit card to provide an online guarantee to make internet shopping easier, and a 0% interest introductory offer on new purchases and balance transfers.

It was also the first UK bank to provide an account aggregation for its services, enabling customers to see and operate all their online financial accounts – whether those accounts are with Egg or not. The company remains committed to growing its business by offering its customers innovative products and services.

The company also innovates in its internal online systems. For example, it has developed an intranet-based system that enables its 1,200 associates to capture feedback from their interactions with customers. Using this feedback, the company has already been able to develop new business propositions and improved customer processes.

Diversity and social responsibility

Egg has a number of policies that support diversity within the organisation including an equal opportunities policy, a flexible working policy, a Work and Parents policy and a Dignity At Work policy. Egg's demographics reflect the areas where it is based. Currently, 48% of its employees are women, of whom 10.6% are in management. Around 12% of employees class themselves as non-white.

On the social responsibility front, Egg aims to develop local talent in four key areas: education, sport, the arts, and regeneration (which can mean anything from fixing the local scout hut roof to painting a narrow boat). Education volunteers at all three Egg sites go into local schools to help with reading and writing skills in the classroom, with sports, and with mentoring pupils to raise their self-esteem and self-confidence.

Egg has also launched a "football skills challenge". As part of this, Derby County Football Club's Football in the Community coaches and Egg coaches go into local schools and deliver football skills training.

Employees are encouraged to fundraise for charities they feel passionate about, and a proportion of Egg's call centre resources are given over to support Comic Relief and Sports Relief. Egg's Community Leave policy allows employees three days' paid time off each year to carry out voluntary work in the community.

Corporate Governance

Egg is managed by a board of executive and non-executive directors. Their decisions are implemented by Egg's executive committee, made up of senior managers, who develop and agree Egg's operating plan. The committee also reviews operating performance, financial performance and change performance against the company's plans.

As a financial services company, Egg is governed by the Financial Services Authority regulations. However, it also has its own core values it seeks to maintain: honesty, integrity and respect for people. All the "people" teams within the organisation – HR, people communications, training and development, community, locations, environment – are expected to support these values through the way employees and customers are treated.

Egg aims to have clear two-way communications channels that ensure its people can have a say about the environment in which they work. Indeed, the company believes it has established good communications forums with its people; for example, the Egg People Forum which has been recognised as illustrative of best practice in the industry, offering 24x7 availability, one-to-one and email contact, wellbeing surgeries, etc. The company is also aware of the Information and Communication with Employees (ICE) legislation, effective April 6 2005, and indicates all its policies will ensure its communications procedures are fully compliant.

Environmental record

Egg has an environmental policy that is signed off at executive level and overseen by an environmental manager. An internal communications team helps to cascade environmental initiatives throughout the group. The company is listed on the FTSE4Good index, which aims to measure how well companies meet globally recognised corporate responsibility standards.

As part of its environmental policy, Egg aims to cut down on paper waste by recycling paper; and has a policy of disposing of furniture responsibly, firstly by trying to re-use it elsewhere in the community, and failing that, through specialist furniture reclamation companies. IT equipment is disposed of via a specialist company according to the latest Waste Electronic and Electrical Equipment (WEEE) legislation.

Though certain employees are offered company cars, Egg tries to encourage use of alternative forms of transport. All staff can take advantage of season ticket loans, and the company also provides cycle-to-work facilities and holds cycle-to-work event days. In a "bike-to-work week", every person who bikes in gets a free breakfast and free bike servicing. At its main centre in Derby, Egg employees are offered public transport subsidies; and there are incentives for car sharing, for example free parking and guaranteed parking spaces. It's a cracking place to work.

Elan IT

Elan Computing
Elan House, 5-11 Fetter Lane, London EC4A 1QX
Tel: (0) 20 7830 1300 **Fax:** (0) 20 7830 1373
Web: www.elanit.co.uk

Pay and Benefits	6.8	Innovation	6.0
Promotion and Development	6.1	Diversity	5.9
Training	5.8	Social Responsibility	5.2
Travel opportunities	6.1	Corporate Governance	5.8
Culture	6.9	Environment	6.2
Total			**58.4**

Elan is Europe's largest IT & T recruitment company by turnover (Ovum Holway ITSA Report, October 2003); providing permanent and contract staff, managed services and training solutions to clients across a range of industries.

Headquartered in London, Elan was established in 1987 and has grown its operations to encompass 51 offices in 16 countries throughout Europe and the Asia-Pacific region. With a 2003 turnover of £237m, Elan currently employs about 550 people and is a wholly owned subsidiary of Manpower, one of the world's largest temporary and permanent staffing specialists.

The professionalism and quality of the service provided has been recognised within the industry, and has seen Elan voted as Recruitment Consultancy of the Year for both 2003 and 2004 (Computing Awards for Excellence).

Executive summary

In 2004, Elan successfully placed over 2,500 IT professionals in permanent positions, and 3,500 contractors.

Elan's objectives are to be the leader in each market they operate in, and to continue to grow and take market share by providing the best IT people and a world-class recruitment service. They aim to do this through:
- Offering a depth and breadth of service that adds value to each client's business
- Supporting delivery to clients with world-class e-commerce solutions
- Delivering a truly pan-European solution to support each client's needs
- Investing in the personal and professional development of the workforce

Elan is a wholly owned subsidiary of Manpower Inc., one of the world's leading employment services companies. Manpower has more than 4,300 offices in 66 countries, and had total sales of US$12.8bn worldwide in 2003. This relationship enables Elan to meet any non-IT requirements that clients have; and use Manpower's global infrastructure to provide local support to deliver services, knowledge of local market conditions and modus operandi to clients.

Elan's culture is very much a dynamic and proactive one, one that embraces innovation and creativity and supports the personal and professional development of their employees. This ensures that retention rates remain high within the company, with subsequent employee satisfaction maintaining a creative, positive and innovative work environment.

Pay and Benefits

Elan has a competitive remuneration and benefits structure in comparison to its industry competitors. The company is able to do this by carrying out regular salary surveys to ensure they remain competitive within the industry.

Flexibility is also an important feature of Elan's approach to reward, which is about more than just remuneration. Reward schemes are designed to meet employees' varied and changing needs by introducing individual choice in how each employee receives their benefits package. This ranges from commission-based rates for sales staff, through to incentive programmes for non-sales staff.

Employees are also offered a gamut of benefits to guarantee their personal and professional wellbeing. These include:

- Pension scheme (with associated pension advice on a monthly basis)
- Health insurance
- Private dental care
- Life assurance
- Childcare benefit vouchers
- Share options (after initial qualifying period)
- Season ticket loans (after 6 months)
- Flexible working hours for employees with dependants
- Provision of tax-free computers to staff for use at home
- Long-service awards are also given for five, 10 and 15 years' service with the company

Elan's competitive pay and benefits structure allows them to attract and retain the best employees in their sector, ensuring continued excellence of service to their client base.

With regards to rewards, a number of prizes are offered on a monthly, quarterly and annual basis to sales staff who over-achieve. Elan also runs an elite sales competition "Elan 18" which rewards the top 18 sales consultants from across the group. This consists of two exclusive prizes: one for the overall top consultant (previous prizes have included a Lotus car and a Harley Davidson motorbike) and one for the top 18 collectively. In previous years, the Elan 18 have been rewarded with trips to Hong Kong and to the Monaco Grand Prix. In 2004, the top 18 flew to the Mardi Gras in Rio de Janeiro, Brazil.

For individuals within the company who are not linked to sales targets, Elan offers discretionary awards for superior performance. For example, this could be demonstrated by exceptional customer service (either to external or internal customers) or the development of a key customer relationship.

Personal Development

The freedom for individuals to express themselves in the workplace is embodied within the Elan company values – people, knowledge and innovation.

All staff are required to undertake a programme of continuous development training courses to ensure that they are familiar with best practices. Elan has established a training academy, which promotes the professional and personal development of all individuals within the organisation.

On joining the company, all employees go through a comprehensive induction programme which consists of standard and tailored elements – this tailoring takes into account any previous experience the new starter brings with them. The induction programme includes workshops, self-taught modules, e-learning, and line manager coaching; complies with the principles of the sales culture; and supports Elan's ambition to be No 1 in every market they operate in. The induction is followed up with further formal training programmes three months later. To ensure ongoing professional development, mentors are assigned to new employees to monitor and encourage assimilation and progression in the organisation.

Elan also runs a number of internal training courses, often delivered by internal subject experts. There is a new training site on the company intranet, offering nearly 1,000 e-learning courses. Employees can take as many of these as they choose, either in their own time or during working hours. The company also gives support for external training; staff are provided with opportunities to broaden their horizons through training in areas not directly relevant to their roles, or otherwise provided with full sponsorship for work-related training.

On the subject of sabbaticals, Elan's HR director, Patricia Asemota, believes talented people are a valuable business resource; and companies that fail to invest in their staff outside the workplace fail to maximise the potential of their workforce. She says that the hobbies and interests of her colleagues develop unique skills that give them the edge in the competitive world of IT.

"We don't know what transferable skills people have picked up along the way – skills that could be useful for mentoring or coaching," Asemota says. "We look at the whole person because people are more than the jobs they do. We want to find out what makes a person unique, because they may have developed something that takes them from being good to being great."

Elan's experience suggests that companies can gain from supporting their employees' outside interests. "We encourage the growth and development of the individual as well as developing their skills for the job," Asemota says.

Elan's proactive attitude to employee sabbaticals ensures that the workforce remains fresh and culturally enriched. Not only does this provide personal development for individuals, but also motivation levels are retained – and this all allows for the implementation of new ideas through employees bringing new knowledge back to the company.

Promotion

All staff are encouraged to discuss their career aspirations with their managers on an informal basis. Every year, they also receive formal performance evaluations; these provide an opportunity to identify their strengths, discuss concerns (both personal and professional), identify areas for improvement, and set targets and goals.

Promotion from entry positions to more senior levels can take place within six to 12 months of joining; after that, it will typically take two to three years to move into a more senior role such as team leader, account director, or even on site with the client. Elan operates on a purely meritocratic basis, and promotes employees who demonstrate excellent performance. Indeed, the CEO and a current member of the executive board both started at Elan as sales consultants.

As a multinational company with employees across 16 countries in Europe, Asia and Australasia, Elan offers employees the opportunity to work and live abroad where the employee displays the requisite competency for the role. As part of the Manpower group, there are also plenty of opportunities across the 67 countries in which Manpower has an office presence.

Company culture

Sean Costello, Elan's chief executive officer, has created a lively and innovative environment within the company. Elan is a dynamic, results-driven culture; where performance excellence is encouraged at corporate, team and individual levels. The contribution of every individual is recognised, valued and rewarded.

Those who thrive within the company will be energetic, motivated and passionate about their work.

Elan seeks to create an atmosphere of partnership and teamwork in which employees can be actively involved in shaping the company's direction. They are actively encouraged to speak out to management about their ideas and opinions. Through its annual "people survey", the company benchmarks its performance against the rest of the Manpower group on areas such as the role of senior management and employee welfare.

Though recruitment is traditionally a young environment, and new recruits are generally graduates, Elan is not just a place for 20-somethings. The company has grown and matured, and there are now a number of long-standing staff that contribute to a growing, successful company culture.

Having the discipline and commitment to deliver excellent service is important within the company; but there is also scope for flexibility, with proactive attitudes to employees with dependants with regards to leave and working hours.

Innovation

Elan is considered to be one of the most innovative and forward-thinking recruitment companies within its sector.

In an extremely competitive market, Elan is constantly striving to improve the solutions within its service offering and the processes and methodologies that underpin them. Elan is credited with pioneering next-generation recruitment services and expanding the remit by which client-supplier relationships have traditionally operated. Elan ReSource, the specialist managed service division, provides bespoke managed service recruitment solutions that include overall responsibility for managing all of their clients' recruitment activity. As pioneers of managed service solutions (which include agency management and master vendor services), these models deliver substantial cost savings, improved productivity and a competitive edge in sourcing quality staff; and free up internal staff to focus on core functions.

Corporate Governance

Elan is committed to using best-practice processes that minimise business risk for clients; is a member of a variety of industry bodies including REC, NCC, SCAT and ATSCO; has ISO 9001: 2000 accreditation; and is committed to CSR Europe. Elan is also being sponsored by the MOD to obtain list X status that will enable them to provide security clearance for candidates.

Diversity and social responsibility

As part of the Manpower group, Elan has a dedicated social responsibility team and is committed to developing opportunities for disadvantaged groups (including disengaged youth, older people, the long-term unemployed and returnees to work). For example, this has included forging a business relationship with Working Links in an effort to break down barriers to a potentially rich source of untapped labour.

As an equal opportunities employer, Elan has a positive approach to recruiting regardless of age, disability, race, gender, religion or sexual orientation. Elan's approach to managing diversity complements their approach to equal opportunities. This is a quality assurance approach. It helps Elan to identify hidden barriers within their organisation, which make it more difficult for people who are perceived as being different from the majority of their colleagues to succeed and develop their careers. It also helps to affect cultural change by creating an environment in which people of all backgrounds can work together harmoniously.

As with equal opportunities, managing diversity allows Elan to ensure that decisions about the employment and training of people support business goals and are objective and meritocratic, relating to individual personal development criteria.

Enterprise Rent-A-Car

Enterprise Rent-A-Car
Enterprise House, Delta Way, Egham, Surrey TW20 8RX
Tel: (0) 1784 221367 **Fax:** (0) 1784 221399
Web: www.enterprisealive.com

Pay and Benefits	5.8	Innovation	6.7
Promotion and Development	6.8	Diversity	7.6
Training	6.6	Social Responsibility	6.6
Travel opportunities	6.0	Corporate Governance	6.2
Culture	6.9	Environment	6.1
Total			**65.3**

US-based and privately owned, Enterprise Rent-A-Car is the largest car hire firm in North America. The business focuses on rental car replacement through the insurance industry; fleet management services for corporations; and recently, in response to customer demand, some airport rental offices. Its multinational operations span five countries – US, Canada, UK, Republic of Ireland and Germany – employing more than 57,000 people (2,900 in the UK). Enterprise has 5,400 offices in the US and more than 600 in the other four countries. Enterprise has operated in the UK for 10 years and currently has 250 branches here.

Executive Summary

Enterprise was founded as a leasing company in 1957 by entrepreneur Jack Taylor, and over the years has added many more services. Unlike other car rental companies, Enterprise focuses on local markets. It specialises in renting to customers who need a replacement car as the result of an accident, mechanical repair or theft; or for a special occasion or short business trip.

Through its 6,000-plus offices worldwide, Enterprise operates a rental car fleet of more than 602,000 vehicles, featuring more than 120 different makes and models. These are big numbers, of which the company is proud, but what makes Enterprise unique is its people who provide extraordinary customer service at every rental location. Its brand awareness is remarkable, fuelled by customer satisfaction and referrals.

"Being privately owned allows Enterprise to make many decisions it couldn't make if it was publicly listed," says Brice Adamson, UK/Ireland managing director. "For example, we are able to look at investment from a long-term perspective, giving us the time needed to build large, profitable networks." Enterprise's turnover in the last financial year exceeded £4.6bn and profitability reached record levels. The company has seen year-on-year growth ever since it began, and it continues to expand its operations. In 2003 alone, more than 500 new branches were opened – that's more than one every business day – a trend the company expects to continue in the future.

Pay and Benefits

Donna Miller, human resources director in Europe, is quite candid about Enterprise's pay structure, particularly for graduates joining its management trainee scheme. "We pay a competitive starting salary – we're not the lowest, but we're not the highest either. Graduates could find higher starting salaries." But this is just an entrée to a reward culture where the company lives up to its name – it's all about enterprise.

Starting salaries range from £14,000 to £18,000 on the management programme, which is usually completed over 9–12 months (it could be shorter). The next step is to assistant manager and a salary increase, plus eligibility for a share of profits in your part of the business (£5,000–£8,000) – be that a branch, area or unit within it. By the third year, another salary increase could be accompanied by bonuses of £10,000. Enterprise graduates find that they quickly outpace their peers elsewhere.

Middle and senior managers regard Enterprise as one of the better-paying companies. Promotion is based entirely on merit and there really is no limit to how quickly you can progress. At group manager level you could be earning a six-figure salary within 7–10 years. Not all wealthy 30-year-olds need be footballers.

The package of benefits includes private health care, life assurance and long-term disability cover. Branch managers and above are entitled to company cars – after all, there are plenty of them around. Enterprise also sets aside 5% of its annual profits to distribute among eligible employees; individual shares vary upon length of service and position. Flexible benefits are being "looked at". Miller says: "Our employee base is very young and they can trade away potentially valuable benefits. We want to make sure that employees are covered with the benefits that they need for something catastrophic; specifically in health and disability cover."

Promotion and development

Enterprise hires graduates, particularly for the all-important customer-facing roles. With a customer service philosophy that is already strong, it means that Enterprise people can take the initiative and solve problems quickly and directly. "Our people are very good – they make the job look easier than it is," adds Miller.

The career ladder progresses through assistant manager, branch manager, area manager, group manager to vice president – the board sits above the VPs. There are also specialist roles and professional functions in IT, finance, marketing, sales, HR and so on – and plenty of opportunities to switch careers without switching companies.

Promotion depends upon performance in four key areas of the business. First, your Enterprise Service Quality index (ESQi) – a measurement of complete customer satisfaction – needs to be above company average. You need to demonstrate profitability, controlling costs as well as boosting revenue and fleet growth (measured by the number of cars in your branch). Finally, developing your team, while less tangible, is just as important.

"Enterprise is serious about its commitment to its customers and employees," says Adamson. "The company offers a multitude of promotion opportunities throughout an employee's career. Most people start at management trainee level, washing cars – just as I did. But the company promises you that there will be continual opportunity. Many companies say that, but not many can actually deliver it. At Enterprise our entire business model is based around it!"

Training is very comprehensive. Enterprise is always recruiting and always training. In 2004, the company hired 1,000 trainees in the UK to feed its management programme. The first two weeks are spent in the classroom and then – armed with a structured training manual – it's on the job, with branch managers responsible for their new charges. Enterprise is a very decentralised company, and each branch may do things a little differently. There will be a further 10–12 days' classroom training dispersed throughout the year. "So many companies contact Enterprise complimenting us on our people and showing interest in our people, which I take as a good sign," says Miller.

Other courses are supported on request and there is an international language programme – perhaps with one eye on its planned international expansion. Transfers within the company – abroad and within the UK – happen all the time. Enterprise doesn't ask people to relocate, but all positions are advertised internally. "In 2003, we moved 425 people," says Miller. "That's a big relocation programme."

Company culture

Enterprise founder, Jack Taylor, looked around his small office one day and saw a handful of co-workers fielding phone calls, calculating rates and washing cars. But he saw something else too: people doing ordinary, everyday things with extraordinary passion and focus, going well beyond their own tasks to get the whole job done right.

Enterprise's phenomenal growth and success over the ensuing decades is based on Jack's simple philosophy: "Take care of your customers and employees first...and profits will follow." But Enterprise's goal has never been to be the biggest car rental company – only the best.

And the thing that Enterprise people talk about most is...Enterprise people. The management style of the company is based very much on being honest, open and up-front – and managers pick up their own phones. "People here do feel comfortable about management. They know that they are hearing the truth and that there are no hidden agendas," adds Miller.

The company's values are underpinned by professional HR policies. Recruitment is a hive of activity but so too is training. Enterprise is looking long-term, identifying the strong leaders of its future. "If we don't provide development, people will leave to find it elsewhere," says Miller. "People can see the tremendous growth in the business," adds Adamson.

Enterprise operates an Alternative Work Arrangements programme – its answer to flexible working. When Diane Lynch was promoted to group manager while on maternity leave, she returned to find it difficult to balance having a child, a husband who worked full time and a demanding job. She asked if she could shrink her hours and be available on her mobile (Enterprise people typically work a 50-hour week, largely because of the business needing to be open from 8am to 6pm). She continued on a reduced schedule for eighteen months and still outperformed her peers (largely men). She was recently promoted to assistant vice president, working directly with Brice Adamson.

Innovation

"We actively encourage our people to make decisions and build their confidence at finding innovative business solutions to day-to-day concerns," says Adamson. "Well-calculated risks are a necessity of a managerial position." With profit share correlated directly to the performance of their branch, innovation focuses on doing those extra little things to make a big difference in customer service.

There's no better illustration of this than the introduction of ESQi. Concerned that it might be sacrificing customer service for growth, Enterprise started to measure complete customer satisfaction – for every branch. That's 200,000 independent customer surveys each month. ESQi scores appear against branch managers' monthly profitability reports. An above-average ESQi is a pre-requisite for promotion, and a below-average score is tantamount to going to "ESQi jail" – "a place you don't want to be," said an insider.

The results were staggering – complete customer satisfaction figures rose from 67% in 1994 to 81% in 2004; and the spread between the top and bottom branch ratings narrowed, showing improved consistency.

Diversity and social responsibility

On diversity, Enterprise is probably one of the most advanced companies in the UK (stemming from being a US organisation, suggests Miller). Some 25% of its workforce comes from ethnic minorities, but what stands out is its diversity training. Other companies might respond "huh?" but in this company, diversity is enshrined in the management development programme. This highly structured course teaches cross-cultural awareness, male-female communication, and the needs of single parents and employees with children. The purpose is to arm managers with the skills to handle real life situations and act as agents of change.

There is also a national Diversity/Career and Family Focus Group, with meetings held quarterly aimed at "finding new ways to make Enterprise a better place to work". Locally, each operating group has its own team to implement fresh ideas.

Social responsibility is a big deal at Enterprise. It's best highlighted by the Jack Taylor Founding Values Award. To qualify, operating groups need to excel in community partnerships, diversity, work/life balance options, and governmental/philanthropic relations. Of 130 people who qualified in 2003, two won a $20,000 grant to put back into a charity project of their choice. It's how Enterprise encourages its people into social responsibility, without issuing any central dictat.

There is also a payroll giving programme, where Enterprise donates 50p for every £1 that employees give to charity.

Corporate Governance

Enterprise is a company founded on integrity and best-practice governance. An internal audit division scrutinises individual business groups annually (an exercise repeated externally through professional auditors) and "digs through everything". On data protection, most is stored in the US head office in St Louis and there is also a "safe harbour" office in the UK. There is a separate company compliance officer, and it is fair to say that Enterprise takes corporate governance pretty seriously.

Environmental record

As a car rental company with a conscious eye on the environment, Enterprise adheres to guidelines set by the Environmental Agency. Enterprise has all the boxes ticked when it comes to the regular, safe disposal and recycling of all waste products. There are recycling bins for ink and toner cartridges, card, paper, cans and cups throughout its UK locations.

Enterprise even cleans its cars in an environmentally friendly way, making every effort to ensure that car washes dispose of the dirty, soapy water safely – rather than pour it into the main drainage system.

Enviros

Enviros, Regus House
1010 Cambourne Business Park, Cambourne, Cambridge CB3 6DP
Tel: (0) 870 165 2400
Web: www.enviros.com **E-mail:** recruitment@enviros.com

ENVIROS

Pay and Benefits	5.5	Innovation	6.4
Promotion and Development	5.6	Diversity	5.3
Training	5.1	Social Responsibility	5.2
Travel opportunities	5.8	Corporate Governance	5.6
Culture	5.3	Environment	7.2
Total			**57.0**

Enviros is an environmental consultancy and software business. It helps organisations in the public and private sector identify and grasp opportunities to improve financial performance, increase stakeholder support and create a better environment. Employing some 400 people across 10 offices in the UK – and three in Barcelona, Prague and Toronto – Enviros is also the founder of a global consulting network. Over the past few years, it has transformed itself from an under-performing consultancy to one of the leading players – with operating profits of £2m up to October 2004 on turnover of around £23.5m. Enviros also practices what it preaches.

Executive summary

Enviros started life 30 years ago as a number of independent environmental consultancies, which came together in 1995 under the Enviros brand. A management buyout in 2001 was followed by a "poor year" in 2002, and a senior management and culture change in 2003. A more integrated management approach from 2003 produced an excellent financial turnaround, and the trend continued into 2004.

Surveys show the environmental consultancy market to be worth £1.2bn in 2004, increasing by £100m each year up to 2007. Enviros is regularly ranked by clients in the top three of UK environmental consultancies. The company is managed on a cross-office basis in line with five market-facing divisions: climate change, corporate services, land and water, risk and resource management, and software solutions. The organisation is a founder member of the CAT Alliance; which, with two European consultancies, is one of the largest European-based providers of due diligence services. The Alliance partners can mobilise consultants and local support in over 50 countries worldwide.

Pay and benefits

"Our pay and benefits package is in the mid to upper quartile range," says Doug Cattermole, head of human resources. "It's difficult to compare salaries as we operate in such a diverse market, with many niche players, where there are no salary surveys. We need people with at least a year's experience, and our employees tend to have at least two degrees."

There is a discrete stock option scheme but no general staff bonus scheme. There's a quarterly recognition scheme where staff are nominated for notable achievements; successful staff receive a recognition award and are reported in the intranet-based Enviros newsletter.

All employees have access to a discounted personal car leasing option. The same car leasing company operates the company car scheme, which is banded by carbon dioxide emission limits. A cash allowance may be taken instead. There's also a hybrid option where relevant employees have access to a pool car as needed and a reduced cash allowance.

As a result of earlier mergers, there were seven pension schemes in operation up to July 2004; then a web-enabled ethically friendly stakeholder scheme was introduced where Enviros contributes 6%, and employees 3% of salary. Employees may flex their contributions upwards if wanted. A pension steering committee monitors the scheme for those employees who eschew a hands-on approach. There is private medical cover, permanent health insurance and life assurance of four times salary. The former may be extended to family members at reduced rates.

"We are looking at introducing a flexible benefits scheme," says Cattermole. "This involves Inland Revenue and NI-friendly systems to lease PCs for home use and bicycles for travel to and from work. We're also considering introducing childcare vouchers. There's an individual approach to any requests from staff for flexible working – 6.5% of staff work part time and 4% are homeworkers."

Promotion and development

With an open management style, staff are encouraged to speak freely with managers. The CEO operates an open-door communication policy. There is a well-defined career development structure in the streams of consultancy and software, business support, and corporate. In the first, there are three levels each of consultant and senior consultant, feeding to commercial consulting group or technical manager and then director. Managers may move between staff management, commercial and technical responsibilities. In business support, there are consultants and seniors; and the professional stream has assistants, professionals, managers and a director/head of discipline. Each route has a grading structure offering progression.

"Managers take responsibility for professional training," says Cattermole. "We have rolled out a course locator on the intranet for individual generic training." On offer are: internal courses in project management, project director training, quality systems, health and safety, and financial awareness; and externally run courses in management development and sales.

Formal appraisals take place in January and July. Coaching and mentoring works on a team basis; and there are strong supportive links between group, technical and commercial managers in non-hierarchical ways. Staff are encouraged to take up professional membership (paid by the company), speak at symposia and conferences, and get published in relevant journals and media. "We have many employees who are leaders in their particular fields and disciplines," says Cattermole.

There is no formal graduate training scheme, but Enviros does offer study support on achieving qualifications such as an MSc.

Company culture

"People like it here because of the interesting range of work we have," says Cattermole. Enviros is seen as a good employer with a considerate, open and informal style of management. As an ethical business, they have an approach based on professionalism and integrity with a strong client and shareholder focus.

There is no formal work/life policy, but the organisation does offer flexible working, parental leave to look after a child, time off for dependants, adoption leave with adoptive parents having the same rights as natural parents, eye tests for users of display screen equipment, homeworking, and a raft of working hours possibilities; enabling the statement "we cater for the individual" to be validated. All in all, there is a good work/life balance and people enjoy working at Enviros. For its part, the company recognises that its people are a valuable asset and assist it in reaching its goals and aspirations.

There are six core objectives for Enviros in its three-year business plan up to 2006. These cover people, quality, client relationships, profit, market position and software products. For people, it is to achieve 90% staff retention and increase the investment in training and development by 10% each year. Overall, these objectives add up to a challenging target of making Enviros a leading player in its field, based on sound profitability and excellent products, with the emphasis on quality and delivery leading to clear recognition of this position from clients.

Innovation

This company's vision is "to help our clients do business today and have the world they want tomorrow".

"We are an ideas business," says Cattermole. "Equally, we have a commitment as a business to be carbon neutral. We pursue market-leading work on advising government and industry on emissions trading."

Enviros is at the leading edge in its work in several key areas ranging from climate change to its work on the effects of nuclear activities. The software side of the business, integrated into the environmental consultancy, enables the organisation to offer distinct services to clients not available elsewhere; for example, 2005 will see software products being launched in the sustainability sector.

The enManage system enables companies to make energy and resource savings with 5–15% reduction in usage costs, from a minimum capital investment with rapid payback. This approach has been successfully deployed to multinational blue-chip clients. Enviros has also looked to diversify in other areas, including a partnership with a leading investment manager looking at brownfield development.

Staff are encouraged to contribute ideas. An example is where staff in Manchester suggested a local car-sharing scheme, which was not only embraced but is being rolled out company-wide.

Diversity and social responsibility

Women make up 40% of all staff and 21% of management. Enviros is "concerned about the levels in management positions" while recognising that it is largely a historical situation, and that the pattern of gender balance at the lower levels has altered.

While there is no formal policy on charitable giving, the company does make a contribution to Future Forests as part of its carbon neutral policy, and sends e-Christmas messages instead of cards. Payroll giving is being considered.

The company's ethical policy contains a commitment to contribute in all that it does to the wellbeing of communities and to avoid harm to people. In offering its service to its clients, it either helps them to contribute positively to human wellbeing, or at least reduces the adverse impacts of their activities. In its own practices, Enviros enables its employees to offer their services free-of-charge during normal working hours – that's expertise, advice or capacity building. Examples include a prize donated for an eco-music festival at Meole Brace Infants School, Shrewsbury; membership of Amnesty International UK Business Group, a body of professionals trying to help businesses incorporate human rights into their activities; an engineering ambassador for a school near Bedford; and free annual seminars at Bristol University on consultants' roles.

Corporate Governance

As well as two executive directors, the board of Enviros comprises two non-executive directors. It ensures the company operates in a manner compatible with corporate responsibility by initiating relevant policies and objectives with the assistance of its strategic adviser.

Responsibility for developing implementation plans, detailed targets and procedures is delegated to an executive board; while all employees have an individual responsibility to comply with them. The board keeps management of the company under continual review and has specific procedures for doing this. It thereby identifies any need to modify policies to improve compliance and/or performance.

There are compliance officers and processes for health and safety, quality, and environmental monitoring systems (EMS); the management systems committee ensures the relevant standards have been attained in all three areas. All competencies are measured through the appraisal system.

A particular investment is the one Enviros makes in its staff. There is no union. "The staff have never asked for unions," says Cattermole. "There is the upcoming Information and Communication with Employees (ICE) legislation, which is effective April 6 2005. We will thus have to formulate a policy to ensure our communications procedures are compliant."

Environmental record

"Our intention is to be a leading environmental company, as would be expected given the nature of our company," says Cattermole. "Our greatest direct environmental impact relates to emissions of carbon dioxide. Our emissions arise from both transport – air and car – and office use." Two separate measures have been introduced – a carbon dioxide cap in the car fleet and a carbon offset scheme.

The company also aims to reduce energy consumption from office-based activities, reduce the paper consumption and disposal in all Enviros offices, and meet all relevant legislative compliance standards on hazardous substances.

Improvements already being progressed include: encouraging employees to travel to meetings by train or explore possibilities of teleconferencing where practicable; recycling office waste paper; encouraging the use of duplex printing capabilities; re-using paper printed on only one side; installing water saving devices, low-energy light fittings and Energy Star compliant computer monitors; and purchasing general purpose paper that has been produced using a chlorine-free pulp process, from a company with an ISO 14001 compliant management system.

"We use Xerox photocopiers because they recycle plastic parts and re-use the chassis," says Cattermole. "Offices in Shrewsbury and Manchester recycle tea-bags." But the best has to be the postcard by the light switch, which states "climate change" and depicts an on/off switch.

Ericsson

Ericsson Ltd
Midleton Gate, Guildford Business Park, Guildford, Surrey GU2 8SG
Tel: (0) 1483 303666 **Fax:** (0) 1483 305899
Web: www.ericsson.com

Pay and Benefits	7.1	Innovation	5.5
Promotion and Development	7.3	Diversity	5.4
Training	6.8	Social Responsibility	5.7
Travel opportunities	7.5	Corporate Governance	6.8
Culture	6.5	Environment	7.0
Total			**65.6**

Ericsson, founded in Sweden, is the largest supplier of mobile systems in the world. The ten largest mobile operators globally are among its customers, and some 40% of all mobile calls are made through its systems. The group provides total solutions from systems and applications to services and core technology for mobile handsets. Today, the group operates in more than 140 countries and employs 50,000 people worldwide, including 1,000 people in Britain. Worldwide headquarters are in Sweden; in the UK, the main office is at Guildford.

Executive summary

Founded in Stockholm in 1876 by a telegraph equipment repairer, Lars Magnus Ericsson, the group's growth and profits accelerated exponentially during the nineties boom in telecommunications. At its peak, the group went from 70,000 employees to more than 100,000 worldwide.

Along with industry competitors, Ericsson suffered a downturn following the crash of the late nineties, and for two years sank below profitability and was forced to implement severe cuts. With rapid downsizing, the number of employees has since halved; in the UK, the workforce was cut from 5,000 to 1,000 people in a redundancy programme that was overseen amicably in conjunction with the trade unions.

"The challenge was to retain Ericsson's heart and soul," comments Phil Hooper, the UK's human resources director. "Together with the workforce and with the union, we did it in a very proactive, positive, involving way. It was a huge challenge, and a hard task, but we managed the process well, came through, and can see the benefits."

In 2003, the company returned, cautiously, to profit; and results released in 2004 show that it may well have weathered the storm, although conditions remain tight. With a still-heavy debt burden on operators, the group is now looking to develop other opportunities, such as managed services and enterprise channels.

Pay and benefits

Ericsson's approach to compensation is fairly standard. It offers base pay that is median within the marketplace, complemented by performance-related pay that brings the total reward into the upper quartile. Pay for key strategic teams within the group – "market hotspots" – may be higher than for others. During straitened times, Ericsson was not able to pay bonuses although it did "maintain the momentum" of salaries. "We want our people to have a good standard of living and not be looking over their shoulders at other companies," says Hooper.

The more senior an employee becomes, the larger the proportion of pay that is variable; senior executives are also rewarded in company shares. The group runs a matched-share scheme where employees who buy a share are given one free in return.

For key contributors and senior executives, that ratio rises.

There are awards for innovation within the business, including financial recognition for high-level ideas that will impact the business. Although many employees have been with the group since graduating, there is no award for long service.

Ericsson still runs a defined benefits pension scheme, for which all employees are eligible. More than 85% of workers are now members of the scheme. Managers are given the option of cash instead of a car, and can sign up for free corporate health insurance – other staff receive a discount on this. While there is no subsidised gym membership, there are sports and social clubs within the group.

Other benefits for employees include subsidised canteens at offices in Guildford, Newbury and Basingstoke; and free tea and coffee throughout the day.

Promotion and development

Ericsson's policy is to develop people within the business as much as possible, and to recruit from within. In times past, it would recruit 200 graduates a year, but in 2004 this figure was down to twenty. However, with the group's global reach, traineeships are still highly sought after.

Some training is outsourced: there is, for example, a formal management programme for "high-potentials" run in conjunction with the London Business School and Manchester Business School; and a small number of executives from across the globe attend bespoke two-week courses at international business schools including Harvard and INSEAD, which focus on broader corporate issues alongside personal development.

"We like to fast-track people," says Hooper. "We send them to an assessment centre and give them a mentor who will work with them over a number of years. We like people to have a rounded set of skills; so someone with the potential to be a managing director will get exposure in sales and in other disciplines."

Sponsorship of training undertaken outside Ericsson's own auspices, such as an MBA, must be linked to the job. The group sees training as an investment, not as a cost; but it "must be a sensible investment". Aspirations towards enterprise are treated sympathetically, says Hooper. "This is a place where you will never hear 'no'."

Overseas placements generally last two to five years and are seen as very much part of an employee's development. Typically, 10% of the UK workforce will be people who are on placement from abroad.

Company culture

Ericsson recently issued all employees with a booklet entitled Our Ways of Working, which outlines the company's vision and values: professionalism, respect and perseverance. The last of these has certainly been tested in recent years, but testament to the group's appeal is the fact that a number of previous employees who were made redundant are now reapplying to work for Ericsson again.

People who work at Ericsson work in a matrix: they tend to be focused, delivery-oriented, and have good influencing and relationship skills. They are people who can cope with both the need to deliver, and the need to adapt to change. Management at Ericsson functions in a similar way – the management culture is results-driven, but prides itself on doing things the right way while taking care to be responsive. Employees meet senior staff through regular Q&A sessions and smaller breakfast gatherings, and are asked to complete an annual satisfaction survey; a mini-survey during the year checks up on whether improvements are being carried out. Meetings with Amicus, the union, are held on a monthly basis.

The group has a "hard work rather than long hours" culture – employees might put in more hours to meet a deadline, but will not work overtime otherwise. As part of the group's commitment to work/life balance, it has teamed up with LifeWorks to offer a counselling service to all employees, dispensing advice and help on medical and lifestyle issues – anything from stress management to help with elderly parents. This service has seen a high take-up, says Hooper.

The group permits homeworking and part-time work for most employees, although managers are required to work the hours that are necessary.

Innovation

The group says that it values innovation as an inherent and vital part of its culture. The establishment of innovation workshops – which all employees attend – aims to tap into creativity and provide tools and techniques to harness this. "It's about mindset change," explains Hooper. "We can get very focused on our tasks, and with these workshops we are trying to give people the mind-space to work in a different way."

This commitment to innovate is echoed strongly within management and with the focus on a move into managed services. "We don't want to repeat mistakes of the past," says Hooper. "We were so busy delivering for today that we didn't see what was happening over the horizon. We are now very aware of the importance of business intelligence – of what our customers are going to be looking for this year and the year after, and how we can help them to become more efficient and make better use of their investment in their networks."

Diversity and social responsibility

As a technology-oriented business, Ericsson is aware that there are "still too many men" within its ranks, and has publicly stated that it wants to increase the ratio of female managers. However, while in the UK there is a new female managing director, progress in raising this profile within the group is hampered by a lack of role models and lack of general interest.

"If only 5% of graduates applying to us are female, then we will have a problem," comments Hooper. "We don't practise positive discrimination, but we are very aware of the issue and committed to addressing this imbalance."

Because of its global reach, a diverse mix of people work for the group and a good proportion of management is non-Caucasian; although as yet there is no specific drive towards diversity other than the standard equal opportunities policy.

Tough times recently have meant that Ericsson, in the UK, has cut back on charitable activities, although it continues to work with local schools offering visits, open evenings and presentations, and giving away its used IT equipment. It will also sponsor employees who initiate their own fundraising events.

On a global level, the group runs Ericsson Response, an initiative aimed at alleviating human suffering caused by disasters. The group has provided specialist volunteers and communications equipment for relief work in Iran, Liberia, Iraq and Algeria; as well as to the UN World Food Programme. The company donated cash and communications equipment, and sent volunteers from the company in response to the tsunami disaster in Asia earlier this year.

Corporate governance

Ericsson endeavours to be "a good citizen", an attitude that stems from its Swedish origins of social democracy (broadly speaking, an awareness of its responsibilities to the community and to the environment).

Recently, the group issued a code of business ethics to every employee, which provided an outline of how the group would operate in the future as an organisation. All employees were asked to sign the document.

"We are looking at where we are compliant and where there are gaps. We are looking at local policies and how they link in to Ericsson's wider policies. We are looking at the legislation, and conducting internal and external audits," says Hooper.

"Corporate governance is increasingly important in business, and we have a worldwide project team of compliance officers whose job it is to make sure that we comply."

Risk is mainly considered at board level. "We are assiduous in checking up on IR35 policies; and if contractors don't fulfil our criteria, they don't work for us," adds Hooper.

Environmental record

On a global level, the group is committed to continuous improvement of the environmental performance of all of its products, services and operations; taking action to reduce the energy consumption of products while in use, and phasing out banned and restricted materials in production. It also consolidated a worldwide Ecology Management recycling scheme to take back and recycle used equipment. Goals for 2004 included evaluating the impact of the EU directive on the prevention of waste of electrical and electronic equipment (WEEE).

In the UK, the group is following all the standard practices of recycling and reducing waste. One decision taken at UK level was to lay on minibuses for employees who wanted to go into Guildford at lunchtimes in order to save fuel, cut down emissions and reduce – if only fractionally – the heavy levels of congestion in Guildford. The minibus service also runs to and from the main train station. Elsewhere in Britain, the group sponsored a local bus service that was free for employees, and available to members of the public for a small charge.

"Reducing the use of cars is something we can make an impact in," says Hooper. "In other areas it can be more difficult, but the intent is there."

Essex County Council

Essex County Council
PO Box 11, County Hall, Chelmsford, Essex CM1 1LX
Tel: (0) 1245 430200 **Fax:** (0) 1245 351324
Web: www.essexxcc.gov.uk

Essex County Council

Pay and Benefits	6.6	Innovation	6.2
Promotion and Development	7.0	Diversity	7.1
Training	6.3	Social Responsibility	6.8
Travel opportunities	3.4	Corporate Governance	6.9
Culture	6.0	Environment	7.3
Total			**63.6**

Essex, the second-largest county in England, is very diverse: London suburbs, army garrisons, new towns, Stansted airport, a long coastline and big rural expanses. Essex County Council provides public services for this region, particularly education and social care; but also roads, spatial planning, trading standards, waste management, and so on. It has a budget of £1.2bn to deliver these services and employs 40,000 people including 25,000 teaching and support staff, and 4,000 in community care. The administrative function is found in Chelmsford town centre. In the government's Comprehensive Performance Assessment, Essex currently rates as "good" overall.

Executive Summary

Conservative-run Essex County Council is focused on providing high-quality, excellent value-for-money services. Council leader Lord Hanningfield sets the tone: "there are a number of challenges to be addressed if we are to make the most of our strengths. We have to balance the needs of housing and transport with creating a cleaner, greener Essex. It's getting harder to find the teachers and social workers we need to improve our services. And for the county council, we have to balance meeting the demands for services with not overburdening the Essex taxpayer."

In addition to its "good" overall rating (which it is striving to raise to "excellent"), Essex has received many national and regional recognition awards for procurement policies; services to the community, including adoption; and equality and diversity.

While there is always talk about regionalisation, the resounding "No" vote in the North East on regional government means that Essex County Council is likely to be around for some time. Services always need providing and managing. However, some things have changed and Essex, like many other councils, is now an enabler rather than a deliverer of many services. Essex's budget is provided by central government grants, and the balance from council tax. It endeavours to keep rises to the minimum.

Pay and Benefits

The Employers Organisation, the national body that negotiates pay for local government, cites the pay structure at Essex as a Best Practice Case Study. While local government pay rates are set at national level, each authority has some leeway to vary local pay rates. So Essex "keeps an eye" on competitors, particularly where there are shortages (teachers and social workers both fit this description); and using the National Pay Awards as a base, tops-up with market factor salary supplements.

For its top 150 managers, Essex has moved away from national negotiations entirely to reward performance. Up to 15% bonus pay can be earned, measured against individual objectives and competencies. Since the Single Status agreement was reached nationally in 1997 for manual and blue-collar workers, they too benefit from a performance-driven component. Middle management has a broad range of grades with many increments. "We have built career pathways through the bands and people can jump increments," says Lorraine Pitt, head of human resources. "The performance element is more important than moving along a scale."

There are many supportive policies and benefits in place. "We look to attract people fed-up with commuting to London," adds Pitt. So term-time working, compressed working hours, flexible hours and career breaks with job return guaranteed are all valued by people who are otherwise difficult to recruit.

There is a good final salary pension scheme, with employees' contributions of 6% doubled by their employer. There is BUPA medical insurance and cars for managers at certain levels. A sports and social club is on site. The excellent staff development programme is seen as a benefit in its own right. The council is also working on options for key worker housing.

Promotion and development

Essex has been quite pioneering in implementing a Competency Framework, which integrates all of its people policies and covers relevant skills such as partnership working, leadership, interpersonal skills and organisational awareness. Delivering against competencies is tied-in with pay.

Around 2,000 people are recruited each year. Councillors make the key decisions on senior people, managers at other levels; with both supported by HR. Essex runs an in-house assessment centre to gauge applicants' abilities. Having moved away from a traditional experience/hierarchy approach, all appointments are made against the competency framework and all promotion opportunities are open to anyone internally.

"It's now all about identifying the abilities in candidates," says Pitt. "We're trying to encourage movement across the old service 'silos', which we're trying to get rid of." The general point is Essex supporting its people to retrain and acquire the necessary qualifications – for example in teaching. "It's not always easy to recruit. Growing our own is a vital plank in our strategy," says Pitt. "Many people have been here a long time and love working for Essex. We're building on that."

The Graduate Trainee Scheme recruits from within and externally. After six months, each spent in four different service areas, graduates are given a year of further support, after which they pursue a "real role". Graduates also take a Diploma in Management accredited by the University of Greenwich. Some continue on to Masters degrees. A £25,000 starting salary is an added attraction.

Modules are offered against each of the 12 competencies, and employees study at their own pace. Professional qualifications are supported financially, as are courses recognised by City & Guilds and the Institute of Management and Leadership. Staff can access the array of adult educational services provided by the council, which also runs its own NVQ centres.

Training is assessed by the needs of the organisation and is designed to help deliver quality services. Around 1% of the salary bill is reinvested into training. "We're trying to give everyone the opportunity to get on the ladder," says Pitt. "The opportunity for development is strong here, and people value that."

Company culture

Inevitably, in such a large and diverse organisation, many cultures happily coexist. But overall, Essex County Council has shifted from being inward-looking to a clear focus on its customers in the community it serves. Everything is designed with that in mind.

The change began five years ago, when a series of hung councils became a strong Conservative majority. Key appointments were made and the council replaced big directorates with a core administrative unit, with customer-facing service heads freed up to deliver services; all backed up by professionals in finance, HR and communications.

HR initiatives put in place to support this include the competency framework, pay structures, and the training and development programme.

Organisational change soon evolved into cultural change. There were many drivers for this: increasing central government assessments and inspections, high expectations from the community, and employees becoming increasingly aware of their rights.

New chief executive Paul Coen's style is very inclusive and non-hierarchical, giving space and empowerment to front-line staff. This is not a top-down culture though. At team briefings, staff are encouraged to give opinions; and staff feedback from roadshows undertaken by Coen and Lord Hanningfield is very positive: "I did not really fancy coming [to the meeting]...but I feel very inspired about what the county council is actually doing and working towards, and feel privileged to be part of it and knowing that what I do matters."

Finding a work/life balance is seen as important in attracting and retaining staff, and the council provides a lot of options on flexible working. It must tie-in with service delivery however, and HR gives managers considerable guidance as to what they can and cannot do.

HR is an integral and valued function. Lorraine Pitt sits on the Strategic Management Board, allowing HR to understand clearly the direction of the organisation and to formulate what the department can do to support it.

Innovation

Essex County Council's Competency Framework is at the forefront of innovative practice in local government. "It's simple, and practical, and helps you measure things," asserts Pitt. Essex has been signed up by the Office of the Deputy Prime Minister to work on a national skills framework for local government. There's been a lot of interest from other local authorities and Pitt is a frequent speaker on the conference circuit.

In social care, Essex County Council's work in conferencing with family members has been acclaimed for its success in getting family members to take responsibility for their actions, and achieving a broader "family sign-up" instead of the traditional one-to-one counselling.

Diversity and social responsibility

An equal opportunities employer without question, Essex County Council stresses that it is more about equal access to service opportunity and delivery – through flexible working, provision for carers, and so on. "We really do want a diverse workforce," says Pitt. "It makes us more effective as a council and reflects the community that we serve. The Competency Framework has been crucial to this."

All councils are required by government to monitor diversity on ethnicity, disability, age and gender. The evidence at Essex is a top rating in the Best Value Indicators on Equality. 50% of the senior managers in the organisation are female – including three of the six-strong Strategic Management Board – and the same can be said of age and ethnic minority mix. The council does a lot of work with "difficult to reach groups"; and with the age discrimination bill due soon, it has already relaxed the requirement to retire at 65.

As to social responsibility, this is the whole reason for the council's being! Going beyond statutory requirements, Essex really provides community leadership; guiding other agencies and listening to what the local community thinks is important – be that the state of the roads or fear of crime. The feedback mechanisms are questionnaires, MORI surveys, focus groups, and a gamut of enthusiastic hands-on councillors and district councils.

Corporate Governance

As a public body, good governance has to be "seen to be open and open to be seen". Everything that the council does is necessarily transparent. Council meetings are public meetings that are reported and publicised. Accounts are published, and the public can see clearly where and how its £1.2bn is spent. There is a range of policies to support employment law including grievance, bullying and harassment policies; disciplinary codes; and dispute resolution procedures. To make this information as digestible as possible, it's all published on the intranet; and support is given to all staff and managers involved in governance procedures.

Essex is inclusive with the trade unions, with whom it has a very good relationship. Regular meetings are held to discuss changes. While there have sometimes been hard decisions to take, the council has been very open in terms of consultation and communication, and the unions have been very realistic – the signs of a good partnership.

Environmental record

Essex County Council is responsible for waste management strategy, including recycling and how local waste is disposed of. Cabinet member, Kay Twitchen OBE, is chairman of the Waste Management Advisory Board, a partnership of all Essex local authorities.

With landfill sites scarce and the Landfill Tax increasing, Essex looks for innovative ways to dispose of waste. Its new waste approach is anaerobic digestion; after recyclable materials have been extracted, the organic waste is ground up and mixed with water to produce a pulp. The pulp is then digested by naturally occurring micro organisms that thrive in the enclosed, anaerobic (absence of oxygen) conditions. A biogas is produced in the digestion process, which can be used to generate heat and electricity.

Internally, the council walks the talk on paper recycling. It encourages car sharing to drive to work (the incentive is free parking) and flexible working is partly aimed at reducing congestion. It is currently working on a new Park and Ride scheme in Chelmsford. There is a large cycle shed at County Hall and a maze of cycle paths in the county.

Eversheds

Eversheds
Senator House, 85 Queen Victoria Street, London EC4V 4JL
Tel: (0) 20 7919 4500
Web: www.eversheds.com

Pay and Benefits	6.8	Innovation	7.0
Promotion and Development	5.5	Diversity	6.0
Training	6.5	Social Responsibility	6.5
Travel opportunities	4.0	Corporate Governance	6.25
Culture	6.25	Environment	5.0
Total			**59.8**

Eversheds may have its roots in the provinces, but "regional" is no longer a tag the firm would recognise. This is the world's third-largest law firm and the UK's largest if you count the number of fee-earners – it has over 2,130 legal and business advisers around the world, most in the UK but 300 in overseas locations (22 offices in Europe, the far east, and the Gulf). It is placed second only to Freshfields in the numbers of FTSE 250 companies it advises, and simultaneously has an impressive client list among SMEs. Its services are backed up by an award-winning Client Relationship Management programme which is unique among conventional law firms; "it aims to turn the old-fashioned way of offering legal advice on its head by putting clients at the heart of our business".

Executive summary

The Eversheds partnership has come a long way very quickly – a regional law firm with a London HQ but a disparate set of local offices has become one of the country's largest commercial law firms; with a coherent national and international portfolio, a demonstrable commitment to all of its staff, and heavy investment in a cutting-edge approach to client relationship management which is now paying dividends.

Turnover for the financial year to April 2004 was up 4% to £296m with net profits virtually static at £56.7m. This is well in line with the industry average; in a year when legal firms were finding markets getting generally tougher, Eversheds' investment in client relationships and its pursuit of overseas business seemed to be paying off.

It is all too easy for a law firm to enforce traditional distinctions between fee-earners and the support staff. At Eversheds the boundaries are more blurred: certainly there is little concern for different status levels within the firm when it comes to staff benefits, and the recent introduction of a profit-linked bonus scheme for all has certainly emphasised the value of the non-fee-earner to the firm's reputation and its ability to deliver.

Pay and benefits

Eversheds aims to provide a total remuneration package that is above average for its market sector, and uses benchmark comparison studies to check this – not just for fee-earners but also for support staff (for the first time in 2004) and for legal advisers and business services (in 2005 and 2006 respectively).

All employees are entitled to the same level and type of benefits, the basic holiday entitlement of 27 days is well above the average for law firms, and childcare benefit is available to all.

There is also an innovative flexible working programme called Lifestyle – anyone at any level is eligible to apply and a whole range of different options are available from career breaks (available for between one and five years, after the employee has completed three years' service) to remote working via shift work, jobshares and self-rostered teams (the team as a whole commits to cover the hours required). Lifestyle is not an entitlement: all requests will be assessed against the needs of the business and some may be rejected. Most applications are approved, however, and applicants are not asked to give reasons for their desire to flexi-work.

The profit-related bonus scheme, which is now in its second year, is open to all qualifying employees and not just legal advisers. The scheme guarantees a minimum bonus if the budgeted profit is achieved; for 2003–04 the bonus payment was £455 for each eligible employee.

The company's Vision and Values Recognition Scheme is just completing its first year. Eversheds rewards outstanding behaviour that supports its values (client-centred, straightforward, teamwork, mutual respect, accountability, continuous improvement). Colleagues nominate recipients who receive a monetary reward allocated to their Choices account. Choices is an online discount shopping site for all staff, accessed through the firm's intranet with a good range of discounts and a wide mix of products and services.

Childcare vouchers are offered as an alternative to providing crèche facilities; this effectively enables employees to make National Insurance savings on approved childcare costs, and participants get discounts at approved nurseries plus access to a parent advice helpline.

Promotion and development

All Eversheds people undertake an annual performance and development review (PDR) with a six-monthly follow-up, which aims to identify individual strengths and development opportunities. Everyone, including partners and senior managers, are required to go through the same review process.

Flexibility in PDRs allows scope for individuals to follow their interests. There's also the imaginative Career Pathways scheme, which provides fully trained in-house careers advisers to provide information and advice to all non-fee-earners, analysing the individual's goals and proposing a suitable career plan to achieve them. Given the firm's size and range of activities, there are many options for a change of direction or a change of geography.

A variety of feedback mechanisms have been developed – a full-company attitude survey ran for the first time in 2003, with smaller and more frequent surveys in 2004. The award-winning Have Your Say programme is designed to elicit general feedback on specific issues, and the managing partner visits local offices regularly to discuss issues of importance with a wide range of colleagues.

There is generous funding for training, with an open-minded interpretation of the value of personal development. Eversheds sponsors MBAs and professional qualifications, and it is keen on NVQs for support staff. In addition to sponsored external learning, they run an extensive in-house curriculum ranging from half-day refresher sessions to intensive three-day residential workshops. On average, Eversheds expects to deliver 10 hours' learning to each person for "soft" skills and 30 hours for more technical learning.

The Eversheds group personal pension scheme, offered to all new employees on joining, is a defined contribution scheme open to all employees, including trainees, aged 18 and over; the firm matches contributions up to 5% of salary. For colleagues with more than 10 years' service, the matched contribution level rises to a maximum of 6%.

Company culture

Traditionally, law firms have not been regarded as providing the ideal working environment – rigid distinctions between fee-earners and support staff led to rudeness bordering on offensiveness, and a lack of mutual respect. Eversheds has done as much as any other law firm to change that image, and has taken the change further than most.

Eversheds promotes a culture of teamwork and mutual respect that is driven from the top. The firm's vision statement – "To be a great place to work and the most client-centred international law firm" – recognises that the quality and attitude of their people is critical to successful, long-term client relationships. It is recognised that investment in the company's people will pay dividends, and in the last year or two the arrival of specific programmes such as the profit-linked bonus scheme has underscored the message.

Working long hours is frowned upon at Eversheds, and it's not unknown for someone who is still in the office at 6.30pm to be advised to go home.

Innovation

Eversheds has introduced some groundbreaking products and services. A DVD explaining data protection is selling well; the firm is a leader in electronic delivery of information; and an extranet for clients is offering everything from document libraries and case management to e-training on competition rules. One argument for this emphasis on online services is that it cuts costs for the client, and makes it easier for them to judge how much Eversheds' services will be costing them.

That is a small example of the heavy investment Eversheds has made in client relationship management systems, particularly delivered via the web. Eversheds.com is a multi-faceted website that offers just about everything a client might need – knowledge banks, sector and business news, legal commentary and analysis, tailored extranet services, an interactive training site ... all from a single home page without separate logins. This multi-award winning technology is a world-class client portal.

Diversity and social responsibility

Diversity is inherent in this company's normal way of working, but there are also some interesting specific initiatives – for example, a Diversity Calendar has been produced highlighting religious and cultural occasions from across the world; Eversheds is actively looking at ways of celebrating both Christian and non-Christian festivals.

There is a detailed equality and diversity policy and an associated complaints procedure (which is rarely used). Eversheds regularly reviews policies, procedures and practices, and is committed to eliminate any unjustified discrimination or victimisation that is revealed by this monitoring process. The HR team is also responsible for some well-regarded material – factsheets and short courses – that explain diversity issues and remove the excuse of ignorance.

Eversheds isn't a place of entrenched attitudes, though. It is an open and outward-looking organisation when it comes to community involvement. For one thing, Eversheds is a member of Business in the Community's National Cares programme, the main business-led employee volunteering programme in the UK. The firm encourages its people to give up working time (though at no cost to themselves) to support local community activities.

The firm has a community service budget (in 2003, worth around £70,000), which is used to support local community charities and events. Eversheds will match donations from individuals who get involved in sponsored events and the like.

Eversheds is also active in providing work experience for school students. Working with local government Connexions teams, the firm provides a two-week work experience placement for students aged 15–17. The scheme allows students to develop work-related skills and appropriate attitudes, while dispelling the stereotypical perceptions of a law firm.

Women make up 62% of the staff and 14% of managers at Eversheds.

Corporate Governance

Eversheds is a Limited Liability Partnership, not a publicly quoted company with shareholders, and as such it is not covered by the codes of practice that the City has been promoting for the conduct of companies and their boards. Even so, a good deal of background information about Eversheds and the way it operates is in the public domain, particularly on the website.

Environmental record

Eversheds introduced an Environmental Purchasing Policy in 2004, part of an ongoing programme to decrease its use of energy and reduce waste. In-house recycling schemes, particularly for paper use, aim to inform and educate employees.

Gallaher

Gallaher Group Plc
Members Hil, Brooklands Road, Weybridge, Surrey KT13 0QU
Tel: (0) 1932 859777
Web: www.gallaher-group.com

Pay and Benefits	6.6	Innovation	4.4
Promotion and Development	6.2	Diversity	4.0
Training	6.4	Social Responsibility	4.0
Travel opportunities	5.4	Corporate Governance	6.2
Culture	5.2	Environment	4.6
Total			**53.0**

Gallaher Group is a tobacco company with a turnover of about £9bn that has outgrown its domestic origins to become an international player – especially in Europe and the CIS nations. The group reckons that every second of every day, over 5,000 people somewhere in the world light up a cigarette made by Gallaher. That translates as 160 billion cigarettes sold to 26 million consumers in 2003.

Gallaher's corporate strategy is to develop a balanced portfolio of interests in markets across Europe, the CIS and Asia Pacific – organically and through acquisitions and strategic alliances – capitalising on the group's proven ability to build brand equity.

Gallaher aims to be "the most effective, efficient, energetic and enthusiastic tobacco company we know". Given that it also operates in an environment laden with regulation and surrounded by health and ethical issues, the group works extremely hard to demonstrate a sense of responsibility and awareness. Gallaher has recently published a guide to smoking-related issues called Behaving Responsibly. This publication provides an overview of Gallaher's position on its corporate behaviour and aims to bring balance to the public debate on the issues surrounding smoking.

Executive summary

Since demerging from an American conglomerate in 1997, Gallaher Group has been transformed into the fifth-largest international tobacco company in the world – it employs around 10,000 people; manufactures in the UK, Russia, Kazakhstan, Austria, Sweden, Poland and Ukraine; sells in 65 countries; and includes brands such as Benson & Hedges, Silk Cut, Memphis, LD, Hamlet and Old Holborn.

Gallaher had turnover of £9bn in 2003 and reported profits of £627m – both over 7% on the year before and part of a continuing pattern of success. Prohibitions on advertising, the strength of sterling, and rises in tobacco duty in Europe are all hitting shares in some markets now; but there's impressive growth in other areas, particularly eastern Europe, where local brands are being displaced by demand for "western" cigarettes.

Gallaher is well aware of the issues surrounding its business, and it puts a lot of effort into being seen as a good corporate citizen. This inevitably includes an impressive degree of transparency in its business dealings, but it also appears in a sense of commitment to its people; Gallaher wants its reputation to be based as much on its approach to employees as on commercial success.

Pay and benefits

Gallaher is prepared to pay for quality; it ensures that it has very competitive salaries relative to the FMCG sector in the markets in which it operates.

Nationally, there are annual bonus schemes for most people. In the UK, all employees receive a variable amount, linked to the company's earnings per share but guaranteed to be at least 8% of salary. For senior management, there are bonus payments linked to appraisal targets and based on group performance.

20% of the group's employees are members of a save-as-you-earn scheme – similar benefits are gradually being introduced worldwide – and 13% have joined the Sharepurchase Share Incentive Plan (as soon as they join the group, employees are eligible to use up to £125 of their pre-tax pay each month to buy shares).

The usual social and sports clubs are available in most locations.

Gallaher's UK health insurance schemes include spouses and children below the age of 18. Each UK employee receives an annual Benefit Statement that details all elements of the remuneration package, share scheme participation, other company benefits and personal financial planning.

Gallaher believes that it operates a high-performance work culture. The company has clear connections between the way in which success in the business is measured and the way that teams and individuals are recognised and rewarded.

Promotion and development

Gallaher is committed to personal development and training, and takes the processes for promotion and development seriously as part of its continuous improvement philosophy.

New recruits are encouraged to have a personal development path with individually selected training as well as intensive and broad-based courses promoted by the HR department.

Sponsorship for MBAs and similar training is available; sabbaticals can be taken; and staff are frequently seconded to local projects such as Business in the Community (free business advice for start-ups). This is not a formalised process; all applications and requests are considered on their merits, but with a degree of flexibility that suggests any serious proposition will be accommodated. Gallaher has a successful Performance Management programme with some in-house management training, and external courses at Ashridge, Cranfield and INSEAD.

Gallaher has Investors In People status for the UK and is looking to apply the same standards to its international operations. The IIP standard requires that every employee should have a regular opportunity to discuss their own development with their employer, and that all personal development is in line with corporate objectives and the employee's development plan. Regular reviews, both internally and for the acceptance body, will ensure that the standard is maintained and improved upon.

Gallaher has grown primarily through international acquisition, and as a matter of policy it seeks to spread a Gallaher culture across all members of the group. The result: significant international opportunities for management.

The management team is relatively young, with senior positions held by people in their 30s and 40s. This inevitably produces an air of relative informality and flexibility. But it is also a long-service company; people tend to stick with Gallaher.

Company culture

The atmosphere at Gallaher's Weybridge HQ is relaxed, but there's a sense of commitment about most of the Gallaher people you meet. There's certainly a consensual management style and a belief that everyone in the business – at whatever level – can make a real difference. Gallaher regards itself as less bureaucratic than its competitors; even relatively junior people will have the opportunity to develop and run real-world projects.

A strikingly flat management structure helps: there are only seven steps from shop floor to executive director level. The CEO tours the international and UK sites each year with an open and informal question-and-answer roadshow where anyone can put any question.

There is a sophisticated approach to HR. The head of group human resources who deals with strategy sits on the group's management committee – the key source of operational strategy – and HR is viewed as having an important contribution to make to the success of the company.

Innovation

The regulatory constraints on marketing, and the ethical and health issues, produce a challenging environment for the company itself and for the people who choose to work in it.

One result is that marketing has to be particularly creative; many of the best-remembered ads have been for Gallaher products (Hamlet, Silk Cut) and Gallaher products are regularly at the top of brand recognition lists (B&H, Hamlet, Old Holborn, Silk Cut).

Another result is a sense of commitment among the management teams – not so much an "us against them" attitude as a sense that the group has to be better than the average company in order to justify its commercial position.

More conventionally, Gallaher has a good track record in process innovation – the Gallaher bag is an industry standard for reusable tobacco sacks. Novel design in product and packaging has also seen successful introductions like a fliptop pack for Amber Leaf rolling tobacco, and through a joint venture, the Reynolds slide pack.

Diversity and Corporate responsibility

There is much emphasis on local, regional and national cultures at Gallaher. The company is aware of the importance of a coherent and consistent image across the group, but the rush of acquisitions – especially in the last five years – could have led to the imposition of a central culture. Instead, the pattern of integration appears to be very smooth; Gallaher policies and best practices are encouraged throughout, but local identities are retained.

More formally, Gallaher has produced and follows a whole range of well-documented corporate, employee, environmental and community policies that demonstrate a commitment to corporate responsibility.

This includes an ongoing community involvement. Gallaher contributes significantly to local community projects, typically selected by a committee of employees.

The company also operates a Give As You Earn scheme; the employee can nominate a charity to receive up to £1,200 a year from their salary, which Gallaher will match.

Gallaher's approach to its corporate responsibility activities goes right up to the top level: there is a corporate responsibility board committee made up of the group operations director, group commercial director and group company secretary.

Gallaher also recognises its responsibilities as a tobacco manufacturer, and acknowledges the health risks associated with smoking. It operates a number of policies governing the group's conduct in the manufacture, distribution and marketing of its products; and while it reserves the right to argue for freedom of individual choice, it is firm in its belief that smokers should be fully aware of the health risks associated with smoking and that children should be dissuaded from smoking. In many countries, for instance, its tobacco products carry health warnings that exceed local requirements.

Gallaher has voluntarily established an online archive of documents as a contribution to the debate on smoking (www.gallaher-docs.com).

Gallaher achieved a score of over 79% in the 2003 Business in the Community Corporate Responsibility Index, making it one of the Top 100 Companies that Count in the UK. The BITC observed that Gallaher demonstrates "leadership in the open and transparent way in which it manages, measures and reports."

Corporate Governance

As part of its commitment to good corporate governance, Gallaher has laid down policies that govern the group's conduct generally and in the specific terms required by the code announced by the Financial Reporting Council in July 2003.

These are underpinned by detailed internal policies that provide operational guidance and direction. During 2003, the board and each of the audit, nomination and remuneration committees started a regime of annual performance evaluations to appraise whether they are operating effectively on behalf of all stakeholders. So far, the results have been satisfactory.

The company secretary has overall responsibility for monitoring and maintaining the required level of corporate governance at Gallaher.

Environmental record

The group's environment policy is published on the company website. It requires group companies to seek out cost-effective opportunities to improve standards of environmental performance.

Gallaher also charges its companies to develop systems for the management and measurement of environmental performance, to be consistent with the principles of internationally recognised standards, and to comply with all relevant national and local environmental legislation.

As a matter of policy, group companies are required to take steps to ensure that wastes which cannot be reprocessed on site are disposed of in such a way that they can (in order of preference) be recycled for the same, or an alternative use; or that the energy they contain can be recovered; or that they are subject to a disposal process which minimises the environmental impact of such waste. Typically, operating locations have waste paper recycling and collection systems in place. Group manufacturing facilities achieved an average recycling rate of 56.8% in 2003.

The group operations director is the board director responsible for environmental and health and safety (EHS) topics group-wide, and the corporate responsibility committee of the board includes these matters within its remit. The group EHS committee coordinates group operational aspects, including monitoring performance against environmental objectives and targets. The group EHS department has advisory and auditing functions. Information about EHS policies and procedures is published on the group intranet in a dedicated EHS area as well as through team briefings, internal publications and location committees. The website features a description of EHS management systems, objectives, targets and performance; including annual EHS reports and statistics.

The group participates in the annual BITC Corporate Responsibility Index, which includes the Business in the Environment (BiE) Environmental Engagement Index. The group is benchmarked in the non-cyclical consumer goods sector of the Index. In the BiE Index for March 2004, the group scored its best ever result (76.73%). It was ranked 14th out of 23 in the sector.

GCHQ

GCHQ
Hubble Road, Cheltenham, Gloucestershire GL51 0EX
Tel: (0) 1242 232912/3
Web: www.gchq.gov.uk **E-mail:** recruitment@gchq.gsi.gov.uk

Pay and Benefits	Innovation
Promotion and Development	Diversity
Training	Social Responsibility
Travel opportunities	Corporate Governance
Culture	Environment

Total - GCHQ is exempt from the scoring system

GCHQ – Government Communications Headquarters – is an intelligence and security organisation based in Cheltenham, with some 4,500 staff. One of the country's three intelligence agencies (with MI5 and MI6), GCHQ is a civil service department. Key customers are the Ministry of Defence, the Foreign and Commonwealth Office and law enforcement authorities; but GCHQ also serves a range of other government departments. The intelligence agencies share an intelligence budget of around £1bn and GCHQ deals in the most sensitive and detailed analytical work. Their work can often be highly time critical, but despite this there's a terrific working atmosphere. "Get what you do right and noone's ever going to know; get it wrong and events could be catastrophic."

Executive summary

GCHQ is not a commercial organisation, but it does have demanding customers. Indeed the phrase "time-to-market" is more critical when applied to GCHQ than it is to commercial organisations as lives depend on deadlines here. GCHQ has two missions – signals intelligence and information assurance. Signals work protects the vital interests of the nation, while information assurance helps keep government communication and information systems safe from hackers and other threats. A £1bn budget is spread across all three intelligence agencies (GCHQ, MI5 and MI6) and GCHQ is "required to make sure we provide the best service we can for the money we get."

GCHQ competes with open source intelligence but it works to priorities set by the Joint Intelligence Committee, and the agency's success can be measured (e.g. the effects on drugs, terrorism, etc.). The department works within a legal framework and is supervised by the Intelligence and Security Committee and the Intelligence Services and Interception Commissioners. The government's continued investment in GCHQ can be measured through the new £308m Cheltenham offices opened in 2003 in a PFI deal.

It's critical for GCHQ to get the best out of its people. The intelligence product is tailored, involving much liaison with customers – meaning GCHQ deals less in general "product" than it does in ensuring a bespoke service to fit customer needs.

Pay and benefits

While there are few disaffected staff at GCHQ, many will not be stampeding there for the money. That said, graduate starting salaries are very competitive (£18,100–£20,500), while for other jobs "competitive" salaries are offered. Senior staff equate to senior civil servants elsewhere in the UK. The key to working at GCHQ is the excellent work/life balance. Retention rates among staff are high – only 1.5% left in 2003–04 (an "exceptional year" as the average is 3.2%). Most of the 4,500 staff are based in Cheltenham, but some are at outstations in Bude and Scarborough. Others may be on assignments. Salaries are in line with general civil service scales and are linked to performance. Pension options are great – a final-salary occupational scheme enabling a maximum of two-thirds final salary after 40 years' service (with 3.5% contribution) or a money-purchase "partnership" scheme with a choice of contribution rates.

Most staff work 5-day weeks of 37 hours with flexitime, accumulation of extra leave and varied start/finish times. As well as 10.5 days' public/privilege holidays, the basic leave allowance is 22 days – rising to 25 days after a year and up to 30 days after 10 years. Benefits include maternity and paternity benefits; a holiday play scheme; a welfare service; help with overseas and domestic relocation; and the Wellbeing Suite, which offers aromatherapy, massage, pilates, yoga, etc. The new building (christened "the doughnut" due to its shape) offers improved catering facilities and cafeterias, a restaurant, shop and breakout areas. An impressive range of sporting pursuits is available through the Cheltenham Area Civil Service Sports Association.

Why stay here? There's no arrogance. It's a team-based organisation with a culture where people recognise ability, not whether your face fits. GCHQ provides you with opportunities based on all you can do.

Promotion and development

Training and development are a big deal here. "You're looking at a mixed economy of breadth, depth and choice – people who aren't satisfied can pursue career paths that press their buttons." Staff are at GCHQ for the business, but the department recognises that a pragmatic approach is required in order to deliver the product and meet the career aspirations of the individual. Certainly the organisation is full of opportunity and change, so a balance has to be struck. The fact is, they've got a really serious job to do.

GCHQ has been accredited to Investors in People since the late 90s, winning many awards. There are other accreditations: to BCS, IEE and IIE; and to maths, linguist and librarian information scientist schemes. There's sponsorship for public service MBA programmes, MSc and MA courses, and Open University degrees (eg someone did a degree in psychology).

Staff enjoy an average of 7.5 working days' training a year. A leadership and management skills development programme has been running since 1998. Senior management courses (for those in position for some time) cover topics such as being better at mentoring, handling conflict, etc. Sharing best practice is encouraged. A government management trainee scheme operates into which anyone can be recruited – there's no block on age, the proviso being that you must give 5 years' service prior to retirement and meet the qualification criteria (variable depending on requirements). People move around the organisation in accordance with a negotiated development plan for each individual, and on average move posts every 3 years or so.

Company culture

In GCHQ, neither age nor length of service is an issue – the things that matter are ability and the individual concerned. GCHQ's values rely on openness and respect for each other. The advice is to challenge senior managers who are not adhering to the values. Senior management has signed up to this, and are not just paying lip service. The key point is that people are empowered to do something if there is a problem and if it cannot be resolved in an informal manner; individuals then have recourse to a formal grievance process, which will deal with the problem independently and objectively.

Everyone's performance is governed and monitored through a series of competencies. Objectives for the year are drawn up, together with a personal development plan and the training needs to do the job. There's a minimum of one formal mid-year review of performance. The thrust is that you know what's expected of you at GCHQ. The culture is not about telling people how bad they are – it is more of a coaching environment.

There's also a general disinterest in bits of paper; for example, if someone has an MBA, the interest is not in the qualification but in the ability of the person. The organisation is more interested in who the person is and what they do. There's no real policy on qualifications except in the professional strands; a trainee auditor, for example, would need to gain a qualification before passing to the next grade because that job cannot be done without a recognised qualification. Careers in the department can be viewed as vocational, except in those areas where professional qualifications are mandatory.

Innovation

While GCHQ is spending public money, it does so wisely. The list of innovative schemes is proactive and engaging, and includes: improving reading and maths in local schools (with its acknowledged depth of mathematical skills, it is well-placed to address difficult matters in schools' programmes); drawing up a business plan for the underprivileged through the Cheltenham Credit Union; working with community projects in a nearby EU Regeneration Area; mentoring people at university; engaging youngsters for careers in engineering through the Smallpeice Trust; arranging a six-month secondment to the Prince's Trust; and running an NVQ management programme. It also takes an active role in the Cheltenham Science Festival. Socially, GCHQ helps a hospice in Devon, and sponsors people to compete in the Challenger Trophy.

In terms of general innovation, the company believes "there are decided things we must do to keep our business alive". GCHQ points to published achievements in maths such as PKC (Public Key Cryptography), which was actually developed in the 1970s by one of GCHQ's senior mathematicians. One can infer GCHQ will be doing more of this.

Over the past couple of years, GCHQ has collected plenty of awards, including Recruitment Awards for Innovation and the Integrated Marketing Award (2002, 2003) presented by the Association of Graduate Recruiters.

Diversity and social responsibility

GCHQ values diversity, and an individual has been appointed to ensure "everything we do is done with a view to ensuring we provide opportunities for all". Policies and practices have been developed to help create a more diverse workforce – such as signing up to the Commission for Racial Equality's Leadership Challenge and being awarded a Gold Star in the Opportunity Now benchmarking exercise. GCHQ takes part in positive action schemes such as the Windsor Fellowship Programme and Civil Service Summer Development Programme (development programmes aimed at providing members of ethnic minority communities with summer work placements and opportunities to work in a government department).

The organisation adheres to the Department of Employment's Disability Two Ticks standard, which is awarded to disability-friendly employers. GCHQ is happy to make reasonable adjustments to assist those with disabilities in the workplace, and provide specialist assistance for those with hidden disabilities such as dyslexia and dyspraxia. Such was its application in this area that it won awards for its dyslexia toolkit, which was developed by GCHQ and a consultant and has now been adopted by the Cabinet Office for use across government. Floor areas near lifts in "the doughnut" have been textured to assist partially sighted users.

Corporate governance

GCHQ is an organisation that looks forward but equally recognises its heritage. It's an organisation that wishes to proclaim its work/life ethos – while doing the most secret work, and simultaneously and actively seeking to maintain a low profile. That's not exactly easy. Staff surveys show more than 90% of the workforce are committed to GCHQ's success, and more than 80% expect to be there for the next 20 years. But there are still lots of things to get better at.

There's a corporate governance team to ensure "we're in line for legal reasons"; and there's a set of systems, independent of everyone, "to keep us honest". GCHQ's statutory foundation is defined by the Intelligence Services Act (1994); and there's obvious compliance with the Data Protection Act, Disability Discrimination, and the Human Rights Act. Legal advice has been beefed up. A corporate planning group ensures everyone does all the right things. The legality of everything that is core to the business is the responsibility of these teams. All that is non-core – say, the running of the building, catering, security, heating, etc. with all its attendant regulations and commitments – is the responsibility of the service provider team, which is part of the PFI consortium.

Environmental record

"The doughnut" has proved a big step up for the organisation in environmental terms; it features solar glass, chilled beam and air recycling technology, and remote presence-sensing lighting controls. It is an intelligent building that has to function 24x7x365. A green transport policy operates – and not only because local council planning rules dictated there would be fewer car parking spaces. GCHQ has invested in cycle paths, lighting, walkways, bus routes, park and ride schemes; and a car sharing service, which is run through the intranet. The percentage of cyclists in Cheltenham is actually higher than the national average, because of the organisation's investments in cycling schemes. The department has also recently been voted "the UK's most motorcycle-friendly employer".

Staff suggested the recycling of cups, newspapers, glass bottles and cans. Printer cartridges are recycled, and some redundant equipment (eg computer monitors) can be donated to local schools. Toilets are designed to flush economically, and schemes to cut down on waste are pervasive.

All of these actions meld well with the sense emanating from GCHQ – of culture and purpose opportunity (you have control and choice), improvement (aim high constantly) and commitment (to a dynamic approach to meet today's threats).

GlaxoSmithKline

G

GlaxoSmithKline
GSK House, 980 Great West Road, Brentford, Middlesex TW8 9GS
Tel: (0) 20 8047 5000
Web: www.gsk.com

gsk
GlaxoSmithKline

Pay and Benefits	7.8	Innovation	7.8
Promotion and Development	6.8	Diversity	7.3
Training	7.0	Social Responsibility	7.4
Travel opportunities	7.5	Corporate Governance	7.4
Culture	7.0	Environment	7.5
Total			**73.5**

GlaxoSmithKline, with a 7% share of the world's pharmaceutical market, is a global leader in research-based pharmaceuticals with headquarters in the UK and 101,000 employees in 117 countries. In 2003, GSK had sales of £21.4bn; with the US, France, Japan and UK the biggest markets. GSK's mission is "to improve the quality of human life by enabling people to do more, feel better and live longer". In 2003, the company spent £338m supporting global community programmes.

Executive summary

GSK is a leader in the provision of pharmaceutical products in four key therapeutic areas: anti-infectives, central nervous system (CNS), respiratory and gastro-intestinal/ metabolic. The company also supplies 23% of the world's vaccine market and has a growing portfolio of oncology products.

The company's Consumer Healthcare business comprises over-the-counter medicines, oral care products, and nutritional healthcare drinks. Famous brands include Panadol, NiQuitin CQ, Aquafresh, Sensodyne, Ribena, Horlicks and Lucozade.

GSK's strategic intent is to become the indisputable leader in its industry, and the company's robust financial performance in 2003 demonstrates the drive to achieve that goal.

GSK has one of the most broadly based product portfolios in the pharmaceutical industry. From 2005 onward, the company expects to show an increase in the number of key new compounds entering final trials from its "most promising pipeline"; and to have one of the lowest exposures to drug patent expiries measured as a percentage of turnover, says J P Garnier, GSK's chief executive officer.

From over 23 locations in the UK, GSK manages five businesses: consumer healthcare, corporate headquarters (communications, finance, human resources, IT and legal), manufacturing and supply, Research & Development (R&D), and pharmaceuticals. GSK is the number one pharmaceutical company in the UK, accounting for 9.5% of the market.

Pay and benefits

TotalReward, GSK's pay and benefits package, is designed to attract, motivate and retain the best talent; it is based on two key principles – pay for performance, and a share in GSK's success. Why is it called TotalReward? Because the reward for working for GSK comprises much more than a monthly pay cheque.

TotalReward recognises an employee's individual contribution to GSK's success through a competitive salary and annual bonus. It also gives employees the opportunity to share in the future success of GSK through share plans offering discounted and free shares.

New employees automatically join the GSK Pension Plan, a defined contribution scheme with generous company contributions and the opportunity for employees to make additional payments, which will be matched by GSK.

How does all this add up? The average salary at GSK is more than £40,000 a year, while the value of the average TotalReward package is closer to £50,000.

GSK's mission to enable people to do more, feel better and live longer extends to its employees. TotalReward's Lifestyle benefits include 26 days' annual holiday, free healthcare plan membership for employees, access to a free and confidential Employee Assistance Programme, a Family Support service offering advice and financial help towards finding suitable childcare, plus corporate discounts on selected products such as mortgages and annual holiday insurance.

Communication and education are important aspects of GSK's approach to reward. Employees receive regular communications about their TotalReward, including a quarterly newsletter, to ensure they understand and make the most of their benefits.

They also have access to personalised and general information about their pay and benefits on the GSK intranet; and the opportunity to learn more at lunchtime seminars, one-to-one meetings, and through online tutorials.

"TotalReward means each employee is valued for their contribution," sums up Jan Fenton, vice president, human resources, corporate.

Promotion and development

All employees have a personal development plan, agreed with their manager and reviewed during the year. Reviews are conducted in each business and function to ensure a diverse talent pool is fully developed to meet future business needs, and successors are identified for key positions.

Comprehensive leadership development opportunities are available to managers at all levels. These opportunities are targeted to help leaders meet the challenges they face in a complex global organisation. They ensure leaders motivate teams and individuals to do their best work.

Individual development is a partnership between the employee and the company. The employee has a responsibility for their own career development, which the company supports by providing training facilities, courses (online and face-to-face) and learning materials accessible through the myLearning intranet resource.

In a management survey carried out in 2004, 65% of UK managers agreed that they were given a real opportunity to improve their skills at GSK. In the same survey, 76% of managers would gladly refer a good friend or family member to GSK for employment, and 79% were proud to be a part of GSK.

With operations in 117 countries, there are opportunities for employees to move overseas where this fits with the needs of the business.

Company culture

Internally, the GSK Spirit aligns employees with a common vision, defining "why we are in business, what our business goal is, what we need to do to succeed, how we do it, and most importantly, each individual's part in making the organisation successful". It comprises the company mission, strategic intent, business drivers, the company's vision for the future, and leadership essentials – which are a guide for acceptable behaviour in demonstrating and reinforcing the GSK Spirit every day. They are: performance with integrity; people with passion; innovation and entrepreneurship; sense of urgency; everyone committed, everyone contributing; accountability for achievement; alignment with GSK interests; and develop self and others. The leadership essentials form part of personal development planning, to ensure employees are rewarded not just for what they achieve, but how they achieve it.

Since the merger between Glaxo Wellcome and SmithKline Beecham in December

2000, the past few years have been spent creating a culture based mainly around becoming a centre of excellence in every clinical area in which GSK operates, which actually means most of them. Underpinning the culture are the two key tenets: an entrepreneurial spirit, and integrity in everything the company does. The key focus has been on developing the best pipeline of new medicines and vaccines in the industry, and on becoming a world-leading consumer healthcare products business.

GSK recognises that people are its most valuable asset and a source of competitive advantage. In 2004, the UK Health and Safety Executive (HSE) awarded GSK with Beacon of Excellence status for the stress prevention programming and resilience processes within the organisation.

A good work/life balance is important. GSK has a proactive approach to flexible working and managing employees with work-related health issues.

Innovation

Pharmaceutical companies in general are currently experiencing a decline in R&D productivity. GSK has tackled this by radically redesigning its R&D organisation. "The new structure, based on seven centres of excellence for drug discovery, is working well and we're developing more high-quality compounds than ever before," says Fenton. The UK is a core R&D base for GSK; in 2003, £1bn was spent in this area. Recent investments include £28m for the Clinical Imaging Centre at Hammersmith Hospital, and £40m to construct a state-of-the-art automated chemistry facility.

There are 10 major products, accounting for £7.6bn of sales. One drug (for asthma and chronic obstructive pulmonary disease) is one of the top 10 global pharmaceutical brands. Recent product launches have included advances in the treatment of diabetes and the first combination HIV/AIDS treatment to be available in a single, once-daily tablet. "We now have 148 projects in clinical development," says Fenton.

Innovation extends beyond R&D and can be seen in the company's global community investment; charitable donations were equivalent to 5.3% of pre-tax profits in 2003. GSK was recognised in the Guardian Giving List in 2003 as the largest corporate donor in the FTSE 100. This £338m investment was focused on achieving lasting change for society's poorest and most vulnerable members through disease programmes, education, employee involvement and medicine donations.

Diversity and social responsibility

The nature of GSK's business is to improve lives, therefore the company is committed to being a good corporate citizen and takes seriously its responsibility to invest in the communities in which employees live and work. Community Partnership activities encompass support for healthcare, education, scientific and medical research, and arts projects. The company is also involved in a number of major global initiatives to combat health problems in the developing world. The company's flagship community programme is its key role in the Global Alliance to Eliminate Lymphatic Filariasis (aka elephantitis) – a 20-year $1bn commitment to eliminate one of the world's most disfiguring and disabling diseases.

"A Corporate Responsibility Committee of non-executive directors has oversight of corporate responsibility matters," says Fenton. "The committee advises the board on social, ethical and environmental issues that have the potential to seriously impact our business and reputation."

GSK's 14-strong board, drawn from a rich mix of backgrounds, has two female members, while the corporate executive team has one. Elsewhere in GSK, the number of female managers worldwide is 34%. The number of ethnic minorities employed in the workplace will be available from 2005 following a push to get all UK employees to report their ethnicity.

Corporate governance

In the 2004 management survey, 91% of managers agreed with the statement: "People in my department show commitment to performance with integrity."

The Financial Reporting Council's Combined Code on corporate governance, which was published in 2003, is fully supported by GSK's board who moved quickly to bring the company's governance procedures substantially in line with best practice.

All employees are required to maintain the highest standards of ethical conduct and corporate responsibility worldwide. Principles such as those enshrined in the UN Universal Declaration of Human Rights and the International Labour Organisation's Core Conventions are robustly embraced. GSK prides itself on the quality and extent of its relationships with its staff wherever they may be located.

GSK's key investment is the one it makes in its staff. Equally key is the emphasis placed by the company on nurturing employees' management and personal skills in equal measures. In this way, GSK and its staff will continue to develop, performing to the highest standards and embracing any challenges the future offers.

As GSK operates in 117 countries, local site and country practices can influence business issues and union relations.

Environmental record

The concept of sustainable development is core to GSK's environmental programmes. Work has begun by mitigating environmental impacts and looking at ways to improve production efficiency. The use of renewable resources, and the overall balance of the consumption of resources with the generation of waste, will be investigated in the future. GSK has a standard on sustainable development that defines the approach from discovery through manufacturing to sales. Environmental sustainability starts with R&D. As part of the support for R&D, a toolkit has been developed to assist in the selection of green chemistries and processes.

GSK is committed to connecting business decisions to ethical, social and environmental concerns. The company believes that solid financial performance is closely linked to ethical business practices. "We understand it's not just how much profit we make that matters," says Fenton. "Stakeholders want to know how that profit is made, and be reassured of the sound ethical basis for the business." GSK is mindful that its business is creating medicines to treat and prevent disease – something society needs and values. Simultaneously, healthcare and the way it is delivered and funded provoke intense debate. GSK is playing its part by, for example, making significant headway in drug treatment donation programmes in the developing world.

GMAC-RFC

GMAC-RFC
Eastern Gate, Brants Bridge, Bracknell, Berkshire RG12 9BZ
Tel: (0) 870 484 4484 **Fax:** (0) 1344 478050
Web: www.gmacrfc.co.uk

GMAC RFC
A General Motors Company

Pay and Benefits	6.8	Innovation	6.4
Promotion and Development	6.9	Diversity	5.9
Training	6.0	Social Responsibility	6.1
Travel opportunities	5.1	Corporate Governance	6.1
Culture	6.1	Environment	5.7
Total			**61.1**

GMAC-RFC (GMAC Residential Funding) is a creator and trader of residential assets. It employs around 700 full-time employees and a smaller number of contractors, mainly in Bracknell. In 2003, it provided loans worth £4.8bn – a total that was projected to increase to over £6bn for 2004.

Executive Summary

GMAC-RFC is part of GMAC Financial Services, the finance division of the General Motors global business group. Specialising in residential mortgage lending, it distributes its mortgages through authorised intermediaries. It also trades and invests its asset base, making it as much a business-to-business player as a consumer-oriented enterprise.

Launched via acquisition in the UK in 1997, the company restructured two years later and has since grown rapidly against favourable market conditions. Today, it is ranked 12th among mortgage lenders and enjoys a 2% market share. However, in order to secure further share GMAC-RFC has extended its focus beyond its core non-conforming (high-risk) products to move into prime (more traditional) products, to redefine itself as an all-status credit lender. It has also moved to automate much of its product delivery processes in order to speed up and simplify the customer experience.

The strategy appears to be paying dividends. Though Britain's property boom has made mortgage lending one of the more attractive industries of recent years, there is a good deal of competition. Yet GMAC-RFC grew 11 times faster than the market – in a market that grew 36% year on year. With a slowdown anticipated, however, the company knows it has to be competitive on price yet strive to maintain margins.

Key areas for the company include the sales and capital markets teams, which deal with investors and corporate customers; the business processing team, which handles new applications right up to completion; credit and risk management; project management; and support services. Post-completion services are outsourced.

Pay and Benefits

As part of a global corporate empire, GMAC-RFC can afford to pay staff well and it does. Base pay is in the median range – it is the discretionary bonus scheme that pushes overall reward into the upper quartile. Two-thirds derive from the achievement of personal objectives; the other third from company performance. Capital markets and sales employees are, unsurprisingly, more heavily incentivised. At entry level, bonus payments can be up to 10% of base pay – rising to over 100% for key executives.

There is a range of conventional benefits including a defined contribution pension plan, a sick-pay scheme and long-term disability benefit. Where the firm is really innovative, however, is in the number of different recognition schemes on offer. Under the Celebrate Leadership programme, employees can nominate high-performing colleagues who, if they are selected, can enjoy a holiday for two organised by the firm. Additionally, employees can be nominated for the Partner programme and enjoy a more visible role in the organisation as well as the opportunity to take a six-week paid sabbatical. Awards are also given to people who have displayed integrity, and for one-off examples of high-quality work or ideas generation.

Promotion and development

The fact that the company intends to diversify its service portfolio translates into a growing number of opportunities. Most of the vacancies at GMAC-RFC occur at entry level and are therefore externally filled. However, all senior positions are internally advertised and currently 60% of promotions are filled internally – a proportion that is steadily on the increase.

For the company, nearly 4% of whose people are in HR and learning and development, having a clear commitment to training and developing people is seen as integral to achieving this. There is a comprehensive three-month induction process for new hires; and all staff undergo an annual appraisal, the purpose of which is to identify personal aspirations and job-related objectives as well as review training and development.

Associates are able to give feedback on the training they receive through a number of channels. As well as an annual employee survey (GMAC-RFC changed supplier in 2004 and are now using Gallup's Q12 survey), there is an elected Employee Council; regular team meetings in all departments; and the CEO and other directors often host informal lunches with employees. Currently, training accounts for 3.6% of payroll.

Mentoring occurs at a number of levels, most notably on the formal graduate programme. Two streams – general management and IT – are on offer and mentors have themselves been trained in mentoring techniques. GMAC-RFC has also identified the need to "embed a coaching culture". Training of supervisors and line managers in coaching skills began in 2004, and at executive level coaches are regularly used on accredited management development programmes to ready individuals for particular roles. Support is also given to employees who wish to undertake further education studies.

Company Culture

Though its association with General Motors means its corporate heritage runs deep, GMAC-RFC is a young organisation and one that has so far seen rapid growth. Maybe it is this that accounts for much of the "buzz" that people who work there speak of. Certainly it is an energetic environment where people work hard to meet targets, yet know they are never taken for granted. At the end of 2003, the company significantly exceeded its growth plans; and in recognition of the strain this had at times caused, staff were given an extra day off at the beginning of the new year to rest with their families. In the second half of 2004, the company was gearing up to comply with Financial Services Authority (FSA) directives regarding statutory regulation of mortgages and took on a significant number of contractors and temporary staff to ensure the transition was a smooth one. A health and wellbeing day was held to manage any stress that was felt; also the staff restaurant was kept open later and a concierge service introduced in recognition of the irregular hours worked by some individuals.

GMAC-RFC has traditionally been a nine-to-five-thirty organisation. However, the changing face of the market now demands a wider range of hours, particularly for customer-facing roles. Because of this, GMAC-RFC has competitive policies on paternity, parental leave and special leave.

Around 2% of employees will travel abroad at least once a year; there are a number of expat managers in international locations, and the Rotational Assignment Framework allows for assignment opportunities in Minneapolis (head office) and central Europe.

It's also the kind of place where personal interaction is valued highly – rather than use email, most employees prefer to talk to colleagues – and this extends beyond immediate teams, right across the organisation. Twice a year there is an offsite round-table meeting at which senior management can brief employees on strategy and developments, but it is also an opportunity to have fun and relax. Staff Christmas parties and fancy-dress days are also arranged.

Innovation

GMAC-RFC's business strategy is predicated on being a leader in its field, and its very identity as a non-typical mortgage lender reflects this. Having built a dominant position in a niche market (non-conforming products), its visibility among mainstream mortgage providers is on the increase and entrepreneurialism is seen as a driving force behind this. People are certainly encouraged to question existing ways of working and to respond to customer feedback. As a product, the mortgage offers limited scope for innovation, yet GMAC-RFC has introduced a range of new criteria and access points.

Some of the best examples of innovation are reflected in the recognition programmes previously outlined. The Smart Award programme rewards associates for coming up with new ideas, while an employee council provides a more formal channel for ideas generation. It was at one of these that the idea to provide staff with transport to ease travel arrangements occurred.

In 2003, the GMAC-RFC Foundation was established. Uniquely aimed at preventing mortgage repossessions for all borrowers, the US-based body is set to support the Citizen's Advice Bureau in this country in the provision of better debt counselling.

Diversity and social responsibility

At a corporate level, social responsibility at GMAC-RFC is reflected in the Community Involvement Programme, which encompasses a range of schemes and campaigns. The schemes reward employees by matching monetary fundraising and providing grants in recognition of time spent volunteering for charities. The campaigns include Share the Magic, where contributions made from employees are matched up to £4,000 a year; and Gift of Time, where the company makes a donation to charity in return for employees having given their leisure time.

In all, the company donates 1% of their net income to community projects. For example, support is given to a specific charity nominated by employees each year (in 2004, the company pledged to fund the installation of a lift in a hospice in Ascot), while a five-year bursary is targeted at causes identified by the Duke of Edinburgh's Outward Bound Trust. The company also commits to following "the hearts of its employees" by these schemes. In addition, charitable funding is also raised through dress-down days, fun runs and sponsored fun events.

With regard to diversity, GMAC-RFC has formal policies on equal pay and equal opportunities, and has recently introduced diversity training for all managers. Just over half of all employees and a quarter of managers are female. Maternity and flexible working policies are currently under review in order that the business can become more family-friendly.

Corporate Governance

GMAC-RFC is part of a global financial institution that has every incentive to be seen to match up to current expectations of sound corporate governance. At a strategic level this means finding a balance between accountability to stakeholders and risk management in locating and developing new business markets. In an organisational sense, the result is a statutory board and a number of sub-committees to deal with issues of assets and liabilities, risk, audit and strategy, and investments. Chaired by the executive chairman, the board meets quarterly and includes two non-executive directors from outside the UK.

In 2004, the company successfully gained authorisation from the FSA in recognition that its conduct in all areas of operation meet the strict criteria laid down by that organisation. GMAC-RFC's cores values are to seek markets, value people, care deeply, balance life and succeed with integrity. These values are embedded into the day-to-day life of the company through its intranet, corporate literature, wall posters and management briefings.

Environment

GMAC-RFC has a formal policy on the environment. Much recent activity has focused on effective waste management practices: all outdated IT equipment is taken offsite to be recycled; toner cartridges are also recycled; and fluorescent lightbulbs and batteries are collected separately for proper disposal. In early 2005, the company was due to benchmark its commitment to the environment against others in its industry sector.

The company now provides a free bus service (for Bracknell-based employees), which travels around the town and to the train station. A car-sharing scheme is also about to be introduced.

HMV

HMV UK Ltd
Film House, 142 Wardour Street, London W1F 8LN
Tel: (0) 20 7432 2000 **Fax:** (0) 20 7432 2134
Web: www.hmv.co.uk; www.hmvgraduates.com

top dog for music·dvd·games

Pay and Benefits	6.5	Innovation	5.9
Promotion and Development	7.2	Diversity	5.3
Training	6.8	Social Responsibility	3.8
Travel opportunities	4.5	Corporate Governance	4.7
Culture	5.6	Environment	6.6
Total			**56.9**

HMV is one of the UK's leading music and entertainment retailers. It sells CDs, DVDs, videos, games and other related products; and has also started to work in the music download market. It opened its 200th store in 2004, meaning it has grown by 20% over two years. This is notable against the backdrop of a changing market – anyone asking about the download market a couple of years ago would have been greeted with polite smiles at best. The long-term effects of this new medium have yet to be felt; for the moment it's certain that HMV is one of the foremost entertainment retailers in the UK.

Executive summary

HMV is one of the best-established players in the entertainment market in the UK, having opened the doors of its first premises in London's Oxford Street in 1921. The current HMV exists as the result of the formation of the HMV Media Group after a management buyout in 1998. The new organisation bought the HMV and Dillon's bookstores from EMI, and acquired Waterstone's from WHSmiths. The Dillon's brand was subsequently absorbed into Waterstone's.

This profile focuses on HMV, the music brand, as the book operation is run separately. Floated on the London Stock Exchange in May 2002, the business has continued to operate profitably and opened its 200th store in 2004. Recent years have shown rapid growth for the company in its core markets in the UK and Ireland in the face of a number of new entrants into its market. It has expanded successfully into the internet for orders as well as for downloads, and will monitor the emergence of the online market very carefully.

Pay and benefits

HMV believes that it offers a very good, competitive package to all employees entering the business for the first time. This includes its graduate training scheme, where salaries started at £18,500 in late 2004. In addition there is a quarterly bonus scheme and a 30% product discount. This is important to most of the company's employees; HR director Liam Donnelly explains that the majority of HMV's employees are also very passionate about the products they sell, and if they weren't working for HMV would be heavy buyers! Discount is therefore valued as a very important benefit.

Holiday allowance is generous for newcomers, starting at 23 days a year, although the company asks that people don't take time off during the busy month of December. Relocation expenses are available when someone is moving store; there is a company pension scheme and a share incentive plan as well as an employee assistant programme. Every individual in HMV is also able to take part in a bonus scheme.

Moving up within the company, the benefits increase. Store managers can expect a competitive salary and excellent benefits – the company's internal surveys suggest that managers consider they get better than average salaries in the retail industry, and the HR department keeps a constant eye on pay levels with all of the current marketing reports. There is an excellent annual bonus scheme for management, 23 days holiday, paid attendance at the company's national conferences, and of course the same discounts and other benefits that are available to employees.

Jobs at head office crop up from time to time, but inevitably they are in shorter supply than opportunities within the numerous retail stores. Nevertheless, if your specialism is within HR, IT, customer services or finance it's worth checking the company's recruitment website as the company will post any vacancies there when they arise.

Promotion and Development

Retail is a busy environment and before entering it, a candidate needs to consider whether they have the application and sheer energy required. Selling music sounds like great fun, but the work is hard and involves long hours with often quite repetitive work. For the right people who are driven to get on and succeed, and who are passionate about both the product they sell and their customers, the opportunities are many at HMV; and the organisation prides itself on the work it does to recruit, develop and hold on to the best people in retail – staff turnover is very low for the industry.

Career development begins with a company induction; staff receive a day's training offsite plus a handbook covering the company's history, the support they can expect from head office and company procedures. This becomes their company workbook and is signed off every month during the induction period. There are then a number of Fast Track development programmes for individuals showing ability and potential, through which literally hundreds of talented people progress each year.

Training is available within the company's different disciplines – it is split into a number of levels according to your role in the business. Core learning is divided into a number of areas including people management, finance and operations – everything an employee would need as a minimum to do their role effectively in either a store or head office role.

As HMV continues to grow, there is a constant need to focus resources, time and effort on bringing talented employees through the career ladder; HMV particularly prides itself on its ability to do this effectively.

At senior level, the company has worked with a range of high-profile business schools, including Templeton College at Oxford University, to work on the skills a regional manager would require. In 2003, the company developed its own management diploma in conjunction with Ashridge Business School, which it intended to run again in 2004. The diploma is designed to develop and challenge high-performing managers for future senior manager roles.

Everyone has a compulsory annual appraisal and a separate developmental meeting, and this entire process has been further reviewed and improved over recent months to ensure each individual receives the appropriate levels of feedback, coaching and support needed to develop their career and maximise their performance.

Company culture

HR director Liam Donnelly stresses that the company is informal yet highly driven. It's informal in its style, although it's clear that the stores are under the control of the managers and there's no room for prima donnas who don't want to shift boxes, man the checkouts or are reluctant to perform any other particular tasks. Commercially, it's an aggressive organisation that does what it takes to maintain and increase its market share, but this doesn't translate into a tough workplace. "The perception is that HMV is a hard place, and commercially there's some truth in that," says Donnelly. "But within, it's a very supportive culture and has a history of nurturing very good managers and leaders." Donnelly adds that "HMV is known both within the company and outside it for having a unique culture, impossible to copy and highly valued by all who come across it – we take this very seriously and protect and nurture the culture to ensure it continues to bring the success through our people that the business has enjoyed over many years."

It's usually clear by the end of two years whether someone is likely to want to stay with the company, but everyone is treated as though they're in for a permanent career from day one. HMV believes this is part of the reason it has only a 25% turnover rate; employees understand that within three or five years they could be running their own store if they put the hours and effort in.

Working hours are decided by head office on a store-by-store basis, with the clear imperative that a shop must honour its commitment to opening hours. Work/life balance is accommodated as far as is possible, although this means so many different things to different people that it's difficult to generalise; the staff retention rates indicate that the company is getting it right.

Innovation

On the technical level, HMV was one of the first retailers to recognise the importance of the MP3 format and to start allowing downloads of music from its website. On the HR front, the company is proud of its recent equal opportunities training (see next section) and also the continuous development programme (CDP), on offer to all staff. This is operated in part through the company intranet, and can be used by staff to build up whichever skills they need to move on to the next stage in their career.

There is also a separate fast track scheme for promising graduates, which is highly rated as an innovation within the company.

Diversity and social responsibility:

Although HMV doesn't operate a quota system for people of diverse origins and abilities, it has recently launched a major equal opportunities initiative called Fair Play at Work, which has been very well received in the business. This initiative has produced ongoing activity and plans to further develop the company's working conditions and opportunities. Fair Play at Work has involved demonstrations of scenarios by actors and role-playing for staff at all management levels in the company. "Every manager will go through it, we're doing it very proactively," comments Donnelly.

The company also plans to alter all of its stores' layouts with accessibility in mind, although this is no light undertaking depending on the building in which a branch is located. Clearly, new builds have accessibility by law, but upgrading the existing stores may cost a considerable amount.

There are no crèche facilities on offer because it would be unfair to offer these to returning mothers only (by law); the company makes efforts to be sensitive to any returning parent's circumstances.

Corporate Governance

HMV is one of the leading retailers of any description in the UK; as such it is bound by trading standards, employee communication, health and safety, and numerous other pieces of legislation. In addition, as a company listed on the Stock Exchange it is regulated by the laws that govern the City. It takes all of its obligations seriously starting at board level and filtering downward.

Environmental record

HMV is well aware of the role a major business can play in safeguarding the environment and has a dedicated environment committee for precisely that reason. The company is passionate about the issues and has obtained discounts on bikes for staff, for example. It recycles and uses recyclable materials wherever possible, and focuses on energy efficiency in its stores.

Further ideas on carrying the company forward in this area are always welcomed from staff.

Huxley Associates

Huxley Associates
75 King William Street, London EC4
Tel: (0) 20 7469 5000 **Fax:** (0) 20 7469 5009
Web: www.huxley.com **Email:** internalrecruitment@huxley.com

Huxley
Associates

Pay and Benefits	6.8	Innovation	6.0
Promotion and Development	6.6	Diversity	6.2
Training	7.2	Social Responsibility	5.8
Travel opportunities	5.8	Corporate Governance	6.2
Culture	6.6	Environment	5.4
Total			**62.6**

Huxley Associates, privately owned, is one of Britain's leading recruitment consultancies. Established to recruit into the ICT (Information Communications Technology) industry, it has recently expanded into the finance and engineering sectors. Its offices are in London (head office), Birmingham, Manchester, Reading and Amsterdam. It expects to open a New York office in 2005 (desk-trading New York placements from London in the meantime); and offices in Frankfurt, Paris, Hong Kong and Singapore within two years. Huxley Associates provides a range of recruitment services, split roughly 50:50 between permanent and contract placements. Huxley Associates has 180 employees – on target to be 280 by the end of 2005.

Executive Summary

Huxley Associates started life in 1995 and has weathered all of the ICT recruitment industry's highs and lows. During the economic downturn in 2001, which had a disproportionate impact on the recruitment sector, Huxley Associates suffered along with the rest of the sector. But this determined company stood firm during the downturn while its competitors recorded losses and shed jobs.

For a start, it still made a profit – a considerable achievement. Remarkably, Huxley Associates has had only two job losses in nine years. And when Enron went down, Huxley Associates paid £750,000 to contractors that it had placed into Enron, to cover lost earnings. Huxley Associates also moved into finance and engineering and took the opportunity to get closer to its clients, such that repeat business increased from 15% to 35%.

In 2001, profit before tax was £5m on turnover of £43.1m. Profits slipped to £1m in 2002 on turnover of £29m, and to a loss of £15,000 in 2003 (after an unused provision of £1.25m for an office move). During 2004, things picked up noticeably – profit for the first ten months was £3.6m and was on target for £4.6m for the full year.

Huxley Associates continued to invest in people, systems and technology while others cut back, using the downturn to "grow up" as a business. Such confidence meant that its people have been trained right up to the hilt, helping Huxley Associates hit the ground running as its markets have recovered.

Pay and Benefits

People join Huxley Associates because the earning potential is better than at its peers. Not only is it the market leader, but it also invests in people's development so that they are better equipped to perform. The infrastructure is in place – in the shape of IT systems or advertising support for placements. It all adds up to real and significant opportunities for very high earnings.

Remuneration is geared towards commission. "The average salary here is around £50,000," says Gary Eldon, managing director of Huxley Associates. "Around 60% of that would be made up of commission." The top recruitment consultants are able to earn in excess of £100,000. A graduate in year one might average £35,000 (but the first 3–6 months are heavily spent in training). In year two this should increase to £45,000–£50,000 as you become better at your job, and after that the sky's the limit. The reward opportunities here are almost limitless.

Commission is based on personal sales, "assists" (where an introduction is made to another consultant), and a management override for team performance. Directors and senior managers also have profit share and hold shares in the business – useful if the company ever goes public.

Company cars are given at four levels and the models are unashamedly aspirational. Expect a Polo or equivalent after 6–9 months and a Mini Cooper S, GTi or MG at the second level. Beyond that, Huxley people drive Porsche Boxters, BMW convertibles, Range Rovers and Mercedes. At the company AGM, the winner in the high achievers prize draw gets the use of an Aston Martin DB7 for a year. This popular car scheme allows young people to drive cars for which they wouldn't otherwise get insurance. Non-drivers can claim a cash allowance instead.

Other benefits include a stakeholder pension scheme, private healthcare and generous holidays. There are free eye tests and free glasses (quirky, but thoughtful – people spend a long time in front of computer screens).

Promotion and development

Huxley Associate's training scheme, from joining to senior director, is perhaps the best in the industry. It envelops each person and every position from the first day they join. Training averages 12 days a year, and in the first year it can exceed 20. The in-house training department is nine strong, supplemented where needed by external training sources and mentoring.

A knowledge of the appropriate business sector is not always assumed upon joining, but you are expected to learn. You are also taught sales-based competencies, client-handling skills, and internal systems; and as you progress into team leader and management roles, leadership skills. Your initial position will be working with someone who has specialised knowledge, and people tend to become specific experts in one product and one region. But people do move around, and having close relationships with specific clients need not hold you back.

A clear structure is set out from day one as to where you can go. Around 80% of Huxley people are consultants. There are also client relationship managers and general management; and the usual professional functions in HR, finance, legal, marketing – and of course, IT. If you want to stay as a fee-earning consultant instead of progressing into management, you can do so. Nothing is forced or prompted; you travel at your own speed.

Each manager has a dedicated coach, with feedback to the board. Everyone receives a monthly business review on roles and activities, and there is a six-monthly appraisal where performance against competencies and long-term business objectives is assessed.

Company culture

When you ask Huxley people to describe their company culture in one word, most say "meritocracy". From the outset, Huxley has had a flat management structure and has preached and practised open communication. It's a young, dynamic company and people are attracted by its straightforward, up-front approach.

The company conducts an annual, independent culture survey on its intranet. Anonymity is offered, and feedback is given through managers and at the AGM. The same meeting is an open floor, where people talk candidly about opportunities and achievements.

Huxley actively encourages people to generate new ideas, and management meetings from junior level upwards have mechanisms to feed in business suggestions. For example, Huxley's move into engineering recruitment – the idea came from the floor.

"Management reaction was initially lukewarm," says Gary Eldon. "But that's the culture of the company. We say, "show us what you can do and give us a business plan". We always look at it." Engineering now represents perhaps 40% of Huxley's business in the regional offices.

HR policies are professional and extensive. The company looks to be as flexible as possible with respect to working hours and holidays. But this is a high-energy business. Sales is quite a demanding task and people are driven by the high earnings potential. It's not an environment for nine-to-fivers; and the type of person who flourishes at Huxley is hard working, honest, positive, ambitious and friendly.

The company certainly enjoys its own company. Huxley's social diary is legendary, but it's about bonding. The whole company regularly debunks for paid-for weekends away – to Dublin, Ibiza, Milan, Marbella, Barcelona, Paris, skiing in Comyeur or Austria – the cost per person running easily into four figures. The Lunch Club for high achievers earns you a table at a top (and they mean top) restaurant on Fridays. There are go-karting events and trips to comedy clubs. It is certainly fair to say that the party culture is ingrained at Huxley. Once a year there is a trip to Las Vegas for those that have performed well over the year, where achievers are treated to an all-expenses stay at the Bellagio and a helicopter ride over the Grand Canyon.

Innovation

Recruitment IT systems – to handle search, logging criteria and databases – are usually standardised and bought off-the-shelf. Born out of a mix of frustration and innovation, Huxley developed its own tailor-made system – at a cost of £3m. The bespoke system is highly intuitive. It weeds out the most appropriate candidates from the thousands of applications received over the internet. It allows an advertisement, once posted, to appear simultaneously on a number of European internet sites. It also allows consultants to monitor sales and performance in real time.

Huxley has pioneered the export of recruitment services from the UK. "The European recruitment market is very different," says Mike Smith, director. For example, in Germany, IT recruitment agencies don't exist in the same sense as they do in the UK; and in Belgium, there is often resistance to move towns for "lifestyle" reasons. Huxley is even placing US candidates into US companies – from London. As well as exporting UK recruitment practices, it also helps export UK skills. "British people are in demand," adds Smith.

Diversity and social responsibility

The company has a diversity policy and also covers issues such as sexual harassment and email abuse. Managers receive training on any diversity issues that might occur. "But it's always about the best person for the job," says Zoe Brent, operations manager. "We're totally blind when it comes to colour, age or gender."

The board directors come from a diverse mix of backgrounds; the top-performing fee-earning consultant is an Asian woman. Huxley Associates is attempting to link with Global Graduate schemes that promote ethnic minorities with degrees. Around 40% of the workforce is female, and the company is currently interviewing more women than men. Age is no barrier, but the required energy levels tend to attract younger people. Huxley is very strict on equal pay for equal jobs, and promotes and rewards solely on achievement and competency.

The annual Huxley Associates Ball raises money for various charities, and managers and many employees donate their Christmas bonuses to buy raffle tickets at the Ball. Dress Down for Charity, or Jeans for Genes, cost employees between £5 and £50 to come to work in denim. Huxley also sends managers to Byte Night, an event run by a homeless charity, NCH Action for Children. Managers attend a presentation by the charity and then spend the night sleeping rough. In 2003, Huxley's participation in this event raised £25,000.

Corporate Governance

Huxley is always fully compliant with all DTI regulations and the Data Protection Act, and all IT systems are developed with all these requirements in place. The legal department ensures compliance and the company is a member of the Association of Technology Staffing Companies. Internal compliance procedures are fully set out for employees to understand, and the company also runs spot checks.

As a recruitment agency placing people into contractual positions, Huxley has fully compliant UK and European business models and a separate European legal team. With the government having targeted IT contractors under IR35, Huxley takes legal matters to the last letter of the law; checking that candidates comply totally with tax regulations and working only with bona fide UK limited companies.

Environmental record

As an office-based operation, Huxley recycles all paper, cups, toner and office materials. All obsolete technical equipment is cleaned of "computer waste" and passed on for recycling.

With its heavy investment in IT systems, and by the very nature of its business, there is little need for paper in Huxley offices. An imminent policy will ensure that there are no files or in-trays on desks and no consultant has a filing cabinet. Time sheets are completed online, and CVs are submitted and forwarded online. There is even a team that calls clients and candidates to obtain email addresses so that all information and communication is made electronically.

Innocent

Innocent Drinks, Fruit Towers, 3 The Goldhawk Estate,
Brackenbury Road, London W6 0BA
Tel: (0) 20 8600 3922
Web: www.innocentdrinks.co.uk **Email:** jobs@innocentdrinks.co.uk

Pay and Benefits	8.1	Innovation	8.1
Promotion and Development	7.8	Diversity	7.9
Training	8.2	Social Responsibility	8.3
Travel opportunities	7.1	Corporate Governance	7.7
Culture	8.8	Environment	7.9
Total			**79.9**

Innocent Drinks describes itself as a "little juice company" – literally, it makes little bottles of smoothie juices in combinations of different fresh fruits and sometimes yogurt and honey. Founded by three City high flyers in 1998, the company now employs 57 people. It has almost doubled its turnover every year, selling through the supermarkets and other retail outlets, and developing the odd sideline – you can buy books and shirts if you wish. The emphasis is on fun, quirkiness and getting the job done by enthusing the staff as much as possible.

Executive summary

The idea for the company came up in 1998 when the founders – Jon, Richard and Adam (Innocent is in some sort of denial about surnames) – decided there had to be more to life than working in the City. They set up a stall at a jazz festival in London and sold smoothies – spending £500 on fruit and setting up two bins for empty bottles, one marked "yes" and one marked "no". Customers were asked whether they should give up their day jobs to make smoothies, and to put their empty bottle in the appropriate bin – so you could argue that Innocent was set up due to public demand!

That at least would account for the organisation's growth. From running in a bedroom, the company turned over £200,000 in 1999, £1.4m in 2000, £3.7m in 2001, and kept growing until 2004 when it made £16.5m. As a private company it doesn't divulge profits but it has made money every year. There is every sign that it will continue to do so, as it expands its Shepherd's Bush HQ and starts to open in France, the Netherlands and elsewhere on mainland Europe.

Innocent Drinks won the National Business Awards employer of the year award in 2004, and was a finalist for the outstanding people development award in the same ceremony the year before.

Pay and benefits

Innocent keeps an eye on the competition, external reports and other sources to keep its pay competitive; and at the end of their first year everyone gets a little share in the company. Private healthcare and a stakeholder pension are among some of the other benefits on offer. There are no company cars, but cereal and toast are on offer free of charge for breakfast.

The company believes it is progressive in terms of flexible working hours and flexible work location – if you want to work from home on occasion that's not a problem. This is common enough, but the approach to hours borders on the revolutionary: "We've never clocked in and out," says Bronte, whose job title is "people person". "Some people just work better if they sleep that little bit longer, some people work better if they come in that little bit earlier and leave earlier." The ethic is to get the job done rather than show your face at regimented hours.

Interest-free loans are available from the company if an employee needs one (probably not a good idea to ask for one at the interview, mind); there is also the possibility of unpaid leave and the "Innocent study fund" – more on that later. If you become a parent you get a £2,000 tax-free bonus.

Family is clearly important to Innocent, which offers extra holiday time for employees who get married. Among the "soft" benefits are nature days (outings to various places) and a weekend snowboarding holiday every year (Italy in 2004 and Bronte was keeping the location of the 2005 event a close secret as this book went to press). There is also a "lunch mate" scheme, which is part of the induction; and on Fridays the staff finish early and go and have a beer. On the social front there are tennis, film, cheese and wine evenings, a culture club and a drum club. If that sounds a little hectic then panic not, you get a monthly massage from Kate; there is also a quarterly award of £1,000 to spend on something life-affirming which has nothing to do with work. You put your case to a Monday meeting and if people vote in your favour, you get the cash!

Promotion and development

It's easy to get the impression that the company is all about having a good time – which it is, but only if it gets its job done and develops its people. Recruitment happens mostly through the website; if you're interested enough to look at the website you're probably ahead of someone who just sees an ad, the business believes. The recruitment process is strict: the organisation wants bright, like-minded people who are going to get on well.

When you start, you're taken to lunch every day for the first two weeks by Innocent people. This enables new employees to build personal relationships, and it also avoids that awful first-day-sitting-with-your-sandwiches-at-the-desk-not-knowing-anyone feeling. After three months you have a chat about your progress. There is then a six-month review and an annual assessment.

Generic skills – IT, negotiation, presentation, time management and people skills – are taught overall, with other skills introduced as and when they are needed. Specific courses on (for example) Dreamweaver and French have been offered for web development and the French operation (the tutors wore berets). In-house training on sales, meeting etiquette, budgeting and other skills are on offer; as are offsite peer-group learning sessions on team management, workload and best practice coaching.

The management team is fully qualified, and primarily it's a young company; the oldest employee was 35 as this book went to print, although this isn't by design – it's by getting the right person into the job.

Company culture

From the moment you walk up to Innocent's door – marked "people" – and look at the window – marked "burglars" – you know that someone here has a sense of humour. It could look forced but somehow it doesn't. As you move further around the office more, slightly offbeat, ideas start to emerge. Customers – anyone – drop in (every bottle carries an invitation to do so). And they phone – there's a number on each bottle that puts you through to a real person if you just fancy a natter. There's no formal reception area. The divisions within the company (marketing, finance etc.) sit together. The board room is called the "bored room", the management team is called the "knitting circle". Everybody is included in the decision-making process. There are meetings every Monday for the whole company, which finish with a quick bout of exercise. Assessments happen upwards as well as downwards (you feed back on your managers as well as vice versa). There are informal reward schemes; an employee of the month is named Lord or Lady of the Sash and gets to wear a top hat or tiara – and has tea made for them for the month and a meal in a top London restaurant. Candidates are nominated by their peers.

People are vital to the company. If you're offered a job you'll get a call the week before you arrive to ensure that you know you're expected. There will be flowers on your desk when you arrive. There are also opportunities to get involved with the company's charitable work.

On reading through this, anyone whose tastes are for the corporate world will be tearing their hair out – and rightly so, this isn't the right place for everyone. But by finding the right match of people, the business has delivered extremely positive results to date.

Innovation:

On the product front, the company prides itself on using exclusively natural and whole ingredients – there is no way anyone will find any concentrates in an Innocent drink; it's 100% fruit and you can get two of your five portions of fruit/veg per day by drinking one.

Concerning people policies, it's hard to find a company policy that's not innovative in some way. Flexible working in terms of location and hours, a budget for learning something completely unrelated to work, free breakfast – Innocent was quite unlike any other company visited during the research for this book. In addition, it has found ways of addressing those little business niggles that really get to people – the "bored room" is not available for booking, instead you pay for it with a meter outside so that you never get that "room is booked but not being used while other people are looking for a meeting place" thing that happens in so many organisations.

On leaving the interview, our researcher noticed that someone had turfed an Innocent delivery van. Somehow he wasn't surprised.

Diversity and social responsibility:

The three founders were male, but the management team – or "knitting circle" – is made up of four women and five men. None of this has been done deliberately, maintains Bronte – the right people are in the right jobs for them.

Innocent is avidly keen on putting something back into the community. It runs the Innocent Foundation, a registered charity run by volunteers from the staff. It has planted trees around the country, for example. Also, the company arranges Fruitstock – a jazz festival for unsigned acts which entertained some 80,000 people in Regents' Park in the summer of 2004 (and whose organiser was trained internally, incidentally). It raises money for Chicks – Country Holidays for Inner City Kids. In 2004, it mobilised a crack force of grannies through Age Concern to knit bobble hats for smoothie bottles "to keep them warm in the fridge in winter", explains Bronte. For every hat the company received, it gave 50p to Age Concern; by mid-December 2004, the business had received around 18,000 hats.

Corporate Governance

In spite of the apparent light-heartedness of so much of what Innocent does, it would be wrong to assume there's anything lax about the operation. As "people person", Bronte takes personal responsibility for the implementation of employee legislation, health and safety, and all of the relevant laws that govern an employer's relationship with its people. Her position includes more than just HR, she confirms; part of the ethic of the company is to value its people above all else, so if there are any regulations in place to protect those people they come under her remit.

Environmental record

As might be expected, Innocent is an environmentally conscious company. It has an electric car. Recycled materials are utilised wherever possible, not only in the packaging – the plastics used for the bottles are 25% recycled, and all bottles are recycled internally. Everything printed is on partly recycled paper.

More unusually, a lot of the furniture is recycled – the room in which the interview for this article took place had walls made of recycled tyres rather than plaster, and shelving was made of reformed wood and old paper.

It's a surprising and refreshing company to visit – and for the right person, working there should be a delight.

J D Wetherspoon

J D Wetherspoon
Wetherspoon House, Central Park, Reeds Crescent, Watford WD24 4QL
Tel: (0) 1923 477777
Web: www.jdwetherspoon.co.uk E-mail: customerservices@jdwetherspoon.co.uk

Pay and Benefits	6.7	Innovation	7.6
Promotion and Development	6.9	Diversity	7.0
Training	6.9	Social Responsibility	7.2
Travel opportunities	2.6	Corporate Governance	6.7
Culture	6.4	Environment	6.2
Total			**64.2**

J D Wetherspoon owns and operates 650 pubs and 11 hotels in the UK. Most of its 18,500 staff are employed in the J D Wetherspoon pubs and Lloyds No 1 bars, while 320 staff are based at the head office in Watford. For its 2003–04 financial year, the company reported an operating profit of £77.6m on turnover of £787.1m.

Executive summary

J D Wetherspoon doesn't brew beer; it's a managed operation, a licensed retailer which buys and sells beer, spirits, wine and food. It was rated Pub Company of Choice by readers of leading monthly magazine FHM, scoring 45% – the closest other managed operator was Yates' Wine Lodge with 19%. Business magazine Management Today placed JD Wetherspoon as the second most admired company in its survey's "restaurants, pubs and breweries" sector, behind Diageo and ahead of Greene King, Allied Domecq and SABMiller.

For the year to July 25 2004, turnover was up 8% to £787.1m with operating profit up 4% to £77.6m. Figures for 2003 and 2002 respectively were £730.9m and £74.9m, and £601.3m and £70m. For the first time in a decade, profits before tax fell 4% – due principally to intense competition from supermarkets. Chairman, Tim Martin says, "Looking forwards, we have several competitive pricing initiatives to drive sales."

Plenty of awards have been secured including British Institute of Innkeeping training awards, Pub Company of the Year, and design and architectural awards for renovating old buildings – for example, Tunbridge Wells' opera house and an old railway station in Aberystwyth. Both are now popular pubs.

Pay and benefits

"Every employee at J D Wetherspoon is eligible for a bonus – that applies from the one-hour a week associate behind the bar up to the chairman," says Su Beacham-Cacioppo, personnel director. "The criteria for the bonus are in terms of profitability and the CBSM standard." CBSM – cleanliness, beer quality, service, and maintenance – are the four key quality standards, rigorously monitored (six CBSM tests every month for pubs) by area managers, headquarters staff and "mystery visitors". Every employee is "bonused" on a sliding scale against CBSM results – if a pub scores 88% and one nearby 95%, the latter gets more bonus. "It's a big incentive to get standards right," says Beacham-Cacioppo. "Customers return if they know the service is good and toilets are sanitary. This is as important to customers as good value prices." Associates can receive 17% of salary rising to 50% for pub managers.

"All employees with more than 18 months' service are eligible for shares, which we issue every six months under our Share Incentive Plan. We give shares, not the option to buy shares, on a ratio of 10% of gross earnings to a cap of £3,000 annually," says Beacham-Cacioppo.

A defined contribution pension scheme operates for all employees. Management grades have contributions matched by the company, capped at 12% of gross basic pay. All management grades receive private medical insurance, which non-management grades can purchase through payroll at the same competitive rates. There are no company cars/petrol, just car allowances based on grade. Flex benefits in operation enable salaried staff to flex 5-week holiday allowances down to 4 or up to 8 weeks. Non-salaried staff receive four weeks' holiday.

Pub managers receive free accommodation, while staff may rent at a discount. There are 50% discounts on drinks and food while working, 20% at other times.

Promotion and development

In this company where most employees are aged under 50, staff turnover runs at 15.2%. "Increasingly we are attracting and retaining older employees," says Beacham-Cacioppo. Employees over 50 can take "sunshine leave" – up to three months' unpaid leave "to help better manage their home and work commitments". The 4% over 50 are mainly at the pub level.

Up to 70% of management positions are filled internally, 95% of pub manager positions and 55% at head office. Hourly-paid associates receive three days' training each year and shift/pub managers 12 days. Some 2% of payroll is spent on training. There are 10 regional training centres spread across the UK. A professional study policy operates in which the company sponsors employees to study for professional qualifications (accountancy, personnel, purchasing, legal, etc.) and ongoing professional development opportunities apply where relevant.

"We identify and develop talent," says Beacham-Cacioppo. "There are appraisals twice a year, development days, talent-spotting days and line management recommendations." At the pub level, J D Wetherspoon is proud of its progress with the nationally recognised qualification, the Advanced Diploma in Leisure Retail Management run with Nottingham Trent University. "The first nine people graduated in summer 2004, another 75 are going through and 75 more are applying," says Beacham-Cacioppo. "Noone else is doing this – the qualification is above HND level and grants exemption to the first two years of a degree course in hospitality management. We pay all fees for the diploma. It's an opportunity for people to study who otherwise wouldn't have the opportunity."

Company culture

The key attribute the company seeks from its 18,500 employees is a can-do attitude. It wants people who'll try anything, who'll get things done, who are open to both in-company and self development, and who are seeking better ways to do things. Beacham-Cacioppo defers to chairman Tim Martin who likens the company to a shark – "it must move forward or die". The company encourages (constructive) criticism. It listens to customers and employees, and constantly asks for feedback. That's how Nottage Hill Chardonnay was introduced. "It's easier to improve 100 things by 1% than one thing by 100%," is the cry. Indeed the company is a stickler for the KISS principle – keep it simple, stupid.

"Work/life balance is a challenge in a business where you are at your busiest while most people are not working," says Beacham-Cacioppo. "We like to limit late-night working and rotate staff weekends off. We were the first pub group to achieve a 48-hour working week. Now we have a working group trialling a 45-hour week. Fixed shifts allow for study, childcare, etc.; plus there's part-time and flexible working."

On average, pubs have 5.5 managers and 25 associates – you need larger management teams to enable shorter working weeks (3,800 of its staff are in pub management). Standard pub licenses run to 11pm, but around 50 pubs have Public Entertainment Licenses – which means they can be open until 2am. "There are people who actively enjoy working these hours, despite them being antisocial," says Beacham-Cacioppo. The company invests in its staff to help build up a long-term quality business.

Innovation

J D Wetherspoon has notched up many firsts. It has featured no-smoking areas for at least one-third of the pubs, and no smoking at the bar, for 10 years. It recently announced that it intends to ban smoking in 60 of its pubs by May 2005, and in all of its pubs by May 2006. It has all-day freshly cooked menus on offer in all its pubs. For the fourth year in succession in 2004, J D Wetherspoon won a Food Development Association award for the content and quality of its pub menus (customers can choose from over 100 dishes in the pubs, from side orders and main courses to desserts).

Fresh coffee has been offered for a decade using proper coffee machines that are on a par with the equipment used in the many high street coffee shops (J D Wetherspoon now sells 250,000 cups of coffee a week, compared with the few cups of 10 years ago) and breakfast is available from opening time (10am). There are 14 airport pubs – air and landside – at key locations, some available for 24-hour operations when necessary, eg during the peak summer season.

"Looking back 10 years, you would have seen most pubs managed by couples," says Beacham-Cacioppo. "Now, more than 75% are single managers – single in the way they work for us that is."

Diversity and social responsibility

A good mix of society is reflected in the headcount, and ethnic origin is now starting to be monitored. Two out of the five directors are female. Overall in the company 49% of employees are female – nearly 40% of junior management and 38% of senior management. The company is very much "female friendly". There is a zero tolerance policy on bullying/harassment, with a hotline confidential phone number posted in every location. It's rarely activated, but zero tolerance really does mean that.

One corporate charity is chosen by the staff each year – currently it's CLIC (Challenging Cancer and Leukaemia in Children) and £500,000 has been raised with the pledge to raise £2m.

A corporate social responsibility group meets monthly to discuss progress. There's glass recycling and packaging recycling. A new warehouse and central distribution facility in Daventry is reducing the hitherto 27 deliveries per week per pub, to 3 per week – cutting down on transport costs and environmental impact.

Work is underway on tackling obesity through diet, low calorie drinks, reducing fat content in meals to under 5%, promoting vegetables and salads, reducing sodium content in children's meals, and better labelling and information for customers. An ethical fund is offered in the pension. There are no unions (noone's asked for one).

Corporate governance

"Different people deal with the various aspects of corporate governance," says Beacham-Cacioppo. "Overall, an internal auditor manages the processes. Data protection issues are handled by the legal department, and financial matters by the finance department. An external agency manages the health and safety issues. We have had a full audit of all of our premises for the Disability Discrimination Act and any work that needed to be done for our premises to comply with the act has been done; for example, we have been installing ramps wherever necessary for wheelchair access. Training videos covering all these essential matters have been distributed to every pub."

"We work closely with the Queen Mother's Foundation and have been highly commended for the last six years, winning EASE – Ease of Access, Services and Employment – awards for four years," says Beacham-Cacioppo. "We also work with charities assisting disabled people in getting back to work."

J D Wetherspoon has taken several positive steps to highlight its commitment to sensible behaviour in and outside its pubs and bars. No company that serves alcohol can be immune from bad behaviour occasionally and the policies the company is implementing should help to reduce its effects. Social responsibility is balanced against company trading policies. Commonsense prevails.

Environmental record

While J D Wetherspoon is listed in the FTSE 200, it's also represented in FTSE4Good, a listing of companies with a good social and environmentally responsible approach – the company has been in it for three years. Examples of its environmental approach have already been discussed – the new Daventry distribution centre workings, for example, also involve lorries returning once their loads have been delivered with a pub's packaging for recycling to save on distribution and overall logistics costs.

The company's award-winning prowess has already been described. Added to this, it has also won Loo of the Year and many training awards. The list is long and will doubtless grow even longer.

Environmental policies and the promotion of sensible behaviour and a pleasant atmosphere at all outlets are bywords. They will also apply to any new development. "We monitor that year by year," says Beacham-Cacioppo. "The driver for all new openings is the availability of quality sites." Overseas? "We're not saying no, but we're not actively pursuing it either."

The goal is to become the UK's largest independent pub operator. It's not just the sites that are required to fulfil that ideal, but sufficient numbers of high-quality people with the supporting company policies. It's got the recipe right, now it needs the ingredients to be kept fresh.

jmc.it

jmc.it
Riverside, Agecroft Road, Manchester M27 8SJ
Tel: (0) 161 925 7777
Web: www.jmc.it **E-mail:** solutions@jmc.it

jmc.it

Pay and Benefits	5.8	Innovation	5.5
Promotion and Development	5.0	Diversity	5.5
Training	6.0	Social Responsibility	5.5
Travel opportunities	3.8	Corporate Governance	5.0
Culture	5.8	Environment	5.3
Total			**53.2**

jmc.it is one of the north's longest established IT resellers, with over 23 years experience. Its consistently strong performance in a competitive marketplace is due largely to the fact that long-term commitment to clients is matched by that shown to its own employees.

An inherent culture that sees the company constantly strive to add value to each client's business, is driven by a six-strong management board that collectively has over 80 years service and has risen through the ranks, living the company's corporate values. Three times re-accredited as an Investor in People, **jmc.it** has a well-defined professional development structure in place for every employee, reinforced by comprehensive training and mentoring programmes across all departments.

The emphasis on teamwork is reinforced through a varied programme of sporting and social activities for employees, helping to further foster a strong corporate pride in the company's achievements and success. As a result, the company is able to retain its highly valued employees. Staff churn is minimal and the average period that the current workforce has worked at **jmc.it** is 7 years, an impressive record of retention in any industry.

Executive summary

jmc.it is an IT reseller based in Manchester that in 23 years of trading has been through both a management buyin, and a buyout. As a company with a headcount of 88, **jmc.it** has a friendly feel; indeed the managing director, Andrew Burgess, knows all members of staff and runs the company as a "family". For the past four years, annual turnover has been static at around £8.2m while profits have increased from £500,000 in 2001 to £1.15m in 2004. This has been achieved by concentrating on higher-margin services. The attraction and retention of clients is key – there are currently over 600 of them. Burgess's view is "the products are important, but clients are core to the business". The statistics speak volumes: 90% of turnover is repeat business, over 90% of clients renew contracts each year, and over 35% of turnover stems from annual support contracts. "There are no casual relationships with clients here," says Burgess. "It all comes down to the quality of our people and we work hard to retain them. The acid test is how long they stay – the average is 7 years, which in the typically transient world of IT is very good."

Pay and benefits

Depending upon position, packages comprise of a number of elements including basic salary, pension contributions, bonuses for individual and company performance, a car or a cash alternative, funds for personal development and entertainment, and a host of other options including the ability to individually flex an element of salary for specific requirements. One popular flex is the provision of tax-efficient vouchers for nursery care. "Overall we believe that the package available is very competitive," says Burgess.

Profit-related pay was introduced in 2004. Burgess believes if **jmc.it** performs well in net profit terms, everyone should feel they have personally benefited. A percentage of profits are put into a pot and equally distributed to employees who've been with the company for more than 12 months – everyone gets the same amount.

Everyone also benefits from an Education and Recreation Fund to which **jmc.it** allocates £160 per year per person. The fund can be used as a contribution to a wide variety of activities including hobbies, interests, personal development, entertainment and keeping fit; and can be used for the benefit of an employee and their family. Recent uses have included scuba diving training, learning Portuguese and mountain bike racing. Any unclaimed funds at the end of each six-month period are donated to a charity selected by the employees. The most recent beneficiary is Cancer Research UK.

Everyone who's been with **jmc.it** for 12 months is entitled to attend the annual weekend away. In October 2004, this was a three-day all-expenses-paid trip to Berlin. "It's a thank you to staff – us saying 'without you we'd be nothing'," says Burgess. A social committee arranges a variety of activities including Christmas parties and an August Fun Day for families. Burgess believes "both employees and families should feel involved in the business". There are 22 days holiday, with one day extra for every two years' employment up to a maximum of 27 days. If an employee has zero days off sick in a six-month period, they accrue an extra half-day holiday.

There is an externally managed contribution pension scheme (**jmc.it** contributes 3% of salary, which employees are expected to at least match). A long-service bonus is offered every two years after a qualifying period of four years, up to a ceiling of £1,500 – 84% of staff currently qualify.

Unusually for a company with 88 employees, **jmc.it** is based in 20,000 sq foot offices, which house a subsidised restaurant and mini-gym.

Promotion and development

The ethos is "promotion from within". All the directors have been with the company for at least 10 years and started at relatively junior levels. Burgess himself joined as a junior salesman in October 1989, and it's the same story for all the senior managers as well. Only once has a senior vacancy been filled through external recruitment, this due to the absence of a candidate with formal marketing qualifications. "We will always look to promote from within," says Burgess. "It is a fundamental element of the bond between the company and its employees."

Sponsorship is available for courses; half-funding if the course is of benefit to the organisation, 25% funding if the benefit is not clear initially but it is likely to help the company in the long run. A number of different options have been supported including business studies degrees and project management certificates.

Typical employees receive between 5 and 25 days' training each year. There are two levels of appraisal and assessment – annual and monthly – which adopt a coaching, mentoring and development approach. The annual appraisal sets the person's goals, training and development needs for the year, taking into account their ambitions. The monthly assessment focuses on the short-term steps needed to achieve these goals.

Company culture

The company is in a top-performing category due to teamwork – everyone is always prepared to help. It's an environment where teamwork really does mean something. While the company complies with all employment legislation, there is no formal HR manager as Burgess instils elements of the HR function into all his managers. The focus is on managing stress and maintaining a good work/life balance (ie pushing the caring family approach). There are no unions as "noone has said they want one" – instead the company has a monthly operations meeting at which representatives of all departments within **jmc.it** get to discuss issues affecting their teams.

All who manage monthly assessments and mentoring have access to an external stress management consultancy to help ensure that any signs of stress are identified early and addressed professionally. The company's own internal stress management training scheme was recently singled out for praise by the International Stress Management Association (ISMA) as one of the most progressive initiatives by any SME in the UK. An anti-bullying policy has also been implemented.

There is no company-wide formal flexitime system as "it would be difficult to make it work efficiently." However, everyone benefits from an initiative that trades a 30-minute reduction in lunchtimes on Friday for a 4.30pm early finish. Out-of-hours' working is kept to a minimum. "It's very much the case that we want people to go home and spend time with their families."

Innovation

"We believe we break the mould for what a company of our size offers employees," says Burgess. "We seek to create a big company feel in terms of the breadth of the benefits we offer, but with the added benefit of the levels of personal attention and development available within a smaller company. Recently, one of our staff received a job offer from a major plc and found the benefits package to be far less comprehensive. He stayed."

As well as the benefits already mentioned, **jmc.it** supports a number of activities including sponsoring its football team, which plays twice a week; circuit training; a lunch time running club; and a mountain biking club taking advantage of the open countryside surrounding its offices.

The creed Burgess works to, and what drives the business, is client retention. Everyone realises that clients can easily find another reseller supplying the same products, and therefore employees are the key asset. The people employed by **jmc.it** genuinely treat the company as their own. They are motivated and enjoy a sense of belonging, which is reflected in the quality of relationships they form with their clients. It speaks volumes for the company when a client knows who they are dealing with by name. "You treat clients in the way you would like to be treated yourself," says Burgess. "True value stems from building long-term client relationships."

Diversity and social responsibility

The company adheres to an equal opportunity recruitment policy in that "people who are good enough to do the job are provided with the opportunity". The only "discrimination" practised is that the company might ask: "are the people good enough to do the job?" Today, the **jmc.it** staff is split 24% female to 76% male, and 17% of managers are female; 3.5% of the staff are from ethnic minorities. "We look at the people we are presented with," says Burgess. "There is no true disability among the staff as few applications are received on that basis."

The company is based on the periphery of Salford and was a founder member of the New Economics Foundation's Inner City 100 Foundation national project – an annual business index and research initiative, which locates and celebrates the 100 fastest-growing inner-city enterprises in the UK. **jmc.it** is proud to be part of this project, which celebrates the role of business in local communities and urban regeneration.

Corporate governance

In March 1994, **jmc.it** was the first IT company in the north-west of England to receive Investors in People (IIP) accreditation; and in celebrating 10 years of achieving the standards required, it is now on its fourth accreditation. The company has also received quality standard ISO 9001:2000 certification, was one of The Sunday Times Top 50 Best Small Companies to Work for 2004, and was a Manchester Evening News Business of the Year 2003 finalist. Aside from these, other current accreditations include those from legal, financial system and technology suppliers – indeed there are over 20 of these. The attainment of such official accreditations is a key element in ensuring the highest standards of service.

This is all formally backed up with compliance with the relevant data protection, health and safety, and disability discrimination legislation. In fact, all these issues are represented on the agenda at every board meeting. The company is too small to employ compliance officers, but is rigorous in ensuring all its obligations are fully met. The stress management and anti-bullying elements are contracted to external specialists for example, under the direction of the board.

Environmental record

The company encourages people to cycle to work. Few walk because of the location. There are five recycling stations around the site for paper, bottles, cans, etc., and these are transported outside to special recycling bins. "We allow clients to recycle computer equipment responsibly through ourselves," says Burgess. "We pass this equipment on to a specialist recycling contractor." All this will be handled in compliance with the Waste Electrical and Electronic Equipment (WEEE) directive, and the Restriction of the Use of Certain Hazardous Substances in Electrical and Electronic Equipment (ROHS) directive from July 2006.

The company is conscious of its responsibility; UN figures show that making the average PC requires 10 times its weight in chemicals (many of them toxic) and fossil fuels. An average desktop PC will have used up the weight of a sports car in materials before leaving the factory!

"With clients capable of sourcing any of the products we supply from numerous other outlets, our people are our greatest asset and fundamental to our success in attracting and retaining our client base," says Burgess. "Our aim is to offer a combination of the benefits of working for both large and small companies, as well as offering an ideal balance between work life and home life. With 7 years being the average length of service of the current workforce, it must be working."

John Lewis

John Lewis Partnership plc
171 Victoria Street, London SW1E 5NN
Tel: (0) 20 7828 1000
Web: www.johnlewispartnership.co.uk

John Lewis Partnership

Pay and Benefits	8.1	Innovation	7.2
Promotion and Development	6.8	Diversity	7.7
Training	7.3	Social Responsibility	8.3
Travel opportunities	4.1	Corporate Governance	8.3
Culture	7.6	Environment	7.7
Total			**73.1**

John Lewis is a UK-based retailer employing over 60,000 "partners". It currently operates 26 department stores and 163 Waitrose food shops whose combined turnover exceeds £5bn annually.

Executive summary

John Lewis began trading in 1864 as a family-owned draper's shop in London's Oxford Street. However, it was not until 1929 that the John Lewis Partnership came into existence, when Spedan Lewis transferred ownership of the business into the hands of its employees. Since then the formal structure of the company has remained unchanged and has underpinned all subsequent growth. Today, John Lewis has a substantial presence across the UK, both in department stores and in Waitrose supermarkets.

According to Andy Street, director of personnel: "Our success has come because our offer on the high street is distinct. Both businesses are about selling high-quality products supported by excellent customer service. What that requires from an HR perspective, is that we recruit people who are capable of delivering that customer proposition. We are looking to recruit people with the right attitude and values that can make a long-term commitment to an employee-owned business."

The last three years have seen growth in both sales and profit for John Lewis, although set against the retail sector as a whole the growth has been relatively modest. Determination to compete led to organisational reviews in John Lewis in which the company had to make some enforced redundancies among its support staff. Acceleration in the growth at Waitrose in 2003 came via the acquisition of 19 stores from Safeway.

Pay and benefits

Two factors dictate the size of an individual's pay packet. The first is the external market; that is, the average rate among retail organisations, which John Lewis aims to match. The second relates to performance. Here, high performance does not trigger bonuses – instead it propels partners on to more favourable pay scales. The company believes this is a progressive, long-term approach to reward in line with its strategic objective of securing loyalty to the business from those it recruits.

John Lewis is especially proud of the benefits package for which all staff are eligible and whose collective value places it in the upper quartile of retailer reward. As an example, a manager earning £25,000 could expect benefits equivalent to £6,000. These are derived from three main components. The first is the bonus reward, which is determined by annual company performance and which is awarded as an identical percentage of overall pay among all partners regardless of rank or seniority. In 2003, it was 12% of base salary.

The second element of the benefits package comes in the form of employee discounts. In Waitrose food shops, the discount amounts to 12% off each retail price; while staff in John Lewis stores enjoy a 25% discount on each item they purchase.

A non-contributory, final salary pension scheme represents the last element of the benefits package. John Lewis has publicly committed itself to maintaining this scheme, which is open to all new members with a minimum of five years' service. In 2003, the company paid £72m into the pension fund.

Partners may also enjoy a range of subsidised social activities. These activities are coordinated through an elected Partnership Council and typically include trips to local shows or attractions, and participation in sports and social clubs. Among the latter there is a well-established sailing club.

Promotion and development

"We would market ourselves as an organisation within which you can fulfil your career aspirations," says Street. "A number of our corporate board members have worked their way through the organisation, which is big enough and varied enough for you to have different development steps."

Most positions at John Lewis are obviously in the core retail function. Yet there is a strong belief in the concept of taking people who understand the values of the business and who have the right personal skills, and putting them in unfamiliar territory. In practice, this means assigning partners to complementary posts in order to develop versatile, well-rounded individuals. Mostly this happens within each individual retail business, though there is also some movement between the two.

Graduates make up only a small number of the total partners and join a structured development programme. Initial development is centrally coordinated, with support from specialist graduate recruitment managers. The bulk of the training is job-related, though there is also a focus on acquiring other skills such as leadership and performance management. Most partners will spend an average of 10 days a year being trained.

Although there is clear preference within John Lewis for developing "home-grown" talent, there is some external recruitment to key positions – however, applicants need to demonstrate empathy with the cultural values of the business. Another example of an outward face is in the operation of the senior academy scheme. Here, executives receive coaching and management education at international business schools in France and the US.

Company culture

The notion of a job for life is, of course, consigned to history now – as much because individuals demand career variety for themselves as because of the reality of the contemporary labour market. Yet at John Lewis it does not seem so fanciful as it does elsewhere. Total turnover of partners currently runs at 22% in the department stores and 33% in the food shops – this in a sector renowned for a high churn rate, and concentrated in a part of the UK where jobs are in plentiful supply. However, after three years the turnover drops dramatically. What is it that drives the longevity of service that John Lewis so prizes among its staff?

Well, whisper it, but in an age where the label "traditional" is often sneered at, John Lewis is traditional – in the best sense of the word – and proud of it. You won't find a relaxed approach to dress in this organisation; people are expected to look smart because they each represent the face of the company to its customers. Having respect for the customer as well as other partners is one of the core values of the business.

Other values that are deeply enshrined are honesty – appraisal is open and transparent and links directly to what people are paid – and teamwork. Of the latter, Street says, "It's the mentality that you're not just an employee, you have a responsibility as a partner for the greater good of the business. Some will want to participate in our democratic institutions, but everyone should contribute to their immediate work team."

Traditional in its values, John Lewis has a progressive approach to people management. Staff can work flexible hours by arrangement with line managers, and can use an in-house occupational health advisory service if they have stress or other work-related problems. A range of employee welfare services includes chiropody – a popular service in an organisation where a lot of walking gets done!

Innovation

Again, from a business perspective John Lewis may trade on a traditional heritage, but it has demonstrated a willingness to explore new areas in order to target customers. Its online shopping service, John Lewis Direct, has proved a success where many similar ventures have floundered; so too the internet grocer Ocado, in which the company has a 40% stake. The latter transports all items from a single warehouse and is now ranked in the top three internet retail distribution businesses by sales volume.

Within the organisation, staff are encouraged to be think of ways to improve the work environment. As well as a long-standing suggestion scheme, the company introduced an annual employee attitudes survey in 2003 – which has generated a lot of feedback, both positive and not so positive. It has also just launched a salary sacrifice scheme, allowing partners to swap remuneration for computer equipment, childcare vouchers and other items.

Diversity and social responsibility

John Lewis serves a diverse range of customers at many of its locations and as such aims to reflect this in its partners. Women currently constitute 60% of staff, and just under half of all managers are female. There is ongoing monitoring of the ethnic diversity of the workforce, 14% of whom are from minority backgrounds. There are also proactive efforts to move partners from ethnic minorities into management positions. The current proportion is 4%, but increasing representation of such partners on the graduate scheme means this proportion is set to rise considerably over coming years.

The company's constitution contains seven core principles relating to purpose, power, profit, members, customers, business and relationships. Though drawn up in 1928, John Lewis believes it anticipates much of the modern CSR agenda. Today the business allocates 2.4% of its profits to social responsibility activities and it is an active member of the CSR network, Business in the Community.

At a local level, each store makes donations to charitable causes chosen by elected charities committees. During 2003–04, these committees gave £430,000 to 3,360 charities – part of £2.88m given in total. The company also operates a sabbatical scheme, whereby support is given to partners who carry out voluntary work at a registered UK charity.

Corporate Governance

"On our main corporate board, we have five of the main directors directly elected by the Partnership Council. So if you want real evidence that the partnership is there to be both commercially successful and act in the interests of the partners, what more could you have?" says Street.

As an equity-owning partnership, John Lewis is not subject to external public scrutiny but it endeavours to set itself the same tests shareholders would. One example of this is the financial return it aims to achieve each year in order to outperform competitors. Street adds, "We also need to satisfy business analysts because we have to raise bond finance, so we have to be self-regulating against very stringent performance criteria."

Environment

With more than half a million different product lines, John Lewis has relationships with a multitude of global suppliers. And in recognition of the emergence of the ethical consumer, it undertakes to be transparent about its sourcing techniques and what it expects of suppliers. The standards it expects were formally set out in 2000, in the company's Responsible Sourcing Principles.

Closer to home, John Lewis is an enthusiastic recycler of waste items – recycling 300 tonnes of packaging in a typical week. Over 2004, waste output was reduced by 20% while the proportion of recycled goods increased by 11%.

Johnson Matthey

Johnson Matthey plc
2-4 Cockspur Street, London SW1Y 5BQ
Tel: (0) 20 7269 8400
Web: www.matthey.com **Email:** jmpr@matthey.com

JM ⊗

Johnson Matthey

Pay and Benefits	7.1	Innovation	6.4
Promotion and Development	6.5	Diversity	5.0
Training	6.2	Social Responsibility	6.2
Travel opportunities	6.7	Corporate Governance	6.3
Culture	5.8	Environment	6.3
Total			**62.5**

Johnson Matthey is a world-leading specialty chemicals company, applying innovative technology to improving the environment and enhancing our quality of life. Today the group has four divisions: catalysts, precious metals, colours and coatings, and pharmaceutical materials. Although it is British in origin, Johnson Matthey is a multinational company selling its products globally. With operations in 34 countries, the company has 7,500 employees worldwide.

Executive summary

Johnson Matthey (JM) has seen its turnover practically double from 1995's £2.27bn to 2004's £4.5bn, and operating profit grow from £100.4m to £206m over the same period. JM's turnover is heavily impacted by the high value of precious metals sold by the group, with the total value of sales each year varying according to the mix of metals sold and level of trading activity. Stripping out the value of precious metals (which provides a more useful measure of returns), sales in 2004 increased by 6% to £1.2bn, and the return on sales from 16.3% to 16.8%. Profit before tax, exceptional items and goodwill amortisation increased by 3% to £195.7m.

JM is a highly successful company that is not particularly well known to the general public. Its customers are usually the largest corporations. Much of JM's business operates in the chemicals sector, and its products go a long way to helping the environment (eg catalytic converters) and people (eg anti-cancer drugs). JM has also gained the Queen's Award for commitment to innovation and excellence 10 times.

Pay and benefits

"JM ranks alongside the best in the FTSE 100," says David Hall, group HR manager. "We offer market median-related base salaries with opportunities for upper quartile total remuneration for superior performance."

Graduates typically start on £20,600 and PhDs on £23,000. Incentive arrangements exist throughout the business, with annual performance-related bonuses for senior executive and middle managers, and profit sharing schemes for most other employees. Those entitled to the provision of a company car have the option of a cash alternative.

Membership of the company's Share Incentive Plan is offered to employees in seven countries, where 85% of eligible employees participate and own shares in a "two-for-one" matched arrangement. Each year, JM contributes over 1.5% of annual profits towards the Share Incentive Plan.

The robust and healthy Johnson Matthey Employees Pension Scheme is a defined benefit final salary pension scheme with membership open to new employees. A pension is provided based on an accrual rate of 1/57th of final pensionable salary for each year of pensionable service. Employees contribute 4% to the scheme while JM contributes 15%.

Normal retirement age is 63 with flexibility of early retirement from 50. Life assurance and dependants pension benefits are also provided.

Procedures exist to encourage fairness and transparency when considering requests for flexible working. Wherever possible, arrangements are agreed which are consistent with individuals' needs and the business's operational and safety requirements. Some staff work shorter weeks or days, and some only in school term times to accommodate family commitments. Childcare voucher purchase facilities are being piloted on a trial basis and are likely to be extended company-wide.

Employees who have given dedicated service for 20 and 30 years are recognised with awards and local social functions. At 35 years, there is an award and presentation function in London, hosted by the chief executive.

"While we cannot guarantee a job for life, JM does offer our people the opportunity to develop enhanced skills and greater employability," says Hall.

Promotion and development

"There are a lot of employees who stay working for the company for many years," says Hall. "JM allows individuals the opportunity to achieve. There is good career progression within the company." As testament to that, the recently appointed chief executive started out as a graduate trainee in 1980. Two of the most recently appointed executive directors are also internal appointments. Staff turnover globally is about 7% each year.

JM sets out to promote from within by drawing on its "high-potential pools of talent". There is a policy to provide personal development opportunities to meet each employee's potential and aspirations. Appraisal interviews take place annually throughout JM and include a review by the employee's manager of achievement against objectives, feedback about success, areas for improvement, and training and development plans. Progress with objectives is discussed quarterly, with each appraisal reviewed by the manager's boss.

"Employee communication at JM is two-way," says Hall. "Employee surveys are conducted locally to investigate employees' attitudes to key business objectives, for example. Employee feedback is encouraged at all levels."

People at JM are encouraged to develop their own careers and will be actively supported. Managers often look across business unit boundaries for talent, and cross-function and cross-division moves are encouraged. Employees can expect 5–14 days training each year. Most graduate entrants attend the Group Business Training Programme (12 two-day modules), which is often followed by practical studies leading to a management certificate, diploma or MBA. Coaching and mentoring procedures are in place to ensure all individuals receive appropriate and agreed training and job experience.

Company culture

People say, "JM is the multinational company with the personal touch". The key words JM typically utilises to describe its culture include continuous improvement, innovation, commitment and teamwork. Staff are valued for being good team players with integrity, on how they use their intellect, the communication skills and rapport they exhibit, and their ability "to make things happen". Continuous improvement is seen at all levels in JM. Most senior management have worked in a number of JM's major business sectors in different parts of the world, and will have spent the best part, if not all of their careers, with the company. The company eschews passing an MBA per se, opting instead for the practical MBA approach indicated earlier. There are over 100 currently studying for the certificate and diploma stages, while a small number have been accredited with MBAs. Some of the company's UK sites have Investors in People accreditation.

Each year, up to 30 people are on the JM management programme in the UK. The key thrust underpinning the management philosophy is to "work smarter not longer" and to prioritise the tasks you are trying to address. To put the work/life balance into perspective, there is a long-held principle within the company that "families come first". Management training encourages an emphasis on time allocation to family and self, with the consequent control over excessive work-related stress beneficial for employees and JM alike. The culture is such that most of the staff tend to stay for a long time.

Innovation

For a company that's so immersed in modern technology – leading-edge fuel cells, the industrial applications of platinum such as emission control catalysis, and the development of platinum-based anti-cancer and acute pain relief drugs – innovation is both a byword and the life blood for JM. The company is a world leader in its fields of activity and is recognised by its peers and customers as such, with the commitment acknowledged through the 10 Queen's Awards it has received. First recognised in 1968 for export achievement, JM went on to secure awards on many other occasions for export, technology, environment and innovation.

A similar philosophy runs through the HR strategy, whose key aim is to enable the business and employees to grow. This is achieved through ensuring that there is minimal bureaucracy, believing in win/win deals, and the marrying of personal objectives with business ones. The philosophy of introducing new ideas is achieved through the well-planned communication of strategy and goals, the training and coaching schemes on offer, teamwork within the company, and problem-solving exercises and methods of instigating continuous improvement. It works. "We instil a wider awareness of the company for staff through two-day group awareness seminars," says Hall. "There's a UK programme which includes employees from Europe and Asia, and a separate US programme."

Diversity and social responsibility

The balance of JM's staff is changing rapidly; 20% of its staff are female, while among new graduate recruits the ratio is 50:50. At the management level, 13% are women. JM operates a flat organisational structure with a distinct lack of hierarchies, which offers opportunities for women to demonstrate their capabilities. "Our equal opportunities policy goes beyond legal requirements in specifying non-discrimination on the basis of age or sexual orientation," says Hall.

Charitable organisations received around £323,000 from JM in the financial year ending March 2003 – excluding payroll giving, staff donations and employees giving their time to specific causes. Since its early days back in the 19th Century, JM has supported the Royal London Society for the Blind. There's also one charitable organisation selected each year as a Charity of the Year. Previous charities that have been supported in this way are: Help the Hospices, Diabetes UK, NSPCC, National Asthma Campaign, British Lung Foundation and Macmillan Cancer Relief.

All JM sites globally strive to play positive roles in the communities in which they operate. For example, in the UK that includes providing newspapers for local schools, repairing a parish church roof, supporting a local school maths initiative, and helping to restore local nature reserves. Good progress has been achieved towards ISO 14001 certification around the world.

Corporate governance

JM applies all the principles set out in section one of the Combined Code on Corporate Governance with reference to the structure of its board, directors' remuneration, relations with shareholders; and the procedures for financial reporting, internal control and audit. The company was in full compliance with the code in its most recent financial year.

All employees are required to maintain the highest standards of ethical conduct and corporate responsibility worldwide. "We fully support the principles set out within the

UN Universal Declaration of Human Rights and the International Labour Organisation's Core Conventions," says Hall. "We are proud of the quality of our relationships with our staff everywhere."

"The company's most important investment will always be the one it makes in its people. JM places total priority on the continuing development of its management talent and the skills of all its employees, to enable them to perform to the highest standards to meet the challenges of the future."

Given the company operates in 34 countries, relations with trade unions are managed locally and are generally considered to be positive and constructive. The trade unions are kept up to date about the company's business issues and are involved both formally and informally according to local site and country practice.

Environmental record

The group's environment health and safety (EHS) management system is applied worldwide and sets standards of performance that go beyond legal requirements. There are policies in place for collecting and recycling waste materials. To be more precise, there are policies for waste minimisation – either through introducing new technologies and processes, or by continuous improvement projects on existing processes. JM's refining business is leading the field in the recovery and recycling of precious metals from industry.

As indicated earlier, good progress has been made in achieving ISO 14001 certification. Today, nearly 50% of employees work at sites with this accreditation.

The company is firmly committed to managing its activities to provide the highest level of protection to the environment. Through its portfolio of products, JM looks to provide the population with cleaner air to live in, clean energy and healthier lifestyles. JM offers employees interest-free loans for the purchase of public transport season tickets, and staff opting for the cash alternative to a company car typically use the money to fund public transport as a preferred means of travelling to work.

"It's about employee commitment to the company – the sense of pride in the role our products play in protecting and improving the environment and public health," says Hall.

Keoghs

Keoghs
2 The Parklands, Bolton BL6 4SE
Tel: (0) 1204 677000 **Fax:** (0) 1204 677111
Web: www.keoghs.co.uk

Pay and Benefits	6.3	Innovation	6.5
Promotion and Development	6.9	Diversity	6.2
Training	6.9	Social Responsibility	6.4
Travel opportunities	3.9	Corporate Governance	6.8
Culture	6.8	Environment	5.8
Total			**62.5**

Keoghs is one of the UK's leading law firms; it specialises mainly in insurance, litigation, insurance fraud, corporate finance, company and commercial law. It has 375 employees, 295 of which are based in Bolton and the rest in Coventry. Keoghs is a privately owned partnership with 25 partners in all. Annual fees average £15m.

Executive Summary

Founded by Joseph Ritson at the end of the 19th century, the modern firm was born in 1968 following a merger with Keoghs (Keogh Ritson became simply Keoghs three years ago). Personal injury litigation has long been the key specialist business area, and 90% of the client base is drawn from big insurance companies. Given the upheaval in the insurance industry in recent years, legal service providers have had to market themselves aggressively in order to secure a foothold on the panels of solicitors used by the main companies. Spiralling costs and increased M&A activity have cut the number of operators, and accordingly the number of law firms instructed. Yet those that have been able to secure a place on the preferred supplier lists have enjoyed greater business volumes – and Keoghs is among their number.

That said, if the last half-decade has seen healthy growth in fees for Keoghs and its people, the current environment is nothing less than challenging. Frances Cross, HR director, observes, "Long gone are the days when you could get fantastic hourly rates for legal services – it's very competitive now. There is a lot of fixed-fee work out there – the fee-earners have to be extremely commercially oriented. Everyone has performance targets, whereas five years ago that was unheard of. Now everything is measured and there is a much greater level of scrutiny."

As a response to market developments, Keoghs strategy has been to diversify its products and services. In particular, the firm has worked to grow its company and commercial division; it operates mainly in corporate finance and acquisitions, and now accounts for 10% of all business. The aim is to establish more of a balance between long-standing relationships with suppliers and customers, and traditional transaction-based dispute-related casework where there is significant pressure on margins. More generally, Keoghs is shifting towards products and services that add value and bring in a premium rate of revenue. A new product team was established in 2003 to underline this intent.

Pay and Benefits

Keoghs regularly benchmarks its compensation policy against equivalent regional law firms, and average basic pay compares favourably with most of the competition. Middle managers can expect to earn around £35,000, while partner remuneration varies from between £60,000 to £140,000. A profit-sharing bonus can add up to 10% of base pay if all company targets are met; in practice, this usually amounts to between 3% and 4%.

The firm is shortly to move to a flexible benefits system; currently every employee is eligible for private medical care, income protection, life assurance and critical illness cover. All equity partners plus other members of senior management get a car allowance.

Also under review is the company pension scheme, which at the time of writing is a stakeholder scheme.

At Keoghs the emphasis is firmly on teamworking, so the reward and recognition strategy is framed accordingly. There are quarterly Team Excellence awards, a monthly Making A Difference award, and ad hoc Extra Mile awards given by team leaders to members who have made a contribution over and above what would normally be expected. Each team also has a budget for teambuilding or social activities. Long-service awards are given at 10 and 25 years.

Promotion and development

As a law firm, Keoghs has a majority of fee-earners who are not fully qualified solicitors. In fact, the firm has a strong track record of promoting secretarial and support staff into fee-earning positions – principally as a response to external market conditions. A number of employees began as modern apprentices, and moved via an assessment centre onto a litigation executive foundation programme. Although much of the litigation they will go on to practice is very process-driven, there are 16 separate training workshops.

Most training provision is in-house and covers anything from teambuilding and leadership to more technical programmes. Individuals will usually undergo a minimum of 16 hours' training annually. The focus is very much now on getting employees to drive their own development needs, and this has been enabled in part through recently installed electronic learning and performance management tools. One result has been a reduction in staff turnover in recent years; it currently stands at 13% – 1% above the target rate.

According to Cross: "Another shift is towards one-to-one coaching. We're looking at identifying our internal experts – and formalising a coaching role for them. We want to put the experience of those in customer-facing roles to real use, rather than rely exclusively on HR-led training programmes." There is some support for non-legal qualifications too; currently the firm is sponsoring two MBA students, as well as a number of support-service qualifications.

Entry-level appointees who do not qualify as solicitors can rise to associate status as early as two years after becoming fee-earners. Those with ambitions to reach equity partner status, however, must be qualified solicitors. Thereafter, it normally takes between three and five years to join the partnership, some of which will be spent on a partner development programme. Here, the emphasis will not simply be on growing billing volumes, but also on acquiring commercial awareness.

Company Culture

Approachability is one of the keywords on which Keoghs sells its services, and this equally extends to the workplace. "We're a very friendly, down to earth organisation," comments Cross.

The belief is that a relaxed, informal environment delivers better results for clients, because while professional standards are always maintained, there is no fear-factor to inhibit people. In fact, the combination of openness and process-orientation is seen as the cornerstone of business success. Mistakes are seen as opportunities for improvement, not blame.

Cross says, "One example of this, is when we had a hiccup with a major client. Following an audit, it became apparent that we hadn't always followed their guidelines; this could have had serious consequences for us, but we worked very closely with the client to fix it. We were very transparent, there was no fingerpointing, and we remapped the whole process. That actually became the model going forward – we now get fantastic ratings from that client."

The grown-up attitude to employees extends to flexible working arrangements, which were brought in long before recent legislation. With women making up a majority of staff, Keoghs has guidelines for returning mothers that wish to work part time. In addition, there is a progressive approach to stress management: as well as carrying out stress audits, the firm has a comprehensive wellbeing programme. Offerings include hypnotherapy, Indian head massages, aromatherapy, chiropody and counselling services.

For the solicitors at Keoghs, building client relationships is an important part of the job description. Whether meeting for a pint at the pub or attending corporate hospitality events – the objective is to ensure visibility of the Keoghs brand, and its values of dependability and total client satisfaction.

Innovation

Innovation is named as one of the firm's shared values, and the concept has assumed increasing importance as the firm looks to diversify its services and add value wherever possible. Clearly the new product team has this remit, but everyone's ideas count and a suggestion scheme has brought about real improvements in case management.

Elsewhere there are business process reengineering teams that work on problem solving in a number of areas; effective transfer of information is an ongoing area of focus. Business unit representatives also meet regularly to exchange information and cascade recommendations down and across the firm. In line with new legislation on consultation, this mechanism is set to be strengthened further with the establishment of a staff forum to enable improved upward feedback on policy and planning issues.

Most training is job-specific, however, there is a social committee to fund extra-curricular subjects, and Spanish evening classes have proved popular in recent times.

Diversity and social responsibility

For most positions, people are recruited locally; Keoghs sees itself as an important part of both the communities in which it is based. The firm supports a number of local charities in Bolton and Coventry, splitting an annual budget of £20,000 between them. Money is raised in different ways: through funds directly allocated to a charity committee, through staff-nominated charity collections on Dress Down Days, and through individual fundraising efforts. In the past these have included parachute jumping, running the Paris Marathon and climbing Mount Kilimanjaro.

The commitment to social responsibility extends to the very top of the organisation. With close links to a number of local schools, chief executive Paul Smith job-swapped for a day with a head teacher at one institution – the experience brought new management ideas to both business and school alike.

In respect of the make-up of staff, Keoghs is very far from being a male preserve. Three quarters of employees are women, who also comprise half its managers. Just over 5% are drawn from racial and religious minorities, and the firm is keen to attract more – particularly through the non-qualified solicitor route.

Corporate Governance

The firm appointed a compliance officer in 2003 to spearhead a drive for good corporate governance. All employees are made aware of issues relevant to their job; for example, accounting procedures, money laundering and data protection issues figure prominently for those undertaking company and commercial client work. Training is designed to be accessible, features various quizzes, and is largely e-delivered.

As part of its commitment to sustaining client relationships, Keoghs issues a monthly newsletter as well as ad hoc client briefs that update developments in this area. Demonstrating a commitment to good corporate governance is now important not only for retaining clients, but often mandatory in tendering for new business.

Awarded ISO 9001 certification and Investors in People, the firm has also received a number of commendations from the British Safety Council.

Environment

Frances Cross comments, "We have an environmental policy statement which is regularly reviewed, and one of the commitments is to both reduce and recycle waste. At the moment we are recycling plastic items after using environmentally friendly cleaning products. Although we don't stipulate that company cars should be environmentally friendly, anyone who car shares is guaranteed a car parking space. And as part of our new range of flexible benefits, employees will have the opportunity to purchase a bike for travel to and from the workplace."

KPMG

KPMG
8 Salisbury Square, London EC4Y 8BB
Tel: (0) 20 7311 1000 **Fax:** (0) 20 7311 3311
Web: www.kpmg.co.uk www.kpmg.co.uk/careers

Pay and Benefits	6.9	Innovation	6.8
Promotion and Development	7.5	Diversity	6.7
Training	7.4	Social Responsibility	7.2
Travel opportunities	7.2	Corporate Governance	7.3
Culture	7.2	Environment	7.0
Total			**71.2**

KPMG is the global network of the professional services firms of KPMG International. With nearly 100,000 people worldwide, KPMG member firms provide audit, tax, and advisory services from 715 cities in 148 countries. In the UK, it employs in the region of 9,000 people, around 500 of whom are partners. Fee income for 2003 was just over £1bn – a drop of 1% on the previous year.

Executive Summary

The firm's roots go back to the 19th century, but the modern KPMG was formed in 1987 with the merger of two leading firms, Peat Marwick International (PMI) and Klynveld Main Goerdeler (KMG). It has since emerged as one of the world's leading brands.

The UK operation is the largest in the firm's EMA region, which covers 86 countries. Although there are strong links between countries – fostered by shared goals and investment – the UK firm operates autonomously, and counts 87% of the FTSE 100 as clients (audit and non-audit services).

In 2002, the firm made 1,000 staff redundant due to a downturn in the British economy. Recently however, it has begun recruiting in greater numbers for staff at all levels. The economic climate may now be improving, but the firm is still having to work hard to maintain volumes. Its fees per professional staff total is the best in the UK, although revenues for the year ended September 2003 dipped slightly to just over £1bn. Profitability rose, however, and there was strong growth in corporate finance and risk advisory services.

The collapse of Andersen cast a cloud over the audit community, and the Sarbanes-Oxley Act that came into force in the US in 2002 signalled much greater regulation and scrutiny of its activities. In response, KPMG clarified its multi-disciplinary offering; in the UK, this included the sale of its consulting practice and the divestment of its legal arm, Klegal, in 2003.

Pay and benefits

Group employee remuneration at the firm is comprised of base and variable pay, and benefits. The benchmark varies according to business area, but for most employees the relevant comparison is with the other "big three" accounting firms. Average base salary is pegged in the middle of that market; but when the firm performs well, bonus payments rise to levels that mean KPMG's package outperforms the market.

The size of bonus payments awarded to individuals is primarily on the basis of an annual performance review, which also helps set base pay levels. Annual discretionary bonus payments are also awarded in line with the financial performance of the business, which determines overall size of the bonus pool. Newly qualified partners can expect an increase of between 25% and 30%.

The firm offers a range of flexible benefits including 25 days' holiday annually, life cover, private medical insurance, and critical illness cover. There is a stakeholder pension scheme that is open to everyone, whose returns increase according to age. Contributions of up to 4% are matched up the age of 30; in the top age bracket, the return is almost double that of the contribution.

Encore! is a recognition scheme for exceptional individual or team performance. Anyone can nominate anyone else; successful nominees receive a prize worth £250 (capped at £1,000 for teams). Prizes range from retail vouchers to a day's outdoor activities. KPMG also funds activities run by employees at a number of sports and social clubs.

Promotion and development

KPMG believes its reputation for developing people differentiates it from its immediate competitors, and a brand review carried out in early 2004 found that clients agreed. Today, however, the focus is not merely about being a better training ground for would-be accountants – it is on taking a longer-term view of development, helping people to develop the leadership capabilities KPMG requires as well as fulfilling their personal and professional aspirations.

Central to the firm's current practice in this area is Managing for Excellence, a programme that recognises that developing and retaining talented people in an atmosphere where everyone can achieve their full potential is not a "nice to have" but a "must have". Coaching, which is a key element of KPMG's learning and development strategy, is also a key element of the programme. Currently, 350 managers are assigned to coaching duties that help grow individuals professionally and personally in line with KPMG's value-set.

In terms of graduate recruitment there are now 15 different entry points, aiming to appeal to a much wider market. Performance appraisals are used to identify strengths and ways of capitalising on them, as well as to determine the key development needs of individuals – most of which will be met through practical on-the-job training. Standards are high and "passengers" are unlikely to be accommodated.

The Emerging Leader programme is an annual programme aimed at high-flying managers and partners – or the top 15% of each grade. Designed to build the breadth and depth of their leadership and business skills, it offers participants an opportunity to test themselves outside their comfort zone. Often this means working in the community, such as in a school or other educational establishment.

The firm supports its people in a range of professional qualifications: accounting, tax and corporate finance obviously figure highly – but so too do non-accounting-related qualifications like human resources, architecture and surveying. Every year it sponsors up to 30 MBA students; it also supports senior executives who want to take time out to study at leading establishments such as INSEAD or the London Business School.

In addition to the firm's leadership development programmes, KPMG spends £24m on learning and development provision in the UK – an average of £2,600 a head. Much of it can be accessed online. The My Learning website contains details on all mandatory and optional training courses, and provides an easy way for each individual to track their learning path.

Company Culture

KPMG's strength lies in its people and the knowledge they possess. Accordingly, self-motivating, intellectually curious people thrive here; this, in turn, means that employees can expect not only a high level of support, but also the freedom to manage their own learning path.

This means that there is plenty of opportunity for movement around the business. Would-be partners will work in KPMG offices overseas as part of their assessment programme; others take their skills into other organisations in the UK, allowing for a different perspective on the services they provide. The firm has strong links with the government, which enables a number of public sector assignments; charities also offer a wholly different environment within which managers can test themselves.

The firm's leadership is keen to ensure operational transparency is matched by transparency within the organisation. To ensure open lines of communication, there are elected employee representatives for each function who act as a sounding board for the executive. Staff are encouraged to contact their representative with any issues they may have, and the minutes of each meeting between representatives and the executive are posted on the company intranet. The focus on robust bottom-up communication is mirrored by a culture of consultation. When the firm underwent a downsizing exercise, affected staff were consulted at every stage and had access to outplacement support.

Since the beginning of 2004, the firm has expanded its offerings in regard to flexible working: options include additional holiday purchase; glide time (a system by which employees can flex their core working hours to earlier or later in the working day); homeworking (properly supported with broadband access etc.); and the more traditional part-time working and job sharing opportunities. Take-up of the offerings has steadily increased since they were made available.

Innovation

The firm's people collectively represent a formidable knowledge base. To provide a framework for sharing this knowledge and creating a climate of innovation, it has established Kworld – an online resource which includes a heavily populated discussion forum. This enables users to access information about new clients and post up their ideas about how to improve the business. KNews is a magazine, which reports on all employee activity in the firm.

Many innovations that affect the practice happen at a local level. One UK business area operates a "'treasure chest" – used to bank ideas for improved client service delivery that cannot be implemented immediately. Last year saw the first annual Client Service Awards, which recognise innovation and creativity in service delivery. The environment department were the overall winners for the efficient use of paper supply in the value chain.

Diversity and social responsibility

As a global organisation with an international client base, KPMG is aware of the business case for reflecting diversity among its people, 48% of whom are women. In the UK, it recently appointed a head of diversity – and has two board-level champions of race and gender. KPMG is a member of the employers' forums Opportunity Now, Race for Opportunity, and the Employers' Forum on Disability. It benchmarks its own work on diversity annually, and has carried out internal research into staff views on diversity. There are Christian, Islamic and Japanese societies; and a gay and lesbian network called Breathe. Nevertheless, at partner level, 88% of employees are male with an average age of 44.

The firm has 2,000 volunteers working on CSR-based activities at any one time. The overarching focus of its social programmes is on employability – and between 2002 and 2004 the firm partnered with other companies on a project to bring homeless people back into mainstream life. Other noteworthy initiatives include a numeracy and literacy programme in local schools, and a mentoring scheme organised through the Prince's Trust. The KPMG Foundation is a fund for education and social projects, which currently totals £8m.

Corporate Governance

"The last few years have been difficult for all of us. We have experienced turbulent capital markets, great economic uncertainty and high-profile corporate scandals. The integrity of our profession has been questioned, and our work is now subject to unprecedented scrutiny." So observes Mike Rake, chairman of KPMG International, in the introduction to The KPMG Way – a booklet outlining the current KPMG work and brand philosophy.

In order to track client-facing activity across all 100,000 people, the firm has introduced more robust systems to ensure there is no conflict between audit provision in one part of the business and audit provision elsewhere. Keen to reduce liability and manage risk in audit provision, the board has also established a separate sub-committee to consider strategic risk. This is in addition to an audit committee, which meets three times a years to discuss risk and reporting issues with other members of senior management.

Environment

A series of programmes covering environmental impact are in place across the firm; KPMG is in the process of integrating these as part of its commitment to environmentally aware business practice. This was underlined in a public policy declaration on the subject in 2000.

The firm has an ongoing commitment to reduce (recycled) paper consumption in its operations; half of any savings made through reduced waste are donated to a charity of employees' choosing. It also operates a mobile phone recycling scheme and has established links with EarthWatch, a global wildlife charity. There is a good deal of local activity too: for example, a bicycle hire scheme is in place at the Watford office so employees can forgo the use of their car if they want to go out at lunchtime.

KPMG's London HQ achieved ISO 14001 certification for environmental management, while the firm as a whole was recently named as one of the top ten environmentally friendly companies in its sector by corporate responsibility agency Business in the Community.

Kwik Fit Financial Services

Kwik-Fit Financial Services
1 Masterton Way, Tannochside Business Park, Uddingston G71 5PU
Tel: (0) 1698 804001
Web: www.kwik-fitinsurance.com **Email:** info@kfis.co.uk

Pay and Benefits	6.8	Innovation	6.9
Promotion and Development	7.8	Diversity	6.9
Training	7.6	Social Responsibility	7.2
Travel opportunities	3.4	Corporate Governance	6.6
Culture	7.0	Environment	6.3
Total			**66.5**

Kwik-Fit Financial Services is an insurance intermediary with a staff of 960 working from a call centre outside Glasgow. It started out ten years ago as Kwik-Fit Insurance (with a primary focus on motor insurance), but it has successfully moved into other areas such as household and pet cover, breakdown recovery, life assurance and utilities; and has re-branded itself Kwik-Fit Financial Services (KFFS). It is one of the biggest call centres in an area of the country that is teeming with call centres – all competing for staff.

Executive summary

Kwik-Fit was founded in 1971 by entrepreneur Sir Tom Farmer. As the company grew dramatically, the client base of motorists with exhaust and tyre needs was there for the taking – so Kwik-Fit Insurance was launched in 1995 (initially selling one product, motor insurance, but now offering a vast array of products). In the current three-year cycle, improvements in financial performance have been significant. There was a pre-tax profit of £109,000 on sales of £35.5m in 2003; this was expected to grow to £131,000 in 2004 and to £156,000 in 2005.

This is from a low in 2002 when there was a loss of £4.2m; the turnaround has been achieved mainly because of a strategic focus on writing business which is profitable.

In the Insurance Times 2004 Top 50 UK Broker report, the company was placed at number 23. Turnover increase per employee increased by 25.7%, the largest of any broker surveyed.

Kwik-Fit is owned by venture capitalists CVC Capital Partners who bought it from Ford in November 2002.

Pay and benefits

There are over 50 call centres in and around the Glasgow area where Kwik-Fit is based, so competition for competent staff is fierce. KFFS works hard at keeping its workforce happy. Keren Edwards, HR director, says: "We sell insurance. You can't taste it, see it or smell it. It is an invisible product. So it is all about our people – they bring in the revenue and make happy customers. One of our major challenges is to attract and keep staff – there is always someone else looking to offer better salaries or benefits. We have to make our working environment better than anyone else's."

Over the past three years, basic salaries have increased by 19%. Starting salaries are in the top 25% of call centres in Scotland. The company's goal is to make it "a fantastic place to work" and with this in mind it conducted a massive staff consultation exercise. This meant losing 630 working days over two months, and resulted in no fewer than 6,550 suggestions.

The result was fundamental changes to employees' everyday working lives. There is now a chill-out room equipped with a pool table, X-boxes, satellite television, table football, board games and books; and a team of volunteers have created a garden.

There is greater flexibility about time off. Annual holidays range from 20 to 25 days a year, including two duvet days to be taken from this entitlement – the employee can phone in the morning to say they won't be coming in, without having to give a reason.

There is an onsite gym at £10 a month; and for £5 a month they can do classes in yoga, salsa dancing and Tai Chi as well as have a massage or a session with a visiting beautician. And as annual sales of £99m show, they still find time to work hard.

Promotion and development

There is an established career path through the main operational areas, moving from consultant to senior consultant, team leader, floor manager and head of department; 100% of those in management positions have been promoted internally. Of the senior managers who report directly to directors, 95% have been promoted internally and 80% started their careers at KFFS. Even within specialist departments, such as HR, internal transfers have allowed employees to move to another department, train on the job, and have the company sponsor their further education.

Promotions are based entirely on merit and not on length of service or age. There is a predominantly young workforce, and the age at which employees are promoted reflects this. The head of customer care – with responsibility for more than 200 employees – was promoted into the role at the age of 29, having left university with an accountancy degree and worked his way up.

Employees go through a six-monthly appraisal, involving a discussion about individual aspirations over the following six months and two years. Combined with the creation of a personal development plan, this prompts a discussion with the appraising manager about the employee's career development and ambitions.

Employees can email the managing director directly via the intranet with their ideas, comments and suggestions. He responds personally to each one received, and passes the responses out for action. The best idea each month earns a weekend break for two.

All directors spend half a day each month in each department on a rotational basis, discussing roles and frustrations – and they do not hesitate to make changes as a result.

Company culture

Can a comparatively young call centre company have a culture? The call centre business does not have a good name. The perception is of masses of people at desks, on the phone, working long hours for little reward and job satisfaction. But KFFS has created a culture that has changed all that. It describes its corporate culture as being people-centred, focused on results and customer oriented.

The 6,550 ideas it distilled from the staff consultation programme, and how it reacted to this, illustrate what it is all about. In two years it became a different workplace with wholesale changes aimed at making KFFS a fantastic place to work. And the changes keep coming – now on the way is a new pension scheme and an onsite crèche.

A Minister for Fun has been appointed, and his job is to organise regular parties and fundraising events. An interior designer was brought in to remove the call centre's "bland and a bit dull" appearance.

Staff turnover has been reduced dramatically. The company was voted fourth best place to work in Scotland for the second year running in the Sunday Times Best Companies to Work for List in 2004.

Other call centre companies now visit KFFS to see how it is done and to learn a few lessons. HR director Keren Edwards says: "We welcome them. I don't believe they can replicate what we have here. We have our own culture – it is all about becoming a listening organisation."

Innovation:

KFFS cites its route to its market as being innovative – the shrewd use of the Kwik-Fit car centres which deal with exhausts and tyres. Within 48 hours of a visit to the garage, the motorist gets a customer satisfaction call – and that is an opportunity to talk about motor insurance. This model has been very successful – the offering now goes well beyond motor insurance, and it won an IFS award for innovation in 2002.

The company is constantly looking for new products and services, and over the last 2 years has added to its customer menu, resulting in an expansion of the business and a change of name to reflect this. It has introduced a Keep Motoring Policy, which ensures the provision of a courtesy car regardless of the reason for the damage to the vehicle – standard comprehensive cover provides a car only in the event of theft or total write-off.

The company is also innovative on the HR front – for example, appointing a concierge to run errands for the staff. Staff are encouraged to come up with new ideas and are rewarded for them. The whole KFFS approach to HR matters is innovative and refreshing.

Diversity and social responsibility

The company policy is to ensure that all employees and potential employees are treated equally and fairly, regardless of their gender, race, religion, national origin, sexual orientation or age. More than half (58%) of the staff are women, as are 41% of the managers.

The overall percentage of female employees is skewed by a large proportion of part-time employees, and a large influx of customer care advisers during the year – they tend to be predominantly female. The area in which the company is located has a low percentage of people from racial minorities so its workforce (with 3% from racial minorities) is in line with the make-up of the local community.

The company strives to improve its links with the local community through charity work, liaison with schools, and providing employment options for those who are long-term unemployed. Most of the employees come from within an eight-mile radius of the centre.

HR director Keren Edwards states: "We believe we have a responsibility to interact with and contribute to the prosperity of our community. We have a detailed programme of visits from schools by both teachers and pupils, we support causes which are local, and are active contributors to the development of policies for social inclusion."

Corporate Governance

KFFS is regulated by the Financial Services Authority, and it is monitored by a full-time compliance manager. It is also covered by the Data Protection Act as well as all relevant employment and health and safety regulations.

The Kwik-Fit values were created soon after the company was established by Tom Farmer and they are: to provide the best products and services possible; to make a fair profit; to provide a climate of trust, respect and support; and to provide opportunities to develop potential. These values are very much part of the way the company goes about its business, but they are being changed and re-appraised as the company now concentrates on the wider area of financial services as opposed to motor insurance only.

It is a target-driven business with set guidelines, which are an essential part of staff training.

Environmental record

A call centre does not have a major detrimental effect on the environment; but this is an organisation employing close to 1,000 people, which means it has to look closely at environmental issues – it does use a lot of paper and energy, for a start.

So, all waste paper and cans are collected and recycled. PCs which are no longer required are offered to a local special needs school, and if they are not wanted by the school then a specialist company is contacted to dispose of them safely and in an environmentally sound fashion.

On the energy front, the company's out-of-town location and poor public transport service mean that staff motor to work; but car sharing is encouraged via the intranet.

The company also uses significant amounts of electricity, so it ensures that lights are switched off in rooms that are not in use. Every little helps.

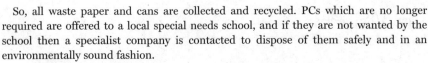

LEWIS PR

LEWIS
Millbank Tower, Millbank, London SW1P 4RS
Tel: (0) 20 7802 2626 **Fax:** (0) 20 7802 2627
Web: www.lewispr.com **Email:** info@lewispr.com

Pay and Benefits	6.5	Innovation	6.4
Promotion and Development	6.3	Diversity	5.8
Training	6.8	Social Responsibility	5.7
Travel opportunities	6.6	Corporate Governance	5.5
Culture	7.3	Environment	5.3
Total			**62.2**

LEWIS Public Relations agency was founded in 1995, following former journalist Chris Lewis's poor experience with a number of public relations companies. He believed he could do better and set the organisation up from his home. It currently employs 135 people (55 at the company's London HQ) and operates in 14 markets. The company now handles international contracts. Its primary focus remains IT-related public relations, but it has also moved sideways into elements of pro bono work for good causes. In spite of vacillations in the market it has continued to grow every year and remains solidly in profit.

Executive summary

When journalist Chris Lewis decided to change his career direction in 1995 he didn't feel he had to look far – just at his in-box full of poorly written press releases and his phone, which would ring periodically as public relations executives called to ask whether he'd received a press release they'd sent three weeks previously. (Non-journalists might like to bear in mind that reporters aren't shy people, they get about 50 releases a day and will call back if it's of interest – so such calls are generally a waste of time).

He therefore set about building his own PR consultancy, and until recently stuck with the technology subjects with which he was familiar. Lately, the organisation has moved into corporate PR and offers profiling services as well as some pro bono work (including clients associated with the rainforests). The organisation's accreditations include being ranked in the Financial Times survey of the best workplaces in the UK. It hasn't gone down the Investors in People route so far as its focus has been on its growth, but it has a lively and often innovative HR department, and forward-looking policies on pay, benefits and much else. PR Week gave it the accolade of No 1 Tech PR agency in the UK for 2004. Also, the company can claim that they have never made anyone redundant in spite of truly tight conditions – although not an award or accreditation as such, that has to count for something.

The organisation has offices in London, Eindhoven, Boston, Copenhagen, Madrid, Milan, Munich, Paris, San Diego, San Francisco, Singapore, Stockholm, Sydney and Washington.

Pay and benefits

So, when would staff in most organisations expect a pay and performance review? Answers like "once a year" and occasionally "every six months" are the most frequent; "once a quarter" sounds extraordinary. It is this frequency that allows LEWIS to keep tabs on just where its staff are in terms of their development and earning potential.

A graduate taken in for the first time will start on the company's basic salary of £15,000. This will move straight to £20,000 after a six-month training period, bringing a recent graduate's salary just underneath the national average wage. The rest is by negotiation over the already-mentioned quarterly appraisals; on reaching partnership status you can expect to start at £40,000–£45,000. "It's a strictly meritocratic business," says HR director Toni Castle.

The rest of the benefits are allocated on a flexible basis. The usual boxes can be ticked: health, dental and travel benefits are all available – but even then things can be different from the norm; if someone is unwell and can't work, LEWIS is as likely to send them to its specialist in Harley Street rather than have them wait for treatment elsewhere. Standard benefits include a transport allowance of £4,000 a year, a pension fund where the company contributes 3% of salary, a mobile phone and homeworking equipment. Childcare elements are worked out on an individual's needs; one person might find it valuable to have help with childminding fees whereas another might want flexible working hours instead.

Overall, within the constraints of serving the business's needs, there should be every reason to anticipate a fast track to a good scale of pay and highly competitive package at LEWIS – if you can prove you have what it takes.

Promotion and development

It's almost a cliché to tell readers they can move up as far as they want to within an organisation and develop their own career; but LEWIS accounts for a lot of people who have done precisely that. HR head Toni Castle is one of them; she joined the company early on, straight from college, and within four years had set up the HR department. People are encouraged to note any specialisms they wish to develop during their appraisals, and there are a number of examples of executives promoted to managerial level before they might have expected because they had done the research and made a business case for their promotion.

The focus is very much on continuous career development – through training, appraisals, secondments and extra responsibilities. People from the London office have been seconded to America, Australia and numerous other areas. Although there is no fixed rule, the HR department reckons to spend £3,000 per year per head on development.

And it needn't be development purely for the company's benefit. If someone wants to take a pottery evening class for their own personal development, LEWIS will look at funding them as it believes in employing well-rounded individuals. It is also sponsoring people to take professional qualifications including Chartered Institute of Marketing and other significant accreditations. Essentially, if you can give LEWIS a good reason it should be developing you in a particular direction, it'll do it.

Company culture

Walking around the company's open-plan office, a visitor is given the impression of a company that's serious about what it does but is happy to have fun doing it. They can have a laugh while they're working; they had an office poll to see what people's favourite words were, and these words were lovingly printed and are now suspended over the various clusters of people while they are at work. The more observant visitor will notice that there is a life-size bear suspended from the ceiling of the corridors; nobody's sure why he's there.

This masks a deep-seated, professional commitment to an American-style pride in being in a service industry. This in turn inspires a team-driven ethic – you are almost as likely to perceive yourself as part of your account team as part of LEWIS itself, since the structure is pretty flat.

Clearly the emphasis is on delivery to the customer, but this is achieved through offering a lot of support to colleagues, in particular beginners. There is a buddy scheme in which new people are attached to someone with experience of the organisation, to whom they can go with any problems. As a result, staff commitment is high and sick leave accounts for a very low 1% at any one time.

The HR department has people undergoing the CIPD qualification, and other accreditations such as MBAs are spread throughout the management. At the time of writing, the organisation was going through a re-branding exercise, but the core values and commitment to customer service will remain the same.

Innovation:

LEWIS prides itself in its complete absence of any redundancies throughout its nine-year history, which – given the state of the industry sector it inhabits – can be seen as an innovation in its own right. The possibility of fast tracking towards higher pay and responsibility marks the company out as unusual, as does their commitment to personal as well as professional development.

A sabbatical scheme is available after two years' service in the company.

Diversity and social responsibility

The company doggedly recruits the "right people", rather than a proscribed racial or sexual mix. This might appear out of step with current thinking, but it was noticeable during CRF's visit to the premises that the sex balance was pretty even and all races were represented – around 10–15% of the staff are from minorities.

Corporate Governance

At the time of writing LEWIS, with 135 people worldwide, did not regard itself as big enough to warrant a compliance officer as such; responsibility for compliance with statutory regulations is shared between members of the board and the auditor for the accounts.

Environmental record

Given that the company is in a service industry, it can be anticipated that it doesn't have any major processes in need of an overhaul for the environment's sake. It recycles paper and card where it can, and is keen to have staff cycle into work whenever that is practical.

It also gives its services free of charge to a number of clients, including cancer research charities, and is keen to contribute to the environment in this way whenever possible.

Loans.co.uk

Loans.co.uk
6 Marlin House, Croxley Business Park, Watford, Herts WD18 8TD
Tel: (0) 1923 655555 **Fax:** (0) 1923 655570
Web: www.loans.co.uk **Email:** info@loans.co.uk

Pay and Benefits	5.8	Innovation	6.0
Promotion and Development	6.3	Diversity	6.8
Training	6.3	Social Responsibility	6.0
Travel opportunities	3.3	Corporate Governance	6.0
Culture	6.5	Environment	5.3
Total			**58.3**

Loans.co.uk is a licensed credit broker employing over 300 people in locations in Watford and Preston. Specialising in loans for debt consolidation, the business is privately owned and has annual sales of £29.6m.

Executive Summary

Loans.co.uk was founded in 1997 by Stephen Hayes and David Cowham Jnr. Launched with seed funding of £500,000, the company helps individuals secure loan and mortgage agreements from clients including First National, First Plus, Paragon and Lloyds Bowmaker. Much of the business is debt consolidation; indeed, its rapid growth is in no small part due to the UK's ongoing property boom and "plastic" consumer spending spree.

Most of the growth has occurred since 2000, the year the company (which was originally called Priority One) changed its name to reflect the importance of the internet as a customer communication channel. According to its owners, an improved conversion rate of loan applications has boosted profits 123% each year from £0.8m in 2000 to an annualised £8.8m in 2003.

The growth in profits has been matched by a corresponding growth in people. Much of the recent expansion has taken place at Preston, where a call centre has operated since 2004. However, Loans.co.uk remains associated primarily with its Watford location. It sponsors the nearby Wycombe Wanderers football team, and its meteoric rise to prominence was recognised locally when it won regional awards in 2004 for Growing Business of the Year and Business of the Year.

Stephen Hayes summarises events: "When we began there were many problems with the industry. It was bedevilled with poor service levels, there were antiquated systems, and very little management information meant people were not sure where the leads were coming from. It took a while for us to show the lenders we were serious and could get results. Now they come knocking on our door, not the other way round."

Pay and Benefits

Loans.co.uk operates in an industry where competition for people is especially fierce, and it frames its reward policy accordingly. Though base pay is comparable to other similar companies, there is plenty of profit-related bonus pay on offer. A new employee can expect to earn £300 extra each month on a £20,000 starting salary, for example. Double bonus payments are given twice a year on average, at traditionally slower business times. There is an additional £1,000 bonus for the employee of the month to spend on specific prizes (a trip to New York for example).

Other benefits include life and health cover; and free social events, which are arranged four times a year. All staff have free use of state-of-the-art in-house gym facilities.

The combination of generous bonus payments and a fun, friendly atmosphere undoubtedly helps motivate the predominantly young workforce. This is reflected in a turnover rate that drops to a single figure percentage after the first three months, and with the company growing rapidly – currently 15 new staff each month – it is an important recruiting tool.

Promotion and development

Training starts quickly at Loans.co.uk with an initial 1-week company induction, which will enable new people to familiarise themselves with all aspects of the business and its culture before being moved into their relevant departments for further in-depth training. The emphasis is very much on making people welcome – as well as being assigned a buddy, new joiners will personally meet all members of the senior management team.

From that point on, training is effectively non-stop, according to Hayes, as most of it occurs on the job. However, provision also takes the form of a number of formal training exercises. Common examples of this include role-play, objection handling, time management and motivational training.

Stand-out performers can move into a managerial role quickly – in fact, team leaders have in the past been appointed within nine months of joining. Currently there are three team leaders in each business area, with a dozen at Preston's new business section.

A high premium is placed on loyalty at the company; this being tangibly demonstrated by a loyalty bonus of 3% of salary awarded to staff members for each year they stay, increasing up to ten years. However, Hayes notes, "Our view is that we don't expect anyone who joins us to work here forever. If they want to leave after, say, two years to progress elsewhere, we'll wish them well, but we won't offer them more money to stay. The reason for this is because if we did, it would imply we weren't already paying them enough."

Company Culture

It is a cliché to say that a company is a fun place to work, but a quick tour of the offices is all the confirmation needed that this is the case at Loans.co.uk. The walls are bedecked with the photos of celebrities who have visited (this happens once a month), sweepstake boards, and paraphernalia associated with various themed events that include anything from the Olympics to Big Brother.

Hayes claims to spend 20% of his time on staff issues, and it is clear he takes the fun side of business seriously. A big part of this is the lively, informal meeting at the end of each month, which features games and competitions. "The prizes are good," says Hayes. "Maybe a holiday for two in Barbados for the winner, and a booby prize of a caravanning holiday in Skegness." Either way, the recipients have to write up a description of their stay and provide photos for Top Dog – the in-house magazine, which reports all the salacious gossip in the firm!

Word-of-mouth recruitment adds to the family atmosphere – literally, in fact, as there are a large number of siblings in the workforce.

Innovation

According to Hayes, the key to the rate and size of growth that Loans.co.uk has achieved, is the way in which information is gathered and managed. Investment in brand new process management technology has further deepened this capacity, and the relationships forged with lenders have helped maintain healthy margins. In other words, the company's profits are not derived from putting customers on to higher rates of interest. This is important because the company's marketing is built around the message that it is not itself a lender, but works on behalf of individuals who want or need to borrow money. The same message is unambiguously conveyed to each new customer who contacts the company.

Hayes says, "In all the time we've been in business we've only got it wrong once. After we did the deal, we had a complaint from a woman in Durham. We looked at it and saw it was wrong, so David (Cowham Jnr) drove up there himself, unravelled the whole deal and put her on the right one."

Diversity and social responsibility

As the company has grown in size it has become more visible in its commitment to social responsibility and the local community. Charity donations are high on the agenda: each year Loans.co.uk gives a minimum of £50,000 to a nominated charity (a muscular dystrophy charity was the beneficiary in 2003–04), while the employee of the month winner receives £1,000 to donate to a charity of their choice.

The company has also forged links with a local school in Watford, where over 60% of the pupils have special needs. It contributed financially in order to help it secure a grant from central government for new equipment. Plans are also in place for a mentoring programme involving volunteers from Loans.co.uk; and will see senior managers organising activities at the school, whose pupils will also have the opportunity to gain work experience at the company.

In terms of the composition of the workforce, the male:female ratio is split fairly evenly. Women managers predominate in the sales and new business areas.

Corporate Governance

Loans.co.uk holds a Consumer Credit Licence issued by The Office of Fair Trading (OFT), and adheres to all guidelines thereof. It is a member of the industry governing body, the Finance Industry Standards Association (FISA), and the Corporation of Finance Brokers (CFB). It complies with client confidentiality requirements through registration under the Data Protection Act of 1998.

The ability of people to effectively manage their financial responsibilities varies wildly, and Hayes is conscious of the ethics that pertain to the company's business practice. Loans.co.uk does not deal with lenders who carry out house repossessions, and equips itself with adequate payment protection insurance. "There is an issue of one person in a family whose credit rating is bad wanting to borrow money and getting another member to apply on their behalf," he notes. "We're aware of this, and always make it quite clear we want to speak to both parties."

Environment

The commitment of the company to the environment is expressed principally through the use of recycled equipment. This extends to all areas of the business. "We send out on average four million mailings a month," says Hayes. "All are made from renewable resources – so, in effect, we replant two trees for every one we use. Everything is environmentally efficient: all of our cartridges, everything in our storeroom, in fact."

London & Quadrant Group

London & Quadrant Group
Osborn House, Osborn Terrace, London SE3 9DR
Tel: (0) 20 8852 9181
Web: www.lqgroup.org.uk **Email:** humanresources@lqgroup.org.uk

L&Q Group

Pay and Benefits	5.9	Innovation	7.5
Promotion and Development	6.7	Diversity	8.3
Training	7.4	Social Responsibility	7.8
Travel opportunities	5.1	Corporate Governance	7.0
Culture	7.2	Environment	6.8
Total			**69.7**

London & Quadrant Group is a charity providing homes to a variety of economically disadvantaged people. It houses 40,000 families in London and the south-east every year. L&Q has diversified into low-cost home ownership and targets key workers as well as providing supported housing for vulnerable residents. With its latest turnover of £121m, up from £112m in 2003, L&Q has a headcount nudging 800. The staff numbers have expanded recently, following a merger that brought the Slough-based Beacon Housing Association into the group.

Executive summary

London & Quadrant's corporate plan of "delivering results" has the key objectives of quality homes, quality service and building for the future; underpinned by the four key initiatives of "our people, meeting customers' needs, financial health and adding value". Funded by government grants, private market loans and rent receipts, L&Q exists to create places where people want to live. It does something about the housing available to those who fall through the net and can't get housed by other means.

L&Q's employment practices have not only secured it a place in the Sunday Times 100 Best Companies to work for list, but also propelled it from 67th to 29th place – making it the second-fastest riser in the charts. The organisation believes its people are its greatest asset and this is reflected in the many awards it continues to accrue: the prestigious Personnel Today Employer Branding 2004 award (it was also nominated for the year's Age Positive award); the National Housing Federation's InBiz award for Employer of Choice in Housing 2004; the Building Quality Houses Best Training and People Development award; plus re-accreditation for Investors in People 2004 with a glowing report.

Pay and benefits

Social housing is not renowned for providing telephone-number salaries as group director of human resources, Sally Jacobson, freely admits. "But as from April 2005 new pay scales come into effect, meaning all salaries are being increased by at least £1,000 – grade 4 housing officers/graduates now start at £20,700 compared to £18,900 a year ago," says Jacobson. "Staff surveys had shown that while staff were happy with the benefits package we provide, they were concerned over the pay scales." Salaries will now be well above the average for this sector.

The benefits here are indeed impressive, and are very family-friendly – which is to be expected given the organisation's laudable role in seeking to improve the lot of the community. L&Q is already ahead of the legislative requirements for family leave, paternity leave, adoption leave, leave for infertility treatment, parental leave, carers leave, flexible working and career breaks. From 2005, employees gain one extra day's leave to be taken when desired – in addition to the standard 30 days – if no days are taken off sick during the year. Plus, L&Q will buy back five days' leave – a gesture that would come in handy during Christmas week.

There are pension, non-contributory life assurance and disability income schemes. Sick pay is above expectations. Car loans are available through a link with Barclays, eye care vouchers are offered, legal and other counselling services are available, and staff can be nominated by colleagues as well as managers for a 2.5% performance-related bonus for outstanding work. The key point to make is that the payback from working at L&Q goes beyond the remuneration – 10 families who would otherwise have remained homeless will have been housed due to the staff's efforts on any given day. That engenders true job satisfaction.

Promotion and development

"We spend £1,100 per year per head on training, which is equivalent to six days' training each year for everyone," says Jacobson. "We recruit trainees at all levels who will develop personally and professionally to become our workforce of the future."

A structured two-year programme introduces graduates to the scope and diversity of L&Q's operations – after two six-month placements, graduates spend one year in a placement of their choice. This gives them the opportunity to acquire in-depth experience and a relevant professional qualification. Professional training schemes are run by L&Q, plus schemes for school leavers.

"We have a great scheme for non-work-related training – we're happy to pay course fees up to £250 for staff with five years' service. Staff have enjoyed pilates, and language and yoga classes. Wellbeing is very important," says Jacobson. "We have a responsibility to develop people for the housing sector in general, not just L&Q. Managers and team leaders can achieve nationally recognised professional management qualifications from Nottingham Trent University. We work with local technical colleges for training staff in maintenance and development positions. There are also opportunities for older staff with courses at the University of the Third Age."

There are secondment opportunities. L&Q works out training plans with each member of staff, plus there's training for coaches and mentors. The organisation's commitment to its people is reinforced with a range of techniques such as succession planning, performance management, work shadowing and volunteering.

Company culture

"At 2%, the sickness rate is very low," says Jacobson. "People enjoy their jobs. We are passionate about customer service and social housing. Professionalism is very important. We like people to have fun at work and enjoy what they do – the core aim being to create places where people want to live and work. Happy staff look after our residents with compassion and fairness, providing excellent customer service."

All the staff at L&Q have one-to-one meetings with their manager every month, plus there are half-yearly and annual appraisals. There is a flat hierarchy and a very stable management team.

The work/life balance at L&Q has been enhanced with the introduction of Vielife Online, a unique health and wellbeing service delivering interactive assessments, engaging content and practical solutions direct to the organisation's 800 staff. The Vielife Online service covers four key areas of health and wellbeing: sleeping well, managing stress, eating healthily, and exercising effectively. Over 50% of staff registered within one month of its launch.

Staff turnover has reduced to 14% from 17% in 2003. As well as the generous benefits package, there are part-time and job sharing opportunities, fully flexible options and counselling services. There is a bullying and harassment policy, and there are good relations with the UNISON trade union.

Innovation

"Some 22% of our staff are aged over 50," says Jacobson. "We've introduced grandparents' leave to provide support to their children following the birth of a grandchild, which comprises two days' paid leave for staff with a minimum of 26 weeks' service." Other benefits include long-service awards, career breaks, carer's leave of five days' paid leave, £100 contribution to health screening, and access to low-cost insurance services. Valuing older workers mirrors today's world, even if deeming someone to be "old" at 50 is questionable. Nevertheless, this move is highly noteworthy, valuable and sorely needed.

People who have been with L&Q for five years qualify for a contribution of £250 towards the cost of non-work-related training, which is undertaken in their own time. Examples of such training include Pilates, yoga and foreign languages. The company does this to encourage staff because "all training is useful".

There is also an innovative approach to working with colleges and universities – providing tailor-made training courses for individuals that are local to where they live and work. It's a development that's proving very popular. The buy back of five days' leave by L&Q is also an innovative move – it can be seen as providing a Christmas bonus through sacrificing five days from an already generous leave entitlement.

Diversity and social responsibility

At L&Q, around 30% of the staff are from ethnic minorities, which mirrors the local community completely; and 62% of the staff are women. L&Q needs a cross-section of society in its staff make-up, as that is the composition of its customer base.

"We tried, in 2004, to raise the profile of housing as an employment option," says Jacobson. "We arranged a conference, entitled 'Making housing an employer choice' in the autumn, the proceeds of which – some £4,000 – were donated to the housing charity, Shelter. We aim to try and raise the profile of social housing as a career option rather than just being a job. Social housing needs beefing up as a profession. It constitutes a fantastic career."

L&Q advertised six graduate traineeships in 2004 and received over 90 applications, from which at least 50% could have been employed. This is the third year L&Q has been taking in graduate entries.

A quote from the first graduate trainee, Sarah Watson, reports on "the privileged opportunity to experience every facet of an organisation that commits itself to groundbreaking ways to improve people's lives." True social responsibility.

Corporate Governance

There is a governing board comprising 16 people who ensure all the relevant laws and regulations are complied with, while L&Q's chairman Robert Appleyard is totally committed and very enthusiastic about the "Our People" agenda for the years ahead. This is all about delivering results, and indeed L&Q's many diverse customers repeatedly tell them that it is an attribute which they associate with the company. Experience shows that organisations that have satisfied staff have satisfied customers. The staff matter. The organisation is aware of the new Information and Communication with Employees (ICE) legislation, effective April 6 2005, and has a formal policy to ensure its communications procedures are totally compliant.

Another key aim has been the fostering of good relations with the unions; this has been achieved with UNISON. There have never been any problems.

Health and safety issues are rigorously addressed, while a quality manager ensures L&Q adheres to all its business promises. There are initiatives in corporate social responsibility embracing health, safety and environmental issues. There is a professionally qualified HR team, plus fully accredited accounting and IT teams. All core corporate functions are managed by professionally qualified competent people.

Environmental record

"We provide eco-friendly and environmentally friendly homes," says Jacobson. The organisation encourages recycling wherever possible. There are recycling initiatives for mobile phones, paper and card, ink cartridges, bottles and cans, etc. When travelling on business, staff are encouraged to use public transport wherever possible. Interest-free loans are available for season tickets. Car loans are available in the link with Barclays, and environmentally friendly vehicles are viewed favourably.

"We view the maintenance of the environment as a vital part of sustainable business development," says Jacobson. "We support responsible environmental and resource management in balance with sustainable business development." The company complies with the relevant environment laws and regulations and makes key commitments in terms of taking account of environmental issues when placing contracts with suppliers; and continuing to introduce energy-efficient systems into its buildings, as well as managing energy requirements sensibly.

One of L&Q's key initiatives now is to introduce a sustainability strategy. There can be no doubt L&Q will be delivering great results in the years ahead.

Luminar Leisure

Luminar Leisure Limited
41 King Street, Luton, Bedfordshire LU1 2DW
Tel: (0) 1582 589400 **Fax:** (0) 1582 589401
Web: www.luminar.co.uk

LUMINAR plc

Pay and Benefits	5.2	Innovation	6.2
Promotion and Development	6.4	Diversity	4.6
Training	6.0	Social Responsibility	6.4
Travel opportunities	2.6	Corporate Governance	5.2
Culture	5.6	Environment	5.6
Total			**53.8**

Luminar Leisure is the largest owner, developer and operator of late night entertainment in Britain; with branded venues such as Oceana, Lava and Ignite, Liquid, Chicago Rock Cafe, Life and Jumpin Jaks, in 159 towns across the country.

Luminar venues provide entertainment in the form of food, DJs, appearances, restaurants – in effect, the facility to dine, dance and drink.

Luminar grew to become the largest ever in the industry after it acquired the venues of its five largest competitors.

In early 1999, Luminar had just 1,150 employees; it now has 10,000 in around 300 venues varying on the seasonal trends.

Executive Summary

Luminar Leisure is not only the largest player in a fragmented industry of owner-operator venues – it's also the clear leader in every sense. This is a story of entrepreneurship and very rapid growth.

The chief executive and the senior management team of the company were colleagues at Whitbread prior to the formation of Luminar Leisure in 1987. They acquired their first discotheque, Manhattan, in Kings Lynn in 1988; over the next two years they added seven more units.

In 1996, the company was established to act as the holding company of the group and became a plc, which injected the investment funds needed for growth. Its strategy projects an annual organic growth of 20%, and with acquisitions, anticipates doubling in size every four years. In 1999, 62 businesses grew to 108 with the takeover of some Allied Leisure units, which had already expanded with the acquisition of European Leisure.

In 2000, the company acquired Northern Leisure (which itself had bought Rank Entertainments) to take the number of operations to 230. The total number of businesses within the estate now stands at around 300.

"We were pulling 8 or 9 G's on the learning curve," says Simon Cacioppo, head of human resources.

This dramatic expansion has meant Cacioppo's team have spent a hectic 18 months consulting and harmonising the business – quite an achievement.

In 2002, Luminar's pre-tax profit stood at £44.1m. This rose to £67m in 2003 but dipped slightly to £62m in 2004, which reflects the pressures inherent in the leisure industry; but Luminar is a long-term thinking, smart company.

"The industry is under a lot of pressure at the moment with competition, price discounting, restrictions and social responsibility issues," says Cacioppo. "Long-term, this pressure will have a positive effect on the industry and our customer base. We tell managers, 'maintain your standards, and don't discount irresponsibly'. Long-term, our approach will see success."

Pay and Benefits

Luminar is in a commercial business, and meeting competitive rates is essential. It operates a flexible policy – varying rates for different job requirements, shifts, seasons and local employment markets in order to remain competitive and recruit the best staff. Employees are offered 22 days' holiday, which increases to 25 after three years' service.

There are incentives for employees within the venues. Business managers negotiate deals with local suppliers for lifestyle benefits that are valued – cinema tickets, restaurant offers and vouchers for music stores. Individual businesses run localised bonus schemes, and many suppliers also offer big-value prizes and competitions for staff.

Managers operate in the field and at the company's two administration centres at Luton and Preston. They are rewarded with bonuses based on performance and the size of the venues they operate. For example, some large venue managers enjoy salaries up to the mid £40,000s, and bonuses can be as high as 50% of their earnings.

General managers actually requested to redistribute a proportion of this bonus to their employees.

There is a money purchase pension scheme, a sharesave scheme, private medical and income protection insurance, and sick pay increasing with service.

Promotion and development

Each venue is run by a general manager, who is accountable for that individual business. Depending on its size, general managers are supported by deputy managers, assistant managers and trainees. Luminar's middle/senior management structure has area managers, managing directors, and a director of operations who reports to Stephen Thomas, the chief executive. Front-line employee teams include bartenders, supervisors, waiting staff and glass collectors; and support staff such as cloakroom attendants and kitchen workers. Door-supervisors, DJs and cleaners are contracted out.

Through its acquisitions, Luminar inherited a number of managers drawn from different organisations. Previously, venue managers scaled heights through the "good lad syndrome". Luminar believes that as the leader in the industry, it should also be the leader in management development, and has put in place a highly visible, structured management programme to produce qualified managers for the future.

"It's easier to develop expertise inside the business," claims Emma Hind, group training manager.

70% of promotion is from within, and those who want to enter management start at the bottom of the ladder. Applicants are initially assessed over a series of modules and then the area manager completes the final selection process. The training department then follows a 12- to 18-month programme involving operational management at each stage.

Graduates are eligible to apply for the position of assistant manager at a venue, where they develop their skills and experience.

Beyond this, there are fast-track pathways to deputy manager and general manager.

Training for these roles focuses on development centres, and involves observed exercises and psychometric testing. To gain promotion to general manager requires considerable focus on the strategic aspects of the business, including marketing.

Development programmes are also in place for area managers. "Some people have gone from trainee to successfully running their own venue as a general manager in just two years," says Hind.

Luminar has spent a large amount of time and investment managing this process, balancing what the business needs with what people need to run the business. Investors in People confirmed that Luminar's development process is "very robust" with clear evidence seen in the field.

Company culture

Luminar recognises that its whole business is about the choice made by the consumer. Customers can choose to go to visit any number of bars or nightclubs in a town.

A good yardstick to measure the success of the package Luminar offers is that despite spending a lot of time working in the venues, many employees return out of work to socialise.

"Luminar is an entrepreneurial business – historically it always has been," says Cacioppo. "It's fast moving and pretty full-on." This stems from the working ethos of Luminar's chief executive, Stephen Thomas.

Luminar will always strive to deliver its objectives. For example, a proposal for a new-build venue received more than 400 local objections; but with a personal approach, Luminar's co-founder, director Steve Dennis, met and dealt with every single objector's concerns. This included paying for a CCTV system and links to the local authority's cameras.

Cacioppo says that this can-do culture brings with it a passion for the business, and encourages Luminar to be a strong force within the town. Feedback from the front line confirms this is a natural, not a top-down, culture. This provides a focus and commitment to developing an entertainment company of excellence. The culture is continuing to evolve with a focus on brand-led strategies.

HR functions, notably personnel and training, are not run from behind a desk. A personal approach is vital, and key staff visit venues during their night-time hours of operation to ensure they are accessible to everyone.

The link with general managers is strong; and HR is integral to personal assessments, promotion, and other reward and recognition events.

"By the very nature of the business, we need people to work outside normal hours," says Cacioppo. "Only a handful of people work nine-to-five. So it's not difficult to offer some flexibility, built into the business need." While hours of 10pm–2am might appear awkward to recruit for, they actually suit a diverse range of people including students, second job searchers and parents looking to return to work.

Innovation

At the latest British Entertainment and Disco Association (BEDA) awards, Luminar grabbed the headlines: Chloe Bellaers won Bar of the Year for Chicago Rock Café in Maidenhead; Richard Taylor won Club of the Year for Lava and Ignite in Burnley; and Peter Bell of Batchwood Hall, St Albans, was recognised for his commitment to a socially responsible club operation.

Design, build, lighting, sound and imagery – you name it, and Luminar is pushing back the boundaries. Customer feedback indicated that females wanted greater floor visibility and security; Luminar designed its Liquid clubs with white ceilings, walls and floors – and with uplights. This may sound bizarre, but it produced an atmospheric, safe and highly acclaimed environment.

Lighting, ventilation and sound systems are top of the range and unique. And Luminar was the first to use DVDs in its clubs at a time when they were new on the market and incredibly expensive.

The company is now at the forefront of the public debate on smoking, building venues where people can smoke in designated areas or on outside terraces.

Diversity and social responsibility

Investors in People say that everything they look for in equal opportunity is ingrained at Luminar. The company doesn't break down diversity figures – there is no need. "Putting people into ethnic boxes doesn't help," says Cacioppo. "We say 'there's the development programme, whoever you are – black or white, graduate or not. Are you up to it?'"

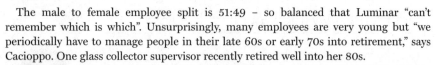

The male to female employee split is 51:49 – so balanced that Luminar "can't remember which is which". Unsurprisingly, many employees are very young but "we periodically have to manage people in their late 60s or early 70s into retirement," says Cacioppo. One glass collector supervisor recently retired well into her 80s.

Luminar is in the vanguard of social responsibility and works closely with The Home Office and the Department of Culture, Media and Sport.

General managers are encouraged to take positions on local committees such as PubWatch, and Luminar has its own Code of Practice that sets standards to exceed government guidelines. "When you go out, you want a good night, a safe night and to get home without any trouble," says Cacioppo.

Chief executive Thomas says, "as the largest late-night operator in the UK, it falls upon Luminar to lead the way in socially responsible operation. We do not believe in simply trotting out warm words. When we commit to act, we act quickly and intelligently." Luminar's Dance Safe initiative is just one example; the company is also rigorous on minimum pricing, and leads the industry on door and dispersal policies. The company has a no-tolerance attitude towards drugs and antisocial behaviour, and is very proactive. Passive and active sniffer dogs are commonplace at its venues and Luminar searches one in ten of its customers within its nightclubs.

Centrally and locally, Luminar does a lot for charity. In 2003–04 alone, it raised over £500,000. Employees have raised over £1m in three years for the company's own children's charity, ECHO (Entertainment Organised for Children's Health).

Corporate Governance

Luminar is fully compliant in all aspects of corporate governance. It has numerous committees dealing with risk assessment, audit, and health and safety. These review and guide how Luminar operates and builds its business. On the self-employed, contractor or payroll issue, Luminar has a number of processes that workers must comply with, and the same applies to overseas workers.

The company has a significant spend to fully meet its responsibilities in employment law. As a publicly quoted company, there is a company secretary and head of legal; and a plc board with non-executive directors who run most committees, including remuneration.

Environmental record

All buildings have recycling bins for collection. Waste management at the venues is contracted out, and as part of these arrangements it is essential that these companies use and recycle the waste.

The venues generate plenty of plastic and bottles on the premises. So bottle banks start immediately behind the bar. Some venues even have holes in the walls for easy and rapid disposal and recycling.

Computer equipment and mobile phones are recycled through a specialist firm or given to charity (or re-used until they don't work any more!). Luminar has even found ways of changing the in-car kits in their vehicles to fit their mobile phones, rather than buy new devices.

Majestic Wine Warehouses

Majestic Wine Warehouses Ltd
Majestic House, Otterspool Way, Watford WD25 8WW
Tel: (0) 1923 298200
Web: www.majestic.co.uk **Email:** info@majestic.co.uk

Pay and Benefits	6.0	Innovation	7.0
Promotion and Development	7.0	Diversity	8.0
Training	7.0	Social Responsibility	5.0
Travel opportunities	7.0	Corporate Governance	6.0
Culture	7.0	Environment	5.0
Total			**65.0**

Majestic Wine Warehouses is the UK's biggest retailer specialising in direct sales of mixed-case wine, with 120 stores throughout the UK. The company differentiates itself through high-quality customer service, the diversity and quantity of stock available to purchase at each store, dedicated onsite customer parking, wines to taste every day, the ability to order in-store or via its website, and free delivery throughout mainland UK. Following 11 successive years of record profits, mid-year results at end-September 2004 were up 7.4% at £74.6m. Add in the many awards Majestic has garnered and you have a robust, vibrant company with great potential.

Executive summary
Majestic Wine Warehouses started in 1981 with two warehouses in London. Now it's the UK's largest chain with 120 outlets, and eight more to be added over the next year. There's also a French operation – Wine and Beer World – in Calais, Cherbourg and Coquelles. Majestic is on target to celebrate its 12th successive year of record profits, demonstrating a rise in pre-tax profits to £4.83m in the six-month period to September 2004, on turnover up 7.4% at £74.6m. Some 28% of this derives from business-to-business sales.

The formula works, as is evidenced through the wealth of awards the company continues to accrue: International Wine Challenge High Street Wine Retailer of the Year (2002, 2003), Retail Week Employer of the Year 2002, OLN Wine Retailer of the Year (2004) and AIM-listing Company of the Year 2002.

Pay and benefits
"We take staff on at trainee manager level. At the store level, there's a flat management structure where promotion is on merit," says Ailsa Thorpe, recruitment and development manager. "Typically each store will have five staff members. Also there are regional manager and head office positions."

"Staff are our most valuable asset, and it is these individuals who assist us in differentiating ourselves from the more traditional wine retailers," says Thorpe. "We are also the only company in the UK wine industry to offer a structured training scheme that includes sponsorship to undertake the Wine and Spirit Education Trust (WSET) Advanced Certificate and Diploma. In 2004, 50 employees were studying for the diploma; while in 2005, 80 are booked onto the course. Looking at other wine retailers offering equivalent positions, we believe we offer packages above the sector average."

Over 20% of staff pay into the company's SAYE scheme, and over 23% have options in Majestic Wine plc. There are sales-related and profit-related bonuses, staff discounts of up to 20%, attendance and performance-related bonuses for distribution staff, a subsidised healthcare cash plan, an annual staff dinner dance, membership of the "10-

year club" to reward length of service, and company cars where needed. There are award schemes for high achievers in trade qualifications. Vendange trips are arranged, staff attend supplier tastings and there are many sales incentives; some 350 staff travelled abroad with suppliers in 2004.

A flexible working policy is in operation to enable the balancing of work and childcare. The company uses the Busy Bees childcare voucher scheme.

There's also a group personal pension plan with the amount of contribution at the discretion of the member of staff – whatever is paid, Majestic will contribute half that amount up to a maximum of 5% of the member's basic annual salary.

Promotion and development

"Everyone joins us as part of a graduate management training programme at trainee manager level, and promotion is usually within 12 months to assistant manager," says Thorpe. "After two or three years, many can become store managers – there's no external recruitment for assistant manager and store manager levels. Nearly 80% of head office positions are filled internally."

"We like to move store managers between stores," says Thorpe. "Staff apply for positions – there are no forced moves." Appraisals take place every three months for trainee managers, six months for assistant managers, and 12 months for store managers. Feedback is vigorously encouraged; there are biannual managers' meetings and a formal ideas scheme where anyone can contact the managing director. Further, the retail and managing directors both aim to visit each store twice a year.

"First-year staff can expect on-the-job training and at least eight days covering everything from basics to customer service, product knowledge and management skills," says Thorpe. "After this, there's training to assist progression through the company, and an option to study for the WSET Advanced Certificate. Where it's relevant to the progression and position of the relevant employee, we would consider sponsorship through other courses."

As Majestic only has 670 staff, the company feels it knows members of staff personally, and considers itself able to identify and measure contributions staff make to the business. Existing, experienced staff members handle all training of recruits. Management skills courses impart guidance on learning and how to train.

Company culture

"For the past four years, we've had a good return rate on turnover, especially from staff returning after having children (91%)," says Thorpe. "Here, there is the opportunity to return on a part-time basis and flexibility is offered around childcare. Each member of staff is treated as an individual with individual needs, and Majestic appeals as a fun and interesting environment." That's very good when seen in the context of the 30% staff turnover, which is low for the retail sector – it's 70%–80% in some parts of the high street.

Majestic describes its culture as product- and customer-service-oriented, sociable, relaxed and informal, motivated, positive and rewarding. People who wouldn't get on here won't like wine, people or working in a team. People who do are positive about customers and will go the extra yard – even metre – for them. Everyone shares knowledge about the way the business is run. People will flourish if they work effectively within teams, enjoy having shared goals and objectives, enjoy customer interaction, and demonstrate enthusiasm about wine.

A weekly memo is distributed every Wednesday to stores, and published on the company intranet every Thursday, to enable employees to access information and provide a forum for feedback. There are opportunities for staff to spend a six-month secondment in Wine and Beer World in France. Add to this sales incentive trips and business travel, and half the staff travel abroad at least once a year. UK staff make up a significant proportion of the management team in France.

Innovation

"We are innovative in how we resource our business and solve problems, and our approach to customer service is award winning" says Thorpe. "That much has been recognised through securing many prestigious awards."

Majestic is rolling out a new electronic point-of-sale system to all its 120 stores in 2005. Rather than passing the work to an outsourced IT company, the intention is to take the four members of Majestic's IT department, and train them in how to install and operate the new system. These four will then visit each store and pass on all the relevant operational knowledge.

The company offers a way into the fascinating world of wine for those with no prior experience, and provides its staff with a high degree of autonomy in managing stores. This translates into the staff acquiring an intimate view of the way the business operates. Plus, the small team philosophy means the work is very much hands-on.

"In the past five years, we've created an award-winning website, acquired and developed a successful business in France, opened a fine wine centre, significantly expanded our corporate sales division, and embarked on a store expansion programme across the UK," says Thorpe.

Diversity and social responsibility

Majestic is an equal opportunities employer and "proud of the working culture" it has in the company. Equal opportunities monitoring is carried out at the recruitment stage and all staff receive an equal opportunities policy in their employee handbook. Currently, 3% of Majestic's 670 staff are from racial and religious minorities. Company-wide, 35% of employees and nearly 40% of management are women. Much effort is spent in ensuring all employees are treated equally and afforded the same opportunities. Diversity in the workforce is encouraged through the company's promotion of employment opportunities at careers fairs such as GRADES (gender, religion, age, disability, ethnicity and sexuality) Diversity Fair.

There is an employee-nominated charity of the year – currently it's CLIC (Cancer and Leukaemia in Childhood). There are in-store charity boxes, tasting evenings/weekends where a percentage of profits is donated, and an annual staff raffle (raising £7,500 in 2004). Staff support local charities at store managers' discretion.

Majestic pays a recycling charge on every bottle it sources, and at store level recycles all unused cardboard boxes and bottles where possible. Majestic is a member of the Portman Group, which promotes the responsible sale of alcohol.

Corporate Governance

Majestic's board has established an audit committee and a remuneration committee. The former is charged with reviewing the interim and final accounts, ensuring the proper functioning of appropriate financial and operating controls, and providing the forum through which the external auditors report to the board. The latter determines the remuneration and benefits of executive directors, plus the operation of the deferred bonus scheme for senior managers.

"Our staff are a key asset so laws and regulations pertaining to employment are important as are those relating to licensing and the responsible sale of alcohol, particularly as we are a wine retailer," says Thorpe. "At Majestic we try to go further than just adhering to the minimum guidelines laid down in law – we endeavour to work to guidelines set out in best practice."

"A major part of our business strategy comprises our core intention to be both a responsible retailer and a responsible employer," says Thorpe. "Both values are intrinsically linked. Everything we do is integrated, from customer service through teamworking to continuing training exercises." The company is not unionised, but then the staff have never asked for it to be so.

Environmental record

"There is no formal or direct policy in place on environmental issues generally," says Thorpe. "However, we do address environmental issues on a case-by-case basis, for example on the use of corks in wine production and the impact of discarded screw caps on the environment. There are no formalised procedures, but we do encourage staff to recycle printer cartridges for charity, and office paper, for example." Bottle banks exist in some stores where space allows, and more critically, where they will be collected and emptied. Wooden port and claret boxes are sold and the proceeds given to charity.

"We reimburse the cost of young person's railcards for all employees, and fund all travel to and from training courses which are held outside the normal place of work," says Thorpe. "Employees are encouraged to use public transport on these occasions due to the nature of the training provided."

While cardboard boxes and packaging will be recycled wherever possible, the company also ensures that wine cases are reused at any available opportunity – carrying away a mixed box of French Cave des Fleurs medium white and Chilean Merlot in a Chassagne-Montrachet Blanc, Bader Mimeur case has a certain cachet. Just like Majestic. Affordable quality.

Masterfoods

Masterfoods
Dundee Road, Slough SL1 4JX
Tel: (0) 1753 550055 **Fax:** (0) 1753 550111
Web: www.mars.com

Pay and Benefits	7.5	Innovation	6.8
Promotion and Development	6.5	Diversity	5.8
Training	6.9	Social Responsibility	5.0
Travel opportunities	5.9	Corporate Governance	4.8
Culture	7.0	Environment	6.9
Total			**63.1**

Masterfoods manufactures confectionery, pet care and main meal products; and is part of Mars Inc., one of the largest privately owned businesses in the world. Mars Inc. has a global turnover of $14bn and employs around 30,000 people across 175 sites in 60 countries.

Executive Summary

Masterfoods is a multinational organisation that offers over 30 brands. Many of the company's brands are internationally famous including Mars,, Snickers,, Twix,, Dolmio,, Uncle Ben's,, Pedigree,, and Whiskas,.

The very first Mars, bar was manufactured in 1932; and today, the same site makes around 3m Mars, bars each week plus a range of top-selling brands. The company built on this confectionery business, moving into pet care in 1935 and main meals in 1962; these three core businesses collectively make up Masterfoods. In addition to this, the UK business also encompasses MEI, a company that manufactures electronic payment systems such as coin-mechanisms.

Pay and Benefits

Masterfoods is renowned for high remuneration, broad training and a very good pensions package. The company has built on these offerings and has developed an increasingly progressive approach to pay and benefits, making it a very attractive place to work compared to other FMCGs (Fast Moving Consumer Goods companies) and a wide range of employers in different sectors.

In setting the level of reward for new recruits, Masterfoods uses a number of different criteria: how well the business is performing, feedback from employees, job size and seniority, and measurement against comparable roles in competitor organisations. Currently, the starting salary for UK-based graduates is £25,000 plus a £2,000 joining bonus, which is well above the average graduate starting salary. Thereafter, pay is defined by a rigorous performance review development process – and the extent to which employees meet their objectives will impact significantly on what they earn. For example, managers who perform well and meet their targets can earn up to 18% of their base salary in bonuses.

Employee benefits also include a non-contributory pension scheme and life assurance; and a private medical scheme, which can be extended to the employee's family for a small premium. There is a 22-day holiday allowance, which increases according to length of service at the company – it can reach a maximum of 32 days. In addition to this, employees can take a year's sabbatical leave once they have established themselves. Oh, and everyone gets a free bag of chocolates at the end of each week!

Promotion and development

Masterfoods sets great store by its ability to nurture talent, and new recruits can quickly experience a range of challenging and rewarding work roles. Working on bestselling brands, talented employees at Masterfoods are presented with opportunities to develop and excel on a daily basis. There are two main types of graduate opportunity at Masterfoods. Firstly, a range of programmes in areas such as research and development, finance, marketing, sales and engineering allow graduates to hone specific skills. Secondly, the European Management Development Programme is aimed at recent graduates who are open-minded about where they want to work in the business, and who want international experience early in their careers. This intake can gain experience at a variety of locations before deciding on a career path. Masterfoods graduate programmes have proved remarkably successful, with 75% of graduates staying on five years after joining.

The company is keen for talented employees to gain exposure to different parts of the business, both within and beyond national borders, and there is a growing trend for associates to take their skills abroad. The UK in particular has become a big exporter of talent around the world, often in helping to establish new sites.

From a graduate perspective, there is a real feeling of community. A research and development placement does not preclude someone from attending a marketing workshop, which may stimulate an interest in another area of the business. Similarly, an alumni system helps to channel advice and support from more experienced hands to newer recruits. In all there are eight reporting levels – which sounds a lot, but in reality employees can move up fairly swiftly through the business if they perform well.

There is a strong focus on learning and development at Masterfoods. A lot of learning occurs on the job from a mixture of challenging assignments, rigorous reviews and clear objectives. Employees also learn from discussions with others, mainly in the context of an individual development plan containing team, functional and personal objectives. And finally, employees can elect to attend external courses. The decision for attending these courses is made in agreement with line managers according to individual needs.

Company Culture

At Masterfoods, the culture is based on Five Principles: quality, responsibility, mutuality, efficiency and freedom. These act as a reference point for any area of business activity and serve as a powerful unifying tool for what is a huge organisation. And as each new generation of the Mars family assumes a leadership position, the principles provide continuity in the face of new internal and external challenges.

A global business it may be, but Masterfoods remains a family concern where everyone is treated equally and egalitarianism is the watchword. All the sites are open-plan, there are no reserved parking spaces, the protocol is first names only, and canteens are used by management and associates alike. Animals are equally well treated – at the site devoted exclusively to pet nutrition, each member of the canine population has their own personal walker!

The friendly, social atmosphere is further driven by a strong emphasis on teamwork. Though very little work is carried out in isolation, there is considerable latitude for individuals to act on business ideas they may generate. The company carries out an annual employee survey and finds a consistently high score awarded to the belief that everyone's opinions count. There are opportunities for flexible working, but most of the workforce take no more than two or three days to work away from the office. This excludes the sales teams, which are largely field-based.

Innovation

Because the Mars family still owns and plays a leading role in the management of the company, it can reinvest profits back into the business and seize new opportunities more quickly. Innovative solutions often arise from the freedom at regional and country level. Masterfoods businesses have to run themselves. A real-life example of this is the ice cream bar market. It was noticed that Mars bar consumers loved putting the product in the fridge during summer and eating it cold. From this came the insight to develop an ice cream with the taste of mars and the refreshing properties of ice cream. This pioneering innovation heralded the birth of what is today a well-known and universally eaten product – the ice cream bar. Another outstanding example would be the transformation of the cat and dog care markets away from cans to fresher and more convenient pouches.

Formal recognition of innovation comes through the annual Making the Difference Awards. Employees can nominate themselves or a colleague for any new or unique contribution. Winners from each Masterfoods location across England and Ireland are then put forward for a national competition, and the winners of this competition are then put forward for the global Making the Difference award. In 2004, it was the UK's turn to win the award as a research and development team were hailed for the development of Frolic, Spiros, – a new product due to be launched across Europe in 2005.

Diversity and social responsibility

The organisation's commitment to social responsibility has long been enshrined in one of the five principles – mutuality. The belief that "a mutual benefit is a shared benefit; a shared benefit will endure" extends to relationships beyond the immediate sphere of business activity. In the UK, the company has built partnerships with many local organisations, particularly at management level. In 2003, it won a special recognition award from Business in the Community for business leadership leading to community impact in Slough.

35% of managers are female – and with ever more scope for flexible working, this figure is rising. In fact, because employees are encouraged to experience a variety of work responsibilities, job sharing is more common than in many businesses.

Masterfoods is an equal opportunities employer; it values diversity and welcomes ethnic minorities. The organisation is a supporter of the Windrush Diversity Awards and also backs the Windsor Fellowship.

Corporate Governance

As a privately owned business, Masterfoods is not subject to the level of scrutiny that a public company would be. However, the company believes that the longstanding mutuality principle has "consistently underpinned the ethics of our corporate governance, and has helped us deal fairly everywhere we are active."

Environment

The company's environmental policy is firmly integrated into all its modes of operation. In that respect, it monitors and seeks to improve upon its performance in this area just as it would aim for quality anywhere else. The company has developed best practice guidelines covering areas such as suppliers, packaging, sales and marketing, distribution, energy conservation, hazardous materials, local environmental impacts, infestation control, waste management, health and safety, engineering design, personnel and organisation, legislation and communication.

Merck

Merck Pharmaceuticals UK
Harrier House, High Street, West Drayton, Middlesex UB7 7QG
Tel: (0) 1895 452200 **Fax:** (0) 1895 420605
Web: www.merck-pharmaceuticals.co.uk **Email:** enquiries@merckpharma.co.uk

ıiMERCK

Pay and Benefits	6.8	Innovation	7.2
Promotion and Development	6.8	Diversity	6.8
Training	6.8	Social Responsibility	6.6
Travel opportunities	6.6	Corporate Governance	7.0
Culture	6.2	Environment	6.6
Total			**67.4**

Merck is a global pharmaceutical and chemical company. In 2003, it had European sales of ½7.2bn, a slight decline on the previous year. Net profit rose slightly to ½208m. It employs 225 people in the UK and over 28,000 worldwide.

Executive summary

Merck is one of the oldest family-owned businesses in the world, with its origins in seventeenth century Germany. Established in its modern form in the UK since 1970, the firm has built a strong reputation in the ethical pharmaceuticals field, notably in oncology, cardio-vascular illness and diabetes. Other key business areas include liquid crystals for display, pigments and reagents.

The bulk of activity at Merck in this country is focused on the marketing and selling of products, with the result that more than half the total workforce is field-based. Most research and development occurs elsewhere, although a small team of clinical research associates (CRAs) carries out pre-licensing clinical retrial work.

In 1995, the Merck family sought to grow the business through a share issue. With 26% of the company passing into the hands of private investors, the company strengthened its corporate brand identity and adopted a strategy of focusing on core business areas. In line with this Merck acquired the Seven Seas healthcare business in 1996. Earlier in 2004, it divested VWR, its loss-making laboratory distribution operation.

The family connection remains strong, however, and this has helped Merck remain relatively stable in an industry often characterised by a high level of M&A activity. Growth has been healthy, particularly in the last three years – 42% organic growth from 2001–2004 – and in 2003, UK turnover was £45m.

Pay and benefits

Merck is by no means the biggest player in the pharmaceutical sector and therefore does not have the resources of some of its competitors. It aims to pay above the median range, with the current minimum graduate starting salary pegged at £22,000.

As a German-owned business, there is a more overtly paternalistic approach to compensation than in many Anglo-American companies. For example, though there are no employee share options on offer, there is a final salary pension scheme – something few companies in this country now feel able to maintain. Merck also grants maternity leave on full pay to employees with at least two years' service, while new fathers have five days' paid leave, set to rise to ten in 2005.

A company car or car allowance is available for all field sales employees, all of whom are eligible for a range of variable incentive schemes based on both individual and business performance. More recently, gym membership was added to the benefits package.

Promotion and development

About 10% of payroll is spent on training at Merck, and it is clear the company places its commitment in this area at the heart of its hiring and retention strategy. New recruits should expect a hands-on approach to development early on, according to John McIlree, head of HR, training and development. He says, "Performance management has always been a very important part of what we do – we think people have to be appraised and assessed the minute they join the company. And as we've assumed more of a global business focus, we realise we need to be sharp about spotting talent. For a long time we were reluctant to have fast-track opportunities and we now realise that was a mistake."

The initial development focus is directed in two areas for graduate recruits (almost all Merck employees are educated to degree level). The first type of training is designed to meet employees' individual professional objectives – to get them accredited in their functional field. This training will also be given to members of the sales team who want to move into specialist areas.

The second area meets the needs of the team and business as a whole; in many cases, this means acquiring the commercial and leadership skills which ultimately ensure Merck remains a dynamic organisation. And as would-be managers develop themselves, the benefits of being a member of a global rather than merely local organisation become apparent. Merck runs its own MBA programme, in partnership with Lufthansa and Deutsche Bank. Successful graduates of the company's Smart Management Programme can move on to an international programme, gaining experience at locations around the world. Senior executive development is run from the Merck University based at head office in Wiesbaden – the two-year programme encompasses study periods at business schools in London, Chicago and Hong Kong.

Company culture

Lots of companies boast that their employees are proud to work there. At Merck, that pride is evident everywhere – not merely because of the way people are treated but because of the ethical nature of the business. According to McIlree, "People here genuinely believe they're doing a lot of good and improving the quality of people's lives. For example, there has been quite a big focus on oncology recently, and people get quite involved when they see what benefits it can bring to cancer sufferers."

Merck enjoys high visibility in its industry yet is much smaller in size than its main competitors (it is not to be confused with Merck & Co.). This allows for a relatively informal approach to people management. In practice, this means that hard numbers are not the only criteria used to identify genuine talent in the organisation; instead, the high level of personal awareness people have of each other means there is a more literal way to get noticed.

Change is afoot, however. Once known as "the company of a thousand islands", Merck has adopted much more of a corporate face since becoming publicly listed. Although national Merck businesses still retain a high level of autonomy, the global brand alignment has widened access to resources and brought increasing operational professionalism. This in turn has given people still more reason to stay loyal to the company. The turnover rate in the sales team averages 17.5% compared to an industry average of 19.5%, and is 7.5% for the company as a whole.

Innovation

In 2003, the company introduced an employee innovation scheme. The idea was to harness the human resource in the business in order to improve aspects of operational efficiency and the collective wellbeing. That year, a total of 330 ideas were submitted, of which half were implemented. The following year almost twice the number of ideas was submitted, with around a third being implemented. Overall, this equates to three implemented ideas for each employee.

Mostly the ideas adopted are small step business improvements. One recent submission involved sharing information on candidates with other similar-sized recruiting companies, which has helped bring advertising savings for the HR team. Other examples include better use of storage space and cost-effective solutions for a more inspiring work environment.

Merck recognises innovation at both a UK and an international level. There are annual Gold Cup awards for the top 10% of high-performing employees, which includes innovation, and a fortnightly in-house magazine also acknowledges contributions in this area.

"One of our major current revenue streams comes from liquid crystal," says McIlree. "It is a Merck invention that dates back to 1904, but its application has changed in recent times – now it is used widely in phone, camera and LCD display screens. Though we have professional research teams working on this kind of product development, we recognise that everyone should have a chance to talk about how we do things. That's why we adopted a formal innovation programme."

Diversity and Social Responsibility

Merck's workforce is split fairly equally between men and women. Just over a third of managers are women, who make up a quarter of the senior management tier. Female representation is on the increase in sales and marketing, where most of the 80-odd staff aged under 34 are employed.

Just less than 10% of employees are non-UK nationals. This number obviously excludes ethnic minority British employees whose representation tends to broadly reflect the local population. People of Asian origin, for example, figure more prominently among London area medical reps than they do among their Scottish counterparts.

Corporate responsibility initiatives are locally driven, with annual donations running at £5,000–£7,000. Head office has forged links with a number of schools in the Hillingdon area, producing a safety programme for the local borough council. In London, financial support has been provided to Great Ormond Street Hospital. A staff welfare fund also exists; this contains money raised for selected local projects, with Merck matching any donation made by employees to the fund.

Corporate Governance

Merck has its own team of internal auditors, which runs checks on the business operation – not only from a financial perspective but also from a process perspective. The company is keen to protect the reputation it has built over many years in both its sector of operation and wider business environment. Accordingly, when Merck employees were found to be involved in irregular pricing practices in the 1990s, the company reacted by implementing a new code of conduct for all representatives. Launched in 2001 – and binding worldwide – the code summarises in 13 guidelines the rules that must be adhered to. This includes the prohibition of unlawful behaviour, care in planning and operating equipment, and the need to respect ethical boundaries.

In the UK, the company secretary has the responsibility of ensuring this code is fully understood and implemented. Merck intends to update this code during 2005. Additionally, through the medical affairs department, the company ensures its people comply with a separate code of practice on industrial safety.

Environment

"Globally, our company has always had a tremendous track record in this area – particularly in Germany where we have a huge amount of production, not just pharmaceutical but all sorts of chemicals. They talked about the company commitment to the environment in the early 70s long before it was fashionable to do so," says McIlree.

Today, the company carries out regular environmental and safety audits at all its 62 production sites. By the end of 2002, 16 of these sites – accounting for four-fifths of total output – had been certified according to the environmental management standard ISO 14001. And in a number of cases, as production has increased, improved efficiency has led to a fall in the level of energy and water consumption.

Merck's distribution network is extensive, and safety of transportation is another key commitment. In May 2004, the company launched a new vehicle risk assessment programme for employees who travel frequently.

Metro

Surrey Quays Road, Rotherhithe, London SE16 7ND
Tel: (0) 20 7651 5256
Web: www.metro.co.uk **Email:** marketing@ukmetro.co.uk

Pay and Benefits	5.4	Innovation	7.3
Promotion and Development	6.5	Diversity	4.6
Training	6.2	Social Responsibility	5.2
Travel opportunities	4.6	Corporate Governance	5.4
Culture	6.4	Environment	5.9
Total			**57.5**

Metro is the UK's fourth-largest national newspaper; it is distributed free to morning commuters in London, Birmingham, Bristol, Edinburgh, Glasgow, Leeds, Manchester, Newcastle and other urban centres. It aims to provide a "20-minute read" founded on fact not opinion, to young "urbanites" in social classes ABC1. Owned by Associated Newspapers (publishers of the Daily Mail, Mail on Sunday and London Evening Standard), it employs about 180 staff, two-thirds of them journalists. Most staff work at the paper's London headquarters; small regional offices produce lifestyle sections for the English regions, and 30 people in Glasgow produce a separate Scottish edition.

Executive summary

Metro describes itself as the ugly duckling which became a swan. The paper was rushed out in London in March 1999 with an uncertain future ahead of it. But the company soon realised that the paper's unique selling proposition – 20 minutes of quality time with a high-spending audience of young, urban middle-class readers – was enormously strong, and it set about turning Metro into a high-value, national media brand.

By January 2001, there were regional editions in Manchester, Birmingham, Edinburgh/Glasgow, Newcastle and Leeds/Sheffield. Bristol and the East Midlands were added in 2004. Circulation passed the one million mark in 2004, taking Metro to fourth place in national newspaper circulation behind the Sun, the Daily Mail and the Daily Mirror.

Advertising space in Metro is at a premium due to the limited number of pages and lucrative audience; unusually, the paper does not negotiate on rates. But Metro's narrow focus on ABC1 urban commuters means that circulation will ultimately reach saturation, so the paper is seeking further expansion by diversifying into books and branded events.

Growth to date has been remarkable. The paper was profitable within four years of its launch, and in 2003–04, profits increased 421% while revenues grew 27% – much faster than other national daily papers. This is a laudable achievement for a young free newspaper.

Pay and benefits

Metro is a company that likes to be different. With a young, urbanite staff reflecting its young, urbanite readership, it is not big on corporate perks such as share options or childcare. "It tends to be more a fun and quirky approach to benefits rather than a traditional one!" says Lara Ashworth, the paper's head of talent.

The sales team hit their bonus target almost every month, which not only earns them a quarterly trip in the UK and annual weekend trip to Europe, but also a substantial bonus. Most people in the commercial wing of the business also have bonuses, which relate to their results and success.

So it's no surprise that in Metro's 2004 staff survey, although just a quarter of staff thought their basic pay compared favourably with the rest of the media industry, four-fifths said their bonus compared favourably. Strictly speaking, this was four-fifths of the commercial and sales staff, since the journalists don't receive bonuses. Although a perceived imbalance between the commercial and editorial parts of the business has often been cited, the company can prove its attempts to redress the balance are becoming successful. Training and development is now offered to all editorial staff, with 81% of the department taking up this opportunity in 2004. An editorial appraisals scheme is now being developed to bring their career planning opportunities into line with those of their commercial colleagues.

Associated Newspapers is a limited company. There are only limited share ownership or stock option schemes. But the very generous final salary pension scheme (5% contributions from employees, 15% from Metro) is still open to new recruits; there is Medisure private healthcare after three years; and cars or car allowances for directors and managers, and for other staff who need them. Most benefits are determined by length of service, not seniority, as are holiday allowances: 25 days rising to 30 after three years. Staff are also eligible for discounts on travel, eating out, eye care and other services.

Promotion and development

Metro recruits new blood by advertising in its own paper. "We want brand champions – people who love the paper and believe in what it does," says Ashworth. But the paper prefers to promote internally, which combined with its rapid growth, means excellent opportunities for anyone with ability.

Within their first few months, trainees can expect a personal development plan to progress them towards the next level. Three-quarters of staff are aged under 35, including several directors. Metro has a flat organisational structure to facilitate communication. This makes formal promotions highly competitive, although there are examples of talented individuals who have been promoted several times within a few years. The company makes up for its fewer formal opportunities by encouraging staff to gain experience of several jobs, or to broaden their remit within their existing role.

Journalists may flit from news to pictures to sub-editing to website design, and if they come up with a good idea they may well find themselves in charge of its execution – as happened with Metro's highly successful collaboration with Rough Guide.

Salespeople are encouraged to run "talent projects": new things the paper would like to do but doesn't have the senior resource available to focus on it. Because the paper is entirely UK-based, there are no foreign travel opportunities apart from one-off press trips or the occasional jolly.

Ashworth's training budget for 2004 was £250,000 – not bad for just 180 staff – and she works hard to identify the best training providers and match them to individuals' needs. When surveys showed hardly any journalists were receiving training, she produced a brochure of courses and encouraged every journalist (including regular freelances) to pick two: one related to their current job and one for interest or career development. The commercial team receive a full skills audit with an annual talent assessment, and training plans are so personally tailored that in 2004 no two people went on all the same courses.

Company culture

Steve Auckland, Metro's managing director, has two whitewashed walls in his office, both heavily inscribed in marker pen. One is the Success Wall, where anybody can write a sentence describing a successful event – whether sales, commercial or editorial. Facing his desk are commercial and editorial targets, and the paper's five key goals for the year – to which he adheres firmly. His nickname is Ronseal, because he does exactly what he promises. "Steve's very empowering," says Ashworth. "He wants you to come to him with solutions, not problems."

The company's unstuffy style is reflected in its open-plan offices, where editorial and commercial staff sit together on one floor. Internal communication is good, with a monthly staff newsletter; quarterly "soapbox" sessions where the editor and managing director give a presentation and answer questions; and an annual staff survey of which management seems to take genuine notice. In 2004, 88% of respondents said: "I'm proud to tell people I work for Metro". Positive feedback is the norm, and the commercial side holds quarterly awards for excellence with cash prizes.

Producing five editions of a national newspaper every week is no picnic. Auckland says, "We believe in stretching our staff and our resources. We want people to produce outstanding results that they never believed they could achieve. We want everyone here to exceed their own expectations and those of our customers."

But Metro belies the image of a stressed-out media company. When the paper was listed in the Sunday Times' 50 Best Small Companies to Work For 2004, researchers found that three-quarters of staff didn't feel under too much pressure. Working hours are modest; 90-minute lunch breaks are allowed (long enough to go swimming or running); and although there is no formal policy on flexible working, the company is sympathetic to requests – one journalist recently started working from home.

Innovation

Metro's most significant innovation is the paper itself: a unique product combining free distribution with national circulation to an upmarket audience – and quickly profitable to boot. Aimed at middle-class commuters aged 18–45, the paper is distributed at underground and railway stations, on buses and trams, and in places where car commuters can be reached (cafes, gyms, even posh apartment developments). It is designed to be read in 20 minutes to fit into the average commuter journey.

As well as regional expansion, Metro is now using its brand to diversify. Its first book, The Rough Guide to 50 Great Travel Experiences, in partnership with Rough Guide and sponsored by the Post Office, was a great success. The first "shopping night", in association with Boxfresh in London and Manchester, gave away twice as many tickets as expected. The paper sponsors Chemistry speed-dating events and the Edinburgh Festival Fringe, and magazine publishing is currently under consideration.

To gather detailed information about its young, urbanite readership, Metro has a 3,000-strong reader panel, Urban Life, which has won awards from trade bibles Media Week and Campaign.

The paper's internal workings are quietly innovative too, with its sales department split into strategic planning and day-to-day selling, and a new performance management programme for the editorial staff – both very unusual in media companies. Having a dedicated head of talent (Ashworth) is also most unusual.

Diversity and social responsibility

Metro's main social project is its partnership with Street League, a charity (London-based but hoping to expand nationwide), which helps young disadvantaged people achieve their potential through sport. The core is a five-a-side football league, plus access to personal development, education and employment. Metro's staff participate actively, and a one-day soccer tournament in 2004 raised £9,000. Regarding involvement in charities, Auckland leads by example as the chairperson of London Cares and an active member of BITC. Staff are also supported in personal charitable projects; one journalist was given a £1,000 scholarship to produce marketing materials for a family charity in Zambia.

The paper's creaking personnel systems (part of the Associated Newspapers legacy) don't allow it to analyse its ethnic balance, and it has no formal policy on diversity – preferring to be a pure meritocracy. However, its staff reflect its "urbanite" brand, and there is a sprinkling of people from ethnic minorities. The gender balance is pretty even at all levels of the company.

Corporate Governance

Metro's slogan is "facts not 'spin", and its emphasis on responsible reporting and the absence of a political or campaigning bias are very effective at keeping the paper out of the libel courts. There is an official query process (seldom invoked) for advertisers who don't like their ad copy or where it was placed, and the paper says it has excellent relations with the National Union of Journalists. Corporate issues – such as data protection, accounting probity etc. – are handled centrally by Associated Newspapers.

Environmental record

Like most newspapers, Metro is largely printed on recycled paper, and wastage rates are very low. The intention is that distribution stands are empty by 10am (by which time young urbanites are at work), and the handful of spare copies are carefully collected up as waste paper is a considerable fire hazard, especially on the underground.

Being based in central London, most staff use public transport; the sales team have season tickets paid for by the company. Office parking is very limited and several staff cycle to work. The paper was named Best Community Cycling Initiative in the London Cycling Awards for its weekly cycling page.

Michael Page

Michael Page International
39/41 Parker Street, London WC2B 5LN
Tel: (0) 20 7831 2000
Web: www.michaelpage.co.uk **Email:** info@michaelpage.co.uk

Michael Page
INTERNATIONAL

Pay and Benefits	8.0	Innovation	7.1
Promotion and Development	8.1	Diversity	7.8
Training	7.1	Social Responsibility	6.4
Travel opportunities	7.5	Corporate Governance	6.8
Culture	7.2	Environment	7.0
Total			**73.0**

Michael Page International is one of the world's leading recruitment consultancies with an annual turnover of £372.6m. It specialises in placing candidates in permanent, contract, temporary and interim positions with clients around the world.

The firm employs 2,435 people in 109 offices across 16 countries in Europe, Asia-Pacific and the Americas.

Its specialist areas are accounting, tax and treasury, banking and financial markets, marketing, retail, sales, legal, IT and technology, human resources, engineering and manufacturing, procurement and supply chain, consultancy/strategy/change, and secretarial work.

Executive summary

Michael Page is unique in its field – and unusual in industry generally – by growing entirely by organic expansion rather than through mergers or acquisitions. Michael Page and Bill McGregor established it 28 years ago as a specialist consultancy, using area specialists to recruit others in their field. In 1979, it started to expand outside London; opening offices in Manchester, Birmingham, Glasgow, Leeds and Bristol. In 1985, it started its overseas expansion by opening an Australian office; and in 1988, was listed on the London Stock Exchange. It has been awarded Business Superbrand status for three years running by the Business Superbrands Council.

In 2003, the firm generated pre-tax profits of £23.5m on turnover of £372.6m. Turnover was down nearly 3% on the previous year, but for the first half of 2004 the company saw an increase in turnover of 13.4% and operating profit grew by 65.9% compared to the same period in 2003.

Pay and benefits

Michael Page aims to offer above-industry-average pay and benefits. Including benefits, the average pay package for sales staff is £45,372 a year. A successful consultant could expect to be earning in the £60,000–£80,000 range, rising to £80,000–£100,000 for a manager. These figures include bonuses that are based on team rather than individual performance.

The salary that new graduates receive varies from region to region: as of summer 2004, graduates in London could expect £20,250; in the south-east, £19,500; and in the rest of the UK, £18,500. After the 4–5 month induction programme, they will usually earn an extra £4,000–£10,000 a year in quarterly performance-related bonuses. On completing their first full 12 months after the training program, they receive a company car or car allowance of £5,000 a year.

Other benefits include private medical insurance, life assurance, personal health insurance, contribution to the group pension scheme, a company car for eligible employees, and stock options (about 12% of employees have a stake in the company). The company offers 23 days' holiday, rising to 28 days with longer service.

Requests for flexible working are considered on their merits; since legislation emerged to ensure requests should be considered, the company has accepted 75% of such requests. The firm currently has 45 people working non-standard hours, including some managers and directors, and most of these started working in this way before the legislation. There are also a few examples of job sharing – for example, two people currently share the role of recruitment manager. Flexible working has also been used to help members of staff return to their previous roles after periods of serious long-term illness. It should be made clear that these figures refer to the UK only.

As well as monetary benefits, the firm likes to reward its employees by holding a series of fun group events. The highest-performing consultants are recognised at the firm's High Achievers Club functions, held quarterly and annually. Organised activities at these functions have included bungee jumping in Zambia and taking the Blue Train down to Capetown in South Africa. Individual divisions also celebrate their achievements by holding "Quarterly Bashes" at their various worldwide locations. Once a year, all Michael Page staff are invited to a black-tie evening event.

Promotion and development

Michael Page is unusual in having pursued a strategy of entirely organic growth. This has been achieved partly through a policy of internal promotion, enabling the firm to reward highly able people and offer them career opportunities both in the UK and internationally. Four out of five executive board members as well as 95% of managers, directors and managing directors started out as consultants.

Most employees join the firm at recruitment consultant level. Once they have proved themselves, there are three possible routes they can take.

Firstly, those who are interested in management can go through a fast-track mentoring scheme to develop their management skills. From management they can potentially progress to director level – a role involving group-wide initiatives and the management of several teams. Secondly, some consultants choose to gain experience in different markets, either by working abroad or within a different discipline. Thirdly, some consultants choose to remain in their chosen field, becoming experienced and knowledgeable in their particular market. Outstanding consultants have the opportunity to continue operating within their specialist markets at an executive level.

New starters at Michael Page get a personal development plan tailored to their individual training needs. All operational employees participate in an induction programme with follow-up modules in all the recruitment cycle skills including candidate management, business development, portfolio and time management, influencing, and temporary-specific workshops.

Experienced consultants participate in an intensive 2-day programme involving a 24-hour virtual office simulation, which allows them to test and extend their skills. In addition, external formal training is offered in such areas as training, motivation, mindset and attitude change, and presentation skills. On promotion to manager level, employees participate in a 6-module management training programme, which complements individual coaching using the competency framework and involves both internal and external trainers. Similarly, directors participate in regular development programmes.

In their first 12 months, employees receive an average 15–16 days' training, decreasing to eight days a year for the next two to three years.

Company culture

Michael Page is now an international business and company culture will, to some extent, vary from country to country. But whichever office you work in, it is a competitive, sales-oriented environment; and the people who thrive in it need a lot of initiative, drive and self-motivation to succeed.

Michael Page's six core values are: pride in one's work, passion, commitment, resilience, teamwork and fun – and it looks to invest in people who share those values.

The first five values are pretty self-explanatory. The last value – fun – is reflected in the firm's policy of rewarding employees with entertaining events as well as money. As well as its High Achievers events and annual employee ball, individual divisions hold "Quarterly Bashes" in all the cities where the firm operates. Recent Quarterly Bashes have included activities such as golfing, spa-days, go-karting, rafting, restaurant outings, racing at Brands Hatch, horse racing; and weekends in Amsterdam, Barcelona and Paris. The activities on offer reflect the firm's predominantly young culture – it recruits straight from university as well as attracting experienced people and most employees are in their 20s or 30s.

Many of these events are held at Michael Page offices around the world, giving staff a chance to mix with their international colleagues. There are opportunities for work-related travel too, although people applying for positions in the UK should bear in mind they'll be predominantly UK-based. There is, however, scope for international transfer.

Innovation

Michael Page has been a trailblazer for many years. It was the first recruitment business to float on the London Stock Exchange, it championed the idea of specialism in recruitment, and it was the first to develop an international computerised applicant network.

The firm is not a believer in innovation for innovation's sake, but is prepared to invest heavily in technology where this will help its business. For example, it recently invested several million pounds on a new global recruitment system. Its website, which has won a number of awards, gives candidates a real-time view on the status of every live job the firm handles – amounting to nearly 13,000 in the UK alone.

Employees are actively encouraged to help the firm come up with innovative business ideas. Five years ago, a new employee suggested the idea of a temporary-candidate management system – the idea was communicated to management, and the system was developed and implemented throughout the UK. In 2000, following a "blue sky" exercise at one of the firm's management conferences, managers suggested a centralised UK training and development function, and the proposal was implemented over a two-year period.

Diversity and social responsibility

Michael Page International is committed to promoting equal opportunities, both as an employer and as a service provider. Discriminatory attitudes or behaviour are unacceptable at any time and Michael Page believes that all staff should have a genuinely equal opportunity to progress within the organisation.

The firm has put in place a number of measures to ensure awareness of equal opportunities. For example, it provides in-house and external training on equal opportunities and diversity issues; seeks to diversify its own workforce; asks all employees and candidates to complete a monitoring form so it can analyse diversity issues; trains consultants in competency-based interview techniques, using behavioural and value-based criteria as well as relevant experience; and appoints, where applicable, a dedicated diversity consultant on specific client account teams.

It also aims to provide services that are welcoming and accessible to all those who might wish to use them. Michael Page wants to achieve an increasingly diverse candidate database through the use of diverse advertising media and non-stereotypical advertising campaigns; to raise its diversity profile through sponsorship and brand awareness campaigns; and to build relationships with organisations supporting diversity.

For example, it joined RFO (Race for Opportunity) in 2004, and will be actively participating in its benchmarking exercises. It has been involved in setting up the Inter Recruitment Diversity Forum where diversity issues and best practice are discussed on a regular basis with eight other major recruitment firms. It also recently hosted a breakfast seminar on the topic of Ethnicity with Global Graduates, became involved with a diversity organisation focusing on training diverse school children, and sponsored the Afro Caribbean Finance Forum in the launch of their 2003 Graduate Careers Fair. In the future, it plans to invite the Employers Forum for Age to host a seminar for employees and clients.

In the UK, 56% of the firm's staff and 38.5% of management are female; 7% of employees come from ethnic minorities, compared to 7.9% in the UK population as a whole. It is developing its own recruitment system to accommodate more detailed diversity monitoring of candidates, and its 2005 graduate recruitment program will use more diverse media including a Diversity Recruitment Fair.

On the social responsibility front, the company does not make official charity donations but supports staff through a Give As You Earn scheme, which matches staff contributions on a pound-for-pound basis.

Corporate Governance

The firm is organised into 11 recruitment areas – for example, engineering, accounting, marketing, and so on. Each discipline has its own MD and board, which reports to the overall board of Michael Page plc.

Each discipline is then organised on a divisional basis, and each division focuses on recruiting in a specific geography, sector or sub-specialism – for example, FMCG Marketing (in London), Risk (in the City), and Pharma Sales (North of England). A manager runs each division with a group of five to eight consultants.

As its entire business centres around permanent and temporary employment services, Michael Page is governed by all aspects of employment law. It also has to comply with the Data Protection Act, since databases containing data on individuals are the main tools of its businesses.

It has two independent accreditations: ISO 9001/MQA01, which relates to marketing quality; and IOS 9002, relating to Quality Systems.

Environmental record

As a service company, Michael Page is not a major polluter, but it recognises that its business activities do have an impact on the environment. The UK MD has board responsibility for group environmental management, which is implemented by the facilities management department.

The firm's policy is to reduce its environmental impact by minimising energy consumption and maximising efficiency; through efficient purchasing which minimises

Moorfields Eye Hospital NHS Foundation Trust

Moorfields Eye Hospital
NHS Foundation Trust, 162 City Road, London EC1V 2PD
Tel: (0) 20 7253 3411
Web: www.moorfields.org.uk

Pay and Benefits	6.3	Innovation	6.5
Promotion and Development	6.2	Diversity	7.5
Training	6.0	Social Responsibility	7.4
Travel opportunities	5.8	Corporate Governance	6.8
Culture	6.7	Environment	5.8
Total			**65.0**

Moorfields is one of the world's foremost centres for ophthalmic treatment, teaching and research, and its name is a byword for eye medicine. Founded in 1805 as the world's first specialist eye and ear hospital, it now employs 1,200 people at 11 locations in and around London. The hospital sees 1,000 patients a day, and although it is a centre for the most complex and innovative treatments, 83% of its work is routine, high-throughput ophthalmology. More than half the UK's ophthalmologists, and many working overseas, received training there. The hospital became one of the first NHS foundation trusts in 2004.

Executive summary

Although part of the National Health Service, Moorfields is run like a business. It has increased its turnover by 8–9% for five years running (to £75m in 2004). Two-thirds of its budget comes from primary healthcare trusts around the UK, but a fifth is earned from private treatment and commercial sales.

The hospital's ability to run its own business affairs was boosted considerably in 2004 when it became one of the first 10 NHS foundation trusts. This allows Moorfields to plan five years ahead, and borrow money and retain budget surpluses (£1.5m in 2004) to invest in new projects and services – such as a new £14.5m international children's eye centre (opening in 2006), and a £13m plant for manufacturing pharmaceutical products.

"We're moving away from being just a building to being a brand name, a byword for excellence in eye care," says Ian Balmer, the hospital's chief executive. This will embrace pharmaceuticals manufacture, private medicine, development of intellectual property and overseas ventures; as well as the hospital's core work in treatment, training and research. Future developments could include partnerships with, or even ownership of, chains of high street opticians – already a trend among US eye hospitals.

Already Moorfields has opened 10 outreach centres in and around London to take its expertise into the community. "As patient choice increases, we want to offer that choice in as many locations as we can," says Balmer. "We believe patient choice will benefit this hospital, because the strength of our brand means many patients will choose us."

Pay & benefits

In many respects, working at Moorfields is its own reward. "If you're a health professional and you want to work in eyes, then you want to work here," says Balmer. There is a definite public service ethos and all the staff, not just the doctors and nurses, are very motivated by the help they can give to patients.

Moorfields is more or less bound by NHS pay scales (including London weighting), and so is unable to match the kind of salaries that both professional and administrative staff could earn just up the road in the City. However, it reckons it pays about average for its location and is not afraid to offer more when necessary. "If we need to buy particular skills, we do," says Ken Gold, the hospital's personnel director. Nobody is on the minimum wage.

There is no performance-related pay, although Moorfields has occasionally paid an ad hoc bonus to all staff. "Our incentives are all around training and development," says Gold. There is an employee of the month award for outstanding service – £250 in shopping vouchers, usually given to one of the lower-grade workers.

The final-salary pension is generous: one eightieth of final salary for each year's service (maximum 40 years) plus a lump sum in return for 6.25% employee contributions. Holidays start at 27 days' entitlement, rising to 29 and 33 days after five and 10 years. There is a little-used employee assistance programme offering counselling etc., but few other benefits.

Promotion & development

"We put a lot of effort into training and investing in our staff," says Gold. "People have the opportunity to grow their skills in the direction they want to take. We like to expand people's horizons. Sometimes we take risks: we spot a job for someone, then see if they can do it." This can range from senior management (one divisional head is project-managing the new children's eye centre) to administrators (like the clerk who redesigned their department's web page). There are career development paths for both clerical and management staff, though it is less usual to jump the gap between the two.

The hospital works hard to counter the hierarchical mindset typical of the NHS, and is developing new job roles as it modernises the way patient care is provided and managed. Apart from the clinicians and technicians, there is a wide range of professional, clerical and manual positions – from IT, finance, procurement and HR to estate management, porters and catering. Vacancies are advertised internally first – but only about 20% are currently filled this way, and the hospital has been deliberately recruiting new blood.

Staff turnover is low, averaging 12% each year, and is much lower in senior positions – only one head of department has left in the last three years. As well as performing conventional appraisals, the hospital recently began a talent audit to ensure a more organised approach to succession planning.

The hospital's three-room learning centre offers classroom and computer-based training, and even provides training to other NHS organisations. Staff are also encouraged to take qualifications: they have taken MBAs and other masters, Open University degrees, accountancy and HR qualifications, NVQs, and basic qualifications in skills such as IT. Anyone doing a degree or professional qualification is encouraged to have a coach or mentor – Gold teaches mentoring for the British Orthoptic Society.

Company culture

"The vast majority of people work here because they want to help the patients," says Balmer. "The hospital is run on the goodwill of its staff – without that it wouldn't survive. I'm always amazed that in very busy circumstances the staff manage to provide such a good patient experience. Patients often say 'it didn't feel like a hospital'.

"It's like a village, with all the pros and cons of village life. Most people know most other people on the staff, and the village gossip machine works extremely well! People understand what their particular effort means to the organisation."

Being a specialist hospital, Moorfields has none of the internecine warfare between clinical departments which blights some institutions – the clinical and administrative sides of the operation work closely together. "You feel that everyone's working in the same direction to the same goal," says Balmer.

As a profession, doctors don't like being bossed around and this gives rise to a culture of persuasion rather than command, which has permeated the whole organisation. Staff at all levels are involved in decision-making – informally and through focus groups and representative bodies – and departmental heads have a lot of autonomy. The result is a culture which is less formal and bureaucratic than many public-sector organisations, and which encourages innovation, suggestion and entrepreneurship.

The environment is quite pressurised and cases of stress are on the increase, although sickness absence is below average. Even though the hospital operates round-the-clock, there is not a long-hours culture – non-clinical staff are usually away by 6pm. There is no formal work/life balance policy but the hospital supports flexitime, homeworking, compressed hours, job sharing and part-time working wherever appropriate. About 60% of staff belong to unions, with whom relations are excellent, says Gold.

Moorfields runs projects in several developing countries including South Africa, Tanzania, Gambia and Ghana; doctors – and sometimes nurses – undertake short teaching secondments abroad, but there are few travel opportunities for non-clinical staff. The hospital has ambitions to expand into China and the Gulf.

Innovation

In partnership with the Institute of Ophthalmology at University College, London, Moorfields is one of the world's premier research centres in eye medicine, so its clinical innovations have been helping patients for generations. One of the latest is a treatment for scarring, a major development which has changed clinical practice in eye medicine and in other fields.

As the healthcare sector moves away from the old "doctor knows best" philosophy, hospitals like Moorfields are radically revising the way they operate and developing "care pathways" which view a patient's treatment and experience holistically. "We're redesigning all our services based on what patients want, rather than on what's convenient for the professionals," says Balmer. For example, some patients may not want multiple treatments to be carried out in a single visit, or they may wish to stay overnight even after relatively minor surgery.

The outreach programme, which has seen Moorfields open 10 regional centres throughout Greater London in the last decade, has enabled patients to choose a more convenient location for treatment and has eased pressure on space at Moorfields. More than 50% of patients are now seen at the outreach centres, which are largely manned by staff based at Moorfields.

Diversity & social responsibility

Almost half of the staff at Moorfields come from ethnic minorities, which roughly reflects the local population (although not all staff live locally). Patients also come from a wide diversity of backgrounds. The hospital gives diversity and disability awareness training to all staff. Women account for two-thirds of all staff, 55% of managers, seven of the 17 senior management team, and one of the five executive directors. The workforce is a relatively mature one, with an average age of 41.

Moorfields has its own charity, the Friends of Moorfields, and works closely with other eye-related charities. It supports the local community through the Hackney Training and Enterprise Network, and the involvement of individual staff members – Gold, for example, has worked with asylum seekers and refugee groups. In the wider world, the hospital supports several community projects, from training doctors in Ghana to telemedicine in the South African bush. Corporate social responsibility is a board-level issue.

Corporate governance

In addition to stringent clinical governance, Moorfields has the same corporate governance procedures as a commercial organisation. It is monitored by more than 100 external bodies – notably, the Healthcare Commission, the Audit Commission, the National Audit Office, and the NHS's foundation trust monitor. A director of corporate governance heads a department dedicated to meeting targets and standards.

There was embarrassment in 2004 when the hospital lost its NHS three-star status owing to an administrative mix-up, but the high quality of its clinical care was acknowledged and the hospital says it has an above-average record on waiting lists. Some departments have gained Investors in People certification, and more will apply during 2005.

Environmental record

Moorfields has a 15-page environmental policy available to all staff members. Disposal of clinical waste from the hospital meets strict regulations. White paper, printer cartridges and old computer equipment are recycled. Transport is contracted out, but most staff (and patients) arrive by public transport and the hospital is enlarging its cycle park.

Morgan Stanley

Morgan Stanley
25 Cabot Square, Canary Wharf, London E14 4QA
Tel: (0) 20 7425 8000 **Fax:** (0) 20 7425 8990
Web: www.morganstanley.com

Morgan Stanley

Pay and Benefits	7.7	Innovation	6.4
Promotion and Development	6.4	Diversity	7.3
Training	7.4	Social Responsibility	6.8
Travel opportunities	6.3	Corporate Governance	7.0
Culture	7.3	Environment	7.0
Total			**69.6**

Morgan Stanley is a leading financial services company. Operating from 600 offices in 27 countries, it is a global provider of investment banking, sales and trading services, private wealth and asset management, and credit services. Headquartered in New York, Morgan Stanley employs more than 52,000 people and has key offices in Tokyo and Hong Kong as well as London, its primary European base. In the UK, the company employs some 6,400 people, mostly working from its purpose-designed site in Canary Wharf. In 2003, Morgan Stanley was named Euromoney's Best Global Investment Bank.

Executive summary

Morgan Stanley was formed in the US in the mid-1930s after the passing of the Glass-Steagall Act. It was established as an investment bank by former employees of JP Morgan (which became a commercial bank). More recently, Morgan Stanley underwent a transformation in 1997 when it merged with the retail brokerage Dean Witter. It celebrated 25 years of operations in Europe in 2002.

In the late 1990s, a period of intense growth was followed by falling revenues – reflective of the sector generally and of the wider economic climate. However, net income pulled back to $3.8bn in 2003, and results for the first half of 2004 were significantly better than in previous years. "We did not reduce headcount in investment banking, and in sales and trading, as sharply as some competitors in 2001–2003," says Philip J Purcell, chairman and chief executive. He believes that this strategy allowed the company to serve clients better during the upturn in 2004.

During difficult times, the company has concentrated on sustaining and maintaining client relationships. "It has been about keeping focused, and being ready for when things start happening again," explains Dawn Nicholson, an executive director in Morgan Stanley's human resources department, based at Canary Wharf. "People associate this brand with top-quality delivery, and top-quality service."

Pay and benefits

Morgan Stanley has a "total reward" approach to pay and benefits; it involves a base salary, discretionary compensation, and for some employees, a component paid in the form of stock units and stock options. This method is standard, and not differentiated by the functions of groups within the organisation.

Base salaries are fixed, while the discretionary element is decided on a yearly basis and judged according to the performance of the firm, the team, the division and the individual, in discussion with department heads. Graduates start on a £35,000 base salary, and in general the company aims to pay at the median-plus level, rising to upper quartile. There is also a profit-sharing scheme, targeted at employees towards the lower end of the pay spectrum and paid in the form of an annual cash bonus.

While the company lacks a specific flexible benefits package, the benefits it does offer have "a lot of flex", according to Dawn Nicholson. These include a pension plan for all employees (with no initial probationary period), life assurance and private healthcare, access to an onsite medical centre, free or subsidised membership of the two onsite gyms, emergency childcare, an online concierge service; and an employee assistance programme which provides help with, for example, caring for elderly parents.

The company's non-financial recognition of employees' achievements includes the President's Award scheme – an award given annually to those who have been nominated by their peers for making an outstanding contribution to Morgan Stanley. In 2003, awards were given to individuals who started up firm-wide networks for women, lesbian and gay employees, and ethnic minority employees. In addition, awards are made for tenure of 10, 15 and 20 years.

The environment it has created for its employees is second to none. "Because we were one of the first companies here, and at that time there was nothing much in Canary Wharf, we had to create a whole infrastructure," explains Nicholson. Facilities on site include a dry-cleaner and tailor, ATM machines, a hairdresser and beauty salon, a nurse triage system, in-house physiotherapy and massage services, and a restaurant and coffee shop.

Promotion and development

Morgan Stanley likes to promote from within, and it's possible for a highly ambitious graduate to progress to vice-president level within six years of joining. "We are a young firm – most of the people in management are in their mid to late forties," says Nicholson. With a rise through management ranks comes plenty of opportunities for development – including coaching – although rather than have a firm-wide policy, the company prefers to respond according to need.

New graduate trainees in investment banking take an intensive three-week induction course; thereafter training and development largely depends on the skills required by departments and any needs that arise. On average, employees receive up to twenty days' training each year in technical and product skills as well as management development. Basics such as time management and effective presentation are overlaid with division-specific programmes. There is an e-learning capability, particularly useful for compliance training. In addition, each employee has a structured personal development plan with regular reviews and 360-degree feedback.

Morgan Stanley has a well-established and popular education assistance scheme, designed to support permanent staff who want to acquire knowledge necessary to further their role in the business. Support varies depending on how the course affects the individual's future, but the company typically provides study leave and pays for books and residential costs, either fully or on a fifty-fifty basis. Courses include MBAs, and professional qualifications such as CIMA.

There are some opportunities to travel and work abroad – short-term, long-term or permanently – but the discipline of working with colleagues in other locations can be equally challenging, says Dawn Nicholson. "One of the challenges is in looking to network outside your own division and to be part of cross-divisional network groups. People in this organisation are very team-focused."

Company culture

As one would expect, Morgan Stanley is committed to the highest possible standards of management; externally, it is regulated by the Financial Services Authority, and internally it maintains checks and balances with a proactive human resources function which in London alone is nearly 70-strong.

Promoting respect and integrity within the company goes more than just skin-deep, says Nicholson. There is, for example, an active Dignity at Work policy, in which training is mandatory. "People can see that we are serious about it. We don't just do it because the law says we should; we do it because it brings palpable business benefits."

BalanceWorks was introduced in 2002 to amalgamate the company's work/life polices. At every level, employees can choose to start and leave early; or to do a flex-fortnight – working ten days in nine and taking every second Friday (or an alternative day) off. The company has been working hard to push forward its work/life balance initiatives.

"There can be an assumption that flexible working means less working," says Dawn Nicholson. "But if an employee wants to be more flexible and the manager says okay, then this says so much more to the employee – it says, 'I trust you, I'm empowering you.'"

People who flourish here tend to be fluid, fast moving, multi-tasking and creative; open to others' ideas and to new challenges; and unafraid to push boundaries. In general, there is a receptive management style that encourages employees to voice their views. An Open programme of internal communications initiatives has proved successful in making senior management accessible, with the European senior management committee participating in regular Q&A sessions, informal breakfasts and "brown-bag" lunches, open to all employees.

Innovation

One of the main areas of innovation within Morgan Stanley has been internal. Over the past three years, the human resources function has begun to actively market the "HR proposition" to all employees – using stylish posters, web-casts and desk-drops for various campaigns such as its diversity programme and BalanceWorks.

In 2003, three new firm-wide employee networks – for women, lesbian and gay employees, and ethnic minority employees – proved immensely popular as a forum for engagement and also for helping with recruitment. A fourth network, for parents, was set up in 2004. Last year, the company's annual diversity week focused on promoting these employee networks; it incorporated talking-head videos, speaker panels, social events and Q&A sessions with members of its European Diversity Council.

In addition, the human resources function is innovating in the realm of training. In 2003, for example, the company put 4,000 of its employees through a theatre-based training programme which involved actors using specific scenarios – such as a mother returning to work, or an incident of bullying – to invoke a response from employees. This kind of training, says Nicholson, "delivers tangible benefits".

Diversity and social responsibility

Morgan Stanley has employed a firm-wide diversity officer, based in the US, for many years; and is extending its diversity programme throughout Europe. It recruited its first diversity officer in London three years ago, and has established a European ratifying council comprised of the heads of the key businesses. "We felt that in order to get real traction in diversity, we needed real business buy-in," says Nicholson. Together with employee networks, she says, these measures go a long way towards promoting a truly diverse and integrated workforce.

The company supports two designated charities each year, currently Barnardo's and the Winged Fellowship, chosen by employees from a shortlist. In addition, a fundraising quiz night has proved popular, with more than 100 teams competing across divisions to raise £20,000 for charity – a sum matched by the company itself.

Employees are encouraged to get involved in "reading partner" and "IT partner" schemes in schools in Tower Hamlets; some are also school governors. Recently, the company brought in the Summer Challenge, where everyone was given a day off each summer to do a community-based or environmental task. "People like to do this in teams," explains Dawn Nicholson. "In 2003, we had a group of senior people in thigh-high waders cleaning the Thames riverbank of flotsam and jetsam; another team was putting up chicken runs in east London. These sorts of activities have the ancillary effect of building up trust between people."

Corporate governance

As one might expect, Morgan Stanley has a department dedicated to compliance issues; and an operating risk committee that evaluates business, product and operational risks. A monthly risk report highlights areas of concern.

Compliance is an increasingly important focus for companies such as Morgan Stanley. "Sarbanes-Oxley has made people even more focused on processes, on any gaps," says Nicholson.

While the company employs some contractors and vendors who have compliance training, it is careful to regulate these through its procurement division. "We have had a number of discussions about the impact of IR35, and we feel that we have got it very policed. If necessary, we seek confirmation from the Inland Revenue," says Nicholson.

Environmental record

In terms of environmental consciousness, Morgan Stanley is working to progress its agenda in this area, although it already has a committee focusing on initiatives that will make the company more environmentally friendly.

It has, for example, installed kitchen points with recycling facilities on all floors, and water for all of its meetings comes from recyclable bottles. There are shower blocks for use by cyclists. In common with many other firms, it offers season ticket loans.

Network Rail

Network Rail Infrastructure Ltd
40 Melton Street, London NW1 2EE
Tel: (0) 20 557 8000 **Fax:** (0) 20 557 9000
Web: www.networkrail.co.uk **Email:** careers@networkrail.co.uk

Pay and Benefits	5.7	Innovation	5.7
Promotion and Development	6.0	Diversity	4.0
Training	5.0	Social Responsibility	5.0
Travel opportunities	3.3	Corporate Governance	6.7
Culture	5.7	Environment	7.0
Total			**54.1**

In 2002, Network Rail took over the ownership, operation and maintenance of Britain's rail infrastructure – including bridges, signalling, tracks and stations – from Railtrack plc.

Network Rail is a private sector company limited by guarantee and run along commercial lines; all profits are reinvested. As a company limited by guarantee, Network Rail does not have shareholders (or share capital), but has members comprising customers, organisations and individuals drawn from a cross-section of the community and wider public interest. It turns over £6bn each year, and is accountable to government regulators and to its members (whose role is similar to shareholders in a plc). Having instigated a major change programme, Network Rail now employs 31,000 people, mostly in the UK.

Executive summary

Towards the end of 2001, after Railtrack plc had gone into administration, three external senior executives – Ian McAllister, Adrian Montague and Iain Coucher – were approached to put together a rescue package. They raised £9bn to buy the company; a year later, a new management team of twelve took the reins of the ailing operation.

McAllister formerly ran Ford Europe; Montague brought experience from the City; and Coucher had been chief executive of Tube Lines, one of the successful bidders for the London Underground PPP. With John Armitt, Network Rail's chief executive, they set about turning around the performance of Britain's railways.

The government's 1994 privatisation of railways created hundreds of external contractors. One of the first steps for Network Rail was to bring work provided by those contractors – and employees of those contractors – back into the company; 16,000 people based in fifty-three locations were transferred over nine months. Additionally, a review of existing employees resulted in various changes.

According to Coucher – who is now deputy chief executive of Network Rail – the change programme, although unsettling, gave the remaining workforce a much-needed boost. "People have seen that not only can we change things if they are wrong, but we are much more unified. There is a real buzz about the place."

The next step was to draw up new organisational charts and separate the seven existing regions into eighteen smaller units, each with a general manager. This structure was designed to increase a sense of ownership, allowing employees to see improvements taking effect.

Pay and benefits

Network Rail's approach to compensation is simple. "We need the very best people to come and work for us," says Coucher. "And if we're going to attract them, we must pay the best – so we benchmark every year all the salaries in various categories and deliberately pay highly competitive packages."

As the company is limited by guarantee, it cannot offer share options. Instead, it gives a management bonus – this comprises a corporate performance-related annual bonus, and a long-term incentive plan designed to replicate a share scheme. Top-level managers can earn 40% on top of basic pay, and board members are eligible for 60% more. Pay across the company is regulated by a banding system.

In addition to the management bonus scheme, there is a general bonus scheme that currently awards employees up to £1,200 annually depending on corporate performance. Other perks of working for Network Rail include discounted travel, healthcare, and a car allowance (in some roles). There is an existing final salary pension scheme. Those joining recently are eligible to enter a defined benefits scheme, but can join the final salary scheme if they stay with the company for five years.

The company holds an annual black-tie celebration, which peer-selected employees attend along with their nominators and partners. "Because being a railwayman is a 24-hour-a-day, seven-days-a-week job – and we like to recognise the sacrifices that partners are making." says Coucher.

Promotion and development

Every front-line employee of Network Rail receives about ten days' training each year because of the need for safety in operating. Other employees receive an average of five days' training. Network Rail's policy is to focus on basic skills, such as project management. It has introduced an apprenticeship scheme, spent £17m on a training centre for front-line maintenance workers, and established two state-of-the-art signalling schools.

For managers, there is currently an executive leadership development programme, but in the near future the company plans to set up a dedicated residential leadership academy in the Midlands, which will cost around £20m. "In our industry, management is a core skill," explains Coucher. Outside training is used if the investment is justified – for example, there are people undertaking specialist environmental courses to fulfil functions relating to certain environmental issues.

Network Rail aims to take on a hundred graduates each year, an increase from the previous intake of twenty-five under Railtrack. Some are sponsored through Sheffield Hallam University's engineering course, and if they join the company they will usually be mentored through to chartered engineer status.

Coaching is undertaken sporadically to help with specific developmental issues. Members of the board mentor those beneath them and there is a formal succession planning process – although, on the board at present, only Coucher is younger than fifty. There is now an emphasis on exposing both high-performers and those who are performing poorly. Managers categorise their workers at appraisals, a ranking that is used to calculate pay rises and identify high-potential individuals.

Company culture

Operating in a safety-critical industry, employees cannot work longer hours than is permitted – indeed, hours worked at the front line are carefully recorded. For those in administrative roles, however, there is considerable flexibility. "People tend to work very responsibly here, and we allow them a great deal of freedom. A number of people work on special contracts – in general, if there is a need, we will respond," says Coucher.

Within Network Rail, there are distinct cultures. Signalling staff tend to be extremely process-driven, while front-line maintenance staff have a hard-working ethos which values camaraderie and loyalty. Meanwhile, in the office, there is a "can-do, will-do" style of working. While the management admits that it is not always easy to find ways to accommodate all three, its approach is "challenging, high-performing and hands-on".

In general, what used to be a traditional, hierarchical culture is becoming a matrix management organisation, which uses targets such as daily performance to "measure, express and reward" loyalty and commitment. Since the change programme, the levels of communication between layers of the company have grown.

"As management, we spend a lot of time going out, visiting workers on the tracks and talking to the signallers," explains Coucher. "Business performance reviews by the executive board with senior managers used to happen quarterly; now it happens every four weeks. Before, people were summoned to London, but now we go out to them. It's been a terrific success as well as a revelation for all of us."

While relations with the unions (the RMT, TSSA and Amicus) can be tricky, particularly in times of change, Network Rail management makes a point of talking to representatives "every day" to maintain good relationships.

Innovation

The most fundamental measures on which the performance of Network Rail is judged are the train punctuality index (PPM) and the number of delay minutes caused by the company's infrastructure. On both indices, the company has dramatically improved – but the board recognises that this is "only a first step" in achieving the target of "basic production". The other steps include ensuring all projects deliver to time and budget.

Further targets for Network Rail are to achieve what it calls "efficient production", which involves implementing a programme of standardisation; and "effective production", which involves investing in a range of technologies to "predict and prevent, rather than find and fix".

In the last two years, the company has innovated in a number of ways. In August 2004, it invested £15m in a new "measurement train", which covers the entire network every two weeks at a speed of 125 mph; it is crammed full of sophisticated equipment and can spot defects in the rails to the nearest 2 mm.

It has also improved the maintenance processes which keep the rails sound; some jobs that used to take a gang of workers eight hours to complete now can be done mechanically in fifteen minutes. Other innovations include a new engineering support centre in Derby, and the installation of basic measurement devices on passenger trains.

Diversity and social responsibility

Only 15% of Network Rail's top management are women, with just two women on the executive committee to four (white) men. Among support and maintenance staff there is a stronger ratio, but Coucher says: "It's not highest priority to get a good diverse mix. It's something that will be addressed over time as our progressive HR policies begin to bite. In our signal boxes, there is a huge range of people and we do not discriminate against anyone."

In the community, Network Rail works to prevent what it calls "route crime" (children playing on the railways) by partnering with football clubs and schools to promote safety. Success has been demonstrated with a clear decline in this kind of activity. There is also a policy of actively stamping out graffiti when it first appears. In addition, the company tries to keep good relationships with the local community by dropping leaflets, for example, in areas that will be affected by rail employees working at night. Recently, Network Rail had the idea of introducing "men in vans" in each of its eighteen areas, whose job it is to sort out problems – this could mean anything from repairing fences to moving an abandoned car or preventing trespass.

The company's charities policy covers seven categories of giving, most of which are railway-related. Employees who raise money for charity can also have their total matched by the company.

Corporate governance

The board of Network Rail – comprising four executive directors and seven non-executives – is not answerable to shareholders, but is accountable to a group of members (currently 113) with no economic interest in the company. The company's main accountability is to a number of regulators including the Office of Rail Regulation and Her Majesty's Inspector of Railways. Network Rail has a safety and compliance director, as well as a director of planning and regulation.

In general, there are constant demands for information; for example, in the offices of senior executives there is a "pager screen" that updates minute-by-minute on every happening on the rail network countrywide. "We tend to be information-demanding," says Coucher. "We always want more detail."

Environmental record

Not many companies have the range of environmental issues that Network Rail faces. Railways are "nature's corridors" and the company is responsible for the UK's largest number of Sites of Special Scientific Interest (SSSI) – home to the likes of badgers, great crested newts, dormice and other protected species. Network Rail says it takes the responsibility seriously; during 2003, one of its activities was to physically mark out the boundaries of SSSIs.

It also runs a large-scale vegetation management programme, which includes the care and sometimes demolition or pruning of trees – an issue which can be sensitive. "We need to keep trees back from signals and so on, so we have an active programme, but the problem is that people don't like to see trees cut back or uprooted," says Coucher.

It has also made progress in other areas, such as using the surface water risk assessment model in a five-year programme to identify, investigate and mitigate surface water pollution risks.

Novartis

Novartis Group
Frimley Business Park, Frimley, Guildford, Surrey GU16 7SR
Tel: (0) 1276 692255
Web: www.novartis.com **Email:** hrrecruitment.phgbfr@pharma.novartis.com

Pay and Benefits	7.1	Innovation	7.5
Promotion and Development	6.8	Diversity	5.8
Training	6.8	Social Responsibility	6.3
Travel opportunities	6.5	Corporate Governance	6.3
Culture	7.5	Environment	6.2
Total			**66.8**

Novartis is a global healthcare group and one of the fastest-growing pharmaceutical companies worldwide. It is one of the top five players in its sector. It was formed in 1997 from the $21bn merger of two rival Swiss pharmaceutical companies, Sandoz and CIBA. Based in Switzerland, the group now employs 75,000 people worldwide. In the UK, Novartis employs 3,000 people; half of these work for the pharmaceuticals arm, Novartis Pharma, which in the UK is based near Camberley. Global group sales in 2003 were $24.9bn, of which operating income was $5.9bn and net income $5bn.

Executive summary

Globally, Novartis has seen steady growth, with worldwide sales up some $6bn from 2001. In the UK, changes in the structure of the National Health Service over the last few years (the establishment of the National Institute for Clinical Excellence, for example, and the development of primary care trusts) have led to interesting times for pharmaceutical companies. "This has always been a highly regulated industry, and while these regulations are of course necessary, it doesn't make working easy," explains Peter Thomas, head of people and organisation development.

The group's biggest strength is its rich pipeline of products. "We are the envy of most pharmaceutical companies globally," says Thomas. "Both companies, before the merger, had very good research and development, and we have a wide portfolio which covers most therapy areas." While there are peaks and troughs in the market, Novartis has "enough products for the next five years and beyond – a position which our competitors would dearly love."

Among their promising products are novel compounds for patients with diabetes, hypertension, cancer and osteoporosis; and for transplantation medicine. In the group's existing portfolio are brands such as the leading myeloid leukaemia drug, Glivec.

Pay and benefits

Novartis's approach to compensation is to provide a good overall package. Base salary is just below upper quartile, and performance-related pay is decided in line with a performance management process in which the employee receives ongoing feedback throughout the year with formal appraisals bi-annually. Managers hold calibration meetings to discuss ratings and ensure that the process is "as robust as possible". Senior executives can be nominated for stock options, and other employees can join an employee share incentive plan (in which one free share is given for every two bought); there is also the opportunity to convert part of a bonus into shares.

Other benefits include BUPA healthcare (with discounts for families), the option to join a money purchase or final salary pension scheme, life assurance, an employee discount scheme; and in some cases, a lunch allowance. Employees who introduce new employees to the company receive a tax-free payment.

Field-based staff, and those whose position warrants a company car, are well served – "Our car policy is seen as one of the best in the industry," adds Thomas.

Membership of the onsite gym at the Frimley site costs £40 per year; and there is an employee assistance programme including access to telephone and one-to-one counselling. A Busy Bees scheme allows employees to exchange part of their salary for childcare vouchers, exempt from NI contributions.

Non-financial recognition includes a peer-nominated Best in Class award ceremony. The UK arm of Novartis also promotes "role-model leadership" on a small scale, and offers reward and recognition vouchers to employees who "go the extra mile". A quarterly Leadership Award with a trophy and the opportunity to guest-edit the staff magazine puts the spotlight on personal leadership at all levels. "We try to engender personal accountability and responsibility, and when we see this, we like to reward it," says Thomas. "Many companies talk about leadership but individuals will often think, 'that's not me'. What we are saying is that anyone can be a leader."

There are also long-service awards; and global awards, depending on function, within the group as a whole. In addition, sales staff have their own plethora of awards, including the ultimate Victory Club: a group of top performers are identified annually and taken, with their partners, for a luxury break in a location such as Monte Carlo in recognition of their achievements.

Promotion and development

Novartis aims to fill three-quarters of key jobs internally, and has done this by prioritising the need to "spot talent and then to develop it". "There is a mentality of development here, and often the people we develop move within the company internationally – we are quite an exporter of talent." However, says Thomas, "it is important for us to also keep an eye out for external talent as we are always looking to hire high-potential individuals."

There is a well-established talent review process in which, every year, each employee can discuss career aspirations with their manager. The employee receives a rating for potential, which is then reviewed by the senior management team in a Talking Talent meeting facilitated by human resources personnel; the cumulative information is linked with future demand for key positions. The resulting "talent pool" is used to feed succession planning.

There is no set amount of training days. Development is seen as an ongoing process, which is not all about attending courses, but includes secondments to other functional areas of the business as well as project-related development. For some, there is the opportunity to participate in European or global projects. However, all development is business-focused: consequently, courses are run tightly in line with actual business needs, and employees can attend those that will help them achieve their objectives.

The group makes extensive use of online and blended learning. For all courses there are four stages: pre-work, the programme itself, practice and performance. Employees attend management development programmes run in association with one of the leading UK management colleges, while senior staff have the opportunity to participate in courses at Harvard Business School and are often linked with a coach. Lower down the organisation, employees pair up to mentor each other informally. Overall, the group wants to move towards a coaching-style culture.

Company culture

Novartis acknowledges that there are "a lot of people here who work hard", but says it takes care to keep a good work/life balance. With "flex days", head office employees can take up to two days of leave each month in exchange for overtime, although more senior employees are not expected to "flex" so much. Those who have worked continuously at the company for five years or more can apply to take a sabbatical; anyone wishing to job share can consult their manager. Thomas adds, "What we say is, let's not discount it...bring us your proposal and we will review its feasibility."

The group has worked on helping its managers to identify signs of stress at an early stage, says Thomas. "We have quite strong policies to deal with poor performance – we endeavour to spot issues early and offer the support required to help people get back on track, and will always try to redeploy people if they are in the wrong job. For those with personal issues, our employee assistance programme provides a friendly voice at the end of a phone. It's a flexible culture – we're not clock watchers – and it's the sort of place people can come to in relatively casual dress, if that's appropriate."

Because of the company's location – just off the M3 motorway – much effort is put into organising social events that can bring employees together (they might live as far apart as Southampton and London). This includes events such as quiz nights, bus trips to Bluewater, Christmas fairs and children's parties.

Innovation

Globally, the group spends more than £50m each year on research and development, aiming to build the most competitive, innovative research organisation in its field.

Internally, there are many initiatives, tools and processes to aid communication and dialogue within the group. "We have worked hard to help employees feel that they can speak up in order to challenge the way we do things or bring new ideas. A good example of this was when we developed our Best in Class vision, which included 1,400 hours of input from employees. Employees' thoughts really count," says Thomas.

Another process is Talk Early! where, each week, ten people from all levels of the business are invited to meet for an hour with two directors over breakfast and discuss items large and small. "Someone pointed out, for example, that we didn't have a recognition award for ten years of service, although we had one for five and fifteen," says Thomas. "The directors agreed immediately we should change that. Another person suggested that instead of sending lots of emails out, all announcements should be posted on the intranet once a week."

Diversity and social responsibility

Each April, Novartis holds a Community Partnership Day in which employees get together to do something for the community. In 2004, for instance, some thirty employees helped to transform a piece of wasteland at a local hospital into a garden, while another thirty took part in "making over" and improving the offices of a local charity, Disability Initiative. Novartis funds such activities and encourages its employees to take time out of the office to participate.

While there is no formal policy on charitable giving, fundraising activities happen throughout the year to raise money for a nominated charity. Worldwide, Novartis has established a foundation for sustainable development, which supports research in Tanzania to eliminate leprosy and to improve access to malaria treatment.

In the UK, the issue of diversity is seen as "important but almost irrelevant in terms of execution", according to Thomas. "Whilst this is a key driver for the business globally, in the UK we don't have to have a real focus on it as a large percentage of senior managers here are women, and we have a number of ethnic minorities. We don't go out of our way to have certain numbers – we treat everyone as equal regardless of gender or race or other personal preferences such as religious beliefs." Around 60% of the company's sales force are women, and because sales reps operate locally, the range of employee backgrounds is wide.

Corporate governance

Novartis has developed a whistle-blowing policy which is "there if people need it", says Thomas. But as an organisation, he believes that issues of integrity are usually dealt with immediately and effectively. "The results from our Employee Opinion Survey back this up – employees feel that we are a very fair company that deals well with the issues it faces."

On a global level, the company's chairman and chief executive, Daniel Vasella, has stated in the group's annual review that "we continue our endeavours to fulfil every regulation, no matter how work-intensive or formalistic it may be… We will comply with every part of the Sarbanes-Oxley Act, thus fulfilling every demand made by US authorities. At a minimum, the transparency of our report will enable our share-owners to assess the current situation, risks and opportunities of the company".

Environmental record

With a sales force of about 500 people in the UK, Novartis by necessity makes extensive use of transport on the roads and actively promotes the use of cars. However, Thomas says, "We do try to be environmentally aware, and do take the time to recycle as much produce as we can. We have different bins around the offices for the different types of waste."

On a global level, the group claims that corporate citizenship is a top priority for Novartis. They say that sustainability is about "managing risks to ensure the health and protect the safety of our employees, neighbours, customers and all others affected by our business activities, as well as protection of the environment".

Office of Government Commerce

Office of Government Commerce
Trevelyan House, 26-30 Great Peter Street, London SW1P 2BY
Tel: (0) 845 000 4999
Web: www.ogc.gov.uk **Email:** servicedesk@ogc.gsi.gov.uk

Office of Government Commerce

Pay and Benefits	7.3	Innovation	6.8
Promotion and Development	6.8	Diversity	7.7
Training	7.3	Social Responsibility	6.3
Travel opportunities	5.7	Corporate Governance	7.2
Culture	6.8	Environment	6.9
Total			**68.8**

Set up in 2001, the Office of Government Commerce (OGC) is an independent Office of the Treasury reporting to the Chief Secretary. Its original aim was to improve the efficiency and effectiveness of central civil government procurement, and to develop and promote private sector involvement across the public sector.

Thanks to its success in achieving its original objectives, OGC has now also taken on a role in helping government departments set up centres of excellence that will drive project and programme management best practice across the whole of government.

It has a network of offices in London, Edinburgh, Norwich and Leeds and employs 400 people.

Executive summary
The Office of Government Commerce (OGC) came into being in 2001, following a review of civil procurement in central government carried out in 1999 by Sir Peter Gershon, then a member of the Board of British Aerospace.

OGC's remit now includes the whole public sector and new business opportunities such as managing the implementation of the government's £21.5bn Efficiency Programme. This programme releases resources for investment in the front-line public services – health, education and criminal justice.

OGC consists of five directorates. The Better Projects directorate oversees more effective implementation of mission-critical projects across government and the public sector. Smarter Procurement is concerned with managing the government marketplace, including relationships with suppliers and procurement strategy. The Efficiency directorate is responsible for overseeing implementation of the government's Efficiency Programme. The Skills and Know How directorate includes a consultancy division who can advise public sector clients in projects and develop delivery skills across government, and a division to help support the relocation of government services out of London and the south-east to promote economic improvement in other parts of the country. Finally, the Corporate Services directorate provides key support services such as human resources, IT and finance to customers within OGC.

Pay and benefits
In most of the public sector, staff can expect a fairly fixed remuneration and benefits package. That's not how OGC works. It recruits a diverse range of staff from both the private and public sector, and pay rates are competitive to reflect the importance of particular skills to the organisation. It aims to pay at the upper quartile.

On top of their basic salary, all staff are eligible for performance-related pay reflecting their contribution to the organisation. In addition, pay progression through annual pay awards is linked to the demonstration of those competencies that are important to OGC's business.

A recognition scheme enables managers to make small recognition payments immediately, rather than waiting until the end of the year, to individuals or teams who are deemed to have gone the extra mile and done outstanding work. These can either be in the form of retail vouchers or cash payments of a few hundred pounds.

OGC also aims to offer a competitive range of non-pay benefits. Employees have a choice of pension schemes, including a final salary option with an employer's contribution of up to 12% of salary. Staff get subsidised access to sports clubs, with an onsite gym at one office. For employees with children, OGC also offers subsidised holiday play schemes and childcare vouchers.

For employees who may occasionally need to work away from home to attend a meeting with clients, OGC meets the additional cost of any childcare. In addition, all staff have access to Family Life Solutions, a telephone helpline service designed to provide information and support for all employees with family responsibilities.

OGC's paid maternity and paternity leave is also generous, and they have a scheme in place to make the transition back to work more flexible – without the loss of pay.

Increasingly, the aim is to offer employees a choice about how they take their benefits. For example, staff can buy and sell annual leave depending on whether they prefer more time off or more pay.

Promotion and development

The skills required within OGC vary widely. Some employees are career civil servants; others have previously worked in the commercial sector or other parts of the public sector such as health or local government.

All OGC employees have an annual appraisal during which they have a chance to discuss their career aspirations and agree a development plan with their manager. To ensure that employees have the opportunity to meet their personal development objectives, there is a development target across the organisation of 10 days "protected time" each year for each employee. Time spent on staff development is reviewed by the board every two months.

At any one time there are external staff working with OGC to transfer skills and develop experience. Similarly, OGC people are regularly sent out to strategic partners to familiarise themselves with the client culture, develop new skills and learn about good practice in other sectors. This means that there is a constant flow of people on secondment to and from the organisation. OGC has formalised this by developing a strategic secondment programme, which aims to ensure that a fifth of all employees are either recruited or developed through secondments. The organisation's investment in secondment will triple over the next two years.

Employees may be sent on a variety of training courses, ranging from familiarising them with working with government ministers through to formal training in programme and project management, or specific skills in finance or HR. Training is mainly carried out by OGC's external training partners. OGC also invests heavily in coaching, carried out externally and by line managers.

The organisation also offers a variety of open learning courses, with resource guides made available on the intranet, on videos, on CD-roms and in books. Open learning may be carried out as part of the employee's development time, but many employees also opt to use their own time.

Company culture

OGC is not your average government department. It offers staff a culture that combines the best of the public and private sectors – a dynamic commercial focus within a public service ethos.

As a young organisation, OGC's culture is still developing, but it aspires to build an environment where employees share knowledge across the organisation and support collaborative working with partners across the public sector – the diverse background of its staff makes for a wide range of skills and knowledge to share. It also aims to remain comparatively small so it can maintain its flexibility and its ability to change and reinvent itself as its clients' requirements change.

Most of OGC's work is within the UK, so there is only limited scope for foreign travel. However, OGC represents the UK at the World Trade Organisation, and is involved in liasing with the European Union. It also regularly hosts visits from overseas governments who are interested in its unique role in the UK public sector.

Work/life balance is an important consideration at OGC and it offers a choice of options for the working week. These include job sharing, part-time working and compressed hours; as well as employment options through fixed-term appointments or secondments.

Though very few employees work from home permanently, many do so from time to time; all staff have remote access to organisational resources via the OGC extranet. OGC has a significant number of mobile workers such as consultants who spend most of their time on customer sites; these employees are given the resources they need to work on the move.

Innovation

As an organisation dedicated to boosting efficiency and effectiveness in the public sector, OGC is innovative by nature. It has piloted a number of IT-based initiatives. These include the use of e-commerce in the public sector; and electronic auctions, which reduce the entry costs for firms competing for government public sector work. In 2003, it launched electronic linkages that enable its departmental customers to synchronise the updating of their property data.

In its first year of existence, the OGC introduced its innovative Gateway Review process. The Gateway Review was designed to tackle the problem of projects failing to deliver their benefits to time and budget. It facilitates a peer review of major projects at critical stages in their lifecycle to make sure they can progress successfully and deliver the best possible service to the public.

Diversity and social responsibility

As a government department, diversity is something OGC takes very seriously. It monitors its workforce in terms of gender, ethnic balance and working options. Women make up 41% of its workforce, 38% of whom are working in management positions.

Currently, 27% of staff come from a non-white background. OGC is actively trying to increase the proportion of minorities in senior positions by encouraging applications and sponsoring talented employees. Talented women managers are assigned female directors as mentors who can guide them in how to develop and progress their career.

Looking outwards, OGC operates a payroll giving scheme whereby any employee can donate a proportion of their salary to charity in a tax-efficient way. It also gives staff time off to engage in a community activity of their choice; for example, staff can be involved in reading and maths schemes at local schools. OGC managers also act as mentors on other organisations' development programmes. One member of staff is currently on a one-year secondment to a major charity. OGC believes that as well as providing their skills to organisations in the community, staff can also learn important skills that enrich the way they carry out their roles on their return to the organisation.

Corporate Governance

OGC is an independent Office of the Treasury with its own chief executive appointed at Permanent Secretary level. OGC reports to the Chief Secretary of the Treasury who is a member of the Cabinet. It is governed by the OGC board, which is made up of the chief executive, OGC executive directors, the chief executive of OGCbuying.solutions, and two non-executive directors.

OGC has a supervisory board chaired by the Chief Secretary to the Treasury and made up of Permanent Secretaries, including the OGC chief executive; the head of the National Audit Office; and senior external representatives. The OGC chief executive also has an advisory group (CEAG), which is made up of a number of departments, executive agencies and non-departmental public bodies.

Environmental record

As an organisation that advises other government departments on how to operate efficiently, OGC aims to "walk the talk" when it comes to energy efficiency. Its environmental policy is a good example of enlightened self-interest, protecting the environment while also making sound business sense.

As part of this policy, it carries out an environmental impact assessment before embarking on any major capital scheme. Its Greener Building programme involves installing more efficient energy management systems, and double-glazing with non-reflective glass surfaces in all offices. It also uses low-energy lightbulbs, and reduced water volume flushing systems in staff toilets. Most offices have recycling schemes for paper, glass and toner cartridges.

The organisation provides interest-free loans to employees who want to buy bicycles to cycle into work, and also aims to encourage uptake of public transport for business use. Staff are encouraged to use its intranet-based public transport booking system. First-class train travel is offered to everyone who needs to travel on business, and is not restricted to directors. Company cars are given only to those who really need them for their jobs, and they do not form part of the official benefits package. Where company cars are provided, OGC aims to buy those that produce the least emissions.

Pannone & Partners

Pannone & Partners
123 Deansgate, Manchester M3 2BU
Tel: (0) 161 909 3000
Web: www.pannone.com **Email:** law@pannone.co.uk

PANNONE
& **PARTNERS**
SOLICITORS
The complete law firm

Pay and Benefits	5.9	Innovation	5.6
Promotion and Development	6.1	Diversity	6.0
Training	5.6	Social Responsibility	6.1
Travel opportunities	4.9	Corporate Governance	5.4
Culture	6.6	Environment	6.0
Total			**58.2**

Pannone & Partners is a progressive full-service law firm with clients split practically equally between businesses and private individuals. Based in central Manchester, Pannone & Partners serves clients throughout the north-west (where it is the largest single-site law firm in the region) as well as nationally and internationally.

Executive summary

Pannone & Partners, which can trace its origins back to 1852, has a headcount of 525 with 74 partners who work within specialist teams. It has grown over the last 10 years from less than 200 people; and seen income grow from £6m to over £29m. Profit has more than doubled per equity partner over the same period (there are 44 equity partners among the 74 partners). Over the past three years, net profit has grown from £6.9m to £10m.

The company is traditionally always in the top five or six in whatever survey or award scheme is running for the region – for example, it ranks highest in billings; 6th in the Sunday Times Top 100 Companies; the top management team in The Lawyer; finalist in the top five regional law firms in Legal Business; and it is recognised by both The Legal 500 Guide and The Chambers Guide to the Legal Profession as one of the leading north-west firms. Many partners in the firm are considered "leaders in their field".

Pay and benefits

"We're not a limited company. We're a partnership," says Joy Kingsley, managing partner. "There's an assumption that those who are leaders will be paid in a way that rewards performance. If it's a good year, the remaining profits – after outgoings and staff salaries, etc. have been paid – are shared among partners to an agreed formula. We are not a meritocracy. To advance to become an owner of the business means you have to be of a particular standard. Initially, new partners receive 50% of a senior's rate, rising to 100% in bands over five years. There are 44 equity partners who own the business. As a law firm we're not allowed to share profits with non-lawyers."

The pay and benefits package is above upper quartile for smaller law firms but comparable to other city-centre firms. Trainee solicitors are paid £20,000 in their first year and £22,000 in their second. There are no bonus schemes, but there is a rewards system that is either individually based or related to the firm's overall performance. Twice a year around 10 people (employees only, not partners) receive a financial award, while simultaneously there are employee of the month and employee of the year selections. People win meals out, trips to Alton Towers, etc. Extra days' holiday are occasionally awarded, and at any time (for doing well financially, hitting targets, etc.) it's "cakes all round" – 525 of them. A lottery draw was arranged when the headcount hit 500, with a top prize of £500.

There's a defined contribution pension scheme, with employees required to contribute a minimum of 2.5%; company contributions average 5%. Private health care applies for everyone, although family members must pay.

There are no company cars or allowances, but car-parking assistance is available. Holiday entitlement is 23 days rising to 33.

Promotion and development

"Theoretically, an office junior here can become a partner," says Kingsley. "There have been secretaries who are now partners. Anyone can aspire to become a fee-earner and then a partner." This is a company where empowerment of the people really means something. There are no glass ceilings.

Every solicitor needs training; employees earn CPD (continuing professional development) points through attendance at recognised courses. There's both internal and external training. Appraisals are conducted annually and followed up rigorously. For the administrative staff (reception, accounts, IT, marketing, secretarial), there are courses in areas such as IT and telephone training, and presentation skills.

It's a "young partnership" – the oldest band is around 53–57 years, and the most usual band is only 30–40 years. To get on the solicitors' bandwagon, says Kingsley, you need a university degree. If your degree is in a non-law subject you need to take a one-year conversion course (known as the CPE), followed by one year on the LPC (Legal Practice Course). If your degree is in law, you can go straight to the LPC. Following this, both routes involve a further two years on a training contract. Pannone & Partners offer 10 training contracts each year to trainee solicitors.

Staff turnover is 8% (excellent for this business – the norm is 15%). Coaching and mentoring are principally managed through the firm's team structure and appraisal scheme, and the process is designed to be as supportive as is feasible within the working environment. An open door policy ensures anyone can speak to anyone else at any time (colleagues, heads of department or senior members of management), while regular departmental meetings allow employees to input ideas and get feedback. It's fair to say a "family feel" pervades.

Company culture

"We're acutely aware our staff are our greatest asset and so we go to great lengths to ensure we recruit lawyers who are not only technically capable but also commercially astute, and secretarial/support staff who are accurate, efficient and think matters through," says Kingsley. Reports from outside testify to this.

Staff are enthusiastic about where they work. The firm was voted 6th in The Sunday Times' poll of the 100 best companies to work for – a survey based on responses from randomly selected staff.

"We were the first law firm to obtain accreditation under ISO 9001, and have retained the quality mark since 1989," says Kingsley.

Words that would equally describe both the atmosphere and the culture are friendly, fair, hard working, rewarding and professional. This is all despite it being a large law firm. There is an excellent work/life balance, with recognition that there is a life outside the firm. Secretaries work 9–5, being paid overtime if necessary. Partners typically work 45-hour weeks. Anyone who takes five days or less off sick a year receives a bonus payment – 25% qualified in 2003. There is a fair but firm policy on absenteeism; and a zero tolerance policy towards bullying and sexual harassment, which has not yet been needed.

The company doesn't educate for the sake of it, but does encourage training in relevant qualifications – as long as you've been with the company for a year and your request has approval from your head of department.

Innovation

"We deliver a comprehensive range of legal services to businesses and private individuals," says Kingsley. "This is unusual, as law firms tend to do one or the other. We intend to remain innovative in the way we deliver legal services through fully utilising IT and excellent client care practices."

The company's products have to be attractive to its clients. An innovative venture reaping many rewards concerns a franchise method of working (to say more would spill the beans). It's been successfully applied in legal practices in Derby, Hull, Southend, Northampton, and on the South Coast; and other companies are ready to sign up. Pannone & Partners receive 5% of any fee income developed by the franchises.

"We aim to make people's life here easier," says Kingsley. "Aside from Dress Down Fridays, we allow judicious use of private email and access to the internet before 9, at lunchtime and after 5. We make occasional checks to ensure it's not being abused." Staff can also take up to 10 days each year to look after their children if they become poorly.

"We encourage staff to come up with new ideas through the open door policy," says Kingsley. "People who come up with something that's acted on are accorded the proper recognition."

Diversity and social responsibility

This is a most female-friendly company. Women account for around 71% of staff, 37% of management, over 50% of the partners, and 30% of the equity partners. Indeed, the Law Society Gazette has noted that the company has the largest number of female partners in any law firm. Within the workforce overall, there is a fair representation of all races and ethnic backgrounds.

The company is well equipped to handle the needs of disabled staff – a paraplegic solicitor underwent his training contract, then worked there for five years. As a result, the offices are adapted for wheelchair users. Today, there is also a blind secretary on the payroll, so the offices have been equipped to comply with the necessary standards required for visually impaired workers.

Pannone & Partners comes across as a very fair company with no glass ceiling in sight.

The law firm undertakes pro bono work for various local organisations, and has contracts with local schools and the university to take students into the firm for work experience. This involves providing placements for 16- and 18-year-olds, and 2nd year university students.

"We're committed to the north-west," says Kingsley. "We play an active role in areas such as local government, infrastructure, the community, regional charities, the arts and regional businesses." The company has won the Greater Manchester Corporate Challenge marathon two years' running (mixed team) and the male individual runner's event.

The equity partners discuss social responsibility issues when required.

Corporate Governance

Pannone & Partners prides itself on providing a quality service to all its clients. This commitment can be demonstrated through it being the first law firm to achieve BS5750 accreditation (now ISO 9001) as well as its subsequent maintenance of the standard for over 13 years. The company has also been awarded the Law Society's Lexcel Qualification for practice management standards; and three of its specialist departments hold public funding franchises (they offer legally aided advice) and therefore have additional quality assessments made by the Legal Services Commission. There are no unions.

"We have sophisticated money laundering procedures, with regular meetings to ensure compliance," says Kingsley. "Risk management is something that's regularly addressed, plus we have a formal complaints system, ensuring any client knows where and how to complain." (It's rarely implemented).

Environmental record

As a law firm, Pannone & Partners has to be careful of how confidential waste paper is discarded and so there are many shredder bins around the building. All waste paper is shredded finely to maintain client confidentiality and the paper is then used in paper recycling processes. Old computers are given to staff for personal use; and PCs, telephones, printers, etc. have been donated to schools or charities in the past.

The company offers season ticket loans so that employees can benefit from the convenience of a monthly repayment, without losing the discounted rate.

While a no-smoking policy is in operation, staff can go outside for short breaks in the morning and afternoons. "We're also considering re-introducing a scheme of assistance to give up smoking, which we ran two years ago," says Kingsley. Full health checks (heart rate monitoring, blood pressure, etc.) are offered to staff.

Pret A Manger

Pret A Manger (Europe) Ltd.
1 Hudson's Place, London SW1V 1PZ
Tel: (0) 20 7827 8000 Fax: (0) 20 7827 8787
Web: www.pret.com

Pay and Benefits	8.0	Innovation	7.7
Promotion and Development	7.3	Diversity	8.3
Training	7.3	Social Responsibility	8.0
Travel opportunities	5.3	Corporate Governance	7.0
Culture	8.0	Environment	7.7
Total			**74.6**

Pret A Manger – "Passionate About Food" – was formed in 1986 by friends Sinclair Beecham and Julian Metcalfe, and remains a private company today. With a reputation for fantastic food using fresh, natural ingredients, Pret is proud not to be considered a chain. It has 125 shops in the UK, with a further 10 in New York and seven in Hong Kong. Shops are concentrated within the M25 and in major cities. Pret's annual UK turnover is £140m; in September 2004, the company reached a milestone – its first "£3m turnover week". Pret employs 2,700 people, including 800 part time and 120 in the central office.

Executive Summary

Sinclair Beecham and Julian Metcalfe's dream was to create a shop selling delicious natural food – served politely, with passion and pride. They worked as team members in the inaugural shop for two years. The founders still own 60% of Pret; McDonalds has 33%, with the balance held by staff and individual investors.

On annual turnover of around £140m in the UK, Pret makes operating margins of 7.5% – heading towards the food retailing industry average of 8–9%. Profit before tax and interest in the UK reached £9.2m in 2004. In 2003, the Pret group made a "small profit" after correcting what the company described as "reckless" overseas expansion over 2000–02. Early in 2003, the founders re-asserted control and appointed a new chief executive, Clive Schlee.

There are good indicators that Pret is doing plenty of things right. Current sales growth is 17% per annum, including 12% from existing or mature shops. Only 2% of this is down to price rises – 6% coming from more transactions, and 4% from an increased product mix. Profitability is on an upward path, and like the food on sale, healthy.

Pay and Benefits

"Pret's pay philosophy is to be best in class," says Andrea Wareham, director of people. "We keep an eye on the competition and pay what we can." Pret participates in an annual pay survey – along with 15 leading retailers – to ensure it offers competitive rates.

Up to manager level, staff are paid each week by the hour. There are some very novel ways in which incentives operate. Each week, every shop receives a mystery shopper visit. If their resulting score exceeds 90%, each team member receives an extra 75p an hour in that week's wages (soon to become £1). This means a lot, and drives people to extraordinary team performance and very low sickness rates.

Shop managers have a Quality Bonus based upon sales, gross profit, personal targets and quality standards that can amount to 30% of salary. Every quarter, Pret identifies those shops that have achieved most in their category. The top five managers have their bonus tripled, and managers 5–10 see their bonus doubled. Pret also offers doubled bonuses for the two best mystery shopper ratings, two best quality surveys and two best Manager Controlled Profit figures.

At Hudson's Place (they don't call it head office), it's the same. Pay is reviewed through an annual survey, peer group comparisons, a check on inflation, and an annual increase – which depends upon individual performance. Bonuses are between 10% and 30%; and are based on profit versus budget, team targets and personal targets agreed with line managers.

There's a Partners In Pret share option scheme with 70 members from all areas of the business, and private medical insurance for the office staff and managers. Pret tops up government statutory payments for maternity pay, and allows its mums and dads to take parental leave as and when they wish. Lunch is free (guess where it comes from?), and is ordered online and delivered in a personalised bag!

Promotion and development

In Pret shops, the starting rate lasts for just the first ten days – after which you receive your first pay rise. And that's only the beginning. Within the shops (where most Pret people work) there is a clear, structured career ladder, which you can climb up quickly.

The ladder begins at team member, through team member star, to trainer (they train the new recruits), and barista (coffee maker – a big deal at Pret). After that come team leader, manager in training, assistant manager, and finally general manager. Each shop has a general manager, and if it is large enough, one or two assistant managers as well. An operations manager looks after every 10 shops (this is fairly unique – in the rest of the industry they cover many more). Each group of ten shops also has a quality trainer – responsible for the training and development of staff, and the quality survey. Most training is on the job.

Pret's policy is to promote internally whenever it can. 50% of staff at Hudson's Place began in a Pret shop, and 75% of shop managers started as a team member. According to Wareham, "Although we promote up the ladder, we also need people from external sources and it's a fine line to get right." It's one reason why Pret opens shops at its own pace. "We don't want to open so quickly that we cannot recruit great managers," says Wareham.

At Hudson's Place, all the usual professional and managerial functions can be found. There's a great emphasis on training and internal communication. The management development programme is comprehensive; it focuses on translating skills and knowledge into personal effectiveness. Pret supports professional studies if they are relevant to your job. People have moved from the UK to overseas shops as Pret extends its international presence.

Company culture

You can read it on the napkins: "At Pret we often refer to staff recruitment as 'treasure hunting'. We are utterly convinced that a well-run Pret shop (delicious food and great atmosphere) is entirely due to the talent and skill of a good manager and a wonderful team."

"Pret is very unusual in the catering industry," says Clive Schlee. "It creates a clear competitive differential in the way that employees handle customers and the way customers see them – as equals." He believes that Pret's culture is an institutionalised "shadow" of its founder, Julian Metcalfe.

Pret has a totally open plan office overlooking Victoria Station – an amazing urban workplace, whose sassy design tells you this is a fun and dynamic place to be. On entering reception, which resembles a Pret shop, it's easy to find yourself asking for a cappuccino by mistake.

Pret sustains its culture by treating people equally, personally, and fairly – which creates real team spirit. Noone is allowed to join Pret after their compulsory trial day without their shop colleagues voting for that to happen. There's an immediate and clearly defined career path "You might have to do things to get there, but they're do-able," says Schlee. "And when you do, you receive rewards to give to the people who helped you get there – which is counter-intuitive."

There's a strong emphasis on the social side of work. Shops are rewarded with staff nights out, and the twice-yearly parties are the stuff of legend. The internal magazine, Pret Star, is uncensored and unviewed before publication!

HR has a set of guidelines – "hate the word policy," says Wareham – that explain in plain English Pret's thinking on various issues. Managers are trained in how to apply them because HR is devolved into the shops. HR's principle role here is to train, support and guide.

Innovation

The founders were always keen on defending the customer and less interested in profit margins. "This is an honourable vision," says Schlee. "But it's where the passion comes from. Julian is passionate about delicious, quality food and would be very upset if he discovered any preservatives."

From passion comes innovation. Everything – and they mean everything – is prepared freshly each day on the premises, in Pret's 150 kitchens. Pret is based on additive-free, "no nasties" food. It publishes nutritional information, and postcards even include the recipes. There's no diet range – they don't serve "punishment food" – so customers are allowed to choose how they take their calories. While competitors have fully stocked shelves early in the morning, Pret's – by necessity – build up towards lunchtime.

It's been said that Pret paved the way for good, healthy eating at lunchtime. Although it's hard to imagine it today, with sandwich shops everywhere, when Metcalfe and Beecham pioneered their idea, the only real alternative was the pub lunch. Pret focuses on not losing that original idea. It could use factories to ship in sandwiches, as its competitors do, but it's keen to retain its innovative point of difference – despite the demands this creates on the supply chain.

Diversity and social responsibility

Pret's workforce is very young. Many people come from abroad, to learn English. "We have dozens of different nationalities working side by side," says Wareham. "It's wonderful to see. A real melting pot." Equal opportunity underpins Pret and very few issues arise.

Pret provides guidance for managers on religion and belief – which festivals there are, when to allow days off, implications for clothing and dress code. "Managers are expected to know so much," says Wareham. "So there's a fact sheet on every religion." Pret does the same for every disability – managers get hints and tips on what adjustments to make for dyslexia, deafness and schizophrenia. Outstanding.

"The culture in Pret is that everyone talks to one another as equals, from top to bottom," says Schlee. Everyone works four days each year in a Pret shop. The chief executive himself had just flown back from New York, where he had worked a 7am to 4pm shift – and was able to spot and inform the team that the cucumbers had arrived unsealed!

Pret concentrates its charitable activities in supporting CRISIS, the charity for the homeless. It donates uneaten food at the end of each day and provides CRISIS with refrigerated vehicles to collect it. The relationship is so close that Pret was even asked if it could leave more sushi! During the Christmas period, 10p from every sandwich sale goes to CRISIS; and Pret has helped the charity set up its own cafe in London's East End.

Corporate Governance

HR keeps things fully up-to-date regarding who it can and cannot employ; they make rigorous Visa checks and train managers on their responsibilities. Recruitment mirrors this – the company tracks applications carefully and makes sure that all necessary forms are submitted correctly.

There is a comprehensive data protection policy, and each year the company performs a data integrity exercise on personal information. There is an external auditor; and twice a year each shop undergoes a financial audit to ensure that all financial, insurance and cash procedures are followed correctly.

Environmental record

Pret does not use food additives, preservatives or obscure chemicals in its food.

As part of British Retail Council accreditation, Pret suppliers are required to have adequate systems for waste disposal. Each Pret shop has a waste compactor.

Pret takes a considered and commonsense view to providing environmentally friendly packaging, while meeting the highest standards of food quality and hygiene. It was the first retailer to move from fully plastic sandwich boxes to cardboard. As a member of Valpak, Pret pays a levy on all its packaged items that goes towards the recycling of packaging waste. It is also investigating the use of recycled plastics and paper in its packaging, and is researching the use of 100% biodegradable materials.

The Restaurant Group

The Restaurant Group plc
20 Irving Street, London WC2H 7AU
Tel: (0) 20 7747 7750
Web: www.trgplc.com **Email:** enquiries@trgplc.com

the
restaurant
group plc

Pay and Benefits	5.5	Innovation	6.2
Promotion and Development	5.3	Diversity	5.8
Training	6.3	Social Responsibility	6.0
Travel opportunities	3.8	Corporate Governance	5.8
Culture	5.7	Environment	5.7
Total			**56.1**

The Restaurant Group (TRG) is one of the largest independent restaurant groups in the UK. It has a portfolio of restaurants, cafes and bars comprising five brands plus The Concession Connection, which is currently operating in five airports, major railway stations and shopping centres. All the group's businesses are in the popular value-for-money food service sector. Some 275 restaurants and bars provide over 20 million meals each year to consistently high standards. Since 2002, TRG has demonstrated significantly improved financial performance, highlighted by the results for the six months to June 2004 showing a 40% increase in profits on a 10% increase in turnover. The group employs 7,000 staff.

Executive summary

TRG operates in three divisions: Leisure Parks (Frankie & Benny's and Chiquito), The Concession Connection (operating mainly in airports, using existing Restaurant Group brands and creating new ones where required), and High Street Restaurants (Garfunkel's, Caffe Uno and Est Est Est). At 25-years-old, Garfunkel's is the oldest brand in the group.

Performance to end-June 2004 saw turnover increase by 10% to £118m while profits before tax and exceptional items increased by 40% to £9.8m. Full-year figures for the previous three years have increased year on year. Profits before tax and exceptional items increased by 15% to £19.3m in 2003 (2002: £16.8m) with turnover increasing by 5% to £227.4m (2002: £216.4m).

This is a young company where most of the employees work in the restaurants; their ages range from "teens to past retirement age". Except for the chairman, the age range of the senior management layer is from late 20s to 50.

Pay and benefits

For senior management at TRG, the salary and benefits package is in "the upper half". The term senior management embraces brand directors, heads of department in corporate functions, and area managers (who look after 10–12 branches). Above this level is the executive committee, which comprises four directors and the executive chairman. The nature of the business TRG is in means that they have a fluid workforce. Branches have a significant range in physical size and typically have a branch manager, assistant manager (sometimes two), head chef, deputy head chef, cook line staff and waiting staff. Branch staff receive basic salaries in line with the best in the restaurant industry, plus a bonus which will depend on the brand and its region. There are also seasonal and part-time workers, particularly at Christmas (which is the busiest time of the year), and these workers are paid by the hour.

A stakeholder pension scheme is available to all employees, and senior employees may be invited to join the company defined contribution pension scheme. Executive share options may be offered down to area manager level. There is a Save As You Earn scheme for all eligible staff (employed for at least one year), which may allow share purchases at a discounted rate.

Five weeks' holiday is available for senior management, and four weeks for all other staff. With the company's restaurants open seven days a week, staff will typically work in shift patterns with regulated days off. A 25% discount on meals and drinks at all group restaurants is available to all staff (and their families or guests) and uniforms are provided, with laundry costs paid for by the company.

Company cars are provided for area managers and above. Employees can opt out of the car scheme and receive a cash allowance instead.

Promotion and development

A "very large proportion" of managers are promoted from within at TRG. The entire management team at the Frankie and Benny's brand has been promoted internally. It is possible to start as a waiter or in the kitchens at TRG and work your way up the company. TRG's largest divisions – Frankie and Benny's and Caffe Uno – have achieved Investors in People accreditation, and the remaining elements of the company are working towards it.

Generally, staff undergo an appraisal at least once a year where career development is discussed and training needs may be identified. In-house training is widely available. Each division has a training department, and there is a company-wide training budget. A study policy operates where contributions are made to employees working to study for professional exams on the corporate side of the business. Financial assistance is given when sitting first exams. The subject being studied, however, must be relevant to the business. Mentoring is provided through ongoing discussion with line management.

TRG is growing rapidly, demonstrating an entrepreneurial and creative streak – and creating job opportunities. The Leisure Park brands are expanding quickly, and the Concessions division constantly develops new brands to match changing customer requirements at airports and in other locations. In 2004, TRG set up the Aqua water bar (customers are increasingly health conscious and want to drink water); and the Pip juice and bagel bar at Gatwick North Airside. Heathrow has seen the opening of Bite offering fresh sandwiches and snacks, and the first appearance of the Est-presso coffee bar.

Company culture

At TRG, the culture is in the brands, and within the brands it's in the branches. TRG can be equated to a holding company in this respect. To work in the company, sought after traits include the ability to manage a team, solid procedural abilities, dynamism, and enjoyment of working with people in a vibrant atmosphere. This is a young company driven by organic growth, which offers all employees the opportunity to go all the way. Vacancies are advertised internally first, then in other divisions, then externally. TRG aims to open 15–20 restaurants, cafes and bars each year.

Bullying, harassment and discrimination are not tolerated. Rigorous action will be taken against anyone who contravenes the policies, which are laid out clearly in the employee handbook.

It is a culture where you are measured on the work done rather than the number of hours spent. The nature of the industry – delighting individual customers – demands flexibility. Hours are varied, with some part-time working and shift work paid by the hour. Area managers visit branches when they are busy – at evenings and weekends – to match the business needs. Each restaurant is run as a local restaurant, with responsibility devolved to each branch including marketing to the local community.

There are internal award schemes. Brands run a branch of the year competition – which reflects on teamwork – as well as awarding a manager of the year and employee of the year, with celebratory dinners as part of the reward.

Innovation

The fact that TRG, in a nine-month period starting in February 2004, developed three separate brands in response to customer needs – Aqua, Bite and Pip – shows a healthy degree of innovation. If sites aren't trading well, management will question what would work there, and different concepts will be investigated. TRG appreciates the restaurant industry is changing. Many people have less time to devote to lunch, being "cash rich and time poor". They want to "grab and go". But when they do sit down to a meal, they want more time. So TRG constantly questions where the industry is going – how are the brands suited to the changing habits among its customers? Quicker and lighter offerings will be introduced to complement traditional full-service concepts. TRG is both proactive and reactive as regards its customer needs and desires.

At least once a year there are cook-offs among chefs to see who comes up with the best meal; and competitions to see who can produce "a meal we can sell", "dishes for a menu" or "chefs' specials". A panel of judges is set up from across the business, and winners receive cash prizes. The competitions represent opportunities for staff to demonstrate what they can do.

Diversity and social responsibility

Of the five executive board members, one is female. Approximately 45% of the staff are female. The workforce is drawn from diverse backgrounds.

Directors regularly attend meetings with employees, and continually review performance, policies and the ways information is disseminated. Where reasonable and practicable within existing legislation, everyone – including disabled persons – is treated in the same way in matters relating to employment, training, career development and promotion.

TRG itself makes no donation to charity but leaves charitable work and fundraising activities to individual restaurants and/or brands. Frankie & Benny's, for example, links up with Children in Need for nominated charitable events. Fancy-dress nights are held with all proceeds going to charity. Caffe Uno has an ongoing commitment to a breast cancer charity. Some restaurants will work with local schools, inviting children in to bake their own pizzas – showing them how a restaurant business operates and teaching nutritional values. While TRG generally encourages each outlet throughout the group to work within their local community, that has to be adapted in an airport environment or city-centre location.

Corporate Governance

TRG is committed to high standards of corporate governance, and has been in full compliance throughout 2004 with the provisions set out in Section 1 of the code of best practice prepared by the Committee on Corporate Governance (the Combined Code).

The board is responsible to shareholders for the proper management of the group and has access to all the required information to enable it to discharge its duties. An experienced senior manager has responsibility for health and safety matters, and manages two fully trained health and safety officers who visit every branch at least twice a year to ensure full compliance with all regulations. There are HR departments for the three key group segments of Leisure Parks, Concessions and High Street. Audits of each TRG site have been undertaken for compliance with the Disability Discrimination Act.

TRG has taken the necessary steps to ensure its communications procedures are totally compliant with the upcoming Information and Communications with Employees (ICE) legislation, which is effective from April 6 2005. As a people-focused business, TRG regards its staff as the key resource that is driving its business success.

Environmental record

TRG acknowledges the importance and relevance of environmental matters within its role in the community. The company particularly seeks to reduce the production of waste in its operations, and to maximise efficiency of water consumption and the use of non-renewable fuels. TRG is working with several key suppliers to ensure environmental concerns are considered alongside economic factors.

The recycling of glass is a further area the company is looking to develop. The recycling of packaging used in the delivery of goods to branches is being considered, as are the key logistics involved in distribution. TRG follows legislation on the use of CFCs and ensures all kitchen equipment is CFC compliant. Redundant computer and office equipment (old PCs, printers, copiers, phones, etc.) are disposed of appropriately following the European Waste Electrical and Electronic Equipment legislation (WEEE).

While the ideal scenario for TRG is to have no waste food products, it is a constant operation and there is inevitably some waste – both from customers' plates and surplus kitchen goods. The group procedures and training provide for this kind of waste to be disposed of securely.

TRG's green credentials mirror its vibrancy and business acumen.

Reuters

Reuters Group plc
85 Fleet Street, London EC4P 4AJ
Tel: (0) 20 7250 1122 **Fax:** (0) 20 7353 3002
Web: www.reuters.com

Pay and Benefits	7.0	Innovation	7.7
Promotion and Development	7.0	Diversity	7.0
Training	7.3	Social Responsibility	7.3
Travel opportunities	8.0	Corporate Governance	7.0
Culture	7.0	Environment	7.7
Total			**73.0**

Reuters is a global information company. It provides indispensable information, tailored for professionals in the financial services, media and corporate markets. Its information drives decision-making across the globe; based on its reputation for speed, accuracy and independence. Reuters has 14,700 staff in 92 countries, including some 2,300 editorial staff in 197 bureaux serving approximately 130 countries, making it the world's largest international multimedia news agency. In 2003, the Reuters Group had revenues of £3.2bn.

Executive summary

Founded by Paul Julius Reuter, who started his business using carrier pigeons to transmit stock price information, Reuters has a long and enviable reputation for being first with information – including news of President Lincoln's assassination in 1865 and the Armistice at the end of the First World War in 1918.

Over 90% of the organisation's revenues come from financial services, but in recent years the group has felt the pinch from an ongoing contraction of the financial services market combined with steady competition from rivals such as Bloomberg. Indeed, both revenues and profits at Reuters declined from 2001 until 2003. Following its first loss in 2002, the group returned to profit in 2003 – making £49m on turnover of £3.2bn.

In response to the downturn, Reuters has launched a far-reaching change programme, Fast Forward, aimed at strengthening the core information business and responding to structural changes within the financial services industry. It will do this by making their information indispensable; moving to a new business operating model; simplifying and segmenting the product line; focusing solutions business around core areas of expertise; reducing and reshaping the cost base; and reinvigorating the culture.

The group is looking to make itself more competitive, focused and profitable; and is looking for cost savings of £440m by the end of 2005. So far it has shed 4,000 people and consolidated much of its operations. Part of this has seen the establishment of new software development facilities in Bangkok, and a content operation in Bangalore. In 2005, the organisation's headquarters will move from the sixty-year-old base on Fleet Street to Canary Wharf, allowing the majority of UK staff to work in one place for the first time.

"We are addressing a number of years of under-investment by improving consistency and standardisation," says Mark Sandham, global head of human resources. "We're also looking at suitable opportunities to move away from core financial services."

Pay and benefits

Reuters pays around the median for base pay, and in the upper quartile in terms of total remuneration. Compensation and benefits are benchmarked against external data;

graduates start on a minimum salary of £24,500. There is a strong element of performance-related pay – agreed on in consultation with line managers – particularly as employees move up within the organisation. "We will always pay for performance," says Sandham. "The more senior you are, the more of your variable pay is at risk".

There are a number of different share plans: the all-employee Save As You Earn (SAYE) plan, with a take-up rate of 68%; and two discretionary plans in which the company selects which employees may enroll as part of the annual review – one scheme is available to senior executives, the other is aimed at the top 25% of employees. Reuters planned to introduce an all-employee profit share plan in 2004.

A recognition programme – part of Fast Forward – awards individuals and teams for "living the values" of Reuters; employees can win up to £1,250 individually or £6,250 as a team. There are also discretionary monetary awards for outstanding performance.

Other benefits of working for Reuters include healthcare, life assurance, car ownership, subsidised sports membership, pension, mortgage and personal loans, a childcare support contribution, an employee assistance programme, and membership of the LifeWorks advice service.

Employees with children under eight (and disabled children under 18) may request flexible working hours. Reuters also promotes "smart" working, with an increasing number of employees working from home. It has a range of family-friendly policies, such as paternity and adoption leave.

"The overall package is extremely competitive, and reflects the calibre of individuals that we try to attract," says Sandham.

Promotion and development

There is an active approach to performance management at Reuters. The cycle starts with individuals setting their own objectives and then, throughout the year, feedback and informal discussions are arranged to ensure that performance is on track. Personal development plans are a key part of this process. Training and development is encouraged through a mix of methods, with a focus on learning on the job.

In 2003, a career development portal was launched to provide employees with a one-stop shop for tools and information regarding career paths within the group. There is also an e-learning tool, Knowing Reuters, which aims to improve employees' understanding of the organisation.

Training takes place on a number of levels, although the group is moving away from a classroom approach towards more informal styles of coaching and mentoring. Executive coaching is provided for senior staff.

There is a company-wide use of "talent review workshops" to identify high potential in individuals, and to develop and retain these employees as well as deploy them most effectively within the group. A large number of vacancies are filled internally.

Reuters has links with the University of Michigan, which delivers a six-day change management training programme four times a year for middle managers from offices around the world. In 2004, some 160 people were selected to go on the programme, designed to engender "a mindset for change".

Given the global nature of the industries in which Reuters operates, many staff are frequently out of the office. In 2003, for example, more than a third of British staff travelled abroad.

Typically, offices are staffed by both local and international staff – a mix designed to combine fresh and objective reporting with local knowledge.

Company culture

The Reuter Trust Principles underpin the activities of the group, although it is currently refreshing the corporate culture with its FAST values: "fast, accountable, service-driven, team (oriented)". "We want to be more fleet of foot, and make our people more accountable," explains Sandham. Employment reviews for senior managers now incorporate 360-degree feedback, and specific feedback about whether people are good role models. "We are a lot more disciplined and a lot more process-oriented. We firmly believe that you can solve your own problems, because you create a lot of them in the first place."

Reuters aims to make the best possible use of technology and recently invested in a thousand new Blackberry hand-held devices for staff, to improve communication. Other web-based communication tools are used to convey strategy to employees, and to encourage them to put questions and give feedback to the chief executive, Tom Glocer.

Management, employees and representatives of the two relevant unions (NUJ and GPMU) meet regularly, and employee surveys are conducted quarterly to evaluate morale and identify issues that demand attention.

In June 2003, more than 250 items of employee feedback were received – covering everything from a request for Earl Grey tea bags in New York to increasing the frequency of performance reviews. Feedback was registered and collected during interactive sessions; by the following month, every issue had been responded to, and many responses contained commitments to action. A year later, Glocer took direct questions and feedback from staff around the globe during three live television broadcasts.

Innovation

Reuters has a long history of innovation in delivering the latest news and information using the fastest technology available. In 1858, the organisation's founder, a German-born immigrant in London, began to open offices all over Europe; seven years later it was registered as a public company; and in the early twenties, Reuters pioneered the use of radio to transmit news internationally. In 1964, the group was among the first to use computers to transmit financial data internationally with the launch of Stockmaster – an innovation which cost them a loss of £53,000 that year (on turnover of £3.5m), but prepared the ground for the new way of working.

Most recently, the group has implemented a comprehensive change programme focused on making the company simpler and more able to compete. This includes an improvement in customer service – according to the chief executive, Tom Glocer, this is "one facet of culture change at Reuters which I will pursue without apology".

As part of the Fast Forward streamlining objectives, the group has made over 80 disposals of non-strategic units and is concentrating its efforts on its holdings in Factiva and Instinet Group.

Diversity and social responsibility

Reuters is dedicated to a policy of equal opportunities for its staff, and opposes any form of discriminatory treatment of employees or job applicants. The group recently appointed its first two female non-executive directors, Penny Hughes and Lawton Fitt. It has also established a global diversity advisory council, building on the success of local diversity efforts across the company. This council will serve as an advisory board to group senior management, and help to drive diversity-related initiatives within Reuters.

As well as matching employee charitable donations pound for pound (up to £250 per person per year), Reuters has also introduced a community volunteering policy that allows employees to spend one working day each year on a community project. The group's first "community events week" took place in 2004, with the participation of more than 1,800 staff in 35 locations.

On a global level, the Reuters Foundation (created in 1982) works to support journalists from developing countries; and embraces a range of educational, humanitarian and environmental causes and projects.

Corporate governance

Reuters has a fundamental commitment to conducting its business in accordance with the highest standards of legal and ethical conduct. Of great importance are the laws and regulations regarding financial services, intellectual property, data protection, employment law and defamation. The general counsel ensures that issues of compliance are observed.

In addition, under the constitution of the Reuters Founders Share Company, the directors are required to act in accordance with the Reuter Trust Principles and to endeavour to ensure that the principles are complied with. The first principle is that Reuters shall at no time pass into the hands of any one interest, group or faction.

Since 1996, Reuters has maintained a European Employee Forum that meets twice yearly to ensure dialogue throughout Europe. Early in 2004, this grew to take account of new countries joining the EU. In response to the upcoming Information and Consultation Directive, the group is also negotiating an information and consultation agreement in order to maintain its good working relationships with the trade unions.

Environmental record

Although the Ethical Investment Research Service classifies the organisation as a low impact business, Reuters endeavours to tread lightly. As a media organisation, it feels the most valuable way to convey support for the protection of the environment is through providing information, and so it works with Planet Ark to enable the public to access environmental news and pictures.

Reuters aims to reduce its environmental impact through a sustained and measured programme, focused on best practices. This means working with suppliers to promote best practice, managing energy supplies more efficiently, minimizing waste production, recycling wherever practicable, and raising awareness of best practice among staff and suppliers.

Rolls Royce

Rolls Royce Group plc
65 Buckingham Gate, London SW1E 6AT
Tel: (0) 20 7222 9020 **Fax:** (0) 20 7227 9170
Web: www.rolls-royce.com **Email:** peoplelink@rollsroyce.com

 **Rolls-Royce**

Pay and Benefits	6.8	Innovation	6.9
Promotion and Development	6.8	Diversity	6.6
Training	7.7	Social Responsibility	7.3
Travel opportunities	6.8	Corporate Governance	6.7
Culture	6.7	Environment	7.9
Total			**70.2**

Having built its original reputation as a maker of fine cars, Rolls-Royce Group is now one of the world's leading providers of gas turbine engines. For a decade it has invested in technology and capabilities that have given it a prime position in four growing global markets: civil aerospace, defence aerospace, marine and energy. While the events of September 11th – followed by the Iraq war and the SARS outbreak in 2003 – affected profits, the group's portfolio approach mitigated the consequent recession in civil aerospace.

Today, Rolls-Royce has a broad customer base comprising more than 500 airlines, 4,000 corporate and utility aircraft and helicopter operators, 160 armed forces, and more than 2,000 marine customers (including 50 navies). The company has energy customers in nearly 120 countries. The group has offices, service centres or manufacturing bases in some fifty countries; and a global workforce of more than 35,000 people, including 21,000 in the UK and 8,000 in North America.

Executive summary

In 1904, the aviator and car enthusiast Sir Charles Rolls met Henry Royce – a manufacturer who he hoped might help him to develop a high-quality car. The meeting led to the birth of one of Britain's most prestigious and enduring brands, which during the First World War won an early reputation for the quality of its aero engines.

While the brand undoubtedly set a benchmark for cars, the company was forced to sell its cars division to Vickers plc when an over-investment in the RB211 engine in the late 60s left it on the brink of bankruptcy. However, this engine was the precursor to the group's acclaimed Trent family of engines, and in 1999, Rolls-Royce came full circle when it acquired Vickers – though the cars are now made by BMW.

In 2001, following devastation in the civil aerospace industry, the group implemented a successful redundancy programme by investing in resource centres to aid the redeployment of some 6,000 workers. A third stayed in the group, a third went to jobs outside, and the rest took early retirement or voluntary severance.

Overall revenues currently stand at just under £6bn with underlying profits at £345m in 2004. In recent years, the group has become more service-oriented, seeing aftercare as a "predictable and growing source of revenue". Indeed, half its turnover in 2003 came from long-term contractual customer relationships.

Pay and benefits

As a truly international employer, Rolls-Royce Group approaches pay and benefits by structuring compensation on a global basis, although salaries vary depending on particular markets. Graduates start on £21,500; other salaries are paid at, or just above, the median. There is an element of performance-related pay for those at senior management level and other selected professionals; and everyone participates in the bonus scheme, which is dependent on the group's overall financial performance.

Many employees opt to take at least part of this annual bonus in shares (senior managers must take a third) and the group also provides Save as You Earn (SAYE) share option arrangements. In all, some 22% of UK employees own shares. "We believe all employees should have the opportunity to build up a long-term interest in the company, and the overwhelming evidence is that our employees value that and keep their shares," says John Rivers, director of human resources.

Corollary evidence of this sort of loyalty can be found in the fact that the average length of employment here is 25 years, a period nevertheless recognised by the group as worthy of a long-service award. In addition, informal arrangements exist to recognise other forms of employee contribution to the group.

Rolls-Royce Group has developed a number of policies to provide opportunities for flexible working; although it acknowledges that flexible working patterns can be difficult to manage on the shop floor. They believe: "where we can be positive in this way, employees will be positive in response". This positive approach, together with the provision of childcare vouchers, fits with the group's aim to attract more women. It also pays pension provisions for those taking career breaks.

While the group has no flexible benefits package, it provides all the usual benefits including company cars, pension provision and employee discounts. The jewel in its crown – and a factor in attracting graduates to work in Derby – is its provision of recreational space: the main site boasts gyms, tennis courts, football pitches, rugby fields, hockey pitches and cricket grounds. There is also a horticultural society, a bowling association and a male voice choir. Some 90% of employees belong to these recreational clubs.

Promotion and development

In 2003, Rolls-Royce Group spent £29m on training and development, not including the salary costs of people attending programmes or on-the-job training. In the past three years it has opened two large new "learning and development" centres to provide all types of training, and there are smaller centres elsewhere.

The group has developed acclaimed training programmes across all disciplines including finance, human resources, engineering, logistics and procurement. There is also "a whole suite of management development programmes" for both young professionals and senior management. These incorporate strategic, operational and performance elements as well as leadership development and training in international business awareness.

Rolls-Royce Group uses a "cell" system for identifying its high-performance high-potential employees, in which managers from various levels meet in small groups at least twice a year to discuss and implement a range of tools for succession planning. There is also a well-developed mentoring function within the group, particularly for new graduates who are working towards accreditation, but available to other employees as well. All managers are encouraged to adopt a "coaching style" and training courses support them in this.

Continuing professional development is key and there are plenty of opportunities to be stretched, both at home and abroad. "More and more people are coming to us because they want an international career," says Rivers. "The amount of movement between businesses worldwide is significant, and many of our senior staff have worked in several different countries. It is a part of our psyche."

Company culture

Rolls-Royce Group is a company that values commitment. In civil aerospace, an order might take 18 months to place and three years to deliver, and the end product could last

25 years. "In this business, our customers expect our people to be deeply knowledgeable so it's an asset to the company that we have long service," says John Rivers. "People here enjoy long careers, with opportunities and responsibilities arising throughout."

The group's three core values are reliability, integrity and innovation. Evidence of good relations internally can be found at the global employee forum; this bi-annual event is attended by employee representatives from around the world, along with the chief executive, and is considered an exercise "which breeds a good deal of trust". Manufacturing and production are unionised; and solid bargaining and consultation arrangements with the unions have been established over the years.

One example of the levels of trust between management and workforce can be seen in the way that the group managed the impact of September 11th. Although the labour force was effectively cut by 20%, the process of redeployment was managed without any disruption.

In another example, future service benefits (the group's pension plan) were successfully renegotiated after consultation with union and non-union members.

Innovation

One of the biggest innovations at Rolls-Royce Group has been the steady removal of traditional demarcations between blue-collar and white-collar workers, together with changes in working patterns. There has also been a move towards self-directed learning, with changes in the role of the supervisor, and an increase in the use of team-based working.

"In recent times we set out plans to invest in modern new manufacturing production facilities in parallel with negotiations to change working practices," says Rivers. The group has moved towards payment systems based on performance and not attendance, which delivers benefits for employees' work/life balance.

"People now work more sensible hours with a better base rate of pay, and we have been able to lay out new factories for more efficient working in better surroundings," adds Rivers. "These are big changes. Noone likes change, but in every place that we have introduced these changes, noone wants to go back."

In addition, customers have now begun to interact directly with the workers who are making and servicing their products. Corporate customers are encouraged to go and see their engines being repaired, which in turn breeds an increased sense of responsibility, ownership and accountability among employees.

Diversity and social responsibility

A sixth of graduate traineeships at Rolls-Royce Group go to non-UK nationals, and across the group, fifty different nationalities are employed. While the group has no diversity officer, it has a well-developed diversity policy and local codes of practice.

Traditionally, the group has found it difficult to attract women workers, partly because of the small number who train as engineers. However, its three-pronged approach – flexible working policies, a mentoring programme, and consistent university liaison – is starting to pay off. "We have links with a dozen or more universities, both on campus and with leading academics," says Rivers.

In functions such as finance, human resources and communications, the ratio of women to men is nearly 50:50; in the group as a whole, 13% of employees and 11% of managers are women.

In the outside world, Rolls-Royce Group takes its responsibilities seriously, coming 10th overall in the 2003 Business in the Community Corporate Responsibility Index. Having recently produced its first community investment report, the group focuses its efforts on causes linked with educational, engineering and scientific objectives. It recently launched an annual science prize, which will be promoted in 40,000 schools.

In 2003, the group gave more than £1m to charity; supporting projects such as The

Prince's Trust, Viva (the orchestra of the East Midlands) and the National Forest. It also acts on a local level, with more than 200 employees acting as school governors; and prizes within its training awards for the best community projects. "Our policy on community affairs is to make donations heavily associated with employee involvement," says Rivers.

Corporate governance

Rolls-Royce Group has no dedicated compliance officers, although it does have risk management systems and well-developed policies in sensitive areas such as remuneration of senior executives.

Rolls-Royce complies fully with the UK government's Combined Code on corporate governance. It has a non-executive chairman and seven non-executive directors, and has separate audit, remuneration and nominations committees.

The board as a whole take collective responsibility in this area extremely seriously, says Rivers. "Rolls-Royce has a strong ethical tradition – it likes to behave properly and wouldn't wish to be associated with failure. Excellence is one of our main values and we have devoted a considerable amount of energy to ensure that we are properly managed. We would regard ourselves as a compliant company."

Environmental record

Rolls-Royce Group combines its policy on the environment with health and safety issues, to which it gives top priority. "Safety has always been of paramount importance in this industry for obvious reasons, so it comes naturally to us to make sure that our operations are safely conducted and that our products are safe and reliable," says Rivers.

When it comes to the environment, the group sets itself ever more stringent standards: aiming to develop quieter, less polluting engines; to increase the recycling of waste metal from production areas and IT equipment; and to reduce the consumption of water and electricity. The group promotes car-sharing initiatives, and has inter-site buses between its main sites in Derby and Bristol.

Rolls-Royce Group participates in the UK Emissions Trading Scheme and the Chicago Climate Exchange. All environmental policies and procedures are controlled as part of the international management systems standard ISO 14001, and the results of audits are reviewed annually. Employees who are involved with significant environmental aspects are given more focused training.

In 2003, Rolls-Royce Group was placed highly in the Business in the Environment index; coming first in the aerospace and defence sectors, second in the general industrial sector, and 32nd overall out of 177 participants.

The Royal Bank of Scotland

The Royal Bank of Scotland Group
42 St Andrew Square, Edinburgh EH2 2YE
Tel: (0) 131 556 8555 **Fax:** (0) 131 557 6140
Web: www.rbs.co.uk

✳✳ RBS
The Royal Bank of Scotland Group

Pay and Benefits	7.8	Innovation	7.1
Promotion and Development	7.9	Diversity	6.8
Training	6.4	Social Responsibility	6.9
Travel opportunities	6.5	Corporate Governance	6.6
Culture	6.9	Environment	7.1
Total			**70.1**

The Royal Bank of Scotland (RBS) is a financial giant, which is getting bigger and bigger. Founded in 1727, it is one of the UK's top 10 companies, Europe's second largest financial institution and the sixth largest in the world. In 2003, it had record profits of £7.1bn and a market capitalisation of £51m.

It is a serial acquirer in America, Europe and in the UK – the last purchase being Churchill Insurance. It employs 135,000 worldwide – significantly more in America than in its home base of Scotland – and it has about 30 million customers.

Executive Summary

The Royal Bank of Scotland was founded by Royal Charter on May 31 1727. Its future was threatened in 1981 with bids from Standard Chartered and the Hong Kong & Shanghai Banking Corporation – but it survived.

When current chairman Sir George Mathewson came in as chief executive in 1987 with responsibility for group development, he promised to expand into England and look carefully at a US acquisition. He has since looked carefully at many acquisitions and made them. Drummond Bank, Williams & Glynn, NatWest, Direct Line, Ulster Bank, Coutts & Co, Citizens Bank in the US, and Churchill Insurance are only some of the many brand names now in the group.

Many of its nine divisions are in a league of their own. Retail banking is a significant force in the UK retail market; the corporate finance division is one of the country's largest owners of aircraft, ships and trains; and Global Travel Money Services is one of the world's largest banknote dealing operators.

More expansion is no doubt on the way, but the main target is increased profitability and that is being consistently met – £4.2bn in 2001, £4.8bn in 2002, £6.2bn in 2003 and £7.1bn in 2004.

Pay and Benefits

RBS has been very profitable over the last few years and this is reflected in a bonus scheme that is related to profits and performance. There is also a performance-driven pay structure, which recognises good performance through increased salary and bonus payments.

Salaries are competitive to attract the best in the financial services marketplace, and they are reviewed and adjusted every year. There are also what they call financially attractive core benefits, including a group profit share scheme, non-contributory final salary pension scheme (a corporate rarity these days), and discounts on the bank's services.

Then there is what RBS regards as the "most exciting" element of its pay and reward structure – RBSelect, a flexible benefits scheme which allows staff to choose the rewards which are most beneficial to their lifestyle.

This can mean increasing the pension, or going for private health care or dental care. It could be money-saving shopping vouchers, or buying or selling holidays. Some of the other benefits are outlined by Adrian Thomas, senior technical partner, resourcing and development: "We have introduced increased opportunities to work flexibly, including compressed hours. There is also paternity leave and part-time working, and it is recognised that some of the best people don't want to work traditional hours so we try, where possible, to match the work with the hours people want to work. We are prepared to do far more than other organisations."

The group's chief executive, Fred Goodwin, has said the aim is to become "the most admired bank". The group's human resources team believe that an integral part of reaching that goal is to become the "most admired employer" – hence a policy of constantly examining, comparing and improving the remuneration structure.

Promotion and Development

Access to Learning (A2L) is a new learning management system designed to support the group's strategic objective of giving employees access to the right amount of training at the greatest time of need. A2L enables employees to key in to a host of lifelong learning tools – they can order books, videos and CD ROMs for personal development and register for role-specific learning programmes and workshops. It also enables individuals to record all completed learning and development online. Defined learning maps can be created to ensure that specific training is completed. Group-wide training, such as with disability awareness, can be added to learning maps to ensure that mandatory courses are completed.

Each employee has a personal development plan, which is reviewed yearly. It sets out a timescale, required skills, objectives, actions to be taken, and the support needed to achieve the goals.

This is HR with good intentions, summed up in this message from RBS to school leavers: "Forget the old clichés about banking. There are no pompous hierarchies here. Everything is flexible – and it's designed to bring out the best in you as an individual.

"Once you've settled in and learned the ropes, we will be expecting you to think about progressing your career. But relax – that doesn't mean sticking to a particular timescale. It just means we want you to show enthusiasm and ambition. We certainly don't want anyone to feel intimidated or left by the wayside."

Company Culture

In a message seeking to entice graduates to come on board, RBS states: "Our activities go way beyond traditional banking. We have big ideas, and make them happen." Adrian Thomas says that a clear example of how they make it happen is that they believe in making and integrating acquisitions extremely quickly. If they think something will fit and complement the rest of the organisation, and the numbers add up, they don't hang about. They will have bought and integrated it before the headline writers have finished their speculation.

Considerable emphasis is placed on what they call approachability. They have put more people into their branches while others have been pulling them out. To be approachable, you have to have somebody to approach, is the theory.

While it employs 135,000 people in 24 different countries, an inherent part of the group culture is its Scottish roots. It holds on to them firmly. At a ceremony in 2003 in Glasgow, awards were handed out to Scottish entrepreneurs and established companies. The winners came from all sectors and sizes and they sold tyres, made celebration cakes, hired kilts and cruised Loch Ness. The winner of the Scottish Business of the Year award was The Royal Bank of Scotland.

An international banking giant it might well be, but it still likes to compete and be respected in its own backyard.

Innovation

Simplicity is the name of RBS's innovation game. Says Adrian Thomas: "We are innovative in that we try to simplify things. We try to lead the banking sector in getting products on to a single platform. Getting things as simple as possible means more competitively priced products. We are one of the best cost/income ratio banks in the world because we do things simply."

And how's this for innovation? The bank is building a new multi-million pound headquarters on the outskirts of Edinburgh, which will house around 3,250 employees – and it is not settling for the usual flagship office. It plans a world-class working environment which will have an executive development centre, an auditorium, a TV studio, a nursery, a street with a Royal Bank branch, a Tesco, a Starbucks, a florist, a hairdresser, a dry-cleaners, photo-developing services, key cutting services, and a shoe repairer.

And here's another bit of innovation for a major new building in Edinburgh – when it opens in autumn 2005 it will be on time and on budget.

Diversity and Social Responsibility

RBS makes it clear that it is committed to promoting and valuing diversity in all areas of recruitment, employment, training and promotion. It says it strives to maintain a working environment that realises the full potential of employees and encourages their creativity and productivity.

A quote from the company Code of Conduct: "All our people have the right to be treated with consideration and respect at work, and we are committed to eliminating each and every form of bullying and harassment. It is our firm intention to maintain a climate free from these unwanted forms of behaviour, one where all people feel confident to raise concerns of this kind and we will have them dealt with quickly, sensitively and effectively."

Board members are informed on equality and diversity policy making, networks and decisions. Managers implement changes in their divisions based on feedback from current and potential employees, and responsibility for adhering to the equality and diversity policies lie with employees at all levels throughout the group.

There are dedicated teams within RBS who are driving forward the bank's community investment programme. This programme is one of the largest in Europe; and in 2003, the group invested £40.1m in the communities it services.

Corporate Governance

It is all spelled out in the impressive 36-page Code of Conduct, which covers everything from alcohol to political activity and is designed to promote honest and ethical conduct, including "the ethical handling of actual or apparent conflicts of interest between personal and professional relationships".

It seeks to have a full, fair, accurate, timely and understandable disclosure in reports and documents that the group files with, or submits to, its regulators; and in other public communications made by RBS.

Compliance with applicable governmental laws, rules and regulations is underlined, and the Code extends to contractors and outside agencies. The need for prompt internal reporting of violations of the Code is stressed.

The Code states: "We are strongly committed to conducting our business affairs with honesty and integrity in full compliance with all applicable laws, rules and regulations. No group employee shall commit an illegal or unethical act or instruct others to do so for any reason."

Those at whose desk the buck stops are listed – the group director, human resources, has primary authority and responsibility for the enforcement of the Code; and if it is relating to the Sarbanes-Oxley Act of 2002, the group secretary and general counsel have responsibility.

Environment

RBS's environmental policy is clear and precise: the group recognises that concern for the environment and the quality of life is an integral and fundamental part of the way in which it conducts its business, and the group is firmly committed to creating strong business growth which is not achieved at the expense of the environment, quality of life or social equity.

The chairman, Sir George Mathewson, takes overall responsibility for the group's environmental performance. He states: "As a financial services group, we impact on the environment in two ways – through our own operations and through our core business, the lending of money to customers. A robust environmental management system has been developed to oversee our internal operations, and environmental considerations are an important part of our decision-making process when lending to customers."

The corporate environmental objectives include the progressive integration of environmental and social considerations into business decisions; raising awareness among staff and undertaking a dialogue with investors, regulators and suppliers; and minimising waste and promoting the efficient use of energy, raw materials, manufactured products and natural resources.

It is also policy to encourage the development of products and services from partners and suppliers who have compatible environmental principles.

Saffery Champness

Saffery Champness
Lion House, Red Lion St, London WC1R 4GB
Tel: (0) 20 7841 4000
Web: www.saffery.com **Email:** info@saffery.com

Saffery Champness
CHARTERED ACCOUNTANTS

Pay and Benefits	6.2	Innovation	5.8
Promotion and Development	6.5	Diversity	6.1
Training	6.6	Social Responsibility	5.1
Travel opportunities	6.3	Corporate Governance	6.3
Culture	5.8	Environment	6.3
Total			**61.0**

Saffery Champness is an old, established and successful accountancy firm serving a mixture of private and commercial clients ranging from charities and professional entertainers to educational bodies and landed estates. One of the UK's top 20 accountancy practices; the firm has nine offices in the UK (London, Bournemouth, Bristol, Edinburgh, Harrogate, High Wycombe, Inverness, Manchester and Peterborough) and one in Guernsey. It has 335 UK staff including 53 partners (half of them in London), plus 90 employees in Guernsey. Since the merger of Saffery and Champness in 1980, the firm's growth has been steady and largely organic. It celebrates its 150th anniversary in 2005.

Executive summary

While some top accountancy firms have struggled in recent years, Saffery Champness has recorded steady organic growth in both revenues and profitability. Fee income grew from around £27m in 2001–2 to £30m in 2002–3 and £32m in 2003–4, without any increase in staff numbers. The firm says profitability has also increased, although being a partnership it does not publish figures.

"We have a reputation for being profitable, and we are ahead of firms close to us in the league tables," says executive partner Philip Hall. He adds proudly that Saffery Champness has not had a round of redundancies for many years, and hasn't failed to give a pay rise in more than a decade – unlike some of its more famous rivals.

Hall ascribes the firm's smooth ride to the nature and loyalty of its client base. "We focus on clearly defined market sectors, and our large private client element makes us less susceptible to economic ups and downs," he says. "Our business is also less cyclical and transactional than in some other firms."

The firm intends to maintain its independence and continue the current pattern of steady organic growth until at least 2008, with projected fee income growth of 8–10% each year.

Pay & benefits

Saffery Champness aims to pay salaries in the top quartile compared with similar firms. It's a common enough claim, but the firm goes to greater lengths than most to deliver what it promises. Instead of having standard salary scales for different grades, the firm uses a wealth of data sources – agencies, published reports, knowledge of other accounting firms, etc. – to devise a personal salary scale for every individual role, from partners to secretaries. This applies to both fee-earners (the accountants) and support staff (IT, HR, finance etc.). If Saffery Champness says you're being paid top dollar, you can bet you are.

There is a significant performance-related element for pretty much everyone except trainees. Bonuses are also paid to everyone above the newly qualified level; more junior people are mostly rewarded for how hard they work, their superiors for how much they achieve. There is also a profit-sharing bonus distributed to all employees equally. Being a partnership, only the 53 partners have a financial stake in the business.

As in most accountancy practices, holiday allowances are relatively meagre – 20 days rising to 25 with seniority – but the benefits package is attractive. The firm actually advises its clients on flexible benefits, so its own scheme is a model one; there is a choice of 19 benefits ranging from BUPA, cars and insurance to child care, health club membership and extra holiday. The money-purchase pension scheme (contributions 4% matched for staff and 5% matched for managers) can be joined after six months' service.

Promotion & development

Saffery Champness recruits about 15 graduate trainees a year, and around half of partner appointments come from outside the firm. Between those two levels, however, you may be lucky to get in – since 80% of vacancies are filled internally, and people stay for six years on average (the industry norm is four years).

Jon Young, head of human resources, puts this down to the variety of interesting work on offer (smaller clients tend to mean shorter audits), and the firm's attitude to its people. "We're small enough to know everybody as individuals," he says. "We've continued to successfully recruit people from bigger firms because they're dissatisfied with the relationships they have there."

Successful accountants can expect to be promoted every couple of years, typically making partner by their mid-30s. Staff progress is regularly on the agenda at meetings, including that of secretaries and juniors, and a "potential partner" programme aims to identify future high flyers. The firm's philosophy is that it would rather see talented people move than leave, and secondments between offices are common. This kind of movement has been key to the firm's development, with regional offices built up by insiders. "It's given us a genuine 'one-firm' culture, and a large proportion of our partners trained with the firm," says Hall.

Care is taken to ensure that trainees experience a wide variety of clients and departments suited to their individual abilities. Their training is as thorough as will be found anywhere in the industry, even at the "big four", claims Young; and their exam results are very good. The firm has a full-time training manager and offers personnel and management training to its clients, so it ensures that more senior staff also receive the training they need to update their professional knowledge and develop their skills. This extends to the support staff, who are treated on equal terms with fee-earners. A few people have MBAs, though advanced technical or professional qualifications are more common.

Formal mentoring covers a quarter of staff, and everyone should receive coaching. The annual appraisal process appears thorough.

Company culture

The island of Guernsey holds an annual charity event unambiguously christened the Mud Run, and among its regular contestants are the four directors of Saffery Champness's Guernsey office. This typifies an attitude that the firm likes to see as fun and unstuffy – at least by the standard of accountancy firms. Hall describes the firm as results-oriented and focused on client service delivery, but also friendly and supportive; it has room for the quietly industrious as well as the overtly ambitious.

The management style is open and accessible, says Hall (he should know, he's on the board), with a marked absence of ceremony and status symbols. For example, when Rob Elliott was elected as managing partner in 2003, he had sit-down lunches in small groups with every staff member from all the firm's mainland offices. The biennial staff survey, which the management board takes very seriously, has shown satisfaction rates triple in the decade it has been running.

Saffery Champness seems to have avoided the culture of excessively long hours and overwork which afflicts many professional firms, and the free stress counselling service it offers is not often used. As people stagger their journeys to avoid rush-hour crushes, the hours are no longer strictly 9–5. Flexible working is supported for parents with young children, and many senior staff (including the vast majority of partners) have been given home computers networked to the office, enabling them to work from home when convenient. Around 25 UK staff work part time, including the majority of female partners.

As well as having a large Guernsey office, the firm takes a central role in SC International – a network of nearly 100 associate firms in 50 countries who refer clients and share expertise. Secondments to other network members have taken staff to Europe, the USA and Australia in recent years, and the firm is keen to encourage this. Staff occasionally travel abroad for UK-based clients with foreign subsidiaries or parents.

Innovation

Accountants are not encouraged to innovate (the term "creative accounting" has a wholly different meaning!), so Saffery Champness's approach to its core accountancy work is pretty traditional. However, the firm says it is always prepared to realign its services to suit the market and it has been keen to exploit opportunities in areas such as private office services, enhanced corporate finance capabilities, and new sectors of VAT work.

Unlike many professional firms, Saffery Champness was quick to see the value of online technologies. It was among the first to use an intranet for managing flexible benefits; and its innovative, internet-based recruitment process allows it to begin recruiting graduates from July, instead of the more traditional October – giving it the pick of strong candidates.

In HR, the firm points to its annual attitude survey, begun in 1994, and its Investors in People accreditation, gained in 1997, as being among the first in the accountancy profession. It also says the scope of its training and development is broad compared with rival firms.

Diversity & social responsibility

Saffery Champness's gender and ethnic make-up is fairly typical of an urban, professional firm. In London, 8% of staff are from ethnic minorities, and the online recruitment procedure helps make the process truly "colour-blind". Only one in seven partners and a quarter of senior managers are women, but this reflects past recruitment and natural dropout rates, not policy. Flexible and part-time working are helping the firm to retain more women, and it is careful to ensure salaries reflect ability and effort, not gender. More than half of graduate recruits are women, though again this is not intentional, and women head three of the six support functions.

The firm has no formal policy on charitable giving, but it is developing plans for a charitable initiative for its 150th anniversary in 2005. Individual offices support local causes, such as the Holborn Partnership in London which is championing Holborn's bid to become one of the UK's first business improvement districts – providing support for the local community as well as local businesses. Individuals (including Young) are given time off to do charitable work.

Corporate governance

As an accountancy firm, Saffery Champness is of course strictly regulated and takes issues of corporate governance very seriously. Issues from money laundering to data protection are championed at the highest level, with partners having specific responsibility.

Messrs Saffery and Champness were both founder members of the Institute of Chartered Accountants (ICAEW) in the nineteenth century, so the firm has a lot to live up to. "It's very important to us to be seen as absolutely beyond reproach in all areas of corporate governance and professional ethics," says Hall.

External accolades have included being only the second nationwide accountancy firm to be awarded Investors in People accreditation in 1997, and the firm scored highly when its accreditation was renewed in 2003. The six-person HR and training department has been awarded a platinum level trainer rating by the ICAEW.

Environmental record

One of Saffery Champness's clients is the World Wide Fund for Nature (WWF). In 2004, as part of a policy to vet its supply chain, the charity performed an environmental assessment on the firm and found that its policies were in line with best practice for an office-based provider of professional services.

The firm recycles as much waste as it can, and is even lobbying its local authority to increase the range of recyclable material it collects. Electricity usage is minimised by switching off unused lights and computers and having flat-screen PC displays, and the firm encourages use of public transport in London by providing season ticket loans but not car parking. The last time it upgraded its PCs, the old ones were sold to staff and the proceeds donated to charity.

Sage

Sage UK Ltd.
North Park, Newcastle upon Tyne NE13 9AA
Tel: (0) 191 294 3000 **Fax:** (0) 191 294 0002
Web: www.sage.co.uk www.sage.com **Email:** hr@sage.com

Pay and Benefits	6.7	Innovation	5.7
Promotion and Development	6.7	Diversity	6.9
Training	6.2	Social Responsibility	6.7
Travel opportunities	4.8	Corporate Governance	5.7
Culture	6.6	Environment	6.6
Total			**62.6**

Sage is the UK's leading provider of business management software to small and medium-sized businesses (SMEs). Over 500,000 businesses in the UK and over 4 million worldwide – from start-ups to multi-million enterprises – rely on Sage to manage their back office functions, including accounting and customer relationship management. Sage has 1,700 employees at its offices in Newcastle (head office), Winnersh (Reading), Manchester and Dublin. The Sage Group plc has over 8,000 employees worldwide in a decentralised, locally based organisation. In the recent European Call Centre Awards, Sage was voted Best Customer Experience and Best Workplace Environment.

Executive Summary

Tracing its origins to a Newcastle quayside printing works, Sage was launched in 1981 when it was among the first to spot the opportunity for "off the shelf" accounting software for small businesses. When the PC took off, so did Sages's sales. In 1989, Sage floated on the London Stock Exchange and the company's growth has been phenomenal ever since. Each year it has reported double-digit growth, having weathered two recessions and the IT stock slide. Since entering the FTSE 100 in 1999, Sage is the only technology stock that remains there to date.

For the year to September 30 2004, pre-tax profit rose 20% to £181m (from £151m in 2003 and £135m in 2002) on turnover of £687m. This reflects the long-term relationships it has nurtured with its customers through support contracts and clear upgrade paths – and also the acquisition of companies in vertical markets.

Sage is the most recognised brand in its sector. 50% of the companies in the UK that replaced their software in 2003 chose Sage – compared to just 12% for Microsoft and 7% for Intuit.

"The customer is number one at Sage", says Paul Stobart, UK managing director. "We take over 10,000 calls a day, providing – dare I say 'Sage counsel' – and best advice as much as technical support. Others say: 'how do you make money?' But we don't regard it as overhead – it's the business. We make products that customers want and give them the support they need."

Pay and Benefits

Sage offers remuneration commensurate with its position as a leading FTSE 100 company. Sara Kaye, UK human resources director, interprets this: "we pay upper quartile total compensation for upper quartile performance. It allows us to give our best people the best packages."

As people progress up the organisation, an increasing proportion of salary and bonus is skewed towards performance. Sales staff receive commission that, although not at "double-glazing levels", could be between 10% and 50% of salary.

Benefits are attractive and extensive – permanent health insurance, life assurance, 25 days' holiday and reduced-price gym membership are but a few; plus, car allowance and private medical insurance are available depending on position. Around 60–65% of the workforce is in one or other of the company's share ownership schemes, which are open to every employee on the payroll on New Year's Day each year. Sage operates a group personal pension scheme with employer contributions between 2% and 10%. The scheme enjoys an impressive 90% take-up – a consequence of the considerable effort Sage puts into communications, forums and pension workshops.

But interestingly, it's the little things that Sage employees talk about most. Like Nice One: a simple thank-you card and bottle of champagne that Sage hands out 20–30 times a month for a job well done – or exceeded. Like Golden Ticket: an employee nomination scheme that rewards great customer service with concert tickets. Employees fondly remember the free cinema tickets sent to them by Sage before they had even joined. The big Christmas party is really a big thank you to all staff, and has become the stuff of legend despite the company's youthful age. As a Premier Partner of Newcastle United, seats in the box often come employees' way in this football mad city. And don't underestimate esteem.

Promotion and development

Sage is the UK's largest software house and employs more software engineers (300 of them) than anyone else. Sales and marketing is crucial to Sage – at least 300 are employed in field and telesales, and a further 100 in marketing (including an in-house studio, and design and product marketing facilities). Customer service is the heartbeat of the company – one-third of the 1,700 UK staff work in this role – but it's anything but a call centre; this is a vital, technical support and advisory service, crammed with qualified graduates, engineers and ex-accountants.

Kaye says: "In the past twelve months, the number one priority has been to retain and develop our staff. It's one of the issues faced by high-growth companies – you're moving so fast, pouring resource in, that you don't always get development right." That's typical of Sage – forever self-deprecating, and trying to improve on an already impressive set-up. Expenditure on training and development has risen by 50% in each of the last two years. Much of this is spent "necessarily" in keeping people at all levels fully up to date on key skills (especially engineering and software development).

Personal career development is put firmly in the hands of the individual – the "manage your own career" philosophy. But the support framework and resources are there in force – delivered through workshops, personal development plans and a range of formal leadership programmes, projects and secondments. Across the company, there is an average of 8.5 days' employee training a year. Sage offers a highly supportive educational sponsorship programme, enabling employees to access courses that are directly or indirectly related to their field of work.

Promotion opportunities are considerable. Previously, the pace of growth was so rapid that external hiring was necessary due to lack of skills bandwidth, and job specifications expanding in size and scope. This has changed, and two recent promotions to the executive board of "local, through the ranks" employees is a sure sign that the indigenous talent stock is strengthening underneath. A clue to promotion? Technical support has often proved to be the primary platform for career progress – there's nothing more useful in Sage than experience of interacting directly with customers.

Sage's business is decentralised – built around local knowledge, local expertise and local customers. Sage is not like a conventional blue chip multinational in that sense. But with technology moving apace, Sage anticipates a greater need for people to move and work across borders.

Company culture

Paul Stobart says: "Sage has a clear vision – to be the business management software company that everyone recommends. This ties back to customer service. If we treat every interaction with customers with the utmost importance and sort out problems quickly, companies will evangelise our products. The power of customer advocacy makes this a circular and proven process."

This vision was not imposed, but came from within the organisation through a host of communications, focus groups and brainstorming. The result is a clear commitment to a vision that places customer service and the power of recommendation at the heart of everything that Sage does.

To support this, Sage has a very clear "people plan" which drives a modern and robust set of policies – evidenced by zero industrial tribunal cases, past or present. Sage even has a whistle-blowing helpline to support its zero tolerance stance on issues such as bullying and harassment.

Employees view their company as being go-getting, opportunistic, hard-working and highly ethical. Sage knows this through its regular culture assessment surveys. These have also revealed a shift in recent years – with the company now seen as more about ownership of values, about customers and the impact you make on your part of the business. As Sage has evolved from an acquisitive, fast-growth company, the impact of change has been felt greatest at management level. "We can see the 'bow wave' effect," suggests Kaye. "In terms of management style, there has been a shift from highly directive to highly collaborative; there are more signs at employee level that they feel genuinely empowered and listened to more."

The company has flexible working options, and more part-time workers than ever before. There are lots of return-to-work initiatives – including bonuses – and maternity and paternity schemes. "Any family-friendly policy you want to pick out, we have it," adds Geary. "We do what we can to encourage people to come back."

Sage's fabulous new open plan head office has been deliberately designed to encourage its culture of openness, interaction and information sharing – with compelling results. A collegiate atmosphere prevails. There are no offices for managers. Out of choice, Sage staff hold business meetings in the open places rather than behind closed doors.

Innovation

Sage was born of innovation and entrepreneurial flair, and the company goes to lengths to support creativity at the coalface. Under the banner GIV (Generating Ideas for Vision), employees are encouraged to contribute ideas to the business. But more than contribute – an online system allows an individual to own that idea, gain business sponsorship for it through to implementation, and gain recognition along the way.

The company is also innovative in the way it listens to customers. With hundreds of staff on the phone to customers all day, it has cleverly built an organic business with a clear upgrade path that makes it easy for customers to grow their software with their business.

Diversity and social responsibility

Sage operates an equal opportunities policy, and being "colour blind", does not carry out ethnic monitoring or set diversity targets. Women represent 50% of its total business population, perhaps surprising for a technical company. There are three female members of the UK executive board of ten, and one-third of senior managers are women.

Sage is proud of its local roots, so it's unsurprising then that it injects a lot back into its local communities. Each year, Sage produces a corporate social responsibility report on its community support activities. One example is a £250,000 pledge to the Tyne & Wear Foundation to provide grants that support education and employment in the region. The new £70m office building was designed and constructed exclusively by local contractors. One nice touch is the in-house coffee shop, run by a local person who approached Sage with a business start-up proposal and now serves "the best" cappuccinos to Sage's workforce. The company has also supported the development of a new national centre for music at Gateshead known as The Sage.

Corporate Governance

Sage is committed to high standards of corporate governance and ensures that it works in accordance with its requirements as a public limited company. The UK executive team meets formally a minimum of six times a year, and people issues are a standing agenda item. In addition, there are a number of specific committees, each chaired by members of the UK executive team – covering disaster recovery, health and safety, and reward, for example.

Environmental record

Sage does everything that it can to be environmentally friendly. There is a high profile and very active recycling scheme at all offices – the main area in which Sage can make a positive environmental impact – with recycling points on every business floor. Everything is recycled. Computer equipment is donated to local schools, associations and employees; and when Sage left its old premises, it gave away the furniture to charities and other groups. The buildings are designed, of course, to be energy efficient.

Samworth Brothers

Samworth Brothers
Chetwode House, Leicester Road, Melton Mowbray, Leicestershire LE13 1GA
Tel: (0) 1664 414500
Web: www.samworthbrothers.co.uk

Samworth Brothers
QUALITY FOODS

Pay and Benefits	5.1	Innovation	6.1
Promotion and Development	5.8	Diversity	5.8
Training	6.1	Social Responsibility	5.9
Travel opportunities	4.5	Corporate Governance	5.2
Culture	6.7	Environment	5.9
Total			**57.1**

Samworth Brothers is a privately owned company selling quality desserts, sausages, pork pies and related meat products to supermarkets and other retailers. It also owns Ginsters – the Cornwall-based company famed for its pasties, sausage rolls and sandwiches – and a handful of less well-known brands. It employs just over 5,000 people at its facilities in Leicestershire and Cornwall, and in recent years has been growing at 12–13%, taking turnover for 2004 to about £400m. The company prides itself on its treatment of its workers and the service it provides its customers in the highly competitive market of food retailing.

Executive Summary

The roots of Samworth Brothers go back more than a century, to a business founded in Birmingham by George Samworth. But the business as it currently exists started in the 1950s. Since then, three generations of the family have built a company that, while little known to the general public, is among the leading players in the British food industry. Still privately owned, it has nevertheless brought in outside management in the shape of Brian Stein – who has been chief executive since the mid-90s and has steered the group from an organisation with about 1,500 people and a turnover of £150m to the 5,000-strong, £400m business it is today.

As a private company, Samworth is not obliged to disclose its profits. But Stein says these have grown every year for the past decade – a fact that has enabled the company to invest heavily in facilities with the aim of prospering in a highly competitive market. It generally invests more than £20m a year, but in 2003 this was increased to £30m. A recent development has been the building of Saladworks – a £25m "snack salad" facility in Leicestershire built specifically to supply Tesco, the supermarket group which accounts for about half of Samworth's sales.

Pay and Benefits

Samworth prides itself on being a fair employer. Employees are required to work hard – particularly at Christmas and other peak periods, when a great deal of flexibility is required – but they are rewarded by good pay and conditions. The result is a high level of employee satisfaction that has in turn made it hard for unions to attract members.

The company's commitment to fairness is reflected in the fact that everybody – from the chief executive down – receives 24 days' holiday. Another sign is the profit pool. 8% of the profit is put into a pool in each business to be shared among the employees. This can amount to an annual February bonus of 2–8%.

A further key benefit is the company's maintenance of a final salary pension scheme at a time when many companies are moving to money-purchase or defined benefits plans. In addition, all permanent staff are covered by a healthcare policy on the grounds that keeping the staff healthy is key to the company's success. Stein thinks this is probably unique in manufacturing, but he believes it contributes to the stable workforce at a company that routinely hands out long-service awards and has many families employed in the business.

The company has deliberately not introduced flexible benefits, taking the view that it brings too much complexity and risks employees taking decisions about benefits that are not in their best long-term interests. "It's paternal, but it's right," says Stein.

While there is not a social club, there are various social activities including celebrations of business openings as well as parties for Christmas and other religious festivals. In keeping with their autonomy, each business is given the freedom to do whatever it deems appropriate. In addition, the rivalry between the group's companies ensures that there are closely fought sports matches.

Promotion and Development

The 80% retention rate among employees ensures that the company has a stable workforce from which it can promote managers. It is not unknown for somebody who starts at the company as temporary labour to become an area manager.

Typically, recruits start with a particular company within the group and gain experience of different operations there. Once established at a senior position in the particular business, the individual would then have the opportunity to move around the group. However, inter-company rivalries mean that there may be a battle for the individual's services; the group's management would then step in to ensure that the employee is not lost to the company overall.

Over recent years, the company has developed a graduate training scheme that sees six to eight university leavers a year join the company. Management is keen to encourage as many as possible into production, but sales and marketing is the most popular destination. Unlike many other training schemes, the emphasis is on the graduates doing a "real" job as soon as possible – "but with quite a lot of supervision", stresses Stein.

Each site has an "academy room" that is used for basic training and to develop staff. The facilities can also be used by individuals for their own development. Books, CD-Roms and other resources can be used to learn foreign languages or even to become more proficient at leisure pursuits, such as fly-fishing.

In view of the fact that many Samworth employees come from Leicester's large Asian community, the company has found the English for Speakers of Other Languages course that it has run with Leicester College especially popular. Nearly 100 employees have gone through it, and the company is considering extending it to members of employees' families.

Company Culture

Samworth's policy is to give a great deal of responsibility to each of the businesses within the group, with the aim of making the managers and staff more motivated than they otherwise would be. "We are very lean and mean at the centre. There's nobody here except the finance director and myself," says Stein. The result of this delegated approach is that each business is highly accountable. "There's nowhere for them to hide," he adds.

The company also makes an effort to make the facilities attractive – they are typically modern buildings set out in landscaped surroundings with plenty of car parking.

Samworth likes to think that it treats its employees well – but it monitors its efforts through an annual satisfaction survey that typically receives a response rate of greater than 80%. It commits itself to dealing with negative comments – on the basis that there will inevitably be occasions when it gets something wrong or fails to appreciate the ramifications of a particular policy or decision.

Absenteeism, the company admits, varies from plant to plant and will also depend on the time of year or the extent of overtime. It aims to deal with it fairly, and to share best practice within the group.

As a company serving the highly competitive food retailing business, where sudden rushes are common, Samworth finds helping its employees achieve a work/life balance difficult. However, managers are encouraged to ease the pain of this sort of situation by communicating the need for overtime as soon as possible, and giving time off when the work is slacker. In recognition of this, Stein himself does not have time off at Christmas.

Innovation

According to Stein, "food is like fashion – you need new ideas all the time". As a result, a lot of attention is paid to innovation. Each company has its own product development operation where chefs, technologists and others work together to satisfy the constant hunger for new foods.

The company – as part of its efforts to control costs and so maintain profitability in the face of pressure from the retailers – is also innovative in terms of processes for producing the food. For example, robotics have recently been introduced extensively. Stein stresses that any labour saved by the new devices has been reallocated to other parts of the business – so nobody has been made redundant as a result of the move.

Strategically, the company is also constantly looking ahead. While Stein recognises that much of the company's growth has been on the back of the extraordinary growth of its biggest customer – Tesco – he and his colleagues have been anxious to reduce the dependence on one customer. Consequently, it has begun to attract business from other supermarket groups, notably J. Sainsbury, Waitrose and Morrisons.

Moreover, Samworth believes its attitude to its staff is ahead of the norm and explains why it is able to recruit the staff it needs to fuel its growth, often from its rivals.

Diversity and Social Responsibility

Samworth Brothers has a highly diverse workforce – in the words of Stein, it is a "replica of Leicester". There are, for instance, 18 nationalities and 25 languages at the Bradgate Bakery plant alone.

While there are obvious issues, such as people from certain backgrounds not being willing to work with specific meats, the company claims not to have any problems stemming from having so many different peoples working alongside each other. In fact, it makes a point when there are disturbances in parts of the world of telling the staff that they should not bring their differences to work.

There are opportunities for people from all backgrounds to progress through the company – one of the company managing directors is Indian, for instance.

Similarly, there is a "good balance" between male and female workers, and three of the managing directors are women.

As far as the community is concerned, Stein chairs Leicester Cares – a local group linking business with the community – and he personally encourages all the companies to find some community activity that "motivates them and their staff". Most of the companies do some work with the schools in their areas, but the company also supports a home for battered women and helps with the rehabilitation of young offenders through placing youngsters in its distribution business.

Corporate Governance

As a private company, Samworth is not subject to the same rules and regulations as a company listed on the stock market. However, proprietor David Samworth has prepared for his retirement by following plc practice and appointing a team of non-executive directors to act as a balance to Stein.

As befits its growing size and the industry it is in, Samworth is careful about who it employs to make sure that all employees – even the temporary staff hired at peak times – have the right credentials and are trained in such key areas as food hygiene.

Environmental Record

Over the past two years, Samworth has established an environmental policy. As part of this, it has installed odour controls in many of its sites and focused on issues such as water use, recycling, energy consumption and fuel conservation.

A key part of its policy, though, concerns recycling of waste. With government regulations now forbidding the feeding of waste to farm animals, the company is looking at ways of obtaining fuel from waste and is involved in projects looking at different approaches. If one looks promising, the company will put money behind it, says Stein.

Scottish & Newcastle

Scottish & Newcastle, 33 Ellersly Road,
Edinburgh EH12 6HX
Tel: (0) 131 528 1858
Web: www.scottish-newcastle.com

Scottish & Newcastle

Pay and Benefits	7.1	Innovation	7.3
Promotion and Development	7.4	Diversity	6.5
Training	7.3	Social Responsibility	7.0
Travel opportunities	6.9	Corporate Governance	7.3
Culture	7.0	Environment	8.1
Total			**71.9**

Scottish & Newcastle (S&N) is one of Europe's leading brewers, and is in the top 10 in the world by sales volume. It is a company of international stature, with strong positions in 14 countries in Europe and Asia. It has three of the top ten brands in Europe – and it exports to more than 60 countries. From its head office in Edinburgh, it operates an international team whose recent goal has been to acquire international businesses. This international reach has seen the company grow rapidly over the last five years and now the challenge is to build leading beer brands such as Foster's, John Smith's Strongbow, Kronenbourg 1664 and Newcastle Brown.

Executive Summary

S&N traces its roots back to 1749 when the Younger Brewery was established in Leith. The Newcastle-half goes back to 1770 with the formation of Newcastle Breweries. In 1960, S&N was formed with the merger of Scottish Brewers and Newcastle Breweries.

S&N has changed considerably – as much as the attitudes and perceptions of the society it serves have changed, so too have the needs of its customers. Group pre-tax profit in 2003 was £159m, up from £146m the previous year, with earnings per share up from 11.5p to 12.8p. Cost-saving initiatives in the UK totalling £60m a year will be completed by the end of 2006 – and that is up from the previous target of £45m.

The beer market generally is in decline but the UK business, known until recently as Scottish Courage, is facing up to that challenge and is managing to grow market share because it has leading beer and cider brands.

It has continuously improved its business performance by not shrinking from painful decisions. In 2003, to tackle production over-capacity, it announced the closure of breweries in Edinburgh and Newcastle – in each case acquiring smaller, more modern and flexible facilities in the same area. This did not go down well with some of the headline writers, but employees seem to have understood and supported the initiatives, as have city commentators.

The company is pursuing a goal of being the best European beer-led drinks company; with sustained revenue growth, and consistently improving returns on capital. All this, whilst making inroads into China and India.

Pay and Benefits

S&N is also careful to keep tabs on pay and benefits to "ascertain our exact position currently relative to the market". It says that in doing this; it will also consider whether it is appropriate to have different positions relative to the market for different areas of expertise.

The plain language for this is "horses for courses" and that's fair enough. There are sweeteners. There is a results-related bonus scheme for executives and senior managers based on overall group performance, UK business performance and individual performance. There are also reward and recognition policies based on improvements in the performance in the business. This could include lump sums to people on an ad hoc basis for specific large pieces of work; and cash, vouchers and Red Letter Day experiences as a thank-you.

There is a share incentive scheme which includes free shares at the company's discretion – these are called "partnership shares" with employees making a monthly contribution and "matching shares" – for every two partnership shares bought with employee contributions, S&N gives a free matching share.

There is also a pension scheme. S&N has not escaped the pressure on company pension funds. The latest actuarial valuation of its pension plan showed a deficit of £424m, but the company has made a special contribution of £223m to show pension plan members that the security of pensions remains a key priority.

Promotion and Development

Coaching has top priority at S&N. It has its own coaching academy – putting "its money where its mouth is" as regards coaching and mentoring. The company is committed to a business-wide coaching culture, with employees given access to world-class professional coaches and mentors.

All new employees at senior management level are expected to embark on professional coaching and mentoring training. All managers are expected, as a minimum, to take a foundation level coaching programme which is linked to other systems such as performance management, selection and employee engagement.

The belief is that the emphasis on coaching in performance management enables employees to focus on being the best they can be in their job – being accountable for their own actions. Individuals will set their own objectives in discussion with their managers at the start of the year, and progress is reviewed regularly.

When being considered for new roles within the company, an individual's potential for coaching and carrying out effective performance management is assessed. This is followed by a short employee survey reporting at team level, which evaluates progress and points the way to further activity at team and organisation level.

As this is a multinational company, there are opportunities for moving internationally – particularly in Europe, where S&N owns interests in France, Belgium, Portugal, Finland and Greece. It also operates a joint venture in eastern Europe with Carlsberg called BBH. There is an international graduate recruitment programme for top multi-lingual business graduates keen to pursue a demanding career.

Company Culture

S&N makes and sells beer, cider and other "long" alcoholic drinks. When you visit its UK headquarters in Edinburgh, what the company does is in your face – the reception desk is two large eye-catching "show" bars, fonts and all. The company showcases its brands in a live environment, and employees can enjoy a relaxing drink there after work.

It is, after all, a drinks company and it takes these responsibilities seriously. Before last Christmas, it took the lead in responsible marketing with a message on its cans and bottles warning drinkers about the number of units they should not exceed. A bit more subtle than the "smoking can kill" warning required of the tobacco industry, but it earned S&N some plaudits. A marketing policy ensures that all promotional activity has a proper regard to responsible drinking – a theme that is part of the wider business culture.

S&N in the UK has been driven by a focus on customer service, and a passion for ensuring its leading beer and cider brands – Foster's, John Smith's, Strongbow and Kronenbourg 1664 – are available at the right time in the right place for trade customers and consumers (drinkers!).

The UK head office gives more clues about the culture. It's a new development and already an award-winner – with an open plan layout, which encourages greater informal communication and interaction. There are enough parking places for only half the employees who might want to drive to work. The company does not allocate spaces in line with grade and status – instead it has introduced a car share scheme, with employees joining registered car share groups and travelling to work together. S&N says it works a treat – but it can't be as much fun as beating the boss to the last parking space.

Innovation

Traditionally, the beer industry has not been good at innovation. But S&N is in a fiercely competitive market, and it recognises that innovation can sometimes give it the cutting edge.

Its technical team caused a revolution in the pub industry by making it simpler for bar staff to pour a creamy, longer lasting head on a pint of Foster's. This was no small achievement – rolled out to other brands in the S&N portfolio, it proved a success with beer drinkers.

S&N says that under-the-counter wizardry also means that beer can be served consistently cold – which is what drinkers want.

S&N has also brought to the bar a new white beer – Kronenbourg Blanc – that will be rolled out across the UK in 2005. Hopes are high that the female market will sup it up.

There are other ways of being innovative. S&N has linked with financial giant HBOS to lead the market in the provision of finance to independent pub owners – in partnership with major competitor Carlsberg – and independent brewing entrepreneurs, providing technical support services to pubs and bars nationwide.

Diversity and Social Responsibility

As a FTSE 100 company, S&N takes its corporate responsibilities seriously. It recognises that this is a crucial element in continuing to make the company successful and profitable. Given the nature of the business, S&N is committed to promoting the responsible consumption of its products. But to survive, it still has to make people buy them. According to Tony Froggatt, chief executive: "Responsibility and corporate success go hand in hand. If we develop and market our products in an irresponsible way, we soon wouldn't have a viable business."

S&N is a founder member of the Portman Group – the industry body which is responsible for promoting responsible drinking – and this has involved the development and introduction of a responsible marketing policy, guidelines to cover all promotions, and the introduction of unit labelling and responsible drinking messages on all products.

The UK business works with a variety of local and national good causes, and was a major supporter of the 2004 British Paralympic team.

It does not just practice diversity. It says that it "celebrates" it. The company policy is that it will not discriminate against any employee or external applicant, and will make full use of the talents and resources of the entire workforce.

Corporate Governance

The company remains committed to high standards of corporate governance and manages its affairs in accordance with the Combined Code issued by the Financial Services Authority. The board is headed by a non-executive chairman and comprises the chief executive, four further executive directors and six non-executive directors. There is an agreed list of matters that are always dealt with by the board, such as the approval of the group strategy plan and group budget, major acquisitions and disposals, and major capital spend.

The roles of the chairman and chief executive are separated. The chairman's role includes maintaining the strategic impetus of the group and developing the appropriate organisational structure for an international business. The chief executive is responsible for day-to-day operational affairs, particularly the challenges of integrating new acquisitions. He also chairs the Executive Management Group, which is responsible for delivering operational objectives.

There is a strong Audit Committee that monitors the integrity of the company's financial statements; it reviews accounting policies, accounting treatments and disclosures in financial reports as well as keeping an eye on the company's whistle-blowing procedures. It also monitors the relationship with the external auditor, including assessing independence and objectivity.

Environmental Record

With its core ingredients being water and agricultural produce (such as barley, hops and apples), the continuous protection of the environment has to be a fundamental way of life for S&N so that it can continue to harness natural products of the highest quality.

A key focus of the company approach is to continuously improve its operations, and to develop its environmental management structures to ensure that the right plans are in place.

As an example, it has identified the consequences of climate change as having the potential to affect the company business in a number of ways. These include changes in agricultural growth patterns, the availability of water and changes in consumer behaviour.

The company is developing a three-year management plan designed to reduce the impact of its operations on the climate. S&N's aims are to operate the business as efficiently as possible and help to reduce emissions of greenhouses gases – while bringing costs down. The company has taken a lead in the UK in dealing with the implementation of the European Integrated Pollution Prevention and Control Directive, and it plans to have all its wholly owned sites in the UK certified to ISO 14001.

Severn Trent Water

Severn Trent Water
2297 Coventry Road, Sheldon, Birmingham B26 3PU
Tel: (0) 121 722 4000 **Fax:** (0) 121 722 4800
Web: www.stwater.co.uk **Email:** recruitment@severntrent.co.uk

Severn Trent Water

Pay and Benefits	6.2	Innovation	6.6
Promotion and Development	7.3	Diversity	7.0
Training	6.1	Social Responsibility	7.0
Travel opportunities	6.0	Corporate Governance	6.1
Culture	6.0	Environment	7.6
Total			**65.9**

Severn Trent Water serves more than 8 million customers across the heart of the UK – stretching from the Bristol Channel to the Humber, and from mid-Wales to the East Midlands. It is part of Severn Trent plc, an international utility services and environmental solutions company that is one of the largest companies listed on the London Stock Exchange. The group, which includes the Biffa waste management company and Severn Trent Laboratories, generates revenues of £2.015bn and employs more than 15,000 people across the United States, the UK and the rest of Europe.

Executive summary

Severn Trent Water Ltd was formed in October 1989. Previously it had been known as the Severn Trent Water Authority, which was created through the merger in 1974 of 137 local authorities, two river boards, 14 joint water boards and two joint sewerage boards.

While many other utility companies change hands and struggle to make money, Severn Trent has been consistently profitable and is one of the best-regarded companies in its sector. In the year to March 2004, it achieved turnover of £945m and made a pre-tax profit of £228m. Since privatisation, the company has spent about £500m a year on capital expenditure projects, mainly involving pipelines and other aspects of infrastructure.

The company is based in Birmingham, but has other offices across the whole of the Severn Trent operation. There are also two sister companies: Severn Trent Retail Services, which offers customers discounts on gas, electricity, phone bills and insurance cover; and Severn Trent Utility Services, which provides the company's expertise to other businesses. It employs about 5,000 staff, mainly in the field.

Pay and Benefits

Severn Trent offers its entire staff a competitive overall package. It uses a well-known human resources consultancy to ensure that its pay remains among the most attractive in its sector. Staff typically have between 28 and 31 days' holiday a year, and have good healthcare cover. A particular plus at this time of uncertainty over pensions is the fact that the company retains its final salary pension scheme for all existing employees. New arrivals have to complete 10 years' service before qualifying.

Another key element is employee share ownership. The company operates an employee sharesave scheme, and 97% of employees own a stake in the company. Staff typically receive 1% of their pay in free shares.

There is also a bonus scheme, under which managers are eligible for payments of as much as 20% of their salary.

The company has also followed the developing trend towards flexible benefits. Employees can, for instance, buy or sell up to five days' holiday a year, and they can also opt for different healthcare arrangements for themselves and their families.

In addition, it is supporting government initiatives to grant employees tax breaks on personal computers and childcare vouchers.

The flexibility extends to working arrangements, too. Many staff work part time or flexitime, or take part in job shares. There is also a career-break option whereby employees can (after five years' service) take up to a year off and return to the same job or a similar role to the one they left.

In addition to an active sports and social club, there is a subsidised canteen.

Paul Stephenson, director of HR services, believes that such elements play a large part in the company having a comparatively low staff turnover rate of less than 5%.

Promotion and development

There are two key aspects to Severn Trent's approach to developing its staff.

First, there is a proper appraisal system for everybody in the company. This not only drives individual performance, but also enables each member of staff to carry out a personal development plan (PDP).

Stephenson stresses that nobody is forced to do a PDP – on the grounds that "some people might be very happy to do the same next year as this". But he says it means that everybody has the opportunity to include in it any desire for training or career aspirations.

The second aspect is the company's succession planning process. This operates on several levels, starting at the top with the directors and senior managers. Regular reviews ensure that the company is doing what is needed to equip talented people with the skills they need to get to the top.

But even before staff reach such levels, they are given a lot of help and support in developing their careers. Each year, 15 to 20 graduates are chosen for a 12-month programme, which involves them being allocated to particular parts of the business. The disciplines will depend upon the area in which the graduate is working, but all must have at least 2:1s. In 2003, Severn Trent won an award for its graduate website for companies recruiting less than 20 graduates.

Once selected, recruits are helped in acquiring whatever professional qualifications are required for their function. They are also given the opportunity to work overseas through secondment in Severn Trent's sister companies.

Company culture

One of the issues for a company like Severn Trent is the sheer breadth of its activities. Because it stretches from a research and development unit employing mainly degree-educated engineers and programme analysts, to a section employing production staff paid to dig holes, there are in fact many different cultures within it.

The company has worked hard recently to build a culture around a simple values statement: "We care" – about colleagues, company, customers and communities. The company directors have concentrated on making sure employees understand the meaning of all the headings. But particular focus has been placed on making the business more customer-focused. While industrial customers have some choice in their water supplier, domestic customers have no choice. Nevertheless, the company wants employees to treat customers more like those of other businesses, and to think in terms of what it is like to be one.

To encourage this, a service champion scheme has been introduced in the past year. Under this, members of the public or fellow employees can nominate members of staff for awards that can lead to them receiving retail vouchers for good work in customer service.

This effort to make Severn Trent "more vibrant and more customer-focused" has been recognised by the industry regulator, Ofwat, which in 2003 ranked the company top in its overall performance assessment – a process that includes such measures as interruptions to customer supply and response to complaints, as well as more technical issues including water pressure. Over the last few years, the company has generally been in the top three.

Innovation

As a technical business, Severn Trent is committed to innovation in such areas as investigating different types of water treatment. This has been rewarded by a Queen's Award for Innovation for a water-testing kit it developed.

The company spends between £4m and £5m a year on research and development; as well as forming links with several universities, it is one of the biggest supporters of UK Water Industry Research, a body formed by one of its former executives.

In addition, Severn Trent seeks to be innovative in its HR practices. It has, for example, put in place a partnership agreement with the trade unions that has won recognition in Downing Street. It was also the first water company to win a five-star health and safety award from the British Safety Council.

It is especially proud of Harmony, a health and wellbeing programme that is open to all employees. It used to operate company gyms – and still offers subsidised health club membership – but feels that this programme (covering such areas as stress, diet and rest as well as exercise) is valuable to a wide range of employees, not least because it enables them to devise personal programmes to promote their health and wellbeing at home and at work.

Diversity and Social Responsibility

Severn Trent is working hard to make its workforce more diverse in terms of race and sex – though Stephenson points out that, with a staff turnover rate of only 5%, it is going to take a while to make an appreciable difference.

In the meantime, it has put in place various programmes aimed at raising awareness of the issue. For example, a booklet has been sent to all employees, and sessions on diversity issues form part of management training. In addition, representatives from all across the business meet every two months to discuss diversity issues.

The company was recently named best newcomer in Race for Opportunity, a Business in the Community project involving more than 180 businesses working to make race and diversity central to their plans.

As part of the company's commitment to communities under its "we care" slogan, extensive links have been formed with schools, charities and other local groups. Among the many corporate schemes is a project working with teachers to promote children's understanding of the water cycle. In addition, the Severn Trent Trust Fund helps those customers who have trouble paying their bills.

The business makes charitable donations and encourages employees to give through payroll deductions; it also allows staff to take time off each year to work with charities or local communities.

Corporate Governance

This is particularly important because Severn Trent operates in a regulated industry. It is required to provide regular reports to Ofwat (the water industry regulator) and the Drinking Water Inspectorate, and to public health doctors and environmental health officers. In general, the company receives a favourable response from those bodies responsible for it.

As a result, it has developed policies on decision-making that are broadly in line with those in similar businesses. There is, says Stephenson, "a huge amount of transparency in the way that the company operates". For example, contracts awarded to suppliers are listed on the company's website.

Environmental Record

Again, as a regulated business operating in the environmental services field, this is a very important area for Severn Trent. As a result, a huge amount of investment goes into the infrastructure of pipes in order to reduce wastage; and there have been great efforts to improve water quality – leading to a 50% improvement in river quality since 1990. This in turn has led to the reappearance of salmon, otters and other species in Midlands' rivers. These efforts have been recognised with various environmental awards, including the Green Apple award for its approach to the environment and sustainability.

In addition, the company has acted ahead of a government aim for businesses to obtain 5% of their energy from renewable sources – they have developed a means of generating power from sludge that produces about 8% of the company's electricity.

The commitment to the environment goes to the top, where Severn Trent's parent company has been named as the leading utility in the Dow Jones Sustainability World Index for the fourth year in a row.

Shire Pharmaceuticals

Shire Pharmaceuticals, Hampshire International Business Park
Chineham, Basingstoke, Hampshire RG24 8EP
Tel: (0) 1256 894 000 **Fax:** (0) 1256 894 708
Web: www.shire.com **Email:** csr@shire.com

Shire

Pay and Benefits	6.5	Innovation	7.9
Promotion and Development	6.5	Diversity	7.1
Training	5.9	Social Responsibility	6.5
Travel opportunities	6.5	Corporate Governance	6.7
Culture	7.1	Environment	7.5
Total			**68.2**

Founded in 1986, Shire Pharmaceuticals is now the third-largest pharmaceutical company in the UK and one of the fastest growing specialist pharmaceutical companies in the world. Headquartered in Basingstoke, the company has a broad portfolio of products and its own direct marketing capability in the US, Canada, UK, Republic of Ireland, France, Germany, Italy and Spain. It sells through distributors to other European countries and the Pacific Rim; and has a regional office in Singapore, which manages its distributors in the Far East. The Shire Group has grown rapidly over the past few years through six mergers and acquisitions. Its revenues for 2003 were $1.24bn – up 19% on the previous year – and its operating income was $394.6m.

Executive summary

Shire Pharmaceuticals was founded in 1986 by a husband and wife team in a tiny office above a shop in Hampshire, and was floated on the London Stock Exchange in February 1996. Over the past six years, it has grown rapidly by merging with six other pharmaceutical companies that brought in new products, new expertise and new strengths.

Shire focuses on building personal relationships with hospital doctors and specialists in three main areas of medicine: central nervous system, gastrointestinal and kidney disease. It has steered clear of high-risk early-stage research, concentrating instead on developing late stage, lower risk projects – often buying in or licensing developing projects and marketed products.

Shire has clearly defined financial goals that include high operating profit, above average annual sales growth and investment in drug development, and aggressive earnings per share targets.

Pay and benefits

Shire aims to pay competitively and uses primarily independent salary surveys – Allen Jones and Towers Perrin – to benchmark its salaries against other companies in the pharmaceutical sector. Pay is generally reviewed annually, but the recently promoted or those on development plans can receive performance-related pay reviews more frequently than this.

On top of this, anyone working in a professional role within the company is eligible for an annual bonus ranging from 10–40% of basic salary.

Shire has three discretionary stock option schemes and a sharesave scheme. Uptake of these is high: around 75% of its employees own shares in the organisation.

There is a company pension scheme, plus a range of other benefits. These include life assurance based on full salary, accident and permanent health insurance which lasts until retirement if need be, and medical insurance. Senior managers are offered company cars or a cash alternative, and company cars are also provided to more junior staff who need them for their work. The Basingstoke office has a restaurant and free gym for employees.

Shire offers generous maternity and paternity leave, and a bonus to help with childcare once employees return to work. It also aims to design flexible working packages – including job shares, part-time working and flexible working hours – to employees who have dependent children, in line with business needs.

Promotion and development

Over the past few years, Shire has grown rapidly through merger and acquisition, giving plenty of scope for upward mobility through the organisation; during 2004, 87 of its 349 UK staff were promoted. There is an annual performance review for all employees.

Shire employs highly skilled and trained people, and so far, the company has been focusing on bringing in external expertise rather than untrained staff. Therefore, there is no formal company-wide graduate training scheme in place.

Sales and marketing is a core Shire competence, which enables the company to achieve maximum revenues through effective targeting of prescribers – sales and marketing people account for nearly half its UK staff. New sales employees undertake a thorough induction programme (lasting 15–22 days), followed by sales training for two days each month with the company's four full-time field sales trainers. They also receive regular skills training and updates on the company's new products.

For the 80 or so research and development staff, training and development is controlled by the Medicines and Healthcare Products Regulatory Agency. They expect to see clear job descriptions and up-to-date training plans, including training in the latest good clinical practice.

For the remaining employees working in corporate roles, job descriptions are too diverse for general company-wide training plans. Development and training is closely tied to their role, so the company works out individual development plans for them.

Company culture

As a dynamic and fast-growing company, Shire does not have the massive infrastructure found in larger pharmaceutical companies. It is not necessarily the place for those who want a quiet life and predictable career progression – but it does offer an open, entrepreneurial, non-bureaucratic culture where initiative and communication are encouraged and rewarded, and new opportunities are constantly opening up. The people who thrive there are energetic, committed, and prepared to work on their own initiative.

Shire's core values are integrity, respect, customer focus and global teamwork. It places high emphasis on communicating with its employees and listening to their views through company newsletters, the global intranet and regular employee meetings. Its 2003 employee survey received replies from three-quarters of the workforce – an exceptionally high response rate reflecting employees' high level of involvement with the company and its goals.

The company recognises that, given the changes the business is going through, it has to work hard to build a globally united company and keep people positively challenged and motivated.

Though Shire is committed to rapid growth and profit maximisation, it also believes in looking outwards and making a contribution to the wider community. This is reflected in its rigorous environmental policy and thriving programme of community involvement.

Innovation

In contrast with larger pharmaceutical companies, Shire gives its employees plenty of scope for personal responsibility and innovation in their work. The business makes extensive use of electronic communications between its global offices. It uses videoconferencing for meetings with international colleagues, and has implemented a global intranet for knowledge sharing.

Shire is not innovative in the sense of carrying out cutting-edge research in high-risk areas. Its strategy is to licence products at a later stage of development, and use its skills in sales and marketing to carry them through to commercial launch. However, it has been responsible for the launch of a number of innovative products including Xagrid (a drug for use in bone-marrow disorders) and Fosrenol (combating the side-effects of kidney dialysis); it is the US market leader in drugs to help with attention deficit and hyperactivity disorders.

Diversity and social responsibility

Shire is an equal opportunities employer committed to a diverse workforce. It believes that a diverse workforce is a more creative workforce – and that creativity is vital to its future success.

Shire's board reviews the company's approach to corporate social responsibility, taking advice from the CSR committee. This was set up in 2003 and is chaired by the chief financial officer. It meets three times a year.

In the Guardian Giving List 2003, Shire was ranked fourth in the FTSE 100 for its charitable giving, up from 17th the year before. It prefers long-term relationships to short-term donations; it prefers to work closely with a smaller number of groups than to give many small donations to multiple charities. It will also match employees' donations to charity; for example, when a group of employees took part in the Race for Life to raise money for cancer research, Shire topped up the sponsorship money they raised.

Shire's charity work often relates to its key research areas, in particular mental health. The company provided funding for Mind's Eye, a not-for-profit Arts in Health Association, to run a series of art workshops aimed at promoting the wellbeing of people who suffer from mental health disorders. It works closely with the Alzheimer's Society and recently funded a social event for Alzheimer's sufferers and their carers.

Employees are encouraged to help local causes in company time. Many of them go out to local schools to read to children, while others are school governors.

Corporate Governance

Shire is committed to high standards of corporate governance. In July 2003, its new Combined Code on Corporate Governance was published and took effect for the 2004 financial year – though the company had already started to comply with it before then.

Shire has an integrated risk management and internal audit function. The head of risk and audit reports to the chief financial officer and attends audit committee meetings. Through its audit committee, Shire has established formal arrangements for financial reporting, internal control and external auditing. The audit committee oversees the company's risk management activities as a whole, as well as the financial aspects of internal control.

Shire has a whistle-blowing policy through which all employees can report concerns about financial disclosure, internal control and other compliance issues. The audit committee has also introduced a procedure for monitoring complaints relating to internal controls.

Shire's board is made up of two executive and six non-executive directors, and meets at least five times a year. It has overall responsibility for managing the company and its strategic direction.

The company aims to provide a safe environment for its employees. In 2000, it started to carry out regular safety audits using British Safety Council guidelines. It has already achieved four stars in the BSC rating system, unusual for a company its size, and is now working towards gaining five stars.

Environmental record

Shire has had a formal environmental policy in place since 2002, and this is reviewed annually. Angus Russell, chief financial officer and chairman of the CSR committee, has overall responsibility at board level for environmental matters. The environmental policy is reviewed regularly; all staff are made aware of it and encouraged to consider environmental issues as part of their role.

The company aims to promote good environmental practice through its purchasing policy and by cutting down its consumption of resources such as energy or water – for example, in its Basingstoke headquarters, the office lighting switches off after a while if nobody is around. During 2004, it held an Energy Efficiency Roadshow to raise awareness of energy-saving issues, and employees who attended were given free 12-year low-energy lightbulbs.

Items such as paper and printer cartridges are recycled. At its key production sites, Shire monitors emissions and discharges with the aim of achieving cost-effective reductions in pollution levels.

All Shire's suppliers are required to comply with environmental regulations, and are monitored to ensure their continuing environmental good practice. Environmental issues are also taken into account whenever the company is planning mergers, acquisitions or business development.

Slimming World

Slimming World,
PO Box 55, Alfreton, Derbyshire DE55 4UE.
Tel: (0) 870 330 7733
Web: www.slimming-world.com **Email:** humanresources@slimming-world.com

Pay and Benefits	6.8	Innovation	7.0
Promotion and Development	7.3	Diversity	5.8
Training	8.0	Social Responsibility	7.0
Travel opportunities	4.0	Corporate Governance	6.8
Culture	6.8	Environment	6.4
Total			**65.9**

Slimming World was founded in 1969 by Margaret Miles-Bramwell, who started with the belief that slimmers like herself needed more and better help than was then available. She remains the chairman and driving force behind the company, which has grown into an organisation of 250,000 members attending 5,500 groups run by a network of 2,500 self-employed consultants around the country. It is the largest independent slimming organisation in the UK. As well as running the slimming groups, it publishes Slimming World magazine – the best-selling diet title in the UK – and has pioneered a referral service with the National Health Service.

Executive Summary

As a private company owned solely by Miles-Bramwell and her husband, Tony Whittaker (who acts as chief executive), the company is not obliged to report details of its financial performance. However, its strong record of growth – including a period between 1989 and 1995, when it doubled in size – is an indication of the company's success. Attractive open plan offices in Derbyshire (with a hair and beauty salon and fitness centre onsite), investment in a state-of-the-art website, and money spent on the training and development of its staff provide further indications.

Moreover, the managing director, Caryl Richards, sees the current national concern about obesity as providing plenty of opportunity for future growth and for the company to move towards its target of 1 million members. Over 25 million people in the UK are overweight, with 7 million of them so overweight that their health suffers. With Slimming World and its chief rivals – Weight Watchers and the Rosemary Conley organisation – only looking after 1 million of them, there is, says Richards, "a significant need for Slimming World to increase our reach and develop our service to potential slimmers".

The focus of Slimming World is firmly on the members – it is supportive rather than judgemental – and people are only recruited to the company if they are felt to have the right attitude towards slimmers.

Pay and Benefits

Slimming World has a highly competitive salary structure. On top of good basic pay packages, the various levels of manager in the field have the opportunity in most cases to double their earnings through bonuses – with the highest-ranking standing to take home about £80,000 a year. The earnings of the consultants running the groups depend upon the size and number of their groups. Individuals pay a few hundred pounds for the licence to operate in a certain area and for the training provided by Slimming World; they can then earn over £25,000 a year for around 20 hours per week through earning commission of 50% on each membership fee (just less than £4 a session).

On top of this, the company provides 26 days' holiday a year plus bank holidays. There are often additional days at Christmas, when there are also parties and presents for all staff and cash bonuses as part of Miles-Bramwell's determination to keep the company a family affair.

The company also pays 50% of nursery fees, offers a stakeholder pension, and provides BUPA medical cover for senior managers. There is a subsidised staff restaurant offering the sorts of meals the organisation recommends for its members and "free-flowing fruits and drinks"; staff receive a discount at the onsite beauty salon; and the new onsite fitness centre is free to all employees.

On the other hand, the company does not pay sick pay – though staff can use up to six of the 26 days' annual holiday as sick leave or as additional paid working days for other reasons if they prefer (which many do). The company has extremely low sickness levels, with a number of staff recently receiving special commendations for not a single day of absence due to sickness in 5 years!

Promotion and Development

Recruitment from within is so important for Slimming World that it makes a point of selecting its managers from members so that they have a total understanding of what the organisation is about, and feel very strongly about the importance of the service. Richards herself started as a member, then ran a group and became an area manager before becoming managing director in 2001.

Though some managers are hired for their expertise in such areas as human resources and information technology, the majority develop within the company.

New consultants are offered a minimum of three days' training at Alfreton headquarters before they start and then two more days within the first 14 weeks, though individuals can return for refreshers as often as they wish. Some go back every year – "it's not an easy job" supporting people who may be suffering from low esteem through a challenging programme, points out Richards.

Individuals are also supported through training in specific roles. For example, those in marketing are encouraged to seek marketing qualifications; while those in facilities management, information technology and accounts train in their relevant disciplines. In addition, many staff have gone through NVQs.

The company also believes in equipping its managers to train the people for whom they are responsible. Richards, in particular, is keen to put senior managers in a position where they can "train and coach everybody they manage" rather than relying on outside training providers. Where outside expertise is used, the company fosters a collaborative approach and prefers long-term partnerships. With managers developing certain specialisms, they have begun training each other's staff in certain skills.

Company Culture

Slimming World recruits employees primarily on the basis of their attitude to slimmers. Recruits have to be able to deal with people in a warm, supportive manner and – importantly – have a sense of fun. Through choosing not to follow the marketing route of its rivals, Slimming World relies on its members succeeding in their aim of achieving weight loss, and recommending the organisation to their friends – about half the company's business comes in this way.

It realises that to achieve this goal requires mutual cooperation and mutual trust, so for example, consultants are given all the support they require to help their clients change often life-long habits.

What this means in practical terms is set out in the company's "management philosophy", which – among other things – states that "the company expects managers to manage in a way which gets the best outcome for the company whilst respecting the needs and rights of the people they manage". It adds: "managers should encourage their teams to take responsibility for their own decisions within the framework of the aims of the company. If they are not doing this, managers need to help people to recognise their capabilities and then motivate them to use those capabilities".

This means that even the call centre is run differently from the norm. Not only are staff allowed to take breaks, but Richards points out that expecting staff to deal sensitively with callers is not compatible with rating them according to the speed with which they deal with calls.

Moreover, bullying or dictatorial management styles are expressly not tolerated.

Innovation

From its early days, Slimming World has worked hard to understand the issues behind obesity and so be in a better position to help those seeking to lose weight. In collaboration with universities and other bodies, it has carried out extensive research into nutrition, the physiology and psychology of slimming, and the lifestyle causes of obesity. This has helped it to develop the Food Optimising concept that enables members to lose weight while still eating a lot.

It helps to spread the word about diet through its highly successful magazine, which is produced by an in-house team at its Derbyshire HQ.

It has also embraced the internet, launching a free online support service for its members, and a separate paid-for service that attracted 6,000 members within its first few months of operation. The company is looking at equipping its consultants around the country with PDAs, so that they can more easily transfer to head office the members' data that is so vital to developing a greater understanding of obesity.

Perhaps most significant, though, is the work it has done to encourage National Health Service doctors to refer overweight patients to Slimming World. Previously, GPs have been reluctant to work with the commercial sector, but with concern about obesity growing, the company has piloted a feasibility study to show how a partnership between health professionals and Slimming World could prove a successful method of tackling the issue.

Diversity and Social Responsibility

Though Slimming World is an overwhelmingly female environment, there are significant numbers of men around. Only 56 of the consultants are men, but there are six team managers and four district managers who are male, while the IT department is largely male. Men are also heavily represented in the finance, facilities, and stock and distribution areas.

As for social responsibility, Slimming World – for all its growth – remains very much part of the community in which its founder lived. It still uses three local printers for its training and marketing materials, while the original semi-detached house in which the business started has been donated to the area as a cyber cafe.

In addition, the company's charity work has raised £1.2m since 1995. Its own charity effort – Slimmers Making It a Little Easier for Someone (SMILES) – was personally set up by Miles-Bramwell; and individual members and employees are encouraged to devise their own means of raising funds as well as taking part in company initiatives.

Corporate Governance

As a private company owned outright by a single proprietor, Slimming World is not really affected by corporate governance rules.

Environmental Record

The company has – for a business – a limited effect on the environment. None the less, it is conscious of its responsibilities in this area and makes an effort to recycle paper. Its planned technological changes could also reduce the amount of paper being used.

St Ann's Hospice

St Ann's Hospice
St Ann's Road North, Heald Green, Cheadle SK8 3SZ
Tel: (0) 161 437 8136 **Fax:** (0) 161 498 3671
Web: www.sah.org.uk **Email:** enquiries@sah.org.uk

St Ann's Hospice

Pay and Benefits	5.7	Innovation	6.5
Promotion and Development	5.7	Diversity	6.3
Training	5.7	Social Responsibility	7.3
Travel opportunities	3.7	Corporate Governance	7.0
Culture	7.1	Environment	6.2
Total			**61.2**

St Ann's Hospice is an independent local charity, which works to improve the quality of life of people living with life-threatening illnesses. Care is provided free of charge to over 3,000 people each year across three sites in Greater Manchester. The organisation employs 300 full-time staff, and up to 50 bank staff who can be brought in to meet operational needs.

Executive summary

The history of St Ann's began in 1971 with the establishment of a hospice in Heald Green. Initially set up to meet demand from the local regional cancer care unit, the hospice became over time a service provider for patients diagnosed with a range of life-threatening illnesses. Specialising in pain control and symptom management, St Ann's was the first modern hospice in the north of England. Demand was sufficiently great for a second unit, which opened in 1979, in Little Hulton. In 1998, St Ann's took over the running of the Neil Cliffe Cancer Care Centre, a day therapy centre offering rehab and support for people affected by cancer.

Maintaining the services offered by the hospice costs about £8.5m each year. About one third of this is government-funded through local primary care trusts. The remainder is sourced through voluntary contributions – some from trade at six charity shops, and some courtesy of a proprietary lottery scheme. There are, in addition, two fundraisers (who assist local organisations in raising funds on behalf of St Ann's), an events organiser, and a corporate fundraiser. Further funding is derived from legacy giving.

With the cost burden of running a hospice so significant, St Ann's places a particular premium on operational efficiency. So much so that the chief executive, Terry McDonnell, can boast, "One of the things I am most proud of is that out of every £1 we spend, 81 pence goes on direct patient care. Our administration and infrastructure costs are significantly lower than most charities of our size."

Pay and benefits

In the recent past, St Ann's was facing an uphill struggle to recruit sufficient numbers of clinical staff – who comprise 85% of the workforce. A key reason for this was its less than progressive approach to remuneration. Although pay scales for consultants, doctors and nursing staff were comparable to those found in the NHS, there was no provision for work during unsociable hours. Today, the hospice has adjusted its remuneration to reflect the irregular work patterns that are a hallmark of the care industry. It also permits staff recruited from the NHS to retain their pension arrangements should they wish to do so. St Ann's own pension scheme is of the stakeholder variety; the organisation will match contributions up to 7% of pay.

Other benefits include free parking for employees, and childcare vouchers which can be collected as part of a salary sacrifice scheme. All full-time staff are entitled to 35 days' paid holiday each year, which – in a nod to flexible working – may include bank holidays. There is a sliding scale approach to sick pay, so that a person with at least one year's service is entitled to up to one month on full pay; a person with two years' service, two months; and so on.

Promotion and development

St Ann's head of education coordinates all training for clinical staff. In-house developmental support covers a wide range of topics, such as drugs and bereavement. The hospice has built a strong reputation for expertise in symptom management and pain control, so employees undergoing training in these subjects may find themselves studying alongside staff from other medical and care establishments. Much of the learning is based on experience, though this complements a classroom-based approach to more technical material (for example, developments in syringe driver use).

Recently, the hospice expanded its overall commitment to staff development by creating a head of training for non-clinical staff. According to McDonnell, the position carries no less weight in the organisation. "It sent out a clear message to those staff about our culture, that they are treated as importantly as anyone else. Patient feedback tells us that the work of non-clinical staff is valued greatly, whatever their role," he says.

While there is a high standard of professionalism at St Ann's, this is not achieved in a coercive or heavy-handed fashion. Accordingly, the Individual Performance Review (IPR) to which everyone is subject is a genuine partnership between individual and supervisor, rather than interrogation masquerading as appraisal. Objectives are agreed and a training plan put in place to help meet them.

All vacancies are advertised internally, though a number of senior staff are recruited from other or similar vocations. Additional online learning tools – for a foreign language, for example – can also be accessed though a LearnDirect hosting facility.

Company Culture

The uninitiated might be forgiven for expecting a hospice that treats people with life-threatening illnesses to be a rather gloomy environment. It's an assumption that McDonnell understands but is keen to correct. "When I first came here I thought the job would be quite heavy, but actually there's an awful lot of laughter here. We have visitors who dread coming through our doors because they think it will be a depressing place, and without exception they say to us 'It's not what we expected at all'."

That it is an upbeat, at-ease-with-itself organisation is doubly significant because just a few years earlier, St Ann's was – by the chief executive's own admission – a very different place. Then cliques, a lack of trust and risk-aversion were the order of the day. Now there is a genuine listening culture; and one single corporate agenda, rather than a number of competing agendas. Above all, there is a high level of communication in all directions. All issues relating to St Ann's operations are covered in a monthly team briefing, which is cascaded down via line managers; the personnel director chairs a regular meeting of staff reps; and there are monthly and quarterly magazines focusing on staff and patient activities distributed to staff, volunteers and supporters.

Many staff get involved in fundraising activities – past events have included a stay in a "haunted" castle and a parachute jump. Last Christmas, nurses staged a panto in which some patients participated.

Innovation

"In terms of our services, we're at the leading edge for palliative care," says McDonnell. "Some of our work with regard to assessment documentation is being adopted by other organisations in developing a package of care for inpatients."

Early in 2005, St Ann's was set to pioneer the practice of including patients in the communications regarding their condition, by copying letters between healthcare professionals. This follows a research finding that patients wanted access to all the information on their health status. It represents a good example of how the hospice lives up to its promise to work with patients to develop an appropriate package of care, rather than act unilaterally.

This applies equally to the growing number of people who want to die at home. McDonnell comments, "We also plan to appoint a user involvement facilitator. This will see someone specifically appointed to ensure that in everything we do, users and carers alike are at the forefront of our clinical practice. It's about building better links with patients when they are at home, or when they are not actively in need of medical attention."

Diversity and social responsibility

St Ann's equal opportunities policy aims to ensure equal treatment of all employees, and states that recruitment and development decisions must be scrutinised to ensure that they do not directly or indirectly disadvantage one group of people against another. Most staff are recruited locally, and with each of the three sites located in an area with little ethnic minority representation, this has tended to be reflected in the workforce composition.

With regard to social responsibility, the hospice has a youth officer whose role is to raise the profile of St Ann's through visits to local schools and colleges. In 2003, the hospice launched a Young Volunteer of the Year competition, and helped organise 25 fundraising activities in educational establishments. Feedback from the participating schools has been very positive, in part because the initiative has helped them to fulfil the citizenship module requirements of the national curriculum.

St Ann's has a number of corporate sponsors, and regularly arranges placements for staff from these businesses who benefit from education on the nature of hospice care.

Corporate governance

Overseeing all the hospice's activities is a board of voluntary trustees from a variety of backgrounds, all of whom are at or near the top of their chosen field. Accounting, legal, HR and health professions are all represented – there is even a vicar for spiritual support.

The board meets every two months, and will receive briefings and reports from three separate strategic committees: audit, finance and staff representatives. In addition, there is an operational group, which examines service governance issues. Chaired by a head of governance, it carries out audits in clinical and non-clinical staff and patient fields. This meets on a monthly basis, as does the risk management committee.

St Ann's has worked hard to turn around what was once an unhealthy organisational culture. Little wonder then that so much emphasis is placed on maintaining professional standards. As well as the hospice's own mission statement on quality care provision, many clinical employees also have their own professional codes of conduct.

Environmental

As with any medical establishment, disposal of clinical waste is an important consideration. At St Ann's, there are checks in place to ensure this happens in the proper manner – namely that it is incinerated offsite – and that the care home inspectors who visit go away satisfied.

The hospice has a car-sharing scheme in operation for staff travelling from one site to another. It also recycles paper, used cartridges and obsolete mobile phones.

St. James's Place Capital

St. James's Place House
Dollar Street, Cirencester GL7 2AQ.
Tel: (0) 1285 640302 **Fax:** (0) 1285 653993
Web: www.sjpc.co.uk **Email:** info@sjp.co.uk

ST. JAMES'S PLACE

Pay and Benefits	7.0	Innovation	6.0
Promotion and Development	7.5	Diversity	6.0
Training	6.0	Social Responsibility	6.8
Travel opportunities	3.8	Corporate Governance	7.5
Culture	6.3	Environment	5.8
Total			**62.7**

St. James's Place Capital is a financial services company specialising in wealth management. Now listed on the London Stock Exchange, it was founded in 1992 as J. Rothschild Assurance when Mike Wilson, a well-known figure in the financial services field, and other founder directors left Allied Dunbar and teamed up with Sir Mark Weinberg and Lord Rothschild. HBOS now holds a 60% stake, but is not actively involved in the management of the company. St. James's Place Capital has in excess of 400,000 clients and £8.6bn funds under management. In the year to December 2003, it made a pre-tax profit of £103.9m.

Executive Summary

As a financial services business, St. James's Capital is very much dependent upon the state of domestic and world stock markets. Accordingly, as group services director Stephen Williams points out, the group enjoyed "terrific year-on-year growth" until 2001. "The market dipped and we dipped with it," says Williams. Since a significant amount of its business comes from single-premium investments made by individuals, any cooling towards the market can have an impact. The result was that in the year to December 2002, the group saw new business drop from £199.1m to £154.1m.

However, once markets began to pick up, so did the fortunes of St. James's Capital. The company believes it was able to weather this tough period better than most. Results for the nine months to the end of September 2004 showed new business up by 27% compared with the same period in 2003. This follows a 24% rise in new business in the last quarter of 2003, when the recovery in new business began. The company hoped that the business would return to the levels before the 2001 market downturn by the end of 2004.

By watching the market, St. James's Place intends to be prepared to make the most of opportunities provided by changes to pension investment rules being introduced in 2006; and by the forthcoming end to polarisation rules, under which investment advisers no longer have to be tied to one company or totally independent.

Pay and Benefits

As part of its aim of recruiting the best people to serve as both administrative and professional staff, St. James's Place is determined to be a top-quartile provider of pay and benefits.

On top of a good basic level of pay, employees receive contributions to a personal pension plan from the day they start (contributions start at 10% and rise to 15% with service), as well as four times salary life cover and death-in-service benefits. They can also make their own contributions to the pension plan. In addition, all staff are given private medical insurance, critical illness cover and permanent health insurance. The package is reviewed annually to ensure that it is in line with what is in the market, but the company has taken a conscious decision not to offer flexible benefits – on the basis that it wishes to ensure that its staff have these benefits available to them.

All staff can also take advantage of a Save As You Earn share scheme up to a maximum of £250 – there is a 70% participation rate for this. In addition, staff at different levels in the company are eligible for share options and bonus schemes in line with Association of British Insurers guidelines.

In view of its size, St. James's Place does not have specific social facilities, but it does have various social events throughout the year. For example, there is a summer barbecue at its head office in Cirencester, and a Christmas party with an overnight stay at a hotel.

Many events are run in conjunction with the St James's Place Foundation, a charity operated by the company that has raised more than £5m for causes such as caring for carers and supporting children with disabilities, degenerative illnesses and terminal diseases.

Promotion and Development

St. James's Place's head office location – in attractive historic buildings in the Cotswolds town of Cirencester – is a significant aid in hiring financial services specialists who are tired of working in the City or other newer towns close by. And once employees are recruited, there is a clear policy for promoting and developing them. Williams says it would rather recruit, develop and promote from within than buy in expertise. A group made up of middle managers reviews promotions. In some cases where specialist skills are required there is a need to go into the market and recruit, although the company tries to keep this to a minimum.

It does not do a lot of mentoring or coaching, though external coaches and counsellors are brought in to help with specific one-off situations.

Because of the size of the company, there is no graduate recruitment programme as such. However, St. James's Place has been working closely with nearby Cirencester College, who have set up a financial academy for A-Level students; the company plans to give students on the three-year course opportunities for work experience.

Within the constraints of the business, there is a focus on encouraging employees to develop within the company, with the idea being for them to spend as much of their career with St. James's Place as possible. "If you're spending good money recruiting people, you don't want to lose them," says Williams.

Company Culture

St. James's Place prides itself on having an open management style. In the early days, there used to be the Monday Morning Meeting, known as M3, at which the managing director would set out what was going on in the business. Now, the business is too big for that; but the ideal is kept alive by having an open-door policy, putting all employees on a first-name basis, and empowering people to "make things happen".

The style of working is set out in a small booklet called Our Approach, which all employees are urged to keep and use as "a code of practice, a charter or simply a series of guiding principles".

Another indication of the management's commitment to this style is its No Hiding Place policy, under which all work and home telephone numbers, fax numbers and mobile phone numbers of the senior management team are made available to everyone.

Employees are expected to work hard, but the company acknowledges the need for a work/life balance and managers are urged to have "the courage to be flexible" by giving employees time off when business is less hectic or when there is a crisis at home. Pointing to the company's low staff turnover and absenteeism rates, Williams says: "We try to create an environment where people come to work because they want to."

He adds: "The objective was always to make St. James's Place a profitable company, but it's our belief that you can only do that by having the right people and looking after them."

Innovation

St. James's Place does not claim to be especially innovative in terms of getting new financial products into the market. But where it does score, is in its approach to serving its clients.

At the centre of client service is the St. James's Place Partnership. The Partners are able to offer a comprehensive range of products and services that clients need in order to provide a complete wealth management service. If they do not manufacture the product themselves, they will look at other providers, products and services and choose the "best of breed" where regulation allows this. The company says the Partners, operating from a network of offices around the country, form "an elite group, made up of many of the most experienced, able and highly regarded professionals working in financial services today".

Called Partners because of their common purpose and shared values, they differ from most sales forces in being highly experienced. On average, they have worked in financial services for 14 years. In addition, some have exceptional expertise in certain areas and are brought in by their fellow Partners to provide extra advice in areas that are often highly technical.

In keeping with the company's focus on wealth management, the emphasis is on maintaining long-term relationships with clients who will typically call on the Partners for advice for an indefinite period. The company says the level of satisfaction with this approach is shown by the fact that a lot of new clients are recommended by existing ones.

Diversity and Social Responsibility

St. James's Place takes equal opportunities and other aspects of the diversity issue seriously. There are clear statements of the company's policy in this area.

While it cannot claim to have a highly diverse workforce, it says that this is not by design. Instead, it is a result of circumstances, says Williams. As a company based in the Cotswolds, its workforce largely reflects the local population. There is one female member of the executive committee, the managing director of the Dublin operation is female, and there are many women in middle management roles.

The company defines social responsibility as "all about being a decent employer, decent in the community, and decent in the sense of charitable giving...having decent values that we all feel we can live by".

The clearest manifestation of the company's commitment in this area is the St. James's Place Foundation, which has raised millions of pounds for a range of charities. The foundation is supported by all employees and Partners – with more than 80% committing themselves to regular deductions from their income.

Corporate Governance

As a company operating in the financial services industry, St. James's Place is highly regulated. As a result, it is in constant contact with the Financial Services Authority about various aspects of its operations.

Williams says great efforts are made to ensure the right corporate governance policies are in place. There are checks and balances designed to make sure executives behave and operate in the right way. For example, the group risk department "is there to ensure people like me are doing the right thing," says Williams.

As a company quoted on the Stock Exchange, St. James's Place is required to meet the various requirements of the Combined Code on Corporate Governance. Accordingly, in the interim report for 2004, departing chairman Sir Mark Weinberg pointed out that the company had complied with these provisions by consulting outside shareholders as well as HBOS on the appointment of former chief executive Mike Wilson as chairman.

Environmental Record

St. James's Place, as a service company, does not have such an obvious impact on the environment as some other types of business. Nevertheless, while it is certain it can do more, it has taken steps to make a contribution to solving the growing problems of waste and global warming by recycling paper and conserving energy use. It has, for example, appointed a member of staff with responsibility for energy use.

Williams says: "We're trying to do what we can, and we treat this as a serious issue."

Taylor Woodrow

Taylor Woodrow Plc
2 Princes Way, Solihull B91 3ES
Tel: (0) 121 600 8000
Web: www.taylorwoodrow.com **Email:** twplc@taylorwoodrow.com

Taylor Woodrow

Pay and Benefits	5.9	Innovation	5.1
Promotion and Development	5.5	Diversity	4.6
Training	5.8	Social Responsibility	4.6
Travel opportunities	5.9	Corporate Governance	4.0
Culture	5.5	Environment	4.9
Total			**51.8**

Taylor Woodrow is a FTSE 250 company and the second-largest UK-based builder of houses. In the UK, it operates through 11 regional offices and trades mainly under the Bryant Homes brand; at any one time, the company is working on over 200 housing developments, and builds around 10,000 new homes each year.

The company also builds around 3,800 new homes in North America, Spain and Gibraltar each year. In Canada, homes are marketed as Monarch; and in the US and Spain, directly under the Taylor Woodrow brand.

In addition to its housing operation, the company has a construction business and a commercial property arm.

Executive summary

Taylor Woodrow's vision is to be the leading developer of living and working environments in the UK and other chosen markets. The company's unique skill base of integrated housing, property and construction expertise ensures that Taylor Woodrow is particularly well equipped to tackle more complex developments, often on brownfield sites in high-profile city centre locations. In 2004, it was voted House Builder of the Year by Building magazine.

The company's turnover for 2003 was £2.6bn, and operating profit was £337.8m. Overall, 95% of the company's turnover stems from house building.

Pay and benefits

"Salaries are generally in the middle to upper quartile at Taylor Woodrow," says Justine Brown, resourcing and contracts manager. "Our reward strategy for staff considers all aspects of salary, incentives and benefits as a total package; with the intention of providing competitive levels of remuneration and enhanced earning opportunities in recognition of business success."

Pay increases are not automatic, but are reviewed at least annually to reflect delivered competence and performance within a role. Basic pay, bonus arrangements and employee benefits are benchmarked against competitors and comparable companies. All employees are eligible for a bonus.

A free income protection plan is offered to all salaried employees. There is a savings-related share option scheme running as either a three or five-year plan. Savings accruing at the end of the defined period are used to buy shares at the plan's start-date prices. A share incentive plan currently running provides "one-for-one" share matching up to a maximum £1,500 each year, plus a low-cost share dealing service is available. A company stakeholder pension plan is provided with life assurance cover of four times salary, and a Give As You Earn scheme is open to all staff.

BUPA Key Health Assessment is provided, plus the company's private healthcare package which can be extended – for a charge – to include partners and unmarried children up to 21, or 24 if in full-time education. Employees who need a vehicle to carry out their duties may be eligible for a company car or car allowance. In some circumstances, to help staff achieve certain professional qualifications, the company will pay annual membership fees for one selected professional institution. Staff are also eligible for a discount on the purchase price of a Taylor Woodrow home (except for directors).

If employees complete 10, 25 or 40 years' continuous service with the company, there are long-service awards to recognise the commitment made and the value of that commitment.

Promotion and development

"At Taylor Woodrow you can develop your own career," says Brown. "Staff are responsible for their own career development and training, with the company providing the necessary tools and support for employees to do this. We hold development reviews every July/August to discuss individual development, and performance reviews – with any development appraisal where necessary – in January to discuss objective setting, and carry out historical reviews."

"People are promoted on merit, and rapidly so if they are ambitious," says Brown. "If you're ambitious and can prove yourself, you will progress."

All training details are on the company intranet. Some courses are mandatory – for example, health and safety issues relating to specific roles. If they want to do something, people are encouraged to pursue training by both their managers and the culture of the organisation. There is potential for staff to move between departments and regions.

"If someone needed to study for further education, it would be encouraged," says Brown. "We have a Leadership Development Programme run with Warwick University, on which we had 16 people in 2004. It's equivalent to an MBA and we invite nominations for places every year, followed by a final assessment. If you pass the assessment you're on the course." Mentoring policies are in place for those on the Leadership Development Programme, and those in supervisory and management positions.

Taylor Woodrow offers apprenticeships lasting 3–4 years, which produce professional craftspeople with NVQ III qualifications. Currently, there are 240 apprentice schemes in operation with 80 being taken on each year. Up to 40 graduates and 30 sponsored students are also taken on each year.

Company culture

"Taylor Woodrow is a growing company, so it attracts ambitious people who are happy to work in a company which is changing and developing," says Brown. Everyone in Taylor Woodrow is expected to perform against core competencies, by adopting the company's key values to guide behaviour and improve performance in a range of vital areas. The core competencies are: teamwork, communication, customer focus, business and commercial acumen, personal drive, innovation, integrity, leadership and strategic vision.

Feedback on all company matters is encouraged in an open environment. Formal internal communications channels include a quarterly magazine, a weekly newsletter and the company intranet; but the culture of the company means that people can feedback informally too. A confidential whistle-blowing hotline is in operation in both the UK and North America. Skip level meetings take place across the company, giving every employee the chance to meet a member of the executive team in an open and informal setting; and regular employee consultation committees give employees the opportunity to feedback on company policies and procedures.

The company actively promotes flexible working policies. There is maternity and paternity leave – employees returning to work after maternity leave are eligible for a returner's bonus of eight weeks salary; while paternity leave of 10 days' paid leave is offered following birth, or on adoption of a child under five years of age. Study leave of five days (paid) is available for those undertaking a relevant qualification. Career breaks of up to two years are offered.

"There are site manager awards for the top three sites in the country," says Brown. "In the long-service awards in 2004, we had five recipients in the 40-year category. That includes the company secretary and an operations director, as well as site-based staff."

Innovation

Taylor Woodrow continues to explore new and innovative ways to satisfy its customers. Its Technology Centre at Leighton Buzzard is a centre of innovation where the company researches new product ideas, eg new types of cladding and insulation. The company is looking at offsite manufacture in housing construction as one way of reducing production costs and compensating for skills shortages within the industry. It's currently being trialled in Manchester.

Taylor Woodrow offers a range of products and services to its homebuyers. Its Bryant Design service provides UK customers with interior, garden and landscape design services; and options for home networks including babycams, TV and audio systems. Buyers typically spend around £2,800.

"We encourage staff to come up with new ideas and suggest improvements on how we do things," says Brown. "It's important in key areas like health and safety where the bar is raised every year."

Diversity and social responsibility

The house building industry has a direct impact on society, the natural and built environment, and the many stakeholders with whom it interacts. Taylor Woodrow has a comprehensive suite of policies in place incorporating corporate social responsibility and sustainability, health and safety, the environment, biodiversity, the community, human rights and ethics. Risk and opportunity management is one of the key processes supporting the company's corporate responsibility agenda.

"We have a big impact on the built environment, so it is important that we continue to build and maintain links with the local communities in which we work and which we help to create. We actively consult with local communities at many different levels, and enter into agreements with planning authorities to provide infrastructure facilities, which offer significant benefits to local communities," says Brown. On active development sites, the company seeks to minimise disruption to neighbours; and public meetings and newsletters are used to keep interested parties informed. On completed sites, and at regional and central offices, the company aims to play an active role in the local community.

Corporate Governance

"Taylor Woodrow is committed to the principles of good corporate governance, and maintains good corporate governance procedures – recognising the part they can play in contributing to enhanced benefits for shareholders," says Brown. "Throughout the accounting period to end-2003, the company has complied with the provisions set out in the Financial Services Authority (FSA) Combined Code on Corporate Governance as issued in June 1998."

The board oversees the audit, remuneration, nomination and executive committees. The group has also established committees to coordinate initiatives in corporate social responsibility, embracing health, safety and environmental matters. The AGM is used as a key opportunity for shareholders to develop a better understanding of company operations.

In July 2003, the Financial Reporting Council published a new Combined Code on Corporate Governance, which will apply for reporting years beginning on or after November 1 2003. The new code now forms part of the listing rules of the FSA. The company has taken steps to anticipate and implement the requirements of the new code, and in so doing has given consideration to the Guidance on Audit Committees (the Smith Guidance) and the suggestions for good practice from the Higgs Report.

Throughout Taylor Woodrow, staff show commitment to performance with integrity.

Environmental record

There are environmental impacts arising as a direct consequence of the company's activities. Areas of significant risk include the potential for environmental pollution during construction, and construction waste. The company's record in respect of environmental pollution is very good. During 2003, management of these issues was reinforced when the company rolled out project environmental management plans across UK project sites. Implementation of a waste management strategy was a key objective for the company's housing sites in 2003.

Such new practices are leading to a reduction in waste disposal costs and an increase in materials recycling. Taylor Woodrow believes it is a leader in its sector in recycling; an increasing proportion of its plasterboard waste from the UK residential sector is now being segregated and returned for recycling (1,928.5 tonnes in 2003, up from 708 tonnes in 2002).

The company's construction arm is certificated to the environment management standard ISO 14001, and the golf course at the Los Arqueros development in Spain has also recently been awarded this standard.

Timspson

Timpson Limited
Timpson House, Claverton Road, Wythenshawe, Manchester M23 9TT
Tel: (0) 161 946 6200 **Fax:** (0) 161 946 0135
Web: www.timpson.com

Pay and Benefits	5.8	Innovation	6.4
Promotion and Development	6.4	Diversity	6.0
Training	6.5	Social Responsibility	6.7
Travel opportunities	3.9	Corporate Governance	6.8
Culture	7.2	Environment	6.0
Total			**61.7**

Timpson began life as a shoe repair chain and is now a unique high street service business with 568 newly refurbished nationwide branches. Based in south Manchester, the business mix is roughly split into: shoe repairs (36%), key cutting (30%), watch repairs (10%), engraving (8%) and other merchandising (16%). Branches are supported by five Excellence Centres.

Executive Summary

The key to cutting it in a traditional craft-based industry is to provide fantastic customer service. On this, chairman John Timpson's message (based on his published style of "upside-down management") is enshrined and clear-cut: "The staff in this shop have my total authority to do whatever they can to give you amazing service." In other words, staff can look after their customers as they see fit – including offering up to £500, without referral, to settle any complaint. An unusual style, which has helped create an extraordinary company.

The original Timpson Company was founded by William Timpson in 1865, well before he got involved in repairing shoes. The core shoe-repairing business is arbitrarily dated from 1903 – "which allowed us to throw a big centennial party in 2003," says Timpson. Since then, the company ownership road has been "bumpy" – encompassing family ownership, boardroom splits, share sales and a management buyout; but has now come full circle and is once again a privately owned, family company. The chairman's son, James, is managing director.

Since the shoe retailing business was sold in 1987, Timpson has added new, improved services and acquired two of its main competitors – creating a growing, multi-service high street business. In 1995, Timpson's pre-tax profit was £700,000. By 2003, it had risen to £6m, and in 2004 was on target for £10m (excluding acquisition costs). Turnover grew from £20m to £100m over ten years.

Pay and Benefits

"We will pay good people more than mediocre people for the same job – because they're not doing the same job," asserts John Timpson.

So there's no formal pay policy and branch managers can be paid differently. While base pay is not the highest in the retail sector, Timpson pays "the right people the right amount" and weekly bonuses can be substantial. Bonuses are calculated on the total wage bill of the branch multiplied by 4.5 – any sales above this threshold are rewarded by 15% commission, shared among the team. Some workers get £400 bonus a week or more. Some earn above £30,000 a year. One manager, through initiative and graft, notched a near-£1,000 bonus in a single week. Timpson publishes lists of the highest bonus earners. "We're turned on by people who are turned on by self-reward," says

Gouy Hamilton-Fisher, company personnel manager.

Managers have the freedom to set their own prices. "The Timpson price list is just a guideline," says Hamilton-Fisher. "Our employees are the local experts, they know their customers best and can charge what they want."

The list of benefits is almost endless and frequently cash-based. There are rewards for long service, product innovation, finding a new site/location, training apprentices and introducing a friend to the company. The chairman has "on the spot" rewards of £500 for deeds of exceptional service. The pension is final salary, and many staff receive life assurance and medical cover.

"Welfare" benefits include staff loans, a hardship fund, company holiday homes, 90% staff discounts on products, an extra week's holiday for weddings and £100 towards the honeymoon. And that's just a selection. On maternity leave, Timpson pays 95% of earnings for ten weeks and adds the other 5% if the mum returns to work. It exceeds government stipulations on paternity leave. No policy is set in stone. "If someone asked, 'can I take two years off?' we'd look at it."

There are loads of social events and each area has a "social fund" to take their people out. Area managers' cars are crammed full of chocolates, wine and goodies to give as rewards. "It all sounds a bit barmy, but it works," says Hamilton-Fisher.

Promotion and development

Of a total of 1,684 employees, 1,487 are full time and 1,002 are non-managers. Each branch has a general manager; and 81 people work in Timpson House in people support, and other administrative and professional functions.

"We used to say 'we need a shoe repairer', but that doesn't happen anymore," says Hamilton-Fisher. Upon joining, people start in a branch as an apprentice, which lasts 16 weeks. There are traditional "stepping stones" to branch manager, above which there are assistant area managers (three for each of Timpson's 21 areas). The area manager is the key person in the field and the main communication link between colleagues and Timpson. There are three regional managers, and then an operations board.

Most managers rise from the branches – they don't "bus in" outsiders very often. "To understand the culture of Timpson, you need to live and breathe the business from the inside," says Hamilton-Fisher.

Timpson has devised its own suite of training programmes and qualifications; the old City & Guilds disappeared and the newer NVQs were regarded as very basic. A timeline is set out for learning, and skill levels are linked to bonuses. "We spend a lot of time training people," says Peter Harris, training manager. "We want to retain them and get them quickly onto the bonus system. You can triple your pay, but you have to work for it, and first you must get the skills."

All training is in-house. Courses are updated and refreshed – for example, the training on transponder keys for modern cars has taken key cutting to new levels. There have been big changes in customer care. "We train people as craftsmen, then we ask them to be caring and smiling. It's about being able to connect with the customer," says Harris. So there are also courses on listening skills, interaction, role-playing with difficult customers, communications, and the value of mystery shopping. "We aim to demystify the whole thing," he adds. There are two-day residential courses where Timpson "throws everything at them".

"We ask a colossal amount of our people – but they are exceptional, unique people," Harris says.

Company culture

This unusual and open organisation stems from the chairman's character, and he has succeeded in generating that most valuable of commodities – trust.

Timpson has put a lot of determined work into looking after employees and looking after customers. The latter depends upon the former – which is where the practical application of "upside-down management" comes in. "It's so obvious, I don't know why everyone doesn't do it," says John Timpson. "You can't achieve good service by the rulebook. You must give people who serve customers the freedom to do what is best. It's sometimes a difficult message to get through. The way we run the business doesn't work for everyone."

Timpson recruits personality, not expertise. "We've been playing around with these ideas for a few years," says John Timpson. "Now the brand should stand for the 'Rolls-Royce' of customer service."

Timpson enshrines a can-do attitude but is also paternalistic – isolationist even. "We look to solve our own problems, and we won't allow anyone or anything to stop individuals and the company from developing," says Hamilton-Fisher.

The Timpson culture is underpinned by extensive people support. Hamilton-Fisher is always galloping up and down the country, listening to people, solving issues and ensuring that everything is running smoothly (don't buy his second-hand car, there's at least 30,000 miles a year in it!). The weekly newsletter is packed with news, information, praise and stories celebrating success in every form. It's sent to people's homes so that partners are informed too.

What about flexible working? "Because of the difficulty we have in recruiting people, it would be economic suicide to make it difficult in any way," says Hamilton-Fisher. "For example, mothers returning to work: if they request a change in hours, we're flexible, we'll look at it – bearing in mind that we're in the retail sector and have to meet customer needs."

Innovation

Timpson was the first company to repair shoes and cut keys in front of customers, which gave pride and confidence back to employees. Encouraging employees is a constant factor. It wants people to input ideas and not be afraid of trial and error – the company champions people who show entrepreneurial spirit.

It's fair to say that in a craft industry, the main area of innovation has been Timpson's bold and unusual style of people management. "We're always grappling with the historical perception of a man in a cellar knocking out shoes," says Hamilton-Fisher. That image is a load of old cobblers because this is a superbly progressive, open organisation that really understands terms like empowerment and customer service while others just talk about it.

Diversity and social responsibility

Timpson does discriminate – between good and bad workers.

But combating perceptions does mean that Timpson strives really hard to attract more women and ethnic minorities. "We look to promote successful female managers as role models. Women are often better communicators." Around 22% of the workforce is female. Timpson produces recruitment advertisements in different languages and goes into local ethnic community centres. It's not positive discrimination, but a positive effort to attract a diverse workforce. It asks women: "what more could the company do to make it an attractive workplace for you?" – and it acts on the answers. Recruitment of ethnic minorities and women is monitored closely.

Timpson is held in affection by the local community, where it has a strong presence. It supports a number of charities that its employees take to heart, but Childline is its favourite. Timpson has raised hundreds of thousands of pounds for Childline. When one particular fundraising target was set, the chairman said he would match it if it were reached! (It was). All tips in the branches are donated to Childline. Timpson also gives footwear away to charities.

In the debate over Sunday shopping, the company was opposed to it – on the basis of the number of days employees would have to work, church and other moral considerations. John Timpson even led a "Cobblers to the Commons" march on the Houses of Parliament!

Corporate Governance

For a company that throws away the textbooks on so many management approaches (John Timpson writes and publishes his own), Timpson does things by the book in corporate governance. Everything is built upon trust and an innate awareness of what is right and wrong. Timpson never breaks the rules. "Only our own," adds John Timpson.

The company does the usual things – the company secretary and finance director ensure that Timpson is compliant in all aspects. The company is fully audited. There are two health and safety officers, an equal opportunity officer and an equal pay officer.

If good governance is about integrity and trust, then Timpson stands out as a company that goes beyond the norm in looking after its people. Trust might have been invented here.

Environmental record

Timpson is a non-polluter – it doesn't manufacture anything. In fact, by encouraging people to repair their shoes rather than buy new ones, it's fair to say: "what could be more environmentally friendly than cobbling?"

Timpson staff are rewarded for keeping stock losses to a minimum. Materials are cut to size, avoiding unnecessary waste.

TNT

TNT Express Services UK & Ireland
TNT Express House, Holly Lane, Atherstone CV9 2RY
Tel: (0) 1827 303030
Web: www.tnt.co.uk

Pay and Benefits	6.5	Innovation	7.5
Promotion and Development	7.1	Diversity	6.8
Training	7.1	Social Responsibility	7.5
Travel opportunities	6.8	Corporate Governance	7.5
Culture	7.3	Environment	7.5
Total			**71.6**

TNT Express Services UK & Ireland is a vital part of TNT Express, the world's leading business-to-business express delivery company whose parent company is TPG – a global express, logistics and mail company that employs over 163,000 people in more than 60 countries. The group started life in Australia in 1946 as a single-truck operation called Thomas Nationwide Transport and grew rapidly into an international operation; it was established in Britain in 1978, and it has become the country's fastest and most reliable business-to-business express delivery company.

Today, TNT Express Services UK & Ireland has annual sales in excess of £750m and employs more than 10,600 people, operates more than 3,500 vehicles from over 70 locations, and delivers more than 40 million items each year. In 2003, the company embarked on an ambitious five-year plan to double the value of the business.

Executive summary

TNT was acquired in 1996 by the de-nationalised Dutch post and telecoms supplier, KPN, but they demerged a couple of years later. The group, now called TPG and based in the Netherlands, is publicly listed on the stock exchanges of Amsterdam, New York, London and Frankfurt; TNT Express is one of its key divisions, responsible for many of the group's product and service innovations.

The present shape of TNT Express in the UK & Ireland owes much to a radical overhaul of the business, started in the late 1980s by the then-new managing director, Tom Bell. Since then, TNT has trebled its customer base and become the market leader in nationwide distribution for the fashion trade. Turnover and profits have increased every year since 1988, out-performing the transport industry in an extremely competitive market (over 3,000 shippers in the UK claim to offer next-day delivery). Service failures have been reduced to almost zero, and the level of staff satisfaction has improved dramatically – now 83% of employees say they are proud to work for TNT. Also, the company has undertaken major investment in infrastructure, people and business processes, which has been highly visible and effective (TNT has adopted the European Foundation for Quality Management business excellence model as a way of working throughout the company).

The mass of industry and community awards that TNT has won provides an impressive benchmark of its progress. It's actually policy to apply for the more demanding awards because the exercise enforces a degree of self-analysis as well as resulting in due recognition.

Pay and benefits

TNT's remuneration packages have been benchmarked by a number of independent surveys as well above average for the sector. Basic pay is competitive, and target-beating performance is rewarded by a variety of incentive and bonus schemes covering all levels.

TNT has a defined contribution group pension scheme that is open to all employees with six months' service – members contribute a minimum of 3% of salary, the company adds a further 7%. Under the executive scheme, the employer's contribution rises to 8% after 5 years, 9% after 10 years and 10% after 20 years. More than 4,000 employees (40% of the workforce) are in the pension scheme.

Holiday entitlement starts at 21 days a year, increasing by one day each year to a maximum of 26. Enhanced maternity and paternity leave and pay are offered after three years' employment, and managers also get free private health care. All permanent employees are covered by free life assurance to a minimum of twice annual salary in the event of death in service. A childcare voucher scheme is due to be implemented in 2005. There is also a range of voluntary benefits and discounts on services and products.

TNT aims to accommodate any request for flexible working – employees can ask to work part time or to job share – subject to the requirements of the business.

Promotion and development

TNT makes no apologies for charging a premium price, and it justifies that by delivering a premium service. The performance and skills of its staff are a key element of this, and since 1989, the company has operated an integrated training plan for all employees.

In fact, TNT's training and development programmes have been winning awards for some time now – including five National Training Awards since 1992. It is certainly recognised as the sector leader in training and development. All employees have access to an impressive suite of training programmes – broadly split into short and more extended courses for management, operations, sales and customer care – and the managerial training can extend to sponsorship for professional qualifications such as MBAs, and Chartered Institute for Management Accountants and Chartered Institute of Personnel Development qualifications.

The company is proud of its Home Grown Timber policy of people development. More than 86% of all supervisory and managerial appointments are made from within, and all but one of the most senior managers have worked their way through the ranks. The managing director, Tom Bell, was himself a TNT driver (he started at the company's Maidstone depot in 1977). 2003 alone saw more than 3,000 positive career moves within the company – not bad for a workforce of 10,600.

TNT is firmly committed to the Investors in People standard. Its first IIP award was in 1994, and in 2004, TNT received Investors in People Champion Status – one of only 16 out of more than 37,000 IIP-accredited organisations in the UK. That's only one of many independent accreditations for TNT; others include the British Safety Council's 5 Star Accreditation and Swords of Honour, a Queen's Award for Enterprise, Chartered Institute of Management Accountants Quality Partner status, and an unsurpassed 21 Motor Transport Awards in the past 19 years.

International assignments are one of the potential benefits of working for a group with worldwide activities, and TNT has often facilitated overseas postings "where the individual's aspirations and skill set are in line with current and potential business needs".

Company culture

TNT operates in a hotly contested market, and its principal sales messages are based on quality and timeliness – that creates a high-pressure environment with no room for passengers, where customer service is the overriding consideration, and where a combination of teamwork and individual responsibility is the way to get things done. Such virtues are highly valued and rewarded by the company. As director of personnel, Suzie Theobald put it: "Our people are always working hard to beat their previous best performances, and the aggregate of all these efforts is a strong market-leading position for the company."

It's a young company – the average age is 36 – and there's a degree of flexibility about the operation. It's important to TNT that all employees at all levels feel able to communicate easily and constructively with each other.

TNT runs an annual employee survey, and the most recent results showed 83% of respondents were proud to work for TNT. Fully 88% would recommend TNT as an employer, 81% said TNT gave opportunities for personal development, and 77% thought TNT provided a satisfactory balance between work and personal life.

Innovation

TNT has always had a good record for innovation. In the 1980s it pioneered guaranteed overnight and next-day deliveries, and provided radios for its drivers to speed up the process. These days the business uses a sophisticated hub-and-spoke system based on three major distribution points and smaller local depots – a system that requires sophisticated routing methods, which also enable the customer to track and trace a consignment during transit.

The track and trace technology helped TNT win the 2003 Motor Transport Award for Best Use of Internet and E-commerce – the company's 21st Motor Transport Award in 19 years.

There have been many other examples of applied technology, including electronic proof of delivery provided via a network of in-cab mobile data terminals that connect directly to the company's central computer. Customers can also use the TNT website to obtain proof of delivery within seconds of a consignment's arrival. A long-running parking dispute with highways authorities in central London has been settled; partly by the use of a technology dubbed Moovit – a light-sensitive sensor on the vehicle's window which is activated by a traffic warden. This sends a warning signal to the TNT driver's pager alerting him that he only has a limited time to complete his collection and/or delivery.

The company has also been able to identify attractive markets for its distribution and logistics expertise beyond the express parcels business – including fashion garments, medicines and healthcare products, car parts, archiving and records management, financial services; and an imaginative sideways step into internal mailroom management, reprographics and confidential waste disposal.

TNT received The Queen's Award for Enterprise – Innovation Category in 2000; having repeatedly revolutionised the UK transport industry with a series of "first to market" services over a period spanning 21 years.

Diversity and social responsibility

TNT has an explicit equal opportunities policy, which is well publicised and enforced by management and formal grievance procedures.

Corporate social responsibility is another major concern. TNT is a member of an elite group of companies – the Business in the Community PerCent Club – that commits at least 1% of their pre-tax profits to charitable causes.

The company's distribution network means individual locations around the UK have many relationships with local community and charity organisations, providing them with both financial resources and direct help. Nationally, TNT is the biggest single corporate contributor to the Wooden Spoon – a charity which funds projects for children who are physically, mentally or socially disadvantaged; and which has received more than £1.1m in cash alone from TNT since 1997. TNT also adds in-kind support; it has provided secondments, funds and logistics solutions to charities such as In Kind Direct and Transaid Worldwide.

TNT is active in supporting road safety initiatives via the UK charity, Brake, and supports Crucial Crew awareness-raising events for schoolchildren around the country.

On the international stage, TNT makes a key contribution in support of TPG's five-year partnership with the United Nations' World Food Programme – enhancing awareness of world hunger, raising funds to feed and educate children in developing countries, deploying volunteers and giving help-in-kind.

Corporate Governance

TNT believe there is only one way a company can win and keep the trust of its employees, customers, shareholders and the public: by being as open as possible about its internal financial reporting, its control systems and its decision-making processes.

The company promotes sustainable development, believes in open and fair competition, and is committed to excellent customer service and preserving the integrity of the business.

Formally, the parent TPG group follows the regulatory requirements for corporate governance that are imposed by the US Stock Exchange. Internally, Project Clarity is a business initiative designed to ensure transparency across all accounting procedures, health and safety, employment law, hazardous goods and taxation.

TPG has also developed a Whistleblower Procedure that enables employees to report concerns within the company, anonymously and confidentially.

Environmental record

The nature of its business means that TNT is operating in environmentally sensitive areas – fossil fuels, urban congestion, air traffic, night time movements – but the company has an excellent record of promoting energy efficiency throughout its operations and says it is "committed to preserving and improving the world in which we live and work".

The company's green credentials are illustrated by a host of examples, including its projects on environmentally friendly vehicles (low-emission LPG fuels, bio-diesel); as well as its preference for minimum-impact vehicles from the current range of offerings – low-noise BAe 146 aircraft have replaced Boeing 727s, for example. Other environmental initiatives include a waste reduction drive in its depots, and a recent commitment to buy 10% of its energy requirements from "green energy" sources.

UNITE

The UNITE Group Plc
103 Temple Street, Bristol BS1 6EN
Tel: (0) 117 907 8695
Web: www.unite-group.co.uk

Pay and Benefits	5.3	Innovation	6.7
Promotion and Development	6.3	Diversity	6.0
Training	6.3	Social Responsibility	6.0
Travel opportunities	4.3	Corporate Governance	6.3
Culture	6.7	Environment	7.3
Total			**61.2**

The UNITE Group develops and manages property for student housing. It is by a long way the market leader in this field, with around 26,000 tenants in 2004; a turnover in excess of £60m; and a property portfolio worth around £1bn that is spread over 100 properties in some 30 of the key university towns and cities across the UK. UNITE expects to continue adding beds at the rate of more than 5,000 a year for the immediate future, and is focused on adding value and service to its existing accommodation offering. Formed in 1991 and headquartered in Bristol, the company currently employs around 600 staff.

Executive summary

Fourteen years ago, the University of the West of England contracted with a local developer for a student accommodation block, and subsequently invited the company to manage the property as well. From that opportunity, The UNITE Group has become the market leader in purpose-built student accommodation, currently with 26,000 tenants in properties worth £1bn right across the UK.

UNITE really has three businesses, though they are closely related. The first is property development – identifying potential sites, new build, conversion and refurbishment of existing premises. The second is accommodation management including traditional facilities management such as maintenance and security, as well as innovative new services for students such as finding and keeping tenants, welfare support for residents, online room booking and allocations, and an informative student website. Its third arm is a manufacturing facility, which produces complete student bedrooms under factory conditions using hi-tech production methods.

UNITE has grown quickly. Four years ago it had just 4,000 rooms; by the end of 2005 the total will be nearer 32,000. Turnover was less than £500,000 in 1996; for 2004 it's estimated at £62m. There's been an operating profit each year, most of which has been reinvested (so minimising borrowings) rather than paid to shareholders. UNITE has had to spend heavily to kick-start the market for commercial student accommodation, but it looks like it is beginning to reap the rewards with a more controlled programme of expansion, and a solid reputation both in the City and among the banks who fund its developments.

For the future, UNITE's market seems secure – the demand is there, the competition isn't – but it will be interesting to see how it copes with the immediate pressures. Because it is providing low-cost housing for students, UNITE is in a strong position to win planning permissions in city centre locations where luxury apartments would be regarded less favourably by planners. UNITE's influence on the nature of the market should also be able to cover the gap between building costs that are rising 8% per year when rents are increasing by only 3%. There's a window of opportunity that the group can grab, economies of scale, and the development of increasingly sophisticated business tools such as yield management systems.

The UNITE Group is probably the world's largest specialist provider of student accommodation – this may open up international opportunities where there are no comparable private-sector suppliers and UNITE may be well poised to consider other markets in future years.

Pay and benefits

UNITE pays above average for the sector and the location, and aims to be in the upper quartile for total benefits. These vary by position, of course, but generally include at least 25 days' annual holiday, private health insurance, a car (or a car allowance) where required, and share options after three years' service.

There's also an annual bonus for all employees, based on divisional and individual performance. Currently, this is 10% of annual salary, and up to 30% for senior managers.

Promotion and development

UNITE says it aims to provide a challenging and meaningful career. It is also policy to recruit and develop the highest quality individuals. It does this by giving staff structured personal and career development plans, and by developing a partnership approach to training and development.

Intensive training starts with a year-long modular programme for management trainees. There's a portfolio of follow-on management courses – these are not mandatory, but there is a strong incentive for professional development.

UNITE is also strong on sponsorship for academic qualifications such as MAs, MBAs and PhDs – around a fifth of senior managers now have a postgraduate qualification.

UNITE doesn't have any operations outside the UK, but it is building business relationships in the US and there is an exchange programme for accommodation managers.

Employee satisfaction at UNITE places them among the top 10 companies in the UK, with almost 80% of employees saying they are satisfied with their job. 90% enjoy the work they do; and key strengths are identified as teamworking, belief in the potential of the business, and personal development.

Company culture

This is a young company: the oldest executive director is 35. So it's no surprise that UNITE has an entrepreneurial feel. This comes, in part, from its CEO, Nicholas Porter – given the approach to business that he has demonstrated in the past, it's difficult for him to say no to good propositions. Working with and for students also helps; so does the business imperative, particularly in terms of finding new development opportunities at a time when city-centre sites are so rare and so expensive.

There's a real sense that creative ideas are encouraged at all levels. It also helps that UNITE people are young enough to understand and sympathise with their key market – it wasn't so long ago that most of them were students themselves.

Innovation

Commercially, UNITE has effectively pioneered a new asset class in the property business. Most other areas of property are cyclical – with seasonal variations through the year, and bigger swings dependent on interest rates and public confidence. But students need accommodation each year; and each year there is more demand for it (especially given the government's stated target for a continuing increase in the student population). A million students currently live away from home, and at present UNITE cares for only 26,000 of them – this is a high-potential business and UNITE is the market leader (its next-largest competitor in this specialised world has fewer than 5,000 rooms).

A key element in its success has been the development of a purpose-built factory in Stroud, which produces pre-fabricated bedroom and bathroom modules under factory conditions. UNITE has the capacity to manufacture a total of 5,000 each year. Designed as stackable units, the modules can be assembled on site with a 40% reduction in build time. This translates into economies in construction, but also means savings on finance charges – a faster build means a shorter period for the external borrowings that pay for it.

Heavy investment in consumer research is another feature that differentiates UNITE from conventional accommodation providers. The annual Student Living Report is the most comprehensive, independent and in-depth study of the views, concerns and hopes of students in the UK – it's also a valuable insight for UNITE into market trends and the needs of its customers.

Diversity and social responsibility

There are no barriers to employment at UNITE, which reasons that it needs to find and keep the best people it can identify.

It also takes its social responsibility very seriously, both nationally and locally. UNITE has an interesting approach here – it estimates that an individual training programme costs around £5,000, and it encourages individuals to return at least that much to the community. Examples include supporting local schools and refurbishment of charity premises.

UNITE provided seed funding and in-kind support to the UNIAID Foundation, a charitable trust set up to help students who wouldn't be able to attend university without additional financial support. In 2004, UNITE provided a programme of accommodation bursaries.

Another charity close to UNITE is the Rainbow Centre, a Bristol organisation that provides support to children affected by cancer, life threatening illness and bereavement. Staff at UNITE have raised money in various ways for the centre, including holding three charity balls.

Corporate Governance

As a plc, UNITE Group follows the standard codes of conduct for corporate governance. Overseeing this is one of the tasks of the remuneration, nominations and audit committees of the board, comprising independent non-executive directors and the chairman of the board. UNITE was a runner up in a recent award by IR Magazine for best corporate governance.

Environmental record

UNITE recognises its responsibilities as a property developer, and also sees how its business can provide opportunities for environmental improvement.

This is particularly relevant because UNITE typically requires inner-city locations for its buildings, and frequently the only economic option is to locate them on brownfield sites or in rundown areas. Certainly, the arrival of a new UNITE development can effectively regenerate a neglected neighbourhood area as new shops and services arrive to cater for the students who inhabit it.

At a more detailed level, the modular construction technique is being used now for any new UNITE building below nine storeys. One effect has been a dramatic reduction in onsite building waste – which is typically destined for landfill – from 5% of the total build cost to less than 0.5%.

UNITE became a member of the FTSE 4Good index in March 2002. Companies are added to the index by an independent committee on the basis of specified criteria – environmental responsibility, positive relationships with stakeholders, and supporting universal human rights. Membership is reviewed every six months.

United Welsh Housing Association

United Welsh Housing Association
Ty Cennydd, Castle Street, Caerphilly CF83 1NZ
Tel: (0) 29 2085 8100
Web: www.uwha.co.uk **Email:** uwha@uwha.co.uk

Pay and Benefits	6.9	Innovation	7.0
Promotion and Development	6.3	Diversity	7.3
Training	7.0	Social Responsibility	6.6
Travel opportunities	4.6	Corporate Governance	6.5
Culture	7.5	Environment	6.2
Total			**65.9**

A not-for-profit organisation with just 125 staff – a quarter of them working part-time – might seem an unlikely candidate for Britain's Top Employers. But the United Welsh Housing Association scored spectacularly in the Financial Times 2004 Best Workplaces Report: it came fifth – the first non-profit organisation ever to achieve a place in the top 10 – and there are very good reasons for that success.

UWHA currently provides over 3,500 homes to rent, 600 of them specially designed for older people and another 500 for people with additional support needs. It also provides homes to purchase under a Welsh Assembly subsidised Low Cost Home Ownership scheme.

Executive summary

Established in 1989 and based in Caerphilly and Cardiff, the United Welsh Housing Association works with a dozen local authorities across south-east Wales. In 2003, the UWHA property portfolio was worth £141m – that represents something over 3,500 homes to rent, typically to people on low incomes or in receipt of Housing Benefit and those with additional support needs.

UWHA also runs a Low Cost Home Ownership scheme, which provides opportunity for home ownership through shared equity. In 2003, the association had income from rents and service charges of £10.5m, recorded a surplus of £2.6m on property revenues, and produced a net surplus of almost £1m after loan interest charges. (Housing associations are not-for-profit organisations, but they still have to operate conventional accounts and show a net surplus.)

2003 also saw some notable improvements in productivity – the turnaround time for empty properties was halved to 12 days, for instance, and rent arrears were down significantly. This compares well with similar organisations and with other local renters.

Housing associations have traditionally been regarded as the provider of last resort for social housing. UWHA aims to be a provider of choice – it wants to be seen as the best alternative in a market that is becoming more competitive.

Pay and benefits

Provision of social housing is not a passport to riches. In UWHA's case, the rewards are certainly there, but they are not necessarily financial. That said, the association regards its pay scales as "very reasonable for the sector".

Equally important is a very real sense of involvement, the feeling that staff at all levels can make a real difference both to the organisation and to the welfare of their tenants.

The quality of working life is also critical. UWHA is prepared to be as flexible as possible in terms of working arrangements, particularly to accommodate staff with families. Several employees have opted for homeworking or flexible working hours; and the Association prides itself on being one of the most family-friendly organisations in Wales – illustrated by the term-time contracts, which allow parents to take a leave of absence to care for children during school holidays.

UWHA participates in the Social Housing Pension Scheme, a multi-employer defined benefits scheme that takes between 2% and 5% from employees' pay (depending on their age) and adds just over 10% from the employer.

Other extras tend to be short-term or one-off benefits – free fruit and subsidised gym membership as part of an ongoing commitment to promoting healthy living, and a paid day's holiday to celebrate the Best Workplace announcement, for example.

Promotion and development

Each member of staff has a personal development plan and an annual appraisal to track progress.

UWHA is keen to offer opportunities for staff to develop – to try different roles on secondment, to train in a different field (a receptionist recently retrained as a support worker, for instance), or to pursue professional qualifications (up to and including MBA sponsorship).

There's also been significant investment in training and staff development at UWHA. This applies at all levels, but in particular the management development programme leads to accreditation by the Institute of Leadership and Management.

Company culture

UWHA realises that it's a service business, and that the delivery of quality services can only be achieved by well-motivated staff.

One aspect of this has been the conscious and systematic development since 2002 of a partnership approach that involves staff in decision-making at a much earlier stage than previously. This provided an imaginative solution to what was a complex and increasingly restrictive agreement that had been signed some time before with the sole recognised union, Unison. It has produced flexible working, improved and speedier decision-making, and a strong sense of shared goals.

The most recent annual staff survey shows that a majority of employees now believe that a high level of trust exists between the staff and management; that the quantity and quality of communication has improved significantly; and that this communication is definitely a two-way process, with staff being encouraged to innovate and even offer (constructive) criticism. Over 80% of staff say they are satisfied with their job, and 85% were proud to work for the association.

UWHA was the first mainstream housing association in the UK to be chosen by the DTI to implement a Partnership at Work project, which aims to modernise the way staff work together and actively encourage staff to take charge of their own decision-making.

UWHA takes pride in describing itself as one of the most family-friendly organisations in Wales. Paternity leave was already in place months before the current legislation was enacted, for example, and the association has pioneered term time contracts, which allow parents to take time off to care for children during school holidays.

Innovation

Previously, the association has had a single-union agreement that was proving increasingly restrictive. Finding a replacement, and a new way of working with staff, has proved a major success for the organisation – the new partnership agreement includes an option-based consultation model, which enables all parties to debate a limited set of pre-agreed options. That short-circuits much of the protracted negotiation that drags out conventional management-staff relationships, fosters posturing and game playing, and encourages both sides to take entrenched positions. The UWHA solution is effective, efficient and apparently well-liked by all.

On the front-line of its operations, UWHA has a strong track record in providing environmentally friendly design within the budget constraints implicit in social housing. It has introduced initiatives such as solar-powered hot water systems at individual developments, for instance; and has pioneered a type of fencing made from recycled PVC. It built the first homes in Wales to achieve the BRE Environmental Standard; and has designed the first "lifetime" houses, which can be adapted internally as the family's needs change.

UWHA is producing a new "pattern book" that aims to standardise environmentally friendly practice in the design of its new homes.

The association has also pioneered a novel supermarket-style loyalty card that rewards tenants for maintaining clear rent accounts and acting in a responsible, neighbourly way. The incentives on offer include discounts at local retailers, entry into exclusive competitions, and £200 cash-back at the end of their tenancy. UWHA hopes that half of its tenants will have signed up to the 5 Star Loyalty Scheme by the end of its first year.

Diversity and social responsibility

UWHA recognises that diversity issues affect all areas of work with its clients, and has developed strategies to pursue equality of opportunity internally as well.

The association has a hands-on approach to community responsibility, organising and supporting numerous events for its tenants – fun days, barbecues, kids' competitions and more. Tenant's associations and consultative committees are funded and promoted; tenants also receive the association's annual report and there is a breezy newsletter, which is jointly produced by UWHA staff and tenants on a quarterly basis.

UWHA has a community services team, which also partners with other local organisations to improve the quality of life in many of the communities where the association works – a long-term work process with several projects that are now producing good results. An example is the work being done in Lansbury Park, Caerphilly – a joint venture with the local borough council and governmental organisations, the work has produced a multi-games area as part of a local housing development and is continuing with a youth club, summer play schemes and more.

The association's staff are ready to give up their own time to undertake fundraising and other activities; UWHA often supports these ventures in kind, and frequently encourages its own contractors and other commercial contacts to help.

The association is a member of Business in the Community.

Corporate Governance

As a non-profit organisation, UWHA is not required to follow the Stock Exchange codes on corporate governance, but it does emphasise that core values are embedded in its structure and procedures – specifically equality of opportunity, empowering staff, being accountable, commitment to growth and improvement, putting customers first and making sound financial decisions. These are communicated extensively via staff handbooks, team meetings, and the many communication channels to tenants and partners. The association is governed by a voluntary non-executive board of management, and subscribes to Codes of Governance issued by the National Housing Federation and the Welsh Federation of Housing Associations.

Environmental record

"We want to be leaders on environmental issues," says the association. At a detailed level: cans are recycled, used IT equipment and furniture are passed on to charitable organisations, and so on.

More broadly, UWHA can point to an excellent record in its housing developments. The association is a member of the South Wales Energy Partnership, providing tenants with lower-cost utilities. It has installed the first solar-powered domestic hot water systems to feature in affordable housing in Wales, and it has built the first homes in Wales to achieve the Building Research Establishment Environmental Standard.

The association has recently been awarded funding to draw up a new "pattern book" for housing. These designs will focus on the efficient use of materials to increase sustainability and minimise waste, the application of renewable energy sources (including solar power and low-energy supplies and fittings), and the use of minimum-impact insulation.

Vanco

Vanco plc
John Busch House, 277 London Road, Isleworth, Middlesex
Tel: (0) 20 8636 1700 **Fax:** (0) 20 8636 1701
Web: www.vanco.co.uk

vanco

Pay and Benefits	6.1	Innovation	6.8
Promotion and Development	6.3	Diversity	
Training	6.3	Social Responsibility	6.1
Travel opportunities	6.8	Corporate Governance	6.5
Culture	6.7	Environment	5.8
Total			**57.4**

Vanco is probably the most successful company to emerge from telecom deregulation.

It is a global Virtual Network Operator– virtual in the sense that it neither builds nor owns the telecoms infrastructure and assets underlying its customers' networks. Instead, it purchases the infrastructure from the most suitable telecoms carriers. This approach has made possible a very impressive growth rate: indeed, its revenue growth has averaged 43% every year since its foundation in 1988. It also has the greatest in-depth global network coverage of any carrier. Vanco employs 500 people worldwide, including 170 in the UK.

Executive summary

Vanco is the brainchild of chief executive Alan Timpany, a "serial entrepreneur". He founded his first business in 1980; Vanco is his fourth, and embodies much of what he learnt about successful businesses en route to creating it in 1988. So, from day one Vanco had in place procedures, structures and schemes more associated with large companies.

Timpany and his fellow directors saw Vanco first as a pan-European company, and then as a global organisation – as he says, "to have a Wide Area Network business, you have to be in lots of places!" It was privately owned until November 2001, when Vanco listed on the full London market – the only full IPO between June and December 2001. It was twice oversubscribed and the share price has doubled since flotation.

Gartner, the world's leading technology research and advisory firm, has positioned Vanco in the leader quadrant in its latest "Magic Quadrant for European Network Service Providers". The company is the only non-asset-based carrier in this leaders' quadrant listing.

Turnover for the year ending January 31 2004 was £76.8m, up 45.5% on 2003; and operating profit was up 490% to £5.5m (2003: £0.9m).

Pay and benefits

Vanco's basic pay is benchmarked to be in the upper quartile. It is also keen on performance-related bonus elements. It has a structure in place whereby, according to grade, £5,000–£10,000 of salary will be performance-related. Sales people have sales plans, but there are also bonus schemes for other staff. These are linked to performance that they have some control over, rather than merely being a function of company profitability – something that Timpany believes has been key to the business's success.

The company has very wide internal share ownership, with two-thirds of its people owning shares. It has just introduced a Save As You Earn share scheme, whereby everyone can save money from salary, and at a later date, take it as either money plus interest or as shares. On the day of the float, everyone in the company became shareholders through a special share issue.

There is a flexible benefits scheme called v:choice. Unusually, this is in place across the company's global operations – something that different local employment laws often rule out. Each employee has an amount to spend on different features (or retain to boost salary). These include holidays, cars, pensions, non-work-related training, PMI, and so on. The scheme was named Most Effective Use of an International Benefits Strategy at the annual Employee Benefits Awards, 2004.

Recognition schemes take two forms. The first is by department. One example is the phone response system that allows every customer to vote on the quality of the service received over the phone. Operators with the highest votes receive recognition. The other is the business executive scheme: twice yearly, employees are put forward to a committee which votes on whether that person should advance. This is an open scheme, so employees know what they're being judged on and can query their verdicts.

There are various social activities, including the car club – for £400, employees have use of Vanco's exciting road cars such as Porsches during evenings or weekends.

The company annually organizes a kick-off conference – at 5 Star hotels, usually in Mediterranean locations – attended by every member of staff from around the world. This creates the opportunity to reward staff and share in the successes, as well as clearly communicate the objectives and challenges for the year ahead. The conference is unusual in that partners are even invited to attend.

Promotion and development

Vanco is definitely a meritocracy. People advance according to their abilities and proven skills. Of around 500 employees, up to 150 are business executives who are key people with substantial responsibilities. Promotion can be rapid – but Vanco is keen to ensure that it is not so rapid that people are promoted too quickly, as was often the case in the dot.com companies. Stephen Mansfield, group HR manager, explains: "Promotion is down to merit and to having done the existing job long enough to demonstrate strength in that role. If you're only in a job for nine months, I don't believe that's long enough to show the effects of your decisions. Eighteen months gives a much better picture."

The company recruits around ten graduates annually: perhaps six in the UK and four elsewhere. Mansfield says, "Graduate recruitment has brought in the level of intelligence and capability we needed. Those recruited ten years ago are now running large parts of the business."

Training is given to people when they need it, not simply to provide training for the sake of it. An in-house training department coordinates that.

All jobs are advertised internally, but with the company growing at such a fast rate, only around 20% of vacancies can currently be filled organically.

The engineering staff are mentored; sales or admin staff are not as such. However, these departments each have a formal process mentor. People can volunteer themselves as Process Champions (and earn an extra £1,000 a year). These people can provide one-to-one or evening training if employees require it.

Company culture

The culture of Vanco can be described as international, open, fun, stimulating and progressive. Managers who bad-mouth employees or are cynical are frowned upon. It's a young company (average age 30); more mature hires are often taken to add balance.

As far as Timpany is concerned, the more staff mobility there is, the better. There is no shortage of opportunities to work abroad – what there tends to be is a lack of language skills! Even those with just the mother tongue, though, can work in Australia, the USA and the Netherlands if they wish.

Vanco has a very strong global management team with staff who were in significant roles in Bell Atlantic, IBM, Unisys, Energis and Equant (which is part of France Telecom). This has been fundamental to creating the positive culture and sense that employees are working for a successful company with a winning team. The organisation has a big company feel as well as big company systems and processes, but does not present itself as being bureaucratic.

Work/life balance is seen as important. Timpany tells every person on the company induction course to go home at night! If people are working too hard, they are advised to take a holiday. After ten years' employment, three- to six-month sabbaticals are sometimes available.

There is no evidence of bullying or harassment, but reporting lines are in place to deal with them if they arise. Stress sometimes occurs, and in these cases, managers are encouraged to look at the individual's workload.

Those who flourish at Vanco are energetic. They are more content creating or making things happen than working in a very structured environment. This is a company in the making, a work in progress, and there isn't a rule book for everything. Instead, people are encouraged to write their own rules and change things if those changes are improvements.

Innovation

Vanco's major innovation was creating the name and the concept of being a Virtual Network Operator; this was a disruptive innovation – like Dell's selling of PCs direct – which changed the status quo of the industry. Andrew Cushing, Vanco's head of marketing, compares the business model with other industries such as manufacturing: "Up until 1988, people assumed you had to own infrastructure to be a network operator. That's like a small steel operator trying to compete with British Steel; it's doomed to fail. But we think the future is virtual. Is Ford a car manufacturer? Most people would think so. But actually it's a design and branding company. It doesn't manufacture many of its parts itself. It is, in effect, a virtual car company, buying the best of the marketplace for its use."

Being a virtual operator has allowed Vanco to grow at a phenomenal year-on-year rate while giving customers what they want in terms of coverage, flexibility and freedom. As a result, Vanco now has customers in 119 countries, and has an excellent record in retaining existing customers. Furthermore, BT now sees Vanco as its number one competitor in managed network space – quite an accolade!

Innovation is also to be seen in such areas as the customer voting system, the global flexible benefits system, and of course much of the company's day-to-day work.

Diversity and social responsibility

Vanco's workforce is 20% from ethnic minorities and 22% female; it welcomes all international groupings, and of course women as well as men. It currently has no female board members, but this is certainly not by design. According to Timpany, three or four of its best engineers are women – including the person who runs one of the most significant engineering areas.

The company supports a number of local charities. In particular, through various initiatives such as the Three Peaks Challenge, Vanco has raised a staggering £1.5m through sponsorship over ten years for Care, a children's charity (formerly known as Children's Aid Direct). It also encourages individuals to support charities.

Corporate governance

Vanco is committed to high standards of corporate governance, and supports the principles of good corporate governance and the Code of Best Practice (the Combined Code). The importance Vanco attaches to this area can be judged by the fact that, before the public float, it ran itself as though it were a public company. It has two principal standing committees – the audit committee and the remuneration committee. It has an internal audit function, and will be one of the first companies in its sector to comply with the new accounting standards – a team of people is already working on that area.

As a significant shareholder, Allen Timpany does not try to dominate proceedings. For instance, the latest changes to the share scheme were put to a free vote with Timpany abstaining.

Environmental record

According to Timpany, the company's record in the environmental area is not advanced – yet it seems to be doing as much if not more as many of its competitors. It does all the basics such as recycling paper and toner cartridges, and in general tries to operate at a responsible level both as a purchaser and a consumer.

Perhaps unusually in today's sometimes cynical business world, Vanco takes its corporate role seriously. It has, for instance, turned down business from companies it believes are acting detrimentally to the environment.

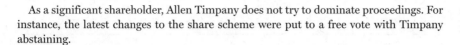

Virgin

Virgin Management Ltd
120 Campden Hill Road, London W8 7AR
Tel: (0) 20 7313 2000 **Fax:** (0) 20 7727 8200
Web: www.virgin.com **Email:** people@virgin.co.uk

Pay and Benefits	7.2	Innovation	6.7
Promotion and Development	6.5	Diversity	6.3
Training	6.0	Social Responsibility	6.5
Travel opportunities	6.6	Corporate Governance	6.6
Culture	7.2	Environment	6.8
Total			**66.4**

Founded upon the genius of Britain's best-known entrepreneur, Sir Richard Branson, the Virgin Group operates as a branded venture capital organisation, raising capital through strategic partnerships. It is the largest group of private companies in the UK, employing 31,000 people in Britain and 9,000 elsewhere. Virgin's portfolio includes airlines, trains, mobile phones, finance – and most recently, space-travel. In 2005, the group expects to make profits of about £650m on a turnover of more than £5.7bn.

Executive summary

Virgin is a unique organisation that operates by Schumacher's maxim: "small is beautiful". "We don't think of ourselves as a company," explains Will Whitehorn, the group's brand development and corporate affairs director. "We are investors in business with a brand name, corporate ethos and management style."

Branson founded his legendary Student magazine in 1967 and ran a mail-order business, as well as recording studios and record shops, before launching Virgin Atlantic in 1984. Following an unsuccessful flotation, he took the group private again and drew up the Virgin charter to safeguard agreements with partner companies.

Virgin Management manages Branson's own interests in the group, and the man himself takes a "hands-on, hands-off" approach to operations – pursuing new business while keeping in constant touch with, on the one hand, a group of trusted senior executives who represent him on company boards, and on the other, the managing directors of the various Virgin businesses.

In 2000, the group was investing heavily in what were then new companies, but recently it has seen profits accelerate with the rapid growth of Virgin Mobile and the success of airline Virgin Blue – now Australia's second-largest carrier after Qantas.

Following the flotation of individual companies, the group has "significant cash reserves – the future is very rosy". It plans to launch its mobile model in Canada, South Africa, Nigeria, China and Mexico; and to enter the US airline market with a low-cost domestic carrier, Virgin America. By 2010, Virgin wants to have spun out "ten or eleven quoted companies" and to be acknowledged among the world's top ten brands.

Pay and benefits

Serious opportunities exist at Virgin for making money. The group operates as a meritocracy, with the opportunity to reap huge rewards – recently, the chief executives of Virgin Mobile and Virgin Blue both made millions when their companies went public. Others benefited too, albeit to a lesser degree, when Virgin Mobile gifted its employees each with shares worth £1,000 to £2,000, depending on how long they had been with Virgin.

"We operate a progressive policy on pay," says Whitehorn. "For example, we are the highest payer of train drivers – our philosophy is that it's important to get good train drivers, and so far that has paid off because we are the only train operating company that hasn't had a serious accident."

While every Virgin company differs, several operate performance-related pay schemes, with employees able to accrue bonuses of between 10% and 20% of basic pay. At Virgin Atlantic, there is profit-related pay; and at Virgin Management, employees can treble their basic salary through various incentives and bonuses.

Senior executives are incentivised through LTIPs (long-term plans based on shadow equity); and for those lower down the scale, perks include the chance of being nominated by one's peers to enjoy a trip to Branson's own Caribbean island, Necker.

The group does not operate its own pension scheme – "one rule we do have is not to self-invest" – but pension contributions are made, and standard benefits are available such as health insurance, subsidised gym membership, and in some companies, free meals. Every employee receives a Virgin Tribe Card, which entitles bearers to a range of discounts on services from plane and train tickets to entertainment products.

Promotion and development

Virgin employees usually receive between seven and ten days of dedicated training each year, much of which – at Virgin Atlantic and Virgin Trains, for example – is offered in-house. Employees who want to embark on an external training course, such as an MBA, might be paid a retainer and offered a job on return, but on the whole the group does not actively sponsor such training.

Virgin's singular structure enables it to develop and retain talent in a way few other businesses can match. While talent is often brought in from outside, frequently through strategic partnerships, all vacancies are advertised internally and "there is a lot of movement within the companies". For example, the person who managed the procurement of Virgin Trains' new super-fast Pendolino moved to Virgin Atlantic in a similar role; and was then seconded to work on the procurement of spaceships for Virgin's fledgling commercial space venture, Virgin Galactic, which plans to offer two-hour flights from a site in the Mojave Desert from 2008.

The youngest managing director of a Virgin company is under thirty, and opportunities for responsibility are many and varied. Managing directors of businesses meet often for briefings, and senior managers in every business are sent "back to the floor" twice a year.

Overseas placements are common, usually on a formalised basis. There are also secondments – young lawyers from the panel of law firms used by the group, for example, are sometimes invited to work with Virgin for six months.

While the group still takes the attitude of "don't whinge about the problem, find a solution", it has made moves to increase the amount of mentoring and coaching that takes place. Succession planning is proactive and extensively supported by Virgin Management, which seeks to identify people who possess sufficient ambition, vision and drive to take the business to new levels.

Company culture

Most of the group's biggest businesses are unionised, and generally Virgin enjoys a good record on industrial relations. Employees are also encouraged to talk directly to the boss if they have a problem or complaint. Branson has an open-door policy and believes that people should not be criticised for communicating with him or telling him about what is happening in the company.

While other large companies use "breakfast with the boss" style events to connect employees with senior management; Virgin trades on its small size and fast-moving nature, expecting this kind of interaction to occur on an everyday basis. "If we find people are cutting themselves off, we are not happy about it," says Whitehorn. "It's a very flat culture in that sense."

The group fosters flexibility in working hours, taking an evangelical approach to job sharing as part of its bid to create a sophisticated but balanced working culture. Cabin crew at the airlines, for example, can take three months' unpaid leave, while others change their hours to suit new family needs. Virgin also takes seriously its regulatory responsibilities. "We do have to be very careful about the work/life balance because of the changes in health and safety regulations," notes Whitehorn. "Because many of our employees do work from home, we have to make sure the environments are safe."

People outside the organisation associate Virgin with ambition, popularity and friendliness. Since the mid-1980s, the general public has also linked the brand with the extraordinary energy and seemingly unshakeable confidence of the group's founder. Common to all Virgin companies are qualities such as flexibility and a drive to improve on existing standards.

Innovation

Innovation is the central ingredient in Virgin's business model – indeed, the brand is known principally for "doing things differently". This attitude is evident everywhere, from the scope of new products – such as space travel – to the management of staff.

Whitehorn points out that Virgin's is a culture in which mistakes are allowed. "Most large companies immediately get rid of anyone who makes an expensive mistake, but here we believe in 'three strikes and you're out'. If you make a major error, you learn a lot from it, and it doesn't make sense to let you go to a rival which then benefits from that knowledge."

In the 1990s, Virgin Direct took on the banks and changed industry practice by offering low-cost index-tracking personal equity plans. More recently, Virgin Mobile revolutionised the mobile phone market by piggy-backing on assets owned by other operators and offering a cheap, understandable model which was supported by top-class customer service.

While acknowledging that its ideas are widely copied, Virgin stays one step ahead by remaining "small". "We see our businesses as being local," explains Whitehorn. "People don't think of Virgin as being a big international conglomerate. Our philosophy is to 'get big by staying small'. It can be an asset not to have assets, and my own view is that this is increasingly how business will be done: with some people owning assets, and other people using those assets."

Diversity and social responsibility

While Virgin has no dedicated diversity officer within the group, it believes it already has a "strong" mix of people within both front-line teams and senior management ranks. "It has come home to us, particularly with working in Australia, just how progressive we are here – although there is always room for improvement," says Whitehorn.

Several of the group's top directors are female – the finance directors of Virgin Trains and Virgin Atlantic, for example – and the group also has a positive approach to hiring women into traditionally male-dominated roles: it recruited the first female pilot (20% of pilots are now female) and the first female train driver. "We believe very strongly that there is no reason why any job is better suited to a man or to a woman."

Virgin purposely avoids using the term "corporate social responsibility", seeing it as potentially "just an exercise in box-ticking". Instead, it operates a discrete function called Virgin Unite, which coordinates all of the charitable and community activity within the group. 1% of all the group's profits goes to charity, and more than six hundred staff are involved in individual volunteering projects.

Corporate governance

Each Virgin company abides by its own legal and regulatory requirements, but in general there is a certain kind of diligence among staff, says Whitehorn. "One of the things about the Virgin culture is that there is no divorce between ownership and control. Most large companies are not controlled by the people who own them, whereas here – even when we take a company public – we always try to keep a minority interest. If there is no divorce of ownership from control, the only person that you are defrauding – if you are not hot on corporate governance – is yourself."

Environmental record

While not especially proactive in promoting environmentally friendly policies internally, Virgin acknowledges that with several of its businesses making a considerable impact on the environment, it must be aware, alert and – where possible – find ways to improve. To this end, it has achieved its goal of making Virgin Atlantic the most efficient airline operator in the world, with the youngest fleet using the least fuel per person out of all fleets globally.

Whitehorn says the group is proud of its track record and "strong approach" and goes further in pointing out that the brand is stronger than any one element of the group. "The Virgin brand is so strong that it polices us. That's why we can genuinely say, for example, that we put safety above profit. It's more valuable to us to make safety a priority than to make money in the short-tem."

Wanadoo

Wanadoo UK plc
500 The Campus, Spring Way, Maylands Avenue, Hemel Hempstead H2 7TG
Tel: (0) 1727 207097 **Fax:** (0) 1727 207169
Web: www.wanadoo.co.uk **Emal:** talentmanagementdirector@uk.wanadoo.com

ⓦ wanadoo

Pay and Benefits	5.9	Innovation	7.1
Promotion and Development	6.2	Diversity	7.1
Training	6.8	Social Responsibility	6.3
Travel opportunities	7.4	Corporate Governance	7.2
Culture	7.0	Environment	6.6
Total			**67.6**

Wanadoo, a brand from France Telecom, is Europe's number one broadband provider. It is also the number one provider of internet services in the UK and France, and the No 2 provider in Spain and the Netherlands. Wanadoo has 9.3 million customers, with 35% of these on broadband. Over 2.4m active accounts are registered with Wanadoo in the UK. Previously known as Freeserve, 500 staff are employed in three UK offices – Hemel Hempstead (head office), Leeds and London. There are 7,600 people in Wanadoo worldwide, and over 218,000 in the giant France Telecom group.

Executive Summary

Wanadoo UK has had quite a corporate journey in its short but sprightly six years. It began life as Freeserve, the UK's first internet service provider to offer "free" internet access. A spin-off and Initial Public Offering (IPO) followed, and in the frantic days of dotcom mania, Freeserve raced into the FTSE 100 Index. In spring 2001, Freeserve was bought by Wanadoo, one of Europe's largest internet companies. In 2004, Wanadoo was bought out by France Telecom, and its shares de-listed.

Much has happened in this time. As part of France Telecom's home division, Wanadoo's strategy revolves around everything internet in the home, focusing on a range of internet products and services, including broadband and narrowband access.

In 2004, the decision was made to rebrand Freeserve to Wanadoo to really exploit the fast-growth broadband market. Since then, Wanadoo's fortunes have taken off and it is now the largest broadband provider in Europe. While BT is still the UK market leader in broadband, Wanadoo – with 4 million customers throughout Europe – is catching up fast. Its introduction of 1Mb home broadband for just £17.99 a month in August 2004 is likely to accelerate this.

In the last two years, Wanadoo UK has become earnings before pre-tax profit positive. It is one of the first internet companies to be in the black, and Wanadoo Group even paid a dividend in 2003. Previously supported by shareholders, Wanadoo is now standing firmly on its feet, with a financially strong and very committed parent in France Telecom.

Pay and Benefits

Wanadoo claims salaries are in the upper quartile, and benchmarks them at least every two years. "Because of the industry we are in, if we're not at the top of the pay scales we don't get the best people," says Norman McQueen, director of talent management. "For some jobs: good, qualified resource is extremely scarce."

There are just four bands for pay – "squashed but broad," you might say, given this industry! This starts at administrative, through professional/team leader/manager, to senior managers and then executive directors. In addition to annual salary reviews, bonuses can be earned in one of two ways – individual "stretch" performance against smart objectives aligned with Wanadoo's values and company goals; and the company meeting its targets. This is split 50:50 for administrative staff, professional staff and mangers; but skewed 75:25 towards company targets for senior executives, whose performance has a greater bearing on Wanadoo's fortunes. Between 10% and 50% of salary can be earned as a bonus depending on pay band.

There were share options before France Telecom bought Wanadoo. These have been replaced by a Collective Incentive Bonus Scheme, with the structure and rewards similar to a share option scheme.

There is a flexible benefits scheme, which is updated every year, with everything from life assurance and critical illness cover to subsidised childcare vouchers and gym membership. These are not given away – instead Wanadoo sets basic salaries "right" (high) and then colleagues can trade in and out the benefits for which the company has negotiated preferential deals. Holidays – the core is 25 days each year – can also be traded up or down. A generous pension scheme is part of the package, and has a 55% take-up. The company encourages everyone to join, even advertising the scheme in the bathrooms!

Promotion and development

There is such a big emphasis on training and personal development at Wanadoo that it is a distinctive benefit of working for the company. "We must spend more per person on coaching and development than is average," says McQueen. Training and development is embedded in each personal development plan, and from top to bottom, it's hard to avoid at Wanadoo.

Management and leadership development is tied into three key things: competency, the company's values, and transference of learning. External coaches are used, and there are mentors inside and outside the business. There are induction programmes and generic courses on time management, presentation, communications and personal impact skills; and as you might expect from an internet company, a lot of e-learning. Wanadoo colleagues receive an average of five days' training a year.

A crucial part of development is "living the customer experience". So each year in the Contact Programme, every single colleague gets to meet customers. This means attending one of the three call centres or listening to live customer communications as well as visiting store outlets or researching a product or service as a mystery shopper. They then report back at team briefings.

There are CIPDs, IMs and other professional qualifications throughout the company, and if requests are relevant to the business, they are supported through the technical training budget. In addition, employees have the opportunity to attend Business and Leadership seminars held by the Institute of Management Studies in Manchester or London.

Wanadoo UK CEO, Eric Abensur, sums it up: "Wanadoo is made up of a talented, multi-skilled workforce and it's down to these people that we're at where we are today. By having things right on the inside, we're in a position to be able to provide our customers with a first-class experience."

Company culture

"This is a great environment in which to work," says McQueen. "The people we want are highly marketable; therefore how we attract, retain and develop their strengths is crucial. We do that well at Wanadoo, and people appreciate that."

Wanadoo people are genuinely committed to Wanadoo's key Four Values – proximity, willingness, optimism and simplicity. This is not mission statement dogma, but real values crystallised from many workshops and feedback mechanisms. McQueen describes Wanadoo as a "brave" organisation. "The executive always seeks feedback and promises actions in response. Not all organisations are that willing to make themselves that vulnerable or personable." Walkabouts by management are expected, so if a director visits a location and doesn't take to the floor, talent management soon gets the feedback!

The original Freeserve culture was inevitably very developmental, innovative and start-up. While many "old timers" still remain, Wanadoo has become a more grown-up company, putting in place the necessary processes. Hard evidence of this is the HR, or talent development department – twenty strong, with its head, McQueen, the only male.

Wanadoo UK has always enjoyed a degree of liberté from its French parents. Asked, "are you becoming French?" chief technology officer, Stratis Scleparis, replied: "We are diluting their culture". But this is definitely a collaborative environment, with both sides learning from a productive two-way relationship.

This is not a nine-to-five culture. Some roles have long hours, but people are attracted to them and want to work hard – driven by thirst, ambition, loyalty and a desire to develop. But Wanadoo certainly does not want burnout. "It's not about staying later than the boss, and we really do try and encourage the balance," says McQueen. Managers take a very flexible approach to individuals setting core hours to accommodate important issues such as childcare – but you must still be able to do your job.

Innovation

Being small relative to its main rival, BT, Wanadoo must innovate to compete – in pricing, products and promotion. Wanadoo's £17.99 1-Megabit broadband package has been a price reduction blockbuster, a "conquest market" initiative that is challenging the company on how to manage the avalanche response. Another innovative product is Livebox – a wireless product for the home, it enables multiple users to connect via broadband simultaneously, for computers, online gaming, on-demand TV and other applications.

And in its busy personal development programme, one of the presentation skills courses involves colleagues taking to the stage to tell corporate stories in a real test of public speaking.

Diversity and social responsibility

Wanadoo doesn't formalise policies on diversity – it doesn't need to. McQueen says, "We recruit the best person for the job. I have never come across anything at Wanadoo that concerns me over diversity – but I have at other companies." Wanadoo breaks out diversity figures in recruitment to support the point.

This is a truly international workforce, partly caused by a UK shortage of skills in certain specialist areas. A technical billing software programme used by Wanadoo has required the company to fly in people for interview from across the world. This team consists of no fewer than 16 different nationalities. The team leader suggested they each put flags on their desk during the football Euro 2004 – a feast for students of vexillology!

Women comprise 37% of the workforce (but adjusted for applications received, recruitment runs above 50%). While Deborah Sherry is currently the only woman on the executive board of nine, recently it was as many as four. Equal opportunity has never been an issue here. Women are encouraged to return after having children, even being offered bonuses to do so. Maternity leave, subsidised childcare vouchers, job sharing, reduced working days or hours are all used positively.

Wanadoo supports the Prince's Trust, regarding this to be an ideal way of getting colleagues involved with the community while aligning with company values. The Prince's Trust needs mentors for the many small businesses it helps establish, and Wanadoo provides this resource. The company supports various local activities – playgroups, a barge for kids, painting a mural on the school playground. A lot of people in Wanadoo ask to get involved and the company is only too keen to back them, including allowing them to use the company's many communications channels.

Corporate Governance

Wanadoo takes good governance very seriously, to meet its best practice aspirations as a company and an employer. Although no longer a UK listed company, Wanadoo UK still follows many best governance practices as set out in the Combined Code, and there is also a separate compliance officer. As a subsidiary company within France Telecom, Wanadoo is required to be compliant with French Securities Regulations and the recent post-Enron Sarbanes-Oxley Act. The group also operates a corporate social responsibility policy, in which Wanadoo is fully involved.

The company is assiduous in checking that contractors do not fall foul of IR35 regulations (it employs a number of freelancers, particularly in content management on its portal).

Environmental record

Wanadoo is not the type of manufacturing company that could pollute the environment, but nevertheless it has environment managers who manage everything the company can do to be environmentally friendly. Wanadoo is diligent in segregating and recycling office waste. Nothing is missed – cartridges, paper and technical materials all find their way to a recycling point. Unwanted mobile phones are given to charities.

As an internet company, as much as possible is generated and kept online, reducing the need for paper. Walking the talk, there are email policy guidelines (why print off emails?), job applications are posted and processed online, and e-learning proliferates.

West Yorkshire Passenger Transport Authority (Metro)

Metro, Wellington House,
40-50 Wellington Street, Leeds LS1 2DE
Tel: (0) 113 251 7272 **Fax:** (0) 113 251 7333
Web: www.wymetro.com **Email:** recruitment@wypte.com

METRO

Pay and Benefits	4.7	Innovation	5.0
Promotion and Development	5.7	Diversity	5.0
Training	6.0	Social Responsibility	5.7
Travel opportunities	2.7	Corporate Governance	5.0
Culture	4.3	Environment	6.0
Total			**50.1**

Metro is the business name of the West Yorkshire Passenger Transport Authority (PTA) and Executive (PTE).

The Authority is made up of 22 elected councillors from the county's five local councils, Bradford, Calderdale, Kirklees, Leeds and Wakefield. The Executive carries out the policies set by the Authority – coordinating and executing the provision of transport routes and services across West Yorkshire. It shapes the framework for a multitude of transport operators, procures services and provides a range of passenger facilities – eg bus stations, bus stops and shelters, travel information services (including a busy call centre), ticketing schemes, and concessions and subsidies. Metro has £750m to spend on capital expenditure over the next three years.

The Executive employs around 350 people, at Wellington House in Leeds, at travel centres and bus stations across West Yorkshire, and at its south Leeds depot.

Executive Summary

This is a Passenger Transport Executive with a difference. While in the public sector, it behaves like an enterprising company. It loves "buzz". It innovates. And an energetic management team is obsessed with providing value-added, quality, and a positive culture for its employees. It can boast awards in abundance, it regularly tops business surveys, and has the most widely recognised logo in West Yorkshire.

Metro is acknowledged nationally as being in the vanguard of transport planning. Metro was named PTA of the Year three years in a row – if it was the World Cup trophy, they'd be allowed to keep it.

Metro, obviously, is financially sustainable. It is funded from Council Tax levies, government transport investment grants, rail grants, and the European Union. It also generates "external income" by selling advertising space; and transport operators contribute to bus stations and information centres. Metro's annual revenue budget is around £150m.

With the government envisaging a greater role for PTEs, developing partnerships, vision and good planning is crucial to Metro. And with successes such as its Yellow School Bus, a groundbreaking real-time passenger information system, and guided buses – it can demonstrate best value through innovation.

Pay and Benefits

The taxpayer funds Metro's activities, so it does not have excessive bonuses – but it does offer competitive salaries, attractive benefits and work/life balance. The evidence is that Metro attracts top people from the private sector, often consultants who have seen Metro in action by working for an operator or another partnership. "This is an organisation where people can make a difference," says Sheena Pickersgill, director of corporate services. "They can realise their full potential here."

There are a variety of roles within Metro, and salaries vary enormously. Pay scales are softened by flexibility; graduates might join a different scale. Metro pays market rates to take into account and attract experience, competencies and specialisms – somewhat unusual for a PTE.

The pension scheme – based on half final salary – is excellent by today's measures. Employees contribute 6%, which is matched or bettered by Metro. Then there is an array of other benefits. Every employee receives a Metrocard for free travel within West Yorkshire. There are childcare vouchers, a BUPA counselling line covering everything from stress management to tax advice, free health checks and flu vaccines. There's even a massage service in-house!

Generous holidays start at 28 days a year, increasing by two days for five years' service and another two for ten years. You can earn an additional day a month if you build up the necessary hours through the flexitime policy, based around core hours of 10–4 and a 37-hour week.

Metro is a very sociable organisation: bonding through parties, quiz evenings, sports teams or just drinks in the pub after work. During the football World Cup, employees were allowed to watch the early morning kick-off games on a large screen at work with breakfast thrown in.

Promotion and development

"People put their heart and soul into their work," says Kieran Preston, Metro's director general. "They don't move from the private to the public sector for 'a rest'. They come to Metro because they can make a real impact and realise their goals. They can see that we are players who punch above our weight. In turn we look for people with drive and ambition."

"Because Metro is always involved with innovative schemes, there's always a challenging new project to work on," says Pickersgill. The corporate services director herself has successfully driven the Yellow School Bus project forward, despite it being in the domain of passenger services rather than corporate services. "Because I wanted to do it," she says.

"We have taken a lot of risks to get ahead of projects," says Preston. "Transport planning skills in particular are in demand." But Metro also turns people into transport planners. "Short, fat courses" are used to augment the personal skills of its bright, energetic people.

Metro is committed to the policies it delivers, and equally to its staff who make all of that possible. Its training and development programme is comprehensive and definitely one of Metro's great strengths. In a recent Leeds University survey of 50 regional companies, Metro ranked top for management development. All new starters are given a thorough induction, and any essential training is given priority and undertaken almost immediately. Every six months, employees have a development review, which evaluates individual performance and what they want out of the organisation, and translates into a training and development plan.

Company culture

Metro is a forward-thinking and fast-moving organisation and has had a Quality Framework in place for years to ensure that it is "fit for purpose". "To deliver quality services, we need a quality culture embedded in the organisation, and that begins with commitment at the top level," says Pickersgill. The constituent parts of the Quality Framework are customer focus, staff commitment, managerial effectiveness, and planning and corporate performance.

Culture is a participative process and one that is under constant review. "If you had the resources, what would you change?" is one question that staff are asked, the answers being fed up the organisation to contribute to service improvement plans. It's also horizontal – looking across the organisation – so people are asked, "what do you need others to do to help you deliver your targets?"

Annual staff satisfaction surveys ensure that the culture is natural and organic, never imposed. With investment in employees, this is a very open, flexible organisation. The mood is friendly and real team spirit is evident. "Buzz is an important word," says Pickersgill. "People who come on site say they cannot believe it is a public sector organisation. The culture here is fantastic."

HR does much to support this positive culture through good, well thought through policies that it regularly updates. "These are not driven by legal requirements," says Jenette Sargent, HR manager. "It's wanting to be the best. And we look at other companies to see what we can introduce. The organisation is unionised, but we encourage people to talk to HR first and we've been successful in achieving that." Communication is key and there's lots of it. Surveys, team briefings, intranet, awaydays and group seminars proliferate. External assessments like Beacon Council and Investors in People are pursued to demonstrate to employees they have an organisation to be proud of.

Metro is exceptional in looking after women with children, new fathers, and people with caring responsibilities. There is no fixed scheme, although Metro pays more than statutory maternity and paternity pay. Metro prefers to listen to people individually and do what it can to help employees manage their lives.

Innovation

Metro far exceeds its brief of making public transport work, and innovation comes as second nature. Its guided buses project – a narrow, segregated strip of road that only buses can use – has been a great success, and Metro has been invited to lead this initiative nationally. In bus station design, its aim is to make them more like airports.

Metro's real-time passenger information project is the most comprehensive scheme with the most complicated execution. Using GPS, a central computer, route identifiers and on-board receivers, "real" real-time information might not be far away – the Big Thing that customers say they want. Information could even be sent to mobile phones and via the internet, as well as on display screens at bus stops.

Four years ago, Metro set out its vision to transform school transport. Its resulting Yellow School Bus project delivers a highly visible bus (it's yellow), a dedicated, known driver, passenger registration, on-board entertainment, and a hotline for parents to call if children are not attending that day. From the pilot scheme in 2002, Metro has proved that it can get children out of cars (and four-wheel drives) with staggering results. Some 91% of children on "My Bus" – as its young passengers have dubbed it – used to travel to school by car. Attendance levels have improved by 5%. One girl used to attend just two days a week; now it's five and her academic performance is rising. After demonstrating this success, Metro has received funding of £18.7m to provide 150 Yellow Buses over the next three years.

Diversity and social responsibility

"We believe hugely in equality as an organisation," says Preston. "We don't need kitemarks to prove that – we've gone well beyond that." Metro is committed to the development of positive policies (not positive discrimination) to promote equal opportunities for everyone in all areas of employment.

For age/gender/colour-blind organisations, real diversity perhaps comes in the type of people working there. Metro has encouraged people of different backgrounds, people who challenge the status quo, who take risks and are "a little bit different".

In the traditionally male-dominated transport industry, Metro is striving to change attitudes. It has tackled and removed any negative attitudes within its own organisation, and now aims beyond. At a recent Journey of a Lifetime conference in Leeds, Metro hired actors to play the parts of drivers on buses transporting delegates, and they gave them a "piece of their mind". A blunt, first-hand experience of what the customer sometimes encounters on the buses, the stunt was aimed at focusing delegates' minds and improving the industry's overall image. "We were priming them for the themes of the conference in an entertaining but slightly challenging way," says Pickersgill.

Corporate Governance

With many different stakeholders, and needing to account for its funding, corporate governance is ingrained at Metro. It works on behalf of the people of West Yorkshire to make public transport reliable, easy to understand and use, accessible, attractive, affordable, efficient, safe and secure. It is also committed to the principles of best value.

"Everyone checks what we do," says Preston. "For example, with the five district councils – we don't have to, but we show and share everything with them." The best type of corporate governance is to have the best people and organisations with a stake in the operation – and that effectively is how Metro works. There are also non-executive directors and a risk management group. Compliance is a given, as is data protection and privacy of information.

Environmental record

Benefiting the environment is fundamental to everything that Metro does. In particular, it aims to reduce the number of vehicle journeys – getting people to use public transport instead of cars. It has succeeded in this to the extent of saving 40m vehicle miles each year. There are 200m bus journeys each year, and it is reckoned that its SuperTram initiative will take out 5m car journeys a year. "It's estimated that traffic congestion costs the NHS around £11bn annually," says Preston. "If we can get people out of cars, we can contribute quite a lot."

Metro must make an environmental impact report on every scheme it is involved in. Knowing this, it tries to sort problems out before they start, planning well ahead. Metro has all the recycling boxes ticked. Paper, toner and cartridges are recycled, and unwanted computer equipment and mobile phones are often given away to good causes.

Whitbread

Whitbread plc
CityPoint, One Ropemaker Street, London EC2Y 9HX
Tel: (0) 20 7606 4455
Web: www.whitbread.co.uk

enjoy!**Whitbread**

Pay and Benefits	6.7	Innovation	7.0
Promotion and Development	7.0	Diversity	5.7
Training	7.3	Social Responsibility	6.7
Travel opportunities	5.0	Corporate Governance	6.7
Culture	6.3	Environment	7.3
Total			**65.7**

Whitbread plc is the UK's leading hospitality business, with major brands in hotels (Premier Travel Inn, Marriott); restaurants (including Brewers Fayre, Beefeater, TGI Friday's and Costa coffee shops); and racquets, health and fitness clubs (David Lloyd Leisure) – giving it a unique portfolio. It acquired the Premier Lodge hotel chain in 2004, but no longer brews beer or owns pubs. Whitbread has around 1,400 outlets UK-wide, and employs 50,000 people; plus 20,000 and a further 600 outlets through its Pizza Hut joint venture. A thousand people work at its administrative centres in Bedfordshire; 35 are based at its London HQ – although this is relocating to Bedfordshire during 2005, in order to bring the brands and head office closer together. Turnover in 2003–04 was nearly £2bn.

Executive summary

After 258 years in the beer business, Whitbread sold its brewing, pub and bar interests in 2000–2001. It was a big wrench, but the company felt the changes were essential to maintain its focus on profitability, earnings growth and increasing return on capital. The group's businesses – in value and upscale hotels; mid-market restaurants; and racquets, health and fitness clubs – give it a unique insight into Britain's leisure habits and the ability to cross-fertilise, says Alan Parker, who was promoted to chief executive in 2004.

The group has achieved double-digit earnings growth for the last seven reporting periods, its share price has roughly doubled in the same period, and it claims to outperform the industry average in every sector.

Asked to account for Whitbread's success, Angie Risley, group human resources director, says: "We've been very clear about our brands, and created a clear and distinctive customer proposition for each one. We're good at anticipating changes in the market, we've focused on investing in our fastest-growing businesses (David Lloyd Leisure, Premier Travel Inn, Brewers Fayre, Beefeater and Costa), and we've moved out of businesses like brewing which weren't in growing sectors. But it's our people who are the key to our success."

The £505m acquisition of Premier Lodge in 2004, and its merger with Whitbread's existing Travel Inn, made the group the largest hotel operator in the UK – but Whitbread's main focus remains organic growth. All three sectors in which it operates are growing, and by 2010 the company plans to nearly double the number of outlets in some businesses – such as David Lloyd Leisure and Costa – and significantly increase others. Its ambition is to double in value over the next five years.

Pay and benefits

"Our people are paid at least median salaries, and where we need to we'll pay top quartile," says Risley. "But we believe our total package is ahead of the market."

Performance-related bonuses are key – based mostly on sales, customer satisfaction and outlet profit achievement for lower grades; more on the balanced score card and group-wide profit achievement for senior people – and can increase a manager's income by 20–80%. There is also a profit-sharing element. Senior people can take advantage of an equity-based incentive scheme, which the company would like to extend; and all told, in excess of 6,000 staff are Whitbread shareholders. In front-line operations, individuals and teams can earn ad hoc incentives linked to performance – ranging from cash and gifts to time off and public recognition. All salaries and benefits are benchmarked.

The benefits package is solid: health and dental care, discounts at all Whitbread outlets and some third party businesses, an employee assistance programme (counselling etc.), cars for senior people and others who need them, and a money purchase pension scheme with company contributions of 4–10% for managers (plus a stakeholder scheme for everyone). Some business units offer more – at David Lloyd Leisure, for instance, all staff get free membership – and holiday allowances also vary. There is no formal flexible benefits scheme, but staff can make choices. There is no provision of or contribution to childcare, though this is under review.

Many staff in Whitbread's pub restaurant businesses are still on the minimum wage, although this is offset by rewards and incentives. Risley is a member of the Low Pay Commission, which shows that the company is aware of the issues.

Promotion and development

Whitbread has a long-standing policy of promoting from within, with about 60% of vacancies filled internally. The average length of service among the 100-odd most senior managers is nine years. For every role in every business unit there is a programme called The Journey, which tells people what they need to do to move up to the next level.

There are plenty of management opportunities – 1,400 outlets require 1,400 managers, while larger establishments also have departmental and assistant managers. The youngest managers are only in their mid-20s. Whitbread offers the opportunity to work within several distinct areas of the hospitality sector as well as in a full range of professional posts, so it's possible to have a varied and challenging career without ever leaving. "We deliberately move people around the business to develop them, and put them on projects to stretch them," says Risley.

Despite this emphasis on nurturing talent, he adds, "we're a growing business so we're continually on the lookout for good new people". Marriott Hotels alone takes on 50 graduate trainees a year, while the Shooting Stars programme in Premier Travel Inn recruits around 30 graduates each year.

Risley describes the company's approach as developing people's strengths. One of the operations directors, for example, was discovered to be very innovative – so he was transferred to a marketing role, which fit better with his natural strengths.

The company supports education at all levels, ranging from its own MBA programme with Oxford Brookes University to the improbably-named Costa Coffee College and David Lloyd Leisure campus which train staff for externally recognised skills qualifications. Across the group, 500 chefs are also on modern apprenticeship schemes.

Whitbread's external training budget is an impressive-sounding £3m a year but this averages just £45 for each person, so a lot of training is on the job. Everyone gets at least one day's training a year, but the company says the average is much higher. This is supplemented by an extensive electronic learning programme.

Company culture

According to Whitbread's annual employee survey, more than 90% of people say they have friends at work. This accords with Risley's view – when asked for words which encapsulate the company's culture, her opening trio are: friendly, decent and fair. She says the kinds of characters who succeed at Whitbread are "people who like the business and the things it does".

The company says it listens to its people and takes careful account of Views surveys, and employee satisfaction is one of its key performance indicators. It has no fewer than 170 HR team members, and several operating units have Investors in People accreditation. Core values of the company, according to Risley, include "belief in people, caring for customers, continuous improvement and a passion for winning".

That said, Whitbread also expects some typically hard-edged, corporate qualities: delivery-focused, results-oriented, playing to win etc. "We pay for performance," says Risley, simply.

Some of Whitbread's establishments, especially hotels, are open round-the-clock. The company tries to make this sound like a virtue rather than a necessity, stressing the opportunities to choose working hours to suit one's lifestyle, which may even include working "the graveyard shift". On the plus side, the company is truly flexible about working hours, especially for staff with families. Mums can work from 10am–3pm, for example, or just one day a week; job sharing and part-time working are encouraged; and homeworking is supported where feasible, particularly by the use of technology. And for team members, there are plenty of David Lloyd Leisure centres to relax in on discounted membership.

Whitbread has outlets in all corners of the UK, and there are a few opportunities for foreign travel. Costa has joint ventures in the Middle East and is starting up franchise operations in China and India; David Lloyd Leisure has operations in Holland and is establishing itself in Belgium and Spain. The company hopes to grow its international operations over time.

Innovation

Ever since it perfected the art of bottling beer for long-distance transportation in 1868, Whitbread has had a history of innovation. Now that ingenuity is being turned to service-based businesses – the company has been quick to spot the demand for cheap, reliable hotels and build up the Premier Travel Inn chain to meet it.

In its business practices, the company says it was one of the first to outsource its IT systems, and among the first in its sector to introduce an ERP (enterprise resource planning) computer system. It is also a pioneer user of voice-activated technology in distribution, and tablet PCs for outlet-based training.

Continuous improvement is one of Whitbread's core beliefs, and staff at all levels are expected to contribute. In 2004, the pub restaurants ran a competition to encourage chefs to dream up specials and new menu dishes, while the Beefeater managing director regularly writes to his team inviting them to contact him directly with feedback.

As further evidence of the group's commitment to its people, Risley, as HR director, is one of only four executive directors (ie Whitbread employees) to sit on the main board.

Diversity and social responsibility

Whitbread does an impressive amount of charitable work at both corporate and local level. It is a founder member of the PerCent Club, which encourages businesses to give at least 1% of their profits to charity. Corporate partnerships include Brewers Fayre with Whizz-Kidz, and Marriott's London hotels with the Prince's Trust; while David Lloyd Leisure provides a variety of community access packages such as free coaching and court time for local schools under its junior tennis programme.

Local initiatives, by outlets or individual staff, are also encouraged; and the company will match fundraising up to £200. Nearly 10% of staff subscribe to the payroll giving programme; and the company has actively supported volunteering around the UK for more than 20 years, through programmes like the Whitbread Young Achievers Awards.

As part of its commitment to equal opportunities, Whitbread says it has worked hard to ensure its recruitment, promotion and succession practices are free of discrimination, even if unintentional. It is taking steps to make its employee population representative of the wider community and of its customer base. Until its ERP system is finished, it doesn't know the racial and religious make-up of its staff. Women make up well over half of all staff, however, and 23% of senior management. The average age of senior management is 42.

Corporate Governance

Whitbread regards all laws and regulations as important in safeguarding the interests of its customers, employees and shareholders. It requires its suppliers to complete a questionnaire about their compliance with key initiatives and to address issues that Whitbread feels are important.

The company began implementing the Combined Code on Corporate Governance a year before it came into effect, and has developed a code of business ethics which is briefed annually to all employees. The code also contains a formal whistle-blowing policy.

The company or its subsidiaries have won many external awards including: Sunday Times 100 Best Companies to Work For (Travel Inn), Brand Revitalisation, Marketing Society Awards (Beefeater), Institute of IT Training Awards (Brewers Fayre and Brewsters), Operator of the Year, Leisure Property Awards (David Lloyd Leisure), and Business Leader of the Year (Alan Parker).

Environmental record

The larger Marriott hotels have invested in equipment to separate, compact and recycle waste; and Marriott has been accredited under the Green Globe Environmental Management scheme. A scheme to recycle cardboard in Whitbread's restaurant businesses will potentially save 7,000 tonnes of waste a year – it won one of the Severnside Annual Recycling Awards and was shortlisted for the National Recycling Awards. Additionally, the group tries to recycle fixtures and fittings when refurbishing outlets, and encourages suppliers to use minimal or re-usable packaging. The group's offices recycle paper and photocopier cartridges, and there is a group-wide glass recycling programme.

Cutting car use is difficult given the location of many of Whitbread's outlets, but it gives season ticket loans wherever applicable, and incentivises staff to choose fuel-efficient company cars. It is switching its vehicles from petrol to diesel to reduce carbon dioxide emissions. David Lloyd Leisure won an Energy Efficiency Council innovation award for its use of combined heat and power. Whitbread has also recently been Energy Efficiency Accredited by the National Energy Foundation in recognition of reductions in energy consumption and emissions.

WL Gore

WL Gore & Associates (UK) Limited
Kirkton South Road, Kirkton Campus, Livingston EH54 7BT
Tel: (0) 1506 460123
Web: www.gore.com

GORE
Creative Technologies
Worldwide

Pay and Benefits	5.4	Innovation	6.8
Promotion and Development	6.4	Diversity	4.8
Training	6.8	Social Responsibility	7.3
Travel opportunities	6.4	Corporate Governance	6.4
Culture	7.7	Environment	6.1
Total			**64.1**

WL Gore & Associates (UK) Limited is the British end of a world-wide company with 6,000 employees in 45 locations. It employs 450 in Scotland – in Dundee and Livingston – in four business divisions: electronic products, industrial products, medical products and fabrics.

Its products have one common thread – fluoropolymers, which are unique among plastics for their chemical and thermal stability and have been used by Gore in thousands of different products – from implantable medical patches to electronic cable insulation. Gore's leadership in the field of fluoropolymer innovation has made it an award-winning international giant.

Executive summary
The company began in 1958 when Bill and Vieve Gore (husband and wife) set out to explore opportunities for fluorocarbon polymers, especially polytetrafluoroethylene (which, mercifully, is now known as PTFE). The founders could see its potential and have exploited it ever since – using it for medical implants, high-performance fabrics that really keep you dry and comfortable, various industrial products, and electronic ribbon cables.

From the outset, the company has steered clear of traditional hierarchy – opting instead for a team-based environment in the belief that this fosters personal initiative, encourages innovation, and promotes direct, person-to-person communication.

By the end of the 1960s, manufacturing sites had been opened worldwide – including Scotland, Germany and Japan – and Gore products were used on the moon.

Gore has repeatedly been named one of the 100 Best Companies to Work for in America, and it is among Fortune magazine's 100 Best Companies.

To the outsider, the way it operates – with no bosses, no hierarchy and equality everywhere – might seem a recipe for anarchy; in fact, it seems to be a recipe for a financially stable corporation with a world-wide presence and one of the 200 largest privately held businesses in America.

Pay and benefits
Gore has no employees. They are all associates. And they will not talk about pay. Its attitude to what it calls "compensation": "Unlike companies which base an employee's pay on the evaluations of one or two people – or supervisors' opinion alone – Gore involves many associates in the process. Our goal: internal fairness and external competitiveness."

Ann Gillies works in human resources in Livingston. She is one of three who do so. But she has no title, and when you ask about pay she says: "I will not tell you about anybody's pay. It is confidential. Pay is not based on job or your job title because we don't have anything like that. It is based on the contribution the associate makes to the enterprise, and contribution is decided by people you work with."

Associates rank their team members each year in order of their contribution to the business, and to maintain competitiveness there is extensive benchmarking and comparisons with pay in other companies.

The menu of benefits is headed by an associate stock ownership plan, which provides equity ownership – and, it is claimed, financial security for retirement. Every year, the company puts an additional 10% of pay into an account, which buys Gore stock for each associate active in the plan. An associate gets this benefit after approximately four years of employment. The stake is valued quarterly, but as the Gore stock is privately held and not traded on public markets, this is not easy.

The rest of the menu includes holidays, profit sharing, a final salary pension scheme, life assurance, medical plans, and long-term disability insurance.

Promotion and development

There are development opportunities aplenty, but there is no promotion. You don't promote when there is no hierarchy. There might be "leaders" but they are said to emerge naturally by demonstrating special knowledge, skill or experience that advances a business objective. Is it meritocracy by another name? There are no chains of command, no career ladders, nobody cracking the whip – anathema in most big businesses. But not at Gore. It says that the most effective way to stimulate growth is to encourage associates to have the confidence to take charge of their own development.

This is done by arranging for them to work alongside others who can complement their skills as well as encourage them to concentrate on their own strengths. Associates generate and follow their own personal development plan. You get on by showing commitment, creativity and entrepreneurial thinking.

Gore says that continuous learning is embedded in the corporate culture. One of its four basic principles – freedom – reflects the importance placed in helping associates to grow in knowledge, skill, scope of activity and responsibility. This can mean taking on tasks far removed from what the associate initially had to offer. In many ways, it is self-development; but being part of an international company, which lives on innovation, provides many development opportunities and a lot of career satisfaction – even though you never actually put a foot on a career ladder.

Company culture

The company has a five-word objective which sums up its culture: "Make money and have fun." It adds a brief elaboration: "Our success in making money and having fun rests on our ability to invent, manufacture, sell and service products our customers value."

This is all done with what founder Bill Gore called a flat, lattice organisation. From the start, he was committed to providing a work environment that encouraged creativity and opportunity with a flat, title-free organisation relying on direct, person-to-person communication rather than chains of command.

This is deemed to encourage hands-on innovation, involving those closest to a project or business in the decision-making. Teams organise around opportunities and leaders emerge.

The culture has an evangelical ring to it: fairness to each other and everyone with whom we come in contact; freedom to encourage, help and allow other associates to grow in knowledge, skill and scope of responsibility; the ability to make one's own commitment and keep them; and consultation with other associates before undertaking actions that could impact the reputation of the company by damaging it "below the waterline".

Gore says that how it works sets it apart – with a unique corporate culture whose core principles are catalysts to participating, communications and creativity.

You know you are moving to a different culture when you visit the plant at Livingston. To the left in the car park there is parking for visitors; to the right it is for "associates" – not for staff, employees or workforce but for people of an elevated status in an equal world.

Innovation

A belief in innovation and a commitment to technical accomplishment have driven Gore for more than 40 years. It has patents throughout the world. The whole point of its unusual culture is to encourage innovation and creativity.

Gore's fluoropolymer products provide innovative solutions throughout industry in next-generation electronics, for medical implants, and with high-performance fabrics.

It creates the next-generation cable assemblies and components for the electronics industry, and sets the standard for outerwear comfort and protection – solving difficult industrial problems with innovative materials and technology. The company states: "We take our reputation for product leadership seriously, continually delivering new products and better solutions for the marketplace of the world."

The company believes that its founders have left a legacy of innovation and that it is an enterprise driven by innovation – and it has a track record of thousands of diverse, innovative products to prove it.

Diversity and social responsibility

Its very beginning is all about diversity. The company believes that because of the lattice organisation it has had since its foundation – with no bosses and where there is equal opportunity for everybody – diversity is automatic; but it does not take it for granted. It organises diversity awareness training for its associates. It believes that to recruit the best and the brightest, diversity goes without saying.

Gore states that to continue to be a leading technology company it needs great talent from all sources, and this means practising diversity with, for example, associate networks – which are groups driving networking, development, education and outreach initiatives which have been piloted among African-Americans, Asians, women and young engineers.

It does not do a lot of community work. It makes sure its properties are attractive and compatible with their surroundings. It supports local charities, but prefers to quietly go about its business – with a workforce that is an example of diversity at its best, operating within the community.

Corporate Governance

This is a tricky one. In a company with no rigid hierarchy and no bosses, who carries the can? In the UK there are three directors – two of them UK-based and the third based in Germany. As directors, they have to carry out responsibilities as laid down by UK law.

But if you want to get down to the nitty-gritty of the financials, you will be told that as Gore is a privately held corporation, most of the financial information is proprietary. Its stock is not available for public trading. Its associates operate according to four basic principles – one of them being consultation with other associates before undertaking actions that could impact on the company by hitting it "below the waterline". This clause is meant to protect the company from inappropriate risk. Noone can initiate projects or business activity involving significant corporate financial commitments without a thorough review and participation by qualified associates.

A final point: Gore did not make it as the best company to work for in Scotland, 1st in the UK as a whole in a Sunday Times list, and 2nd in the US Fortune list without its corporate governance being tickety-boo.

Environmental record

Everything is done by the environmental book – and more. There are no patronising pronouncements about the environment, but an impressive and constantly growing product and patent list, which shows that the company knows all about and understands the environment and how to cope with it. Or live with it.

Its products provide solutions to environmental pollution; and they meet the demands of defence, aviation and satellite industry customers by providing lightweight radiation- and temperature-resistant products that perform in the harshest environments – from battlefield conditions to the extremes of outer space.

That puts the environment at the core of Gore.